Profiling the European Citizen

Cross-Disciplinary Perspectives

Mireille Hildebrandt • Serge Gutwirth
Editors

Profiling the European Citizen

Cross-Disciplinary Perspectives

 Springer

Editors

Mireille Hildebrandt
Erasmus University Rotterdam
The Netherlands
&
Vrije Universiteit Brussel
Belgium

Serge Gutwirth
Vrije Universiteit Brussel
Belgium
&
Erasmus University Rotterdam
The Netherlands

ISBN 978-1-4020-6913-0   e-ISBN 978-1-4020-6914-7

Library of Congress Control Number: 2008926740

Cover image:

SACCO, Joseph
Oeil de jeune femme (Eye of a young woman)
1844
Tempera on ivory mounted on leather in glass and gilt frame placed in leather case with brass fillets and velvet lining
Photographer: Hickey-Robertson, Houston
Credit Line: The Menil Collection, Houston

Printed on acid-free paper

9 8 7 6 5 4 3 2 1

springer.com

FIDIS (Future of Identity in the Information Society) is a NoE (Network of Excellence) supported by the European Union under the 6th Framework Programme for Research and Technological Development within the Information Society Technologies Priority (IST). The network comprises of 24 research institutes throughout Europe (for further information see www.fidis.net), with a variety of disciplinary backgrounds. They share their research findings regarding (emerging) identification technologies, privacy enhancing technologies, the adequacy of the legal framework and identity management systems. Within the FIDIS network a special workpackage has been dedicated to investigate the implications of profiling technologies, taking into account that these technologies are preconditional for smart applications and Ambient Intelligence. This volume is the academic validation of the work done within this workpackage.

Contents

      Behaviour and Social Values 111
      Simone van der Hof and Corien Prins

      6.1   Introduction 111
      6.2   Setting the Stage: Personalisation and Profiling 112
      6.3   The Dark Side of Personalisation and Profiling 115
             6.3.1   Personal Data, Identities and Behaviour 115
             6.3.2   Transparency and Quality 118
             6.3.3   Inclusion, Exclusion and Control 120
      6.4   Concluding Remarks 123
      6.5   Reply: Online Personalisation. For the Bad or for the Good? 124
             Thierry Nabeth
             6.5.1   Online Personalisation: Dr Jekyll and Mr Hyde? 124
             6.5.2   van der Hof and Prins' Perspective 125
             6.5.3   Our Comments on the Work of van der Hof
                      and Colleagues 126
      6.6   Bibliography 127

Part II   Applications of Profiling

7   Biometric Profiling: Opportunities and Risks 131
      Vassiliki Andronikou, Angelos Yannopoulos,
      and Theodora Varvarigou

      7.1   Introduction 131
      7.2   Opportunities 133
             7.2.1   Current Biometric Systems 133
             7.2.2   Future Applications 133
      7.3   Risks 136
             7.3.1   System Attack 136
             7.3.2   System Performance 137
             7.3.3   System Capabilities 137
      7.4   Conclusions 139
      7.5   Need for Legal Analysis of Biometric Profiling 139
             Els Kindt
             7.5.1   Introduction 139
             7.5.2   Definition 140
             7.5.3   Legal Aspects 141
             7.5.4   Distinction Between 'Soft' and 'Hard'
                      Biometric Characteristics 142
             7.5.5   Informational Privacy 143
             7.5.6   Discrimination 144
      7.6   Bibliography 144

Contributors

Vassiliki Andronikou obtained her MSc with the highest honour from the Electrical and Computer Engineering Department of the National Technical University of Athens in 2004. She has worked in the National Bank of Greece and the Organisation of Telecommunications of Greece. Since 2004 she has been a research associate and PhD candidate in the Telecommunications Laboratory of the NTUA. In 2005 she was awarded with the Ericsson award for her thesis on Mobile IPv6 with Fast Handovers. Her research focuses on the fields of biometrics, content management and grid infrastructure.

Bernhard Anrig is professor of Computer Science and director of studies at the Division of Computer Science of the University of Applied Sciences of Bern, Switzerland. He is also a lecturer at the Department of Computer Science at the University of Fribourg, Switzerland.

He studied Mathematics and Computer Science at the University of Fribourg, Switzerland. During his PhD on "Probabilistic Model-Based Diagnostics", he focused on the processing and management of uncertain information with respect to diagnostic processes at both the quantitative and the qualitative level. He worked as a senior researcher in the group "Theoretical Computer Science" of Prof. J. Kohlas at the University of Fribourg, Switzerland on reasoning under uncertainty, especially probabilistic argumentation systems and information systems, information and probability algebras as well as the connections between reliability analysis and diagnostics.

Since 2003 he is a member of "Virtual Identity, Privacy and Security" V.I.P, a research centre at the University of Applied Sciences of Bern. V.I.P represents a wide range of skills in computer science and applied mathematics and covers subjects that deal with security and privacy, cryptology, identities and virtual identities, PETs (privacy enhancing technologies), pseudonyms, anonymisation and data mining techniques as well as applied statistics in a sensitive environment (for example in the medical domain).

His current domain of research and activities covers security and privacy, identities and virtual identities, anonymisation and web-service security. He is a contributing author in several deliverables of FIDIS.
email: *Bernhard.Anrig@bfh.ch*
web: *prof.ti.bfh.ch/arb1*
web: *www.vip.ch*

James Backhouse was educated at Andover Grammar School, Hampshire, UK, the Universities of Exeter and Southampton and in 1990 he completed his thesis on 'Semantic Analysis in the Development of Information Systems' at the London School of Economics and Political Science (LSE). He has taught extensively at all levels of the education sector before coming to the LSE as a lecturer in information systems in 1987. He is the author of over 50 publications in the field of information and security and has published in, amongst others, *Management of Information Systems Quarterly, Communications of the ACM, Journal of the Association of Information Systems, Journal of Financial Crime, Information Systems Journal and Journal of Money Laundering Control.*

He leads the research and teaching at the LSE in information risk and security, focusing on the social and organisational aspects of information security and to date has supervised 18 doctoral students in this subject area, many of whom have gone on to faculty posts in established universities or to global management consultancies and international companies.

Dr. Backhouse is active in standards development and professional best practice in information security and was a member of the Confederation of British Industry working group for developing web security guidelines for the British Standard BS7799, the Code of Practice on Information Security Management. He is also concerned about the wider issues of higher education and serves on the Council of the University of London and chairs its Study Board for the Social Sciences.

He has led a number of key research projects for industry – European and UK research councils and funding bodies, raising over £1.3 million to further his study into information security, consumer protection in online finance, compliance and control of money laundering and more recently identity and interoperability. He was a founding member of the FIDIS EU research network of excellence.
He researches the subject of money laundering with a focus on profiling and behavioural modelling, creating research consortia that include banks, regulators and law-enforcement agencies from countries including Eire, UK, Italy and more recently Greece, Switzerland and Cyprus. His current work is developing organisational strategies for combating money laundering and terrorist financing

Emmanuel Benoist is a full professor in the computer science department of the University of Applied Sciences Bern (Switzerland) since 1999, where he is teaching courses in algorithmic and web technologies He also takes part in the FIDIS project (NoE of 6th Framework Programme of the EU). He is active in the project Memdoc, a web-based database for the documentation of orthopaedic cases. This project is effectuated in cooperation with the medical faculty of the University of Bern and Qualidoc – a spin-off of the University.

From 1997 to 1999 he co-founded the web agency *Norm@Net* and participated in the creation of numerous web sites.

From 1996 to 1999 he worked as a research assistant at the University of Caen (France) in the Computer Science Department. His research activities were focused on Theoretical Computer Science. The title of his PhD thesis was "Polynomial time solution generation for SAT problem".

Will Browne's research interests include architectures of learning systems by analogy to cognitive systems. Diverse and practical applications of novel learning systems have ranged from data mining to mobile robotics.

His mechanical engineering degree from the University of Bath led to an industrial doctorate developing a learning classifier system for data mining in a steel hot strip mill. His post doctoral research was into the capture of human, plant and data knowledge for an on-line supervisory control of an aluminium plate mill. Dr Browne was appointed to a lectureship in Cybernetics, 2001, University of Reading.

Dr Browne has been involved in UK and European research projects which together were worth over £1.5 million. Relevant learning and cognitive projects include 'Abstraction in games playing algorithms' (Nuffield Foundation) and 'Development of a Novel Learning System for Data Classification' (EPSRC CASE award) [Thales Research Technologies Ltd]. Additional projects include 'A Modular Robot Colony for Mapping and Exploration' (Leverhulme Trust) [Ruiz, Browne], Control stabilisation of a model Harrier aircraft in conjunction with Exciting Radio Controlled Models Ltd [Harwin, Becerra, Browne] and the development of a novel learning system for the control of an autonomous flying vehicle (Nuffield Foundation).

Dr. Browne has published 23 research articles in international journals, conferences and as book chapters. Dr Browne is on the programme committee for evolutionary computation and robotics conferences (e.g., IEEE Ro-Man, Congress on Evolutionary Computation, Genetic and Evolutionary Computation Conference and Hybrid Intelligent Systems) and has acted as a referee for a number of international journals. His management skills have been demonstrated as the Project Coordinator for the European Framework V project, CONMAN. He successfully organised the 'Future Directions of Learning Classifier Systems' workshop during the Parallel Problem-Solving from Nature Conference 2004. Dr Browne was PI and UK organiser for the EPSRC & NSF International workshop on Cognitive Robotics, Intelligence and Control (COGRIC), which brought together internationally leading figures in order to discuss latest advancements and direct future research.

Roger Brownsword is a graduate of the London School of Economics.

Since September 2003, he has been Professor of Law at King's College London and Honorary Professor of Law at the University of Sheffield. He is director of a newly formed research centre (TELOS), based in the School of Law at KCL that focuses on regulation, ethics and technology.

Professor Brownsword acted as a specialist adviser to the House of Lords' Select Committee on Stem Cells. Since autumn 2004, he has been a member of the Nuffield Council on Bioethics, where he is currently on the Working Party on Public Health and he is a member of a recently convened Academy of Medical Sciences committee on Brain Science, Addiction and Drugs.

He is the co-author, with Professor Deryck Beyleveld, of *Law as a Moral Judgement* (1986), *Mice Morality and Patents* (1993), *Human Dignity in Bioethics and Biolaw* (2001) and *Consent in the Law* (January 2007). He co-edited (with Professor Cornish and Dr Llewelyn) *Law and Human Genetics: Regulating a*

Revolution (1998) and, supported by a Leverhulme Trust Fellowship, he is working on a new book for Oxford University Press entitled *Rights, Regulation and the Technological Revolution*.

His recent journal papers in the areas of biolaw, regulation and bioethics include: "Stem Cells, Superman and the Report of the Select Committee" (2002) 65 *Modern Law Review* 568-587; "Bioethics Today, Bioethics Tomorrow: Stem Cell Research and the 'Dignitarian Alliance'" (2003) 17 *University of Notre Dame Journal of Law, Ethics and Public Policy* 15-51; "An Interest in Human Dignity as the Basis for Genomic Torts" (2003) 42 *Washburn Law Journal* 413-487; "Regulating Human Genetics: New Dilemmas for a New Millennium" (2004) 12 *Medical Law Review* 14-39; "Reproductive Opportunities and Regulatory Challenges" (2004) 67 *Modern Law Review* 304-321; "Stem Cells and Cloning: Where the Regulatory Consensus Fails" (2005) 39 *New England Law Review* 535-571; "Code, Control and Choice: Why East is East and West is West" (2005) 21 *Legal Studies* 1-21 and "Ri-connessione Interpretativa, Rivoluzione Ripproduttiva e Stato di Diritto" (2005) 10 *Ars Interpretandi* 141-175.

In addition to his interest in law, ethics and technology, Professor Brownsword has written extensively about the law of contract, including *Contract Law: Themes for the Twenty-First Century* (2000 and 2006); he is the general editor of the *Understanding Law* series of books in which he has co-authored two titles with Professor John Adams; he is co-editor of a four-volume set on *Global Governance and the Quest for Justice* (published by Hart), which includes his own edited volume on *Human Rights*; and, for the last two years, he has co-edited the articles section of the *Modern Law Review*.

Ana Isabel Canhoto is a Fellow in Marketing at Henley Management College and a visiting fellow in the London School of Economics. Her major area of research and consulting is Information Processing and Decision Making in environments of high uncertainty. Ana researches the role of technology, mental stereotypes and social norms on decision making. She has investigated this topic in fields as diverse as technology adoption and customer profiling. Most recently, Ana has been investigating the mining of large transaction databases and how that may be influenced by the value judgments and task constraints of the individuals participating in the profiling activity. The study stresses the role of formal and informal norms in the profiling process, the relative weight of different norms, which norms prevail in case of conflicting directions and the process by which the agent selects which norms to abide by. Additionally, she has researched and consulted on consumer responses to emerging technologies such as automated houses or mobile Internet. Ana Isabel is a member of the 'Future of Identity in the Information Society' Network of Excellence, supported by the European Union under the 6th Framework Programme for Research and Technological Development.

Prior to joining academia, Ana worked as a management consultant for the telecommunications industry, where she conducted market overviews, oversaw market research and formulated entry strategies. She also worked as a portfolio manager at a leading media and entertainment company, where she organised and controlled all aspects of copyright management of the organisation's movies and electronic games portfolio.

Paul De Hert (1965) studied law, philosophy and religious sciences. After several books and articles in law and a productive decade of research for the Flemish Funds for Scientific Research, the Belgian Justice Department, the Department of Interior Affairs and the Brussels University Research Council in areas such as policing, video surveillance, international cooperation in criminal affairs and international exchange of police information, he broadened his scope of interests and published a book on the European Convention on Human Rights (1998) and defended a doctorate in law at the Free University of Law in which he compared the constitutional strength of eighteenth and twentieth-century constitutionalism in the light of contemporary social control practices ('Early Constitutionalism and Social Control. Liberal Democracy Hesitating between Rights Thinking and Liberty Thinking' (2000, Promoter: Prof. Dr Bart De Schutter)).

In Brussels, Paul De Hert holds the chair of human rights, legal theory and European and Constitutional Criminal Law at the Free University of Brussels, he is Director of the VUB-Research group on human rights (HUMR) and a core member of the VUB-Research group Law Science Technology & Society (LSTS) which is devoted to the research subjects linked to the topic of his fellowship, i.e., sciences and technology in a democratic constitutional state (see: *www.vub.ac.be/LSTS*).

Lothar Fritsch is a researcher in business informatics and privacy technology at Johann Wolfgang Goethe University's chair for Mobile Commerce and Multilateral Security in Frankfurt. He focuses on the integration of privacy protection and identity management into information systems with an interdisciplinary view. Additionally, his research approaches questions in mobile applications such as location-based services.

Lothar Fritsch received his degree in computer science from the University of Saarland, where he specialised in computer security. He gained international experience at the University of Missouri, studying computer science and journalism. He worked as a product manager for a company in the e-commerce and e-banking security field before focusing on his current research on privacy support in IT infrastructures

Mark Gasson is a senior research fellow at the University of Reading, England. His research predominantly focuses on user-centric applications of developing technologies and he has been actively engaged in a range of UK, EU and US funded research projects. Dr Gasson has specific interest in pushing the envelope of Human-Machine interaction and has been active in the development of Ambient Intelligence Environments and Neural Interface techniques for human augmentation. Dr Gasson considers public engagement of science as an essential component of the scientific endeavour and as such has had an active involvement spanning over ten years. Dr Gasson frequently delivers invited public lectures and workshops internationally, aimed at audiences of varying ages. Dr Gasson is also part of a dynamic group which aims to bridge the void between art and science through public installations derived from collaboration between artists and scientists.

Serge Gutwirth is professor at the Faculty of Law and Criminology of the Vrije Universiteit Brussel (VUB), where he studied law, criminology and obtained a post-graduate degree in technology and science studies. He is also a part-time lecturer of jurisprudence at the Erasmus University of Rotterdam. Since October 2003 Gutwirth is holder of a 5-year research fellowship in the framework of the VUB-Research contingent for his project 'Sciences and the democratic constitutional state: a mutual transformation process'.

Gutwirth founded the VUB-*Research group Law Science Technology & Society* (LSTS) which he chairs and which is devoted to legal research on the mutual transformations of sciences and/or technology and the democratic constitutional state, with a particular focus on privacy related issues (see: *www.vub.ac.be/LSTS*). Currently, Gutwirth is the promoter of the participation of LSTS in three FP6 research projects including academic and non-academic partners from all over Europe. These projects include 2 *Integrated Projects* (REFGOV, 29 partners and SPICE, 25 partners) and a *Network of Excellence* (FIDIS, 24 partners). Next to this Gutwirth is promoter of the LSTS-participation in the interdisciplinary research project on *FLEmish E-publishing Trends* (FLEET, 5 partners) granted by the Institute for the Promotion of Innovation by Science and Technology in Flanders (IWT-SBO), promoter of three research projects granted by the Research Council of the VUB (*Ambient intelligence and data protection, An individual right to free settlement* and *Law and autonomic computing*) and co-promoter of the Prospective research in Brussels postdoctoral project on *Multiconviviality and social exclusion*.

Gutwirth is the author of 3 books, including *Privacy and the information age*, (Lanham/Boulder/New York/Oxford, 2002). He is also the (co)-editor of 10 thematic anthologies such as *Quel avenir pour le droit de l'environnement?* (Brussels, 1996); *Science, Technology and Social Change* (Brussels/Dordrecht 1999) and *Privacy and the criminal law* (Antwerp/Oxford, 2006). Gutwirth has further (co-)authored numerous scientific articles, book contributions and research reports in Dutch, French and English.

Ruth Halperin holds a PhD in Information Systems from the London School of Economics and Political Science, where currently she is a Research Fellow in the Information Systems and Innovation Group of the Department of Management. Her research interests include design and implementation issues in learning technologies and the analysis of technology mediated learning practices. Her current research focuses on the social aspects of Identity in the Information Society. She is a member of the EU Network of Excellence FIDIS and has co-edited and authored research reports and articles in the areas of Interoperable Identity Management Systems and Profiling. Prior to joining the LSE in 2002, she was a Project Manager of a leading software development company specializing in E-learning and KM technologies.

Mireille Hildebrandt is Associate Professor of Jurisprudence and Legal Theory and teaches law and legal theory at Erasmus University, Rotterdam. She wrote a PhD in legal philosophy and criminal procedure in 2002, publishing on criminal law and philosophy, e.g., 'Trial and Fair Trial': From Peer to Subject to Citizen', in *The Trial on Trial. Judgment and Calling to Account*, A. Duff, L. Farmer, S. Marshall and V. Tadros (eds.) (Oxford and Portland, Oregon, Hart. **2**: 15-37). She is part of the editorial board of *New Criminal Law Review* (UK Journal) and co-editor of the Criminal Law and Philosophy (US Journal).

Since 2002 she has been seconded to the 'Centre for Law Science Technology and Society studies' (LSTS) at Vrije Universiteit Brussel, to work on research projects with a focus on the relationship between science, technology, democracy and rule of law. From 2004 she is, together with Serge Gutwirth, work package leader on Profiling in the IST project on the 'Future of Identity in Information Society' (FIDIS). Since 2006 she coordinates the project on 'Law and Autonomic Computing: Mutual Transformations', at LSTS.

From 2003-2006 she was professor of 'Critical perspectives on comparative and European law' in the LLM course of the Institute of European Studies at the Vrije Universiteit Brussel.

From 2006 she has been Dean of Education of the 'Research School for Safety and Security' at Erasmus University, Rotterdam.

Her main research interests are the implications of emerging technologies on identity, agency and liability as presumed by democracy and the rule of law. This includes rethinking the contemporary technological embodiment of legal rules in the script (its dependence on written law), exploring the need to articulate legal rules in technological devices and infrastructures and stressing the need to reinvent democratic procedures to build consensus on the introduction of new technologies.

David-Olivier Jaquet-Chiffelle's current position is full professor of Mathematics and Cryptology at the University of Applied Sciences of Berne in Bienne, Switzerland, since 1997. He is a lecturer at ESC (School of Criminal Sciences) at the University of Lausanne, Switzerland and gives regular postgraduate courses in cryptology.

David-Olivier Jaquet-Chiffelle is also head and founder of V.I.P, Virtual Identity and Privacy research centre (one of the partners in the European project FIDIS, an NoE of the FP6) since 2001.

After having received his PhD in Mathematics, David-Olivier Jaquet-Chiffelle spent a post-doc at Harvard University (Boston, USA) where he was also a lecturer in the Department of Mathematics. He strengthened his experience in cryptology while working for the Swiss government as a scientific collaborator at the Swiss Federal Section of Cryptology.

David-Olivier Jaquet-Chiffelle has a long experience in projects related to security, privacy and identity; he currently participates in FIDIS, a network of excellence of the FP6. David-Olivier Jaquet-Chiffelle conceived the system that is now used by all Swiss hospitals to anonymise (while allowing recognition of multiple hospitalisations) the data they must transfer to the Swiss Federal Office of Statistics. David-Olivier Jaquet-Chiffelle intervenes as an expert in security and cryptology for Swiss television (scientific TV-programmes, news, etc.) and acts regularly as an expert for the European Commission.

His current domain of research and activities covers security and privacy, identities and virtual identities, PETs, (biometric) pseudonyms, anonymisation, applications of mathematics and cryptology to protect privacy.

Meike Kamp is a lawyer. She works at the Independent Centre for Privacy Protection (ICPP) in Kiel. Within the ICPP, which is the office of the privacy commissioner of the State of Schleswig Holstein, she is head of the division concerned with supervising private enterprises. She has worked on several studies concerning consumer protection, one of which was focused on scoring systems in the banking sector.

Meike holds a Masters of Law (LL.M) in Legal Informatics from the University of Hannover and has graduated from Georg August University, Göttingen, completing her first state exam in 2001. Before entering the ICPP she attended a two-year legal clerkship followed by her second state exam in March 2005.

Els Kindt is a legal researcher at the Interdisciplinary Centre for Law and ICT (ICRI – IBBT) of the Faculty of Law of the Catholic University of Leuven, Belgium. She obtained a candidate in philosophy degree and candidate in law degree in 1984 and graduated in law in 1987 from the K.U. Leuven. In 1988, she obtained a Master of Laws (LL.M) in the United States. She is a member of the Brussels Bar and practiced law as a leading member of the IP/IT department of a major international law firm in Brussels from January 1989–August 2003. She has over 15 years of experience in the information technology and communications law practice, advising large software and hardware suppliers, ISPs and traditional industry on various kinds of IT law matters. In 1999, she was listed as an expert for Belgium in Euromoney's Information Technology Advisers Guide. Since December 1, 2003, she has been a contract legal researcher with ICRI. Her research at ICRI presently concentrates on the use of new technologies, data protection and privacy, with a focus on biometrics. She has been involved in several national and EU research projects, including BioSec (Biometrics and Security) and Fidis (Future of Identity in the Information Society).

She is a frequent speaker on information law topics and has published several articles on recent developments in IT law. She is also a member of the editorial board of 'Computerrecht' (Kluwer) and of the advisory editorial board of 'Privacy en Informatie' (Kluwer).

Bert-Jaap Koops is Professor of Regulation & Technology at the Tilburg Institute for Law, Technology, and Society (TILT), the Netherlands. His main research interests are law and technology, in particular criminal-law issues in investigation powers and privacy, computer crime, cryptography and DNA forensics. He is also interested in other topics of technology regulation, such as information security, identification, digital constitutional rights, 'code as law' and regulation of bio- and nanotechnologies. As of 2004, he co-ordinates a research programme on law, technology and shifting power relations.

Koops studied mathematics and general and comparative literature at Groningen University, the Netherlands. He received his PhD at Tilburg University and Eindhoven University of Technology for a dissertation on cryptography regulation in 1999. He has co-edited four books in English on ICT regulation: *Emerging Electronic Highways* (1996), *ICT Law and Internationalisation* (2000), *Starting Points for ICT Regulation* (2006) and *Cybercrime and Jurisdiction: A Global Survey* (2006). He has published many articles and books in English and Dutch on a wide variety of topics.

Koops' WWW Crypto Law Survey is a standard publication on crypto regulation of worldwide renown. In 2003, he gave invited lectures in the U.S. at the University of Dayton, Ohio and George Washington University, Washington, D.C.

Koops is a member of *De Jonge Akademie*, a branch of the Royal Netherlands Academy of Arts and Sciences with 50 young academics. He is also a senior researcher at Intervict, the Tilburg institute for victimology and human security.

His key publications are: Koops, B.J. (1998), *The Crypto Controversy. A Key Conflict in the Information Society*, diss. Tilburg, 301 p. Kluwer Law International, The Hague etc., 1998; Brenner, S. & B.J. Koops (2004), 'Approaches to Cybercrime Jurisdiction', *Journal of High Technology Law 4* (1) 2004, p. 1-46; Koops, Bert-Jaap & Ronald Leenes (2005), '"Code" and the Slow Erosion of Privacy', *Michigan Telecommunications & Technology Law Review 12* (1), p. 115-188, http://www.mttlr.org/voltwelve/koops&leenes.pdf; Koops, Bert-Jaap, Miriam Lips, Corien Prins & Maurice Schellekens (eds.) (2006), *Starting Points for ICT Regulation. Deconstructing Prevalent Policy One-Liners*, IT & Law Series Vol. 9, The Hague: T.M.C. Asser Press 2006, 293 pp.

Contact data:

Prof. Bert-Jaap Koops, Tilburg Institute for Law, Technology, and Society (TILT), P.O. Box 90153, NL-5000 LE Tilburg, The Netherlands

telephone: +31 13 4668101

fax: +31 13 4663750

e-mail: e.j.koops@uvt.nl

web: http://rechten.uvt.nl/koops/

Barbara Körffer studied Law in Hamburg (First State Examination in Law 1999, Second State Examination in Law 2001). From 2002 to 2006 she has been working with the Independent Centre for Privacy Protection, amongst others as Head of Division of IT-Privacy Seal. Since 2006, she has been on secondment to the Federal Ministry of Justice as desk officer in the division of Data Protection Law.

Ronald Leenes is associate professor in IT, law and (new) technology at TILT, the Tilburg Institute for Law, Technology and Society (Tilburg University). His primary research interests are privacy and identity management, regulation of and by technology. He is also involved in research in ID fraud, biometrics and Online Dispute Resolution.

Dr Leenes (1964) studied Public Administration and Public Policy at the University of Twente. He received his PhD for a study on hard cases in law and Artificial Intelligence and Law from the same university. At the University of Twente, his research areas included (public) electronic service delivery, e-voting and legal knowledge based systems. Since 2004, he works at TILT were he broadened his research interests to technology (including IT) and law.

Ronald was Secretary of IFIP WG 8.5 'Information Systems in Public Administration' and Secretary/Treasurer of the International Association for Artificial Intelligence and Law (IAAIL). He was a member of the programme commission of various international E- government and AI and Law conferences.

Ronald participates in several EU FP6 programmes: the Network of Excellence 'Future of IDentity in the Information Society' (FIDIS), the PRIME project and the Network of Excellence 'Legal Framework for the Information Society' (LEFIS).

Nils Leopold (LL.M. Legal Informatics) has Law School Degrees from the Federal State of Baden-Württemberg in 1996 and in 1998 from the Law School at the universities of Constance and Freiburg/ Breisgau. Since 1998, he has been a lawyer in Berlin. In 2000 he followed the Master studies (Legal Informatics) at the university of Hannover and the University of Oslo, Norway. During 2002-2003 he was the chief privacy officer of ID-Media AG, Berlin and during 2003-2004 he became the managing director of the German civil liberties union, Berlin. Since 2004 he has been the head of the section data protection in the business world at the independent centre for data protection Schleswig-Holstein, Germany.

Martin Meints studied chemistry and computer science at the University of Kiel. He has worked in various enterprises and public organisations as an IT project manager and in technical management functions. The main focus of his latest work is the preparation and implementation of security concepts for large private networks (LAN and WAN) and the integration of mobile computing solutions based on the methodology of Baseline Protection from BSI, the German Federal Office for Information Security. Since 2004 he has been a researcher for the Independent Centre for Privacy Protection, Schleswig-Holstein (ICPP); he is mainly involved in the project "FIDIS – Future of Identity in the Information Society".

Thierry Nabeth
Research Fellow, Centre for Advanced Learning Technology, INSEAD France.
url: *http://www.calt.insead.edu/?thierry.nabeth*
Thierry Nabeth has been working at INSEAD as a researcher since 1993, in relation to the application of advanced information technologies (in particular agent enhanced, personalised, collaborative digital environments and knowledge management systems) to support new forms of learning (experiential learning, learning communities, human factors and knowledge dissemination) and new models of organisations (agile, distributed and knowledge intensive organisations).

The current focus of his work is related to the design of the next generation of cognitively informed collaborative virtual environments providing an advanced level of personalisation. Thierry Nabeth is particularly interested in the design of next generation knowledge management systems incorporating ideas inspired by the Web 2.0 evolution (collaborative environments, wikis, blogs, social networking, tagging etc.) that are more personalised, decentralised, active and able to provide support to the social process.

Thierry Nabeth is or has been involved in a variety of European research projects related to the design of intelligent learning systems and advanced knowledge management systems. He is the initiator and the coordinator of the AtGentive project, a STREP European project investigating the support of attention in agent enhanced e-learning systems. Thierry Nabeth is also a work package leader in the FIDIS (Future of Identity in the Information Society) Network of Excellence, where he is responsible for the elaboration of the FIDIS Identity Wiki, aiming at the definition of the concept of Identity in the consortium.

Before joining INSEAD, Thierry Nabeth worked for several years at Bull Systems in the field of Computer Aided Engineering and at Alcatel in the field of object-oriented technologies (methodologies, persistence, distribution, etc) and Artificial Intelligence (constraint propagation, DAI). He holds a DEA in Artificial Intelligence (Master's degree) from the University of Paris 6 and a DESS in Management (Master's degree) from the University of Paris 1. His master's dissertation (in 1990) in AI was related to the use of constraint propagation in an agent-based architecture for the resolution of a combinatorial problem (in the context of firmware memory allocation problems in a processor).

Corien Prins holds a degree in law as well as Slavic languages and literature from Leiden University. As of 1986 she worked as a researcher with the Department of Law and Informatics, Leiden University as well as the Institute for Central and East European Law at Leiden University. Subsequently, she was a visiting professor at Hastings Law School, University of California, San Francisco (1993). In 1994 she was appointed professor of Law and Informatisation at Tilburg University at the Institute for Law, Technology, and Society (TILT:). She headed this institute from 1994 until 2006.

Corien Prins is a member of the Council Board for Social Sciences (MAGW) of the Dutch Scientific Council (NWO) and a member of the Advisory Board of the Netherlands ICT Research and Innovation Authority (ICTRegie). She is also a member of the board of the Dutch Society of Legal Professionals (Nederlandse Juristen Vereniging).

In the past she was a member of the programme committee of the National Programme on Information Technology and Law (ITeR) of NWO. Her present research topics include (international) regulatory questions of ICT and new technologies (biotechnology, ambient intelligence and nanotech), commodification and propertisation of information, consumer protection in an ICT society, biometric technology, e-government, NGO's and new technologies, privacy and anonymity, identity and on-line personalisation.

Wim Schreurs obtained his law degree at the Vrije Universiteit of Brussels in 1996 and obtained an LL.M. in Intellectual Property Law at the Katholieke Universiteit of Brussels in 1999. Since 1998, he has worked at the Bar of Brussels as an attorney at law in the field of intellectual property law. He is currently a researcher at the Vrije Universiteit of Brussels and a member of the LSTS group, where he is preparing a PhD on the relation between data protection and ambient intelligence.

Els Soenens (1980) has been a member of the *Law, Science and Technology Studies* (LSTS) group at the Vrije Universiteit Brussels since autumn 2004.

She followed a specialisation training in *International and European Studies* at the Vrije Universiteit Brussels (2002-2004), after obtaining a sociology degree at the University of Ghent (1998-2002). In September 2006 she followed the bi-annual summer school *Technology Assessment* organised by the Dutch Rathenau Institute.

Since October 2004, she has been involved in the European Union IST Project FIDIS, where she works partly as a project assistant for the Work Package on Profiling and partly as a researcher. She has participated in several FIDIS deliverables with contributions in the domains of mobility and identity, web personalisation and the social aspects of profiling and Ambient Intelligence. She is also interested in (participative) Technology Assessment Studies and in the developments and the implications of e-Health in relation to Identity.

Sarah Thatcher is a professional lawyer specialising in law and social policy, with particular emphasis on the Information Society. She works in the United Kingdom Parliament as a legal specialist serving the House of Commons, giving legal advice to Select Committees engaged in pre-legislative scrutiny and the scrutiny of law and government policy more generally. Following an undergraduate degree in Jurisprudence from Oxford University in 1995, Sarah was admitted as a solicitor in England and Wales in 1998. She went on to practise commercial litigation at two of the top six law firms in the City of London, handling a broad range of commercial disputes, including High Court and international arbitration proceedings. In 2001, Sarah received an MPhil in Criminological Research from Cambridge University, after which she commenced doctoral studies at the London School of Economics. Her doctorate, completed in 2006, examined the social construction of cyberterrorism and the uses made of the concept by political and media élites. During her doctoral studies, Sarah was part of the team teaching the Information Technology and Society course run by the Department of Information Systems at the LSE and has been involved in the FIDIS project since its inception. Her research interests include the social aspects of information security, legal regulation of the electronic environment, cyber-delinquency and cyberterrorism.

Jean Paul Van Bendegem is at present a full-time professor at the Vrije Universiteit Brussel (Free University of Brussels) where he teaches courses in logic and philosophy of science. He is director of the Centre for Logic and Philosophy of Science (www.vub.ac.be/CLWF/) where currently eleven researchers are working. He is also President of the National Centre for Research in Logic (http://www.lofs.ucl. ac.be:16080/cnrl/), founded in 1955 by, among others, Chaïm Perelman and Leo Apostel. He is the editor of the journal Logique et Analyse (http://www.vub.ac. be/CLWF/L&A/).

His research focuses on two themes: the philosophy of strict finitism and the development of a comprehensive theory of mathematical practice. A forthcoming publication, edited jointly with Bart Van Kerkhove is Perspectives on Mathematical Practices. Bringing together Philosophy of Mathematics, Sociology of Mathematics, and Mathematics Education (Dordrecht: Springer/Kluwer Academic, 2006).
His personal website is to be found at: http://www.vub.ac.be/CLWF/members/jean/index.shtml.

Simone van der Hof is Assistant Professor Regulation of Technology at TILT - Tilburg Institute for Law, Technology and Society of Tilburg University, The Netherlands. In December 2002, she received a PhD at Tilburg University for her dissertation titled "International on-line contracts. Private international law aspects of on-line business-to-business and business-to-consumer contracts in Europe and the United States" (in Dutch). Her research covers a wide range of topics in the field of law and information and communication technologies. Her primary focus of research is currently on the social and legal implications of Identity Management in e-Government. Moreover, Simone van der Hof recently participated in a new and highly interesting area of research on the legal and social implications of personalisation of online public and private services. Furthermore, she is interested in the regulation of ICTs in the area of private (international) and public law (PhD research on international online contracts, other research on consumer protection, electronic signatures, trusted third parties, information security and e-Government). Internationally, she is known as an expert on the regulation of electronic signatures (especially through the online Digital Signature Law Survey). Over the years, Simone van der Hof has, moreover, coordinated research on the concept of "openbaarheid" (the public nature of information) in a networked environment and the availability of public-sector information. She has participated in numerous European projects, including PRIME and FIDIS and in two large comparative-law projects on ICT regulation.

Simone van der Hof coordinates and teaches the course Electronic Commerce: International Legal Aspects to foreign and Dutch students. She is a member of the editorial board of the Digital Evidence Journal and country correspondent for the Computer & Telecommunications Law Review. She is a member of the legal expert group of the Platform for eNetherlands, ECP.NL. In 2006, she was a national reporter on e-Government at the XVIIth World Congress of Comparative Law on e-Government.

Michaël Vanfleteren has a degree in Law from Université Catholique de Louvain and a post-graduate degree in Law (LLM) from University College, London. In his previous working experiences, he held: a position as legal assistant within the British Institute of International and Comparative Law, where he worked on setting up a Data Protection Research and Policy Group; a traineeship in the data protection unit of the European Commission and a position as legal researcher at the Interdisciplinary Centre for Law and ICT of the Katholieke Universiteit Leuven. There, he was involved in two 6th framework projects dealing with the concept of Identity: PRIME ('Privacy and Identity Management for Europe') and 'FIDIS' ('Future of Identity in the Information Society'). It is in the framework of the latter that the published paper has been elaborated. Michaël Vanfleteren is currently legal adviser to the European Data Protection Supervisor.

Theodora Varvarigou received a B. Tech degree from the National Technical University of Athens, Greece in 1988, a MS degree in Electrical Engineering (1989) and in Computer Science (1991) from Stanford University, Stanford, California and a PhD degree from Stanford University in 1991. She worked at AT&T Bell Labs, Holmdel, New Jersey between 1991 and 1995. Between 1995 and 1997 she worked as an Assistant Professor at the Technical University of Crete, Chania, Greece. Since 1997 she has worked as an Assistant Professor at the National Technical University of Athens. Her research interests include semantic wed technologies, media streaming and casting, scheduling over distributed platforms, parallel algorithms and architectures, fault-tolerant computation and content management.

Kevin Warwick is Professor of Cybernetics at the University of Reading, England, where he carries out research in artificial intelligence, control, robotics and biomedical engineering. He is also Director of the University KTP Centre, which links the University with small to medium enterprises and raises over £2 million each year in research income for the University. Kevin took his first degree at Aston University, followed by a PhD and a research post at Imperial College, London. He subsequently held positions at Oxford, Newcastle and Warwick universities before being offered the Chair at Reading. He has been awarded higher doctorates (DScs) both by Imperial College and the Czech Academy of Sciences, Prague. He was presented with The Future of Health Technology Award from MIT (USA), was made an Honorary Member of the Academy of Sciences, St. Petersburg and received The IEE Achievement Medal in 2004. In 2000 Kevin presented the Royal Institution Christmas Lectures. He is perhaps best known for carrying out a pioneering set of experiments involving the implant of multi-electrodes into his nervous system. With this in place, he carried out the world's first experiment involving electronic communication directly between the nervous systems of two humans.

Angelos Yannopoulos is a research engineer at the National Technical University of Athens, where he is also about to complete his PhD studies. His research interests merge Artificial Intelligence disciplines (both "numerical" intelligence, e.g., neural networks and "symbolic" intelligence, e.g., semantics and knowledge engineering) with media disciplines [from basic multimedia to modern tools that can deliver new kinds of media and experiences, e.g., biometrics and ambient intelligence for contextualisation and adaptive delivery] leading to long-term research objectives in the area of Arts and Technology.

Chapter 1
General Introduction and Overview

Mireille Hildebrandt and Serge Gutwirth

1.1 Introduction

In the eyes of many, one of the most challenging problems of the information society is that we are faced with an ever expanding mass of information. *Selection of the relevant bits of information* seems to become more important than the retrieval of data as such: the information is all out there but what it means and how we should act on it may be one of the big questions of the 21st century. If an information society is a society with an exponential proliferation of data, a knowledge society must be one that has learned how to cope with this.

Profiling technologies seem to be one of the most promising technological means to create order in the chaos of proliferating data. In this volume a multifocal view will be developed to focus upon what profiling is, where it is applied and what may be the impact on democracy and rule of law. Based on the work done within the European Network of Excellence (NoE) on the Future of Identity in Information Society (FIDIS),[1] a set of authors from different disciplinary backgrounds and jurisdictions share their understanding of profiling as a technology that may be preconditional for the future of our information society. As the title of this volume highlights this is a European endeavour, focusing on the impact of profiling on the identity of European citizens. Evidently, data mining techniques are also used on a global scale; there is nothing typically European about profiling in today's world. However, we focus on European citizens since this volume has been written by European scholars and is mostly based on research in the European regulatory context.

The book is composed of 17 chapters, starting with a summary overview and ending with a set of concise conclusions. Chapters 2 to 15 are divided into three parts: part I investigates what is profiling, part II discusses a set of applications and part III evaluates the implications of these technologies for democracy and the rule of law. These chapters take the form of a main text followed by one or two replies.

Vrije Universiteit Brussel, Erasmus Universiteit Rotterdam

---

[1] See *www.fidis.net* for information on the network.

M. Hildebrandt and S. Gutwirth (eds.), *Profiling the European Citizen:*
Cross-Disciplinary Perspectives.
© Springer Science + Business Media B.V. 2008

The replies offer reviews, mostly from another disciplinary context, thus fostering cross-disciplinary perspectives. The last chapter has been written on invitation by Roger Brownsword, who has published extensively on related issues from the perspective of legal philosophy.

In this introduction we will discuss the content of the three different parts of the volume, introducing the issues that emerge from the different contributions. At the end of the volume we will present a set of conclusions as to the kind of research that needs further attention. The foremost conclusion is that a paradigm shift is needed from privacy and protection of personal data to discrimination and manipulation and transparency of profiles. For this reason it is claimed that lawyers should start thinking about the legal status of profiles, these profiles being a type of knowledge rather than data, while technologists should start thinking about ways to make the knowledge presented by profiles contestable, whether in a court or law or elsewhere: the technological devices to access and assess profiles still need to be invented.

1.2   Part I: What is Profiling?

Instead of stipulating a definition we have devoted the entire first part of this volume to the question of what is profiling. This should allow a gradual focus on the types of profiling that are central in this volume: the construction and the application of profiles that have been generated by means of data mining techniques. **Chapter 2** raises the question of to what extent profiling generates a new type of knowledge. After providing working definitions of central terms like profiling, data subject, subject and data controller *Hildebrandt* develops a generic understanding of profiling as *pattern recognition*. She introduces key distinctions between personalised and group profiling, elaborating on the crucial difference between distributive and non-distributive group profiling. This last type of profiling can be understood as a kind of non-universal categorisation or stereotyping, which some claim to be a necessary reduction of the overwhelming complexity we are faced with in our everyday lives. Referring to the work of biologist and philosopher Francisco Varela, Hildebrandt claims that pattern recognition is a basic feature of all living organisms to survive in and co-constitute their environment. Such pattern recognition does not presume conscious thought and this is what IBM's project on autonomic computing actually builds on when it refers to the way our autonomic nervous system *sub-consciously* regulates our internal environment. Hildebrandt concludes that profiling or pattern recognition can thus be understood as a cognitive capacity of organisms in their environment. She then moves to the distinction between *autonomic behaviour* (of machines, animals and humans) on the one hand and the capacity for *autonomous action* (ascribed to human agents) on the other and takes this to be crucial for an assessment of the impact of automated profiling on human agency.

In his reply, *Nabeth* stresses the segregating function of profiling and the implications this may have in the case of non-distributive profiling. He agrees with

Hildebrandt that in itself such a segregating function is inherent in all social processes, long before automated profiles came about. As to Hildebrandt's notion of organic profiling – taking an ecological perspective on the capacity to profile one's environment – Nabeth points to the implications of such an approach, referring to Sci-Fi author Philip K. Dick whose universe blurs the border between the online and the offline world. He wonders to what extent such blurring will lead to a world ruled by machines, whereas conscious deliberation is entirely replaced by autonomic computing. Moving away from such dark scenarios Nabeth suggests that profiling may in fact disclose the unjustified bias we develop in what he calls instant cognition (what psychologists call stereotyping). This would mean that profiling could in fact diminish our reliance on unjustified categorisations. Despite the dark scenarios pictured in movies like Minority Report, he urges further exploration of profiling techniques in order to, for instance, support individual learning processes, thus raising the interesting question whether such support could in fact enhance our capacity for autonomous action.

The second replier, *David-Olivier Jaquet-Chiffelle*, focuses on the terminology around profiling, aiming to refine the working definitions provided by Hildebrandt. For this reason he introduces two new distinctions. Firstly, he discriminates between an actual subset of elements sharing one or more correlations with other elements and the generalisation of this subset into a category. The actual subset can be the predefined class of data used to make a query in a database, resulting in a statistical overview of the attributes of this class. The subset can also be a cluster that has been discovered as a result of data mining techniques. The generalisation of the subset results into what Jaquet-Chiffelle calls a 'virtual person' or category. The scope of a category moves beyond the actual subset, thereby enabling predictions concerning elements of the category that were not part of the original subset. Secondly, he discriminates between direct and indirect profiling. In the case of direct profiling the profile that is derived from a particular subject (human or non-human, group or individual) is applied to the same subject; in the case of indirect profiling the profile that is applied has been derived from another subject. One could argue that the introduction of the virtual person or category is what makes indirect profiling possible, as it generalises from the original subset to a category. This also indicates the weak spot of profiling: in the case of non-distributive profiles the generalisation is non-universal and may in fact be applied to a subject to which it does not apply. The distinction between direct and indirect profiling is also of importance because data protection legislation protects personal data, leaving a lacuna in the case of the application of profiles generated from other people's data, a point elaborated upon in chapter thirteen.

In **chapter 3** behavioural profiling is described in more detail as a key example of group profiling. After discussing the relationship between data, information and knowledge in terms of pattern recognition in data sets, *Canhoto and Backhouse* describe the technical process of knowledge discovery in databases. This process is analysed as a reiterative sequence of five steps: problem specification, data selection, pre-processing, data analysis and interpretation of the outcome. In their reply *Anrig, Gasson and Browne* elaborate on this with reference to an emerging industry standard, stressing the reiterative process of data mining. After the technical process, Canhoto and Backhouse move into the social process that informs the technical one, highlighting the role of the data analyst at every step of the process. The analysis of the profiling process is extended by distinguishing three types of norms that guide the use of technology: technical norms, formal norms and social norms. The relevance of the distinction is made clear by a discussion of the application of profiling techniques in a financial institution that seeks adequate profiles of behaviour to detect financial crime. Canhoto and Backhouse thus demonstrate how the construction of profiles is determined by the affordances and social norms of individual data analysts, enabling personal bias to inform the outcome of the profiling process. By explaining that automated profiling is not the outcome of a mechanical process, they raise the question of to what extent Nabeth's idea that profiling could disclose unjustified bias, needs qualification.

In **chapter 4** *Anrig, Browne and Gasson* move into a more detailed analysis of one of the steps in the process of profiling discussed in chapter 3, namely data analysis. This is the use of data mining techniques – algorithms – to discover relevant patterns in data that can inform a decision-making process. One important distinction they make is between structure testing and structure exploration. Structure *testing* is about checking whether a certain structure is in fact reflected in the data, structure *exploration* is about discovering whether any structures can be detected in the data. After discussing some of the intricacies of data preparation the authors provide an overview of the output of structure exploring algorithms. This output takes the form of a decision procedure allowing the user to classify a new instance according to the newly discovered structure. Different types of decision procedures are presented, indicating which type suits a particular context and summarising some of the implications of the choice for one or another type. Next, the authors describe commonly used deterministic algorithms and a range of probabilistic algorithms. In fact they conclude that using non-deterministic algorithms improves results by incorporating additional human knowledge. This conclusion highlights the importance of understanding profiling in terms of complex human-machine interactions, as argued in chapter 3. In view of this Anrig, Browne and Gasson provide an overview of the choices to be made between different types of algorithms (technological norms), depending on the available resources (data, time, money) and the purpose of the data mining exercise (testing, exploring, learning), being affordances and social norms. The first replier, *Van Bendegem*, moves into the domain of mathematics, explaining the extent to which inconsistencies in a database cause insurmountable problems, highlighting the trust we put into the use of algorithms. Checking whether a programme actually does what we think it does demands a more complex programme, raising the same issue (does this programme do what it is supposed to do?) at an even higher level of complexity. Van Bendegem refers to the major societal impact of this problem, for instance in the case that harm is caused by a malfunctioning programme. Other major drawbacks are discussed, such as the increase of false positives in the case of widespread application and the fact that constructing rich profiles with many features will augment the probability that different profiles overlap, rendering them less effective instruments of identification.

Most interestingly, Van Bendegem raises the issue of responsibility: if profiles produce knowledge that facilitates illegitimate discrimination or causes unforeseen effects, who should be called to account?

The second replier, *Meints*, discusses privacy preserving data mining (PPDM) as a special type of profiling. The objective of PPDM is twofold: being compliant with privacy standards and producing valid data mining results. The state of the art shows a variety of techniques developed to achieve these objectives, mainly based on data modification but the lack of standardisation renders them ineffective for large scale application. Nevertheless the replier argues that PPDM is a promising instrument to counter some of the privacy risks put forward by data mining techniques.

In **chapter 5** *Angelos Yannopoulos, Vassiliki Andronikou and Theodora Varvarigou* provide an overview of one of the most fascinating emerging technologies in the field of Ambient Intelligence, being behavioural biometric profiling. Within the scope of biometric profiling (further discussed in chapter 7) the aim of behavioural profiling is to detect relevant patterns that allow identification of a person and his or her habits or preferences. Other than non-biometric behavioural profiling, the topic of chapter 3, the authors deal with profiles inferred from data collected by sophisticated sensor technologies that record, store and aggregate machine-readable data of behaviours like speech, facial expression, key-stroke behaviour, gait, gesture, voice and handwritten signatures. Though the authors recognise the current technological and social limitations on wide spread application, they conclude that especially the technological restrictions may be resolved sooner than some sceptics profess. Grid technologies are expected to solve most of the restrictions pertaining to the technological infrastructure, while developments in the context of the semantic web should allow for more intelligent types of pattern recognition, not yet feasible in current applications. Lastly, the authors have high expectations of the integration of pattern recognition devices that mine data of multiple modalities, such as speech recognition on the basis of both voice registration and recording of lip-movements. As should be clear these authors have high expectations of a technology they consider preconditional for the real time monitoring and customisation of the vision of Ambient Intelligence. The replier, *James Backhouse*, is more sceptical, confronting the authors of the main text with assumptions they may not be aware of, explaining how their discourse is infused with a kind of technological determinism that has inspired earlier dreams about artificial intelligence. By claiming that our behaviour is a manifestation of certain parameters that pre-exist their interpretation, the authors according to Backhouse, presume what they claim to prove: that certain data actually express certain types of behaviour, irrespective of the context in which they are registered. Speaking in terms of the extraction of knowledge from data the authors are said to reiterate the language of chemical engineers, popular during the first wave of artificial intelligence. Backhouse argues that quite apart from technological or other limitations to be overcome, the entire perspective should be turned around, returning the process of machine readable pattern recognition to its societal context, acknowledging its dependence on social interaction that cannot be reduced to what machines can register.

As is clear from chapter 3, this does not imply that profiling is rejected but should rather be considered as an incentive to more modest claims and better study of the social context in which such technologies (should) function.

The last chapter of part I, **chapter 6**, develops a comprehensive view on personalised profiling, exploring potential impacts on personal identity, social interaction and some of the values we cherish. The authors, *van der Hof and Prins*, aim to trace the broader and fundamental implications of increased personalisation of services, based on categorisation, creation of identities, (re)structuring of behaviour and the shaping of information flows within society. Personalisation fits the trend from mass production to mass individualisation, being essentially an organisational strategy in business and government alike. While discussing the dark side of personalised profiling the authors focus on the impact on identity construction rather than only paying attention to abuse. They highlight the potential effects of personalisation rather than concentrating on personal data per se. According to the authors personalisation may affect societal values like autonomy and diversity, requiring transparency of the way profiles are constructed and adequate guarantees for the quality and integrity of the personalised services. Pointing to the integration of personalised services into the vision of Ambient Intelligence, van der Hof and Prins discuss the potential pitfalls of inclusion and exclusion, made possible on a more refined scale. The crucial issue at this point will be who is in control, while the authors suggest that the discussion should go well beyond protection of personal data, taking into account autonomy, transparency, discrimination and diversity. In his reply, *Nabeth* summarises the arguments provided in the main text, pointing out the complexity of the process of personalised profiling and the fact that most people are not aware of the way their data are being processed. With van der Hof and Prins he finds that personalisation may deliver great advantages, while having far reaching implications for issues of personal identity and individual freedom.

1.3   Part II: Applications of Profiling

In the second part of this volume, specific application domains are investigated to give the reader an idea of how profiling technologies actually work. Attention is turned to specific technological applications such as biometric profiling, location based services, web user profiling, e-learning, customer loyalty programmes, scoring practices and profiling in the context of employment. Together with the generic description of profiling in part I this provides material for the assessment of potential implications for democracy and rule of law in part III.

In **chapter 7** *Vassiliki Andronikou, Angelos Yannopoulos and Theodora Varvarigou* analyse the risks and opportunities of biometric profiling. Other than the investigation made in chapter five this chapter deals with both behavioural and physical biometrics as part of advanced group profiling, linking biometric profiles with other data to create sophisticated profiles of human subjects in a variety of contexts. The authors discern three types of risks: firstly they discuss the security risk of a system attack, secondly they point to the level of system performance which in many cases still produces an unacceptable rate of false positives and false negatives and thirdly they assess the system capabilities for extensive monitoring, resulting in electronic traces that may generate refined discrimination practices. They express a clear need for legislative control to minimise such risks. In the reply *Els Kindt* moves into the legal implications of biometric profiling, taking note of the fact that few legal authors specialise in this field, due to the need to have a basic understanding of the technical aspects. After discriminating between soft and hard biometrics (describing characteristics that are less or more capable of individuation) she explains why the storage of soft biometrics needs legal attention, even if the use of hard biometrics obviously warrants stringent legal protection. Referring to the recommendations of the article 29 Working Party that guides the implementation of the EC Directive on Data Protection, she highlights the loss of control of individual data subjects regarding the storage of their biometric profiles and agrees with the authors of the main text that the specific risks of the availability of such profiles need to be met in law. With regard to discrimination on the basis of biometric characteristics she notes a lack of legislative protection. The legal implications of both issues (informational privacy and discrimination) are relevant for most instances of profiling and will be discussed in detail in chapter thirteen.

In **chapter 8** *Fritsch* discusses the relationship between profiling of mobile phone users and location based services (LBS) in the light of privacy enhancing technologies (PETs). Referring to Gary Marx, Fritsch starts by linking location and identity, explaining that potential privacy threats will arise from linking location and time with other attributes. The challenge for identity management will therefore reside in a combination of a measure of identity control for the user while still providing enough identity data for the service provider to be able to reach and re-identify the user. The author describes how profiling on the basis of a time stamped location track - using data from GIS (geographical information systems) and POI (points of interest) - can amount to a detailed behavioural profile of a person. When combined with other data it will allow refined segmentation of relevant markets, providing ample opportunity for undesired discrimination. The author discusses three components for adequate protection: identity management, camouflage techniques and a social and legal framework. In his reply, *Ronald Leenes* differentiates between *location based services* based on existing profiles that are triggered by location data, and *location based profiling*, meaning that profiles are inferred from location data. Compared to web profiling, location based profiling – as described by Fritsch - provides a permanent stream of data, allowing the construction of very informative profiles if combined with other data. Leenes estimates that location based profiling is not likely to catch on with commercial service providers, because the complexity involved raises the costs of the exercise while not providing enough added value to ordinary location based servicing. However, the state may be interested to invest in the collection of such rich profiles, claiming a need for them in the fight against terrorism and other types of serious crime.

Chapter 9 takes on the most evident form of profiling in the age of Internet: the profiling of web users. *Emmanuel Benoist* starts from the fact that many web users have a sense of anonymity that is entirely mistaken. He then describes the architecture of the web to enable an adequate understanding of what is and what is not possible. This provides the background for a discussion on the legitimate use of statistical queries and more advanced profiling techniques, aiming for the implementation of logins and shopping carts or targeted servicing. Benoist then moves into privacy threats and counter measures, which he situates in the way data or profiles are used. He especially warns against the sale of information to third parties, a thing that the web user may not be aware of. The best protection available, according to Benoist is the so-called Platform for Privacy Preferences (P3P), which allows the exchange of machine readable data on the privacy policy of a website and the user's privacy preferences. In this way a user's machine can automatically compare the policy with the user's preferences and advice the user (or simply not access a site). The problem with the P3P is that the user's proxy has no way of finding out whether the site in fact follows the policy it claims to apply. In her reply, *Els Soenens* discusses web personalisation for Customer Relationship Management (CRM). She starts by stipulating a distinction between personalisation, defined as the result of data mining techniques, and customisation, defined as based on declared preferences. After warning against potential drawbacks of personalisation (especially the non-awareness of web users and the impact personalised services may have on identity building), she surveys the available tools for protection: privacy enhancing technologies (PETs) like P3P and anonymizer.com. After a critical discussion of these instruments that aim for data minimisation she turns to discuss the principle of minimum data asymmetry. Instead of only trying to reduce the exchange of personal data, this principle focuses on establishing a balance between the information in the hands of the user and the information in the hands of data processors. This should allow web users to access the profiles that have been applied to them, giving them the opportunity to change their preferences. Such a competence would empower consumers, who could turn personalisation into customisation.

In **chapter ten** *Thierry Nabeth* moves away from the dark sides of profiling, highlighting the opportunities for attention support for schools and work. Nabeth starts by detecting an 'attention challenge' in our information and knowledge society; the overload of information requires skills to select relevant information from incoming data and to allocate one's cognitive resources. Profiling could provide support for this process of filtering and cognitive focus, by directing attention to what is of interest for a particular person or group. After a discussion of the concept of attention, the efficient management of attention is qualified as crucial for both learning and work performance. Supporting attention can take place at the level of perception, of reasoning and at the operational level. Such support enables a more productive way of dealing with multitasking, for instance because we become aware of the manner in which we divide our attention across a diversity of tasks and their interruptions. Nabeth then gives an account of the EC funded Adgentive Project in which agent-based ICT tools are used to support students and knowledge workers. The author concludes that the next generation of e-working and e-learning systems will not support their users *more* but serve them *better*, which may be mainly due to the possibilities generated by advanced profiling technologies. The replier, *Ruth Halperin*, discusses these supportive technologies from the perspective of constructivist approaches to learning that emphasise the diversity of individual learning processes. While agreeing there is high potential for personalisation by means of profiling, the replier is more sceptical about the actual application of such technologies, casting doubt on the possibility to provide unambiguous interpretations of actual states of attention. As for profiling to support a community of students, Halperin claims that this in fact produces resistance, as people will probably feel watched over.

Meike Kamp, Barbara Körffer and Martin Meints explain the findings of studies on customer loyalty programmes and scoring practices in **chapter 11**. Describing the findings of a study by the Independent Centre for Privacy Protection (ICPP) 'Kundenbindungssysteme und Datenschutz', the authors check the relevant articles of the European Data Protection Directive and provide a good practice example, the LN-card. This card does not define additional purposes to process personal data, meaning the data can only be used for limited purposes; also contracts with vendors and external services must contain precise definitions of rights or obligations with regard to the use of personal data. Regarding credit scoring the authors describe the purpose and technical details, followed by a legal analysis that assesses the criteria that have to be met to comply with the Directive and the conditions under which scoring practices fall within the scope of art. 15 of the Directive that attributes a right not to be subject to a decision exclusively based on automated processing of data. The authors interpret art. 15 as a prohibition to take automated individual decisions, a position that is challenged in chapter 13. The reply, by *Ana Canhoto*, looks into the context of the customer loyalty programmes and credit scoring, to explain how one legal initiative, the EC Data Protection Directive, results in different technical solutions, depending on the strategic objective that is involved. In the case of customer loyalty programmes the focus is on producing incentives for customer's actions that are found to be profitable by the enterprise. In the case of credit scoring practices the objective is to discourage or exclude certain types of behaviour. The processing of data for customer loyalty programmes will thus be exploratory and could be rather invasive, while the processing of data for credit scoring practices will be directed to classification, less invasive but may tend to discrimination. This difference has consequences for the technical solutions (types of data mining techniques) and affects the application of legal norms (for instance to what extent consent is required).

In **chapter 12** *Nils Leopold and Martin Meints* discuss the use of profiling in employment situations. The contract between employer and employee is one of authority of one over the other with respect to the work to be done. This does not imply the suspension of human rights such as privacy. Employers may want to monitor their employees and claim legal grounds for this in the contract, but – the authors claim - data protection legislation empowers employees to gain access to the information that is being processed. At the same time they acknowledge that the consent required in art. 7 of the Data Protection Directive can hardly be qualified as freely given in employment situations. They plead for sector specific regulations of the extent to which data may be processed and discuss a set of case studies to elucidate legally compliant implementation of profiling in the workplace. In his reply *Paul De Hert* takes a more sceptical view of the effectiveness of the Directive, claiming that its application boils down to a series of procedural technicalities, not amounting to the substantive protection called for, especially the merging of the public and the private that is taking place as a result of ICT creates a dynamic that is not adequately met by the Directive. This is the case because the Directive focuses on protecting the individual person, while the employment situation demands collective solutions like those developed by labour law. De Hert thus agrees with Leopold and Meints that the focus on individual consent is a token of the inadequacy of the Directive for the domain of employment. Other than the authors of the main text, De Hert advocates more radical solutions, like the intervention of criminal law, to provide effective protection in an environment that seems to foster monitoring and surveillance.

1.4   Part III: Profiling Democracy and Rule of Law

In this part we will look into the relevant legal frameworks and access the adequacy of the existing framework in terms of democracy and rule of law. The focus will shift from an extensive analysis of positive law in chapter 13 to a discussion in terms of legal theory and legal philosophy in chapters 14, 15 and 16. The last chapter has been written on invitation by a well-known scholar from outside the FIDIS network of excellence, Roger Brownsword of King's College London. Brownsword is one of the few scholars of legal philosophy confronting the challenges of advanced ICT as formulated by scholars such as Lawrence Lessig.

In **chapter 13** *Wim Schreurs, Mireille Hildebrandt, Els Kindt and Michaël Vanfleteren* discuss the lack of legal certainty regarding the applicability of data protection legislation in the case of automated profiling practices in the private sector. The authors structure their analysis by discriminating between the collection of data, the construction of group profiles and the application of profiles to an individual person. One of the crucial issues is that the definition of 'personal data' in the EC Data Protection Directive restricts the protection to data concerning an identifiable person. The authors wonder whether the Directive is of any use in protecting European citizens against unfair, illegitimate or illegal exclusion on the basis of group profiling, especially in the case that profiles have been inferred from anonymised data or from the personal data of other people. In the second part of the chapter the authors discuss the applicability of anti-discrimination law, concluding that also in this case it is unclear to what extent such law provides adequate protection. In her reply *Sarah Thatcher* discusses the need for legal protection against unfair, illegitimate or illegal application of profiles in the public sector. Pointing out that the EC Data Retention Directive as well as the public order exemptions made in the EC Data Protection Directive are highly relevant to an assessment of the legal framework, she concludes that the logic of data protection is countered by the logic of data retention and she agrees with the authors of the main text that, in the case of data that cannot be linked to an identifiable person the present legal regime seems to offer little or no protection from profiling practices. She, however, goes further than the authors by arguing that the possible solutions they propose are unlikely to be of any substantial use to the data subject for a variety of socio-cultural and commercial reasons. Her ultimate conclusion is that the mechanism of data processing is no longer a suitable basis on which to construct protections for the individual and that the framework for a new protection regime should be based instead on the purposes and impacts of data processing.

In **chapter 14** *Serge Gutwirth and Paul De Hert* present their extensive analysis of privacy and data protection against the background of the democratic constitutional state. The core of their analysis is the distinction between legal opacity tools that protect individual citizens against attempts to make their private life transparent and legal transparency tools that empower citizens by making transparent the processing of their personal data in the case that opacity is not the default position. For them, the default position of the protection of privacy through human rights and constitutional law is an opacity or 'shield' position: as a rule, interferences with the individuals' privacy are prohibited. In data protection however the default position is the transparency of the data controller, who is conditionally allowed to process personal data and is made both accountable for the legality and legitimacy of the processings of personal data in his power, and subject to controls by the data subjects and special supervisory bodies. Regarding profiling, Gutwirth and De Hert argue a need for transparency tools, claiming that the present default position which allows extensive processing of personal data is justified if such transparency and the ensuing accountability of profilers are made possible. In his reply *Ronald Leenes* starts from the position that data protection must be differentiated from privacy for other reasons – namely because the one is a tool to protect the other. Other than Gutwirth and De Hert he doubts that data protection is an adequate tool of protection against profiling practices, especially when the link between a person and the profiles that may be applied is opaque. The opacity Leenes refers to concerns the link between non-distributive group profiles and the persons to whom they may be applied. In that case the profile is not inferred from the personal data of the categorised person but inferred from a large amount of often anonymised data of many other people. Only after the application of the profile to an individual may it be considered a personal data, falling within the scope of the Data Protection Directive. This implies that the protection offered in the form of a right to transparency is only available after the fact. Even with the help of privacy enhancing technologies (PETs) citizens have no access to non-distributive group profiles before they are applied. Leenes concludes that profiling does not warrant protection of one's personal data but against unfair stereotyping and proclaims that at this point in time we do not have effective legal or technological tools to provide such protection.

In **chapter 15** *Mireille Hildebrandt* discusses some of the risks of profiling practices. Both continuous monitoring by government authorities (dataveillance) and processes of normalisation and customisation initiated by private actors like service providers are assessed in terms of their impact on personal identity and individual freedom. Personal identity is understood as a mix of ipse-identity and idem-identity. Ipse (or self) identity is the irreducible sense of self of a human person; idem (or sameness) identity is the objectification of the self that stems from comparative categorisation. This means that identity is understood in dynamic terms, necessitating a mix of negative and positive freedom to reconstruct one's identity in the course of time. Profiling may impact negative freedom (absence of disclosure, coercion and interference), as it provides refined descriptions of one's life style, habits and desires, allowing profilers to target and even manipulate one's preferences. Profiling may impact positive freedom (the possibility to act), because the use of profiles may impact one's autonomy and facilitate unprecedented discrimination. After assessing the legal framework as ineffective Hildebrandt concludes that a new generation of transparency tools is needed, integrating legal and technological tools in order to allow effective anticipation of the profiles that may be applied. In the first reply *Bert-Jaap Koops* critically analyses the claims made by Hildebrandt, stressing the focus should be on abuse rather than on profiling per se. He suggests two alternative solutions to the risks posed by profiling, calling for paradigm-shifts in protection: the first is building legal protection into the technology, the second is a focus on redressing wrongs like unfair discrimination rather than a focus on preventing abuse or on violations of privacy. In the second reply *Kevin Warwick* reiterates the point that profiling machines allow unprecedented classification, compared to what a human mind could master. This means that the way others categorise us is amplified in the case where these others are machines: "we are faced with a global/networked structured definition of who we are". Warwick detects two ensuing issues: firstly, we may not even know how we are being defined and, secondly, we may have no way of changing the way these machines (and their masters) define us. In fact, he claims, the only way to have an impact on the way we are being categorised is to become part of this global network of machines, taking the next step in human (or cyborg) evolution?

In the last chapter of Part III, **chapter 16**, *Roger Brownsword* takes up the challenge of shedding light on all this from outside the FIDIS community. In doing so he develops a normative position on profiling. His analysis is based on the idea of a moral community in which agents respect the generic rights of fellow-agents and he furthermore builds on the fact that a privacy conception based on the actual privacy expectations cannot provide independent arguments for much privacy protection in times when privacy is actually being eroded. His first aim is to draw a line on privacy, determining when privacy is not at stake despite the fact that others do know things about a person. The answer is found in the concept of a reasonable expectation of non-disclosure that is informed by the question whether such disclosure (without consent) stands in the way of the flourishing of agency. The second aim is to decide to what extent the State should be allowed to use profiling techniques as part of its criminal justice strategy. Here Brownsword claims that in as far as the use of such techniques would take away the moral choice of (non)compliance with the criminal law this strategy should be rejected because it would erode the agency of those that form the moral community.

This volume would have been unthinkable without the challenging cooperation within the FIDIS workpackage on profiling and the wider FIDIS community. The editors would like to thank all authors for their recurrent and intense discussion of relevant topics and for their willingness to tune their contributions across a variety of different disciplines within the broader domains of the computer sciences, the social sciences and the humanities. We also like to thank Els Soenens for her patient work on the index and bibliographies.

Part I
What is Profiling?

In this part the process of profiling will be identified and analysed. After defining what type of profiling will be the subject of this publication, the process of group profiling will be described and the role of algorithms will be explicated as this is at the heart of profiling technologies. After this, full attention will be given to personalised profiling and related issues, starting with a contribution on behavioural biometric profiling.

Chapter 2
Defining Profiling: A New Type of Knowledge?

Mireille Hildebrandt

In this first chapter a set of relevant distinctions will be made to explore old and new ways of profiling, making a first attempt to define the type of profiling that is the subject of this publication. The text explains how profiling or pattern recognition allows us to discriminate noise from information on the basis of the knowledge that is constructed, providing a sophisticated way of coping with the increasing abundance of data. The major distinctions discussed are between individual and group profiles (often combined in personalised profiling), between distributive and non-distributive group profiles and between construction and application of profiles. Having described automated profiling we will compare such machine profiling to organic and human profiling, which have been crucial competences for the survival of both human and non-human organisms. The most salient difference between organic and machine profiling may be the fact that as a citizen, consumer or employee we find ourselves in the position of being profiled, without access to the knowledge that is used to categorise and deal with us. This seems to impair our personal freedom, because we cannot adequately anticipate the actions of those that know about us what we may not know about ourselves.

2.1   Introduction

Profiling occurs in a diversity of contexts: from criminal investigation to marketing research, from mathematics to computer engineering, from healthcare applications for elderly people to genetic screening and preventive medicine, from forensic biometrics to immigration policy with regard to iris-scans, from supply chain management with the help of RFID-technologies to actuarial justice. Looking into these different domains it soon becomes clear that the term profiling is used here to refer to a set of technologies, which share at least one common characteristic: the use of algorithms or other techniques to create, discover or construct knowledge from huge sets of data. Automated profiling involves different *technologies* (hardware), such as RFID-tags, biometrics, sensors and computers as well as *techniques* (software), such as data cleansing, data aggregation and data mining. The technologies and techniques are integrated into profiling *practices* that allow both the construction

Vrije Universiteit Brussel, Erasmus University Rotterdam

M. Hildebrandt and S. Gutwirth (eds.), *Profiling the European Citizen:*
Cross-Disciplinary Perspectives.
© Springer Science + Business Media B.V. 2008

and the application of profiles. These profiles are used to make decisions, sometimes even without human intervention. The vision of Ambient Intelligence or ubiquitous networked environments depends entirely on autonomic profiling, the type of profiling that allows machines to communicate with other machines and to take decisions without human intervention.

In this chapter we will start with the identification of profiling as such, providing working definitions of profiling and some related terms. After that we will discuss the difference between group profiling and personalised profiling and the way they are mixed up in practice. On the basis of this initial exploration of automated profiling, such technological (machine) profiling will be compared with non-technological forms of profiling, in particular organic and human profiling. This should enhance our understanding of the difference between machine and human profiling, which is crucial for an adequate assessment of the opportunities and risks involved.

2.2   Identification of Profiling

In this volume the focus will be on automated profiling, which is the result of a process of data mining. Data mining – which will be discussed in detail in chapters 2 and 3 - is a procedure by which large databases are mined by means of algorithms for patterns of correlations between data. These correlations indicate a relation between data, without establishing causes or reasons.[2] What they provide is a kind of prediction, based on past behaviour (of humans or nonhumans). In that sense profiling is an inductive way to generate knowledge; the correlations stand for a probability that things will turn out the same in the future. What they do not reveal is why this should be the case. In fact, profilers are not very interested in causes or reasons, their interest lies in a reliable prediction, to allow adequate decision making. For this reason profiling can best be understood from a pragmatic perspective: it aims for knowledge that is defined by its effects, not for conceptual elaboration.[3] Another way to articulate the particular kind of knowledge produced by profiling is to see profiles as hypotheses. Interestingly, these hypotheses are not necessarily developed within the framework of a theory or on the basis of a common sense expectation. Instead, the hypothesis often *emerges* in the process of data mining, a change in perspective that is sometimes referred to as a discovery-driven approach,

---

[2] Correlations can of course be spurious (see http://www.burns.com/wcbspurcorl.htm), however, this does not mean that non-spurious correlations necessarily establish causal or motivational relationships between data.

[3] According to the founding father of American pragmatism, Charles Saunders Peirce, the Maxim of Pragmatism reads as follows: 'Consider what effects that might conceivably have practical bearings we conceive the object of our conception to have: then, our conception of those effects is the whole of our conception of the object' (Peirce, 1997:111). A pragmatic approach of knowledge should not be conflated with a populist or naïvely 'practical' attitudes to knowledge.

as opposed to the more traditional assumption-driven approach.[4] 'Data mining provides its users with answers to questions they did not know to ask' (Zarsky, 2002-2003:8). After correlations (hypotheses) have surfaced they are tested when the profiles are applied. This is why the construction and application of profiles are entangled in profiling practices (complementing the inductive process of generating profiles with the deductive process of testing them on new data).

Before supplying a working definition of profiling we need to define three terms, which are central in the context of profiling: data subject, subject and data controller. The central position in profiling is taken by what is called the *data subject*, which we define as the subject (human or non-human, individual or group) that a profile refers to. In the case of group profiling this means that the data subject may be the result of profiling, not necessarily pre-existing as a group that thinks of itself as a group. For instance, a category of blue-eyed women may emerge as a data subject, because as a category they correlate with a specific probability to suffer from breast cancer. This implies that we use the term data subject in a different way than is usual in data protection legislation, as in the case when the data subject is defined as 'an identified or identifiable natural person'.[5] We define a *subject* as the human or nonhuman individual of which data are recorded which are used to generate profiles and/or as the human or nonhuman individual to which a profile is applied.[6] The next – equally central – position is taken by the *data controller* (sometimes called *data user*), which we define as the subject (person or organisation) that determines the purposes of the processing of the data and the use that will be made of them (including the sale of data or of the profiles inferred from them).

A simple working definition of profiling could be:

> The process of 'discovering' correlations between data in databases that can be used to identify and represent a human or nonhuman subject (individual or group) and/or the application of profiles (sets of correlated data) to individuate and represent a subject or to identify a subject as a member of a group or category.

To understand the meaning of profiling, it may be helpful to add the purpose of profiling. Besides individuation, profiling mainly aims for risk-assessment and/or assessment of opportunities of individual subjects. This, however, cannot be taken for granted. If the interests of the data controller and subject differ it may well be that the interests of the data controller, who pays for the whole process, will take precedence. Thus – in the end – what counts are the risks and opportunities for the data controller. For this reason the purpose of profiling can best be formulated as:

---

[4] Custers (2004: 46), referring to B. Cogan, *Data Mining; Dig Deep for the Power of Knowledge.* Internet publication at www.BioinformaticsWorld.info/feature 3a.html.

[5] Par. 2 (a) Directive 95/46 European Community (D 95/46/EC).

[6] This means that in this context the term data subject is used in a different way compared to the way it is used in Data Protection legislation. What is called a subject in this text, is called a data subject in D 95/46/EC, meaning the subject whose data have been processed.

The assessment of risks and/or opportunities for the data controller (in relation to risks and opportunities concerning the individual subject).

This raises the question whether it is possible to empower a human subject to make her a data controller in her own right, with regard to profiles that can be inferred from her data and profiles that may be applied to her.

2.3 Group Profiling & Personalised Profiling

2.3.1 Groups: Communities and Categories

Profiling techniques generate correlations between data. For instance, a correlation may be found between people that are left-handed and have blue eyes and a specific disease or a correlation may be found between people that live in a certain neighbourhood and have a particular level of income or a correlation may be found between one's individual keystroke behaviour and regular visits to a specific type of pornographic website. To generate such correlations in a reliable way we need to collect, aggregate and store the relevant data over an extended period of time, perhaps by integrating different databases that contain such data. In the examples given, the correlations concern data of certain categories of subjects, for instance the category of people with blue eyes that are left-handed or the category of people that live in a certain neighbourhood. Once the process of data mining establishes the correlations, two interrelated things happen: (1) a certain category is constituted (2) as having certain attributes. The category is usually called a group and the set of attributes are called the group's profile.

Another possibility is that the data of an existing group of people, who form some kind of community, are collected, aggregated, stored and processed in order to find shared features. For instance, the members of a local church or the students living in a certain dormitory can be the target of profiling. In this case the process of data mining will not establish them as a group (which they already were) but it may generate correlations and certain attributes between them, such as a typical way of dressing, particular eating habits or specific travel habits.[7]

Group profiling can concern both communities (existing groups) and categories (e.g., all people with blue eyes). In the case of categories, the members of the group did not necessarily form a community when the process was initiated; in the case of communities the members of the group already formed a community (however unstructured). The fact that profiling may establish categories as sharing certain attributes may in fact lead to community building, if the members of such a category become aware of the profile they share. The fact that data controllers may target the members of a category in a certain way – without them being aware of this – may of course impact their behaviour as members of this category.

---

[7] Cp. Zarsky (2002-2003:9-15) on clustering and association rules.

2.3.2   Distributive and Non-distributive Profiles

To understand some of the implications of group profiling we have to discriminate between distributive and non-distributive profiles. A distributive profile identifies a group of which all members share all the attributes of the group's profile. This means that the group profile can be applied without any problem to a member of the group – in that sense it is also a personal profile. An example of a distributive profile is the category of bachelors that all share the attribute of not being married. A less tautological example is the category of oak trees that all develop a certain type of leaf. Being a member of a group with a distributive profile has potentially pervasive social and legal implications because the profile will apply without qualification to all members.

It should be obvious that apart from groups that are *defined* in terms of a shared attribute (e.g., the group of bachelors that share the attribute of not being married), most groups do not have distributive profiles. A non-distributive profile identifies a group of which not all members share all the attributes of the group's profile.[8] For instance, Hare's checklist for psychopaths is a non-distributive profile. It contains 20 items e.g., absence of guilt, superficial charm, pathological lying and poor aggression control, that have to be checked and scored on a 3-point scale (0: does not apply; 1: applies to some extent; 2: applies). A person whose profile counts 30 points or more is considered a psychopath, a profile that is said to be – statistically – predictive of violent criminal recidivism of released offenders. The category of persons who score 30 points or more on Hare's checklist has a non-distributive profile, because not every person in this group shares the same attributes. From a social and legal perspective this is very instructive, because it implies that one cannot apply the profile to members of the group without qualification (Edens, 2001).

It is important to realise that treating members of a group that has a non-distributive profiles as fitting the entire profile may have interesting effects. For instance, if people fit the profile of a high-income market segment, service providers may decide to offer them certain goods or provide access to certain services, which may reinforce their fit in the category. If the group profile is non-distributive and they in fact do not share the relevant attributes (e.g., they may live in a certain neighbourhood that is profiled as high-income, while in fact they have a very low income, being an au pair), they may actually be 'normalised' into the behaviour profiled as characteristic for this group.[9]

2.3.3   Actuarial Approach in Marketing, Insurance and Justice

The use of non-distributive profiles (the usual case) implies that profiles are always probabilistic. They basically describe the chance that a certain correlation will occur

---

[8] In terms of Wittgenstein, the members of the group have a family resemblance, they cannot be identified by means of a common denominator. Cp. Custers, 2004; Vedder, 1999.

[9] Cp. Vedder, 1999.

in the future, on the basis of its occurrence in the past. As indicated above, the correlation does not imply a causal or motivational relationship between the correlated data, they merely indicate the fact that the occurrence of one will probably coincide with the occurrence of the other. For instance, in genetic profiling, we may find that the presence of a certain gene correlates with a certain disease. Depending on the exact correlation (the percentage of cases in which it occurs) we may predict – in terms of probability – the chance that a person with the relevant gene will develop the relevant disease. In reality, of course, the correlations may be very complex, e. g., depending on a whole set of different factors in a non-linear way. The exponential increase in computer power, however, enables the storage of a nearly unlimited amount of data and allows computer scientists to develop very complex algorithms to mine these data.[10] This has led to relatively new developments in marketing, insurance and justice, based on the targeted assessment of consumer preferences (leading to spam), targeted risk-assessment (concerning financial credibility) and on criminal profiling (leading to actuarial justice). In all three fields it becomes possible to take decisions (in customer relationship management, on refined types of price-discriminations, on categorised or even personalised interest-rates and insurance premiums, on targets for criminal investigation and on sentencing modalities) that are based on highly informed predictions of future behaviour. This approach to customers and citizens can be termed an actuarial approach, because it builds on highly sophisticated assessments of the risks and opportunities involved. The caveat of this approach is that it extrapolates from the past to the future on the basis of blind correlations, tending to see the future as determined by established probabilities, possibly disabling potentially better solutions that lie in the realm of low probabilities.

2.3.4   Personalisation and Ambient Intelligence

Mining the data from a variety of people allows categorising them into different types of groups, generating high rates of predictability concerning the behaviour of categories of people. Apart from group profiling, however, a second type of profiling has evolved, that mines the data of one individuated subject.[11] Behavioural biometrics is a good example of such profiling (discussed in detail in chapter 5).

---

[10] Data mining by means of algorithms or heuristics (see chapter 4) works with a set of instructions that has to be followed chronologically, this is called conventional computing. The end result of such a process is entirely predictable, even if our brains do not have the computing powers to apply the algorithm in as little time as the computer does. According to Stergiou and Siganos (1996), data mining by means of neural networks works with 'highly interconnected processing elements (neurones) working in parallel to solve a specific problem'. They claim that one of the advantages of this emerging technology is that problems that we do not understand can still be solved, while for the same reason the resolution of the problem is not predictable.

[11] In terms of the reply of Jaquet-Chiffelle this would be 'direct individual profiling'.

For instance, profiling the keystroke behaviour of one particular person may enable a service provider to 'recognise' this person as she goes online because of her behavioural biometric 'signature' and allows the service provider to check her online behaviour (discussed in detail in chapter 9) and thus to build up a very personal profile that can be used to offer specific goods and provide access to certain services. The profile can also be stored and sold to other interested parties, or be requested by the criminal justice or immigration authorities.

Such personalised profiling is the *conditio sine qua non* of Ambient Intelligence (AmI), the vision of a networked environment that monitors its users and adapts its services in real time, permanently learning to anticipate the user's preferences in order to adapt to them.[12] Ambient Intelligence presumes an RFID-tagged environment, and/or an environment enhanced with sensors and/or biometric appliances, all connected with online databases and software that allows a continuous process of real-time profiling. The intelligence is not situated in one device but emerges in their interconnections. The online world with its seemingly limitless capability to collect, aggregate, store and mine behavioural data thus integrates the offline world, creating a new blend of virtual and physical reality (ITU, 2005).[13] AmI environments may know your preferences long before you become aware of them and adapt themselves in order to meet those preferences. The AmI vision promises a paradise of user-centric environments, providing a continuous flow of customised services by means of ubiquitous and pervasive computing.[14] However, one does not need an overdose of imagination to foresee that such highly personalised profiling engenders unprecedented risks for users to be manipulated into certain preferences, especially in the case that users have no feed-back on what happens to the data they 'leak' while moving around in their animated environments.

2.4 Automated and Non-automated Profiling

2.4.1 Categorisation, Stereotyping and Profiling

Long before computers made their way into everyday life, criminal investigators composed profiles of unknown suspects, psychologists compiled profiles of people with specific personality disorders,[15] marketing managers made profiles of different

---

[12] As elaborated in chapter 6, personalised profiling can be a combination of individual and group profiling, or in terms of the reply of Jaquet-Chiffelle 'direct and indirect individual profiling'.

[13] See Mark Weiser's pioneering work on ubiquitous computing, for example, Weiser (1991: 94 – 104).

[14] The AmI vision has been propagated mainly by Philips and the European Commission, see for example, Aarts and Marzano 2003; ISTAG (Information Society Technology Advisory Group), 2001.

[15] On psychometrics (psychological testing), see for example, Rasch, 1980; Thorndike, 1971.

types of potential customers and managers profiled the potentials of their employees for specific jobs.[16] Adequate profiling seems to have been a crucial competence of professional occupation and business enterprise since their inception, perhaps most visible today in marketing and criminal investigation.[17] However, profiling is not just a professional, business or government preoccupation. As Schauer (2003) convincingly demonstrates in his *Profiles, Probabilities and Stereotypes*, profiling is a form of generalisation or categorisation we all apply routinely to get us through life. Habermas would probably speak of *Kontingenzbewältigung*, being the reduction of complexity in an environment that demands continuous choices of action, which would swamp us if we were to reflect on each of them. Schauer professes that categorisation is mainly a good thing, especially if it is based on a 'sound statistical basis' and his position has a strong appeal to our common sense. How could we move on in life if we did not take certain generalisations for granted, if we did not live by certain rules that are based on such generalisation – even if they do not always apply? Schauer warns against attempts to look at each and every case in isolation, attending to the particular instead of the general, glorifying what lawyers in Germany once called 'Einzelfallgerechtigkeit'. In his opinion routine assessments on the basis of generalisation are not only necessary to cope with complexity and multiplicity but they also provide *just* instead of *arbitrary* decisions, because of the appeal to a general standard, which creates a type of predictability (essential for e.g., legal certainty). In psychology the need to reduce the weight of recurring decisions is thought to be the cause of 'stereotyping', a healthy way to deal with the growing complexities of life. It means that we – unconsciously - group different events, things or persons into categories in order to assess what can be expected and to be able to decide how to act. Stereotyping allows anticipation. Following this line of thinking, categorisation and stereotyping are a kind of everyday profiling, based on experience and practical wisdom and if we believe Schauer, it also produces a kind of justice. In the next section I will take this line of thought one step further in claiming that profiling is not only a part of professional and everyday life but also a constitutive competence of life itself in the biological sense of the word.

However, before describing the process of profiling from the perspective of the life sciences, we need to make some comments on Schauer's defence of categorisation and its relationship to profiling. In the introduction to his book he discusses 'Generalization Good and Bad'. He starts by drawing a distinction between generalisations with and without a statistical or factual basis; those without he calls *spurious*. He qualifies this distinction by indicating that in everyday life we may pronounce many generalisations without intending them to be taken as absolute. For instance, when

---

[16] See for example, Rafter and Smyth, 2001.

[17] For a history and overview of criminal profiling, see for example Turvey, 1999. For a history and overview of data mining in academic marketing research see for example Wilkie, William and Moore (2003: 116-146). For more practical research see for example, Peppers and Rogers, 1993 (about the integration of data mining and CRM (Customer Relationship Management) to achieve mass customisation.

we say that 'Bulldogs have bad hips', this – according to Schauer – may be a good generalisation, even though a majority of bulldogs do not have bad hips. 'As long as the probability of a dog's having hip problems given that the dog is a bulldog is greater than the probability of a dog's having hip problems given no information about the breed of dog, we can say that the trait of being a bulldog is *relevant*, and we can say that generalizing from that trait meets the threshold of statistical (or actuarial) soundness' (Schauer 2003: 11).[18] Thus we have what he calls universal generalisations, which denote a group of which all members share the generalised characteristic and non-universal generalisations, which denote a group of which a majority or a relevant minority share the generalised characteristic. Schauer then moves on to discuss prejudice or stereotype as a kind of generalisation, recognising that these terms are often used in a pejorative way. He seems to conclude that the use of a non-universal generalisation must not be rejected, while admitting that - depending on the context (sic!) – sometimes such prejudice or stereotyping can indeed be morally flawed. One example he gives is the case of racial profiling, though he seems to suggest that in this case the generalisation is not based on sound statistical or empirical evidence. The reason for the fact that acting on a nonspurious non-universal generalisation may – under certain circumstances - be morally wrong is that 'equality becomes important precisely because it treats unlike cases alike' (Schauer, 2003: 296). So, even if most ex-convicts or a relevant minority of them, are prone to commit crimes again, we may decide we want to treat them equally when they apply for a job, insurance or try to rent a house - equally to non-ex-convicts. A principle such as the presumption of innocence has the same function: even if we are quite sure that a person has committed a certain crime, government officials cannot treat this person as an offender until guilt has been proven according to law. I am not sure these are the examples Schauer would endorse to demonstrate the importance of the moral evaluation that may interfere with justified generalisation but he has explained in a clear voice how generalisation, equality and even community relate to each other. In the remainder of this chapter we can use some of the salient distinctions he makes to clarify the complexities of automated profiling and the implications it may have for fairness and equality.

2.4.2 Organic Profiling: A Critical Sign of Life

After concluding that profiling is part of professional as well as everyday life of human beings, I would like to make a brief excursion into the life sciences to highlight the importance of profiling for living organisms. As Van Brakel (1999) writes, biology and information theory have developed into an integrated domain, part of the life sciences. This is an important development, which may help us to understand the way automated (machine) profiling can generate knowledge, although not human knowledge.

---

[18] Emphasis of Schauer.

Both 'organic profiling' and automated machine profiling concerns the production of implicit knowledge, or at least knowledge that has not reached a human conscious.

In 1987 Maturana and Varela published a little book, *The Tree of Knowledge*, explaining *The Biological Roots of Human Understanding*.[19] For our purposes the theory of knowledge argued in their book is interesting because it explains knowledge as something that an observer attributes to *an organism that effectively deals with its environment*. For Maturana and Varela knowledge is constituted by the interactions between – for instance - a fly and its immediate environment, if this interaction is successful in the sense that it sustains the life of the fly. Their understanding of knowledge is enactive (knowledge and action 'cause' each other): only by acting, an organism finds out about its environment and in that sense even perception is a form of – entirely implicit - action.[20] To be more precise one could say that all living organisms, in order to survive, must continuously profile their environment to be able to adapt themselves and/or to adapt the environment. Profiling in this case means the process of extracting relevant information from the environment. However, *what counts as information depends on the knowledge the organism has built* on the basis of continuous interaction with its environment, because this knowledge determines what type of information is relevant and valid. This means that what counts as information at one point in time may be noise at another point in time and what counts as noise for one individual (organism) may be information for another. It also means that knowledge depends on both the environment and the organism and must be understood as fundamentally dynamic and context-dependent. Knowledge in this sense is always local knowledge. This does not mean that generalisation is out of bounds, quite on the contrary. To be able to act in an environment adequate generalisation is *necessary* but the question of which generalisation is *adequate* will depend on the context (and on the organism).

What is crucial at this point is that (1) profiling the environment happens without involving a conscious mind (2) profiling provides feed-back necessary to survive (3) profiling extracts information, depending on knowledge that allows one to discriminate between noise and information (4) profiling transforms information into knowledge and (5) information and knowledge always depend on both the organism and its environment, there is no view from anywhere.

2.4.3 Human Profiling: The Meaning of Autonomous Action

The small excursion into profiling by nonhuman organisms allows us to develop a keener eye for what makes knowledge *human* knowledge. If perception, information

---

[19] Revised edition of 1998. Matuna and Varela coined the term autopeiosis in 1973 to describe the process that constitutes living organisms. In *The Tree of Knowledge* they expound on their theory of biology by investigation the relationship between living organisms and their environment.

[20] Their theory of knowledge thus combines pragmatism and embodied phenomenology, rejecting both mentalism or naïve empiricism.

gathering, feed-back and even knowledge are not specific for the human animal, what is? Could it be that consciousness is the discriminating attribute, and if so, what difference does this make for profiling? Compared to a plant, a dog seems to have a different kind of awareness of the world. We may be inclined to call this awareness a consciousness. This is not the case because the dog is aware of being aware but because it seems to embody a unified self that is absent in a plant. The philosopher Helmuth Plessner (1975) described the difference by pointing out that all mammals have a central nervous system that seems to allow for a centralisation of the awareness, giving rise to a conscious presence in the world. The difference between humans and other mammals, according to Plessner, is the fact that a human is also conscious of being conscious, conscious of herself. This reflective attribute, which is often thought to derive from the fact that we use language to communicate with each other, is absent in other mammals or present to a different degree.

To assess why this difference is relevant for our study of profiling we need to connect our capacity for reflection with our capacity for intentional action (which we suppose to be less evident in other mammals).[21] Reflection implies that we can look back upon ourselves, which also implies that we can consider our actions as our actions, as it were, from a distance. Such reflection can be incorporated into our actions – even before we act. We may thus consciously reflect upon different courses of action and intentionally prefer one alternative to another. This is what allows intentional action and this seems to be the pre-condition for autonomous action: an action we have freely decided upon, an action within our own control. Auto is Greek for self, nomos is Greek for law so human autonomy implies intentional action and conscious reflection, two conditions for positive freedom.

Before moving on to the relevance of intentional action and conscious reflection for profiling, we need to keep in mind an important fact. *Most of our actions are neither intentional nor conscious.* We can move around freely in this world because we have acquired habits that are inscribed in our bodies, allowing us to act in a number of ways without giving it thought. However, the very small amount of actions we actually consciously intend, are distinctive for our moral competence – taking into account that conscious reflection is the incentive to create new habits which will again move out from the zone of intentional action, but did originate from it.

2.4.4 Machine Profiling: The Meaning of Autonomic Machine Behaviour

In 2001, Paul Horn, IBM's Senior Vice President, introduced the idea of *autonomic computing*. Interestingly, he chose a term that refers to biology, to the autonomic

---

[21] We cannot be too presumptious here, see for example de Waal, 2001.

nervous system, because it 'governs our heart rate and body temperature, thus freeing our conscious brain from the burden of dealing with these and many other low-level, yet vital, functions' (Kephart and Chess, 2003: 41). One of the objectives of autonomic computing is to prevent or resolve the advancing software complexity crisis, by creating a network that is capable of self-management: self-configuring; self-healing; self-optimising; self-protecting (CHOP). Visions of Ambient Intelligence (AmI), pervasive computing or the RFID *Internet of Things* depend on extended interconnectivity and we are being warned that without self-management the design of the integrated network architectures will become entirely impossible. Another objective is to allow the user of the system to collect the fruits of ubiquitous computing without being bothered with the flow of minor and major adjustments that need to be made to keep the system operational. Kephart and Chess (2003: 42) distinguish different stages in the development of autonomic systems, starting with automated functions that collect and aggregate data and ending with automation technologies that can move beyond advice on decision-making, taking a large amount of low-level and even high-level decisions out of human hands.

To target the difference between organic, human and machine profiling it is interesting to discuss automated profiling in terms of *autonomic machine behaviour*. With autonomic machine behaviour I mean the behaviour of machines that are part of a network of machines that exchange data and make decisions after processing the data. This need not incorporate the entire concept of autonomic computing with its CHOP attributes, but is based on what is called M2M talk (machine to machine communication) (Lawton, 2004:12-15). 'Machine' can be anything, such as a RFID-tag (radio frequency identification tag), a PDA (personal digital assistant) or a PC (personal computer). I call the behaviour autonomic in as far as the network of machines processes data, constructs knowledge and makes decisions without the intervention of a human consciousness. This autonomic machine behaviour will be part and parcel of ambient intelligent environments, which monitor subjects and adapt the environment in real time, necessitating autonomic machine decision making.

The most simple form of automated profiling is when profiles are generated and applied in the process of data mining, after which human experts sit down to filter the results before making decisions. In this case we have no autonomic machine behaviour, because decisions are taken by human intervention. It may, however, be the case that these decisions routinely follow the machine's 'advice', bringing the whole process very close to autonomic machine profiling.[22]

---

[22] Art. 15 of the Directive on Data Protection 95/46/EC attributes a right to 'every person not to be subject to a decision which produces legal effects concerning him or significantly affects him and which is based solely on automated processing of data intended to evaluate certain personal aspects relating to him, such as his performance at work, creditworthiness, reliability, conduct, etc.'. The fact that usually some form of routine human intervention is involved means that art. 15 is not applicable, even if such routine decisions may have the same result as entirely automated decision making.

2.4.5   *Organic, Human and Machine Profiling: Autonomic and Autonomous Profiling*

After discussing organic, human and machine profiling we can now draw some prudent conclusions. It seems that most organic profiling does not involve conscious reflection or intentional action. It is important to note that an important part of human existence itself is sustained by the autonomic nervous system, which continuously profiles its environment inside and outside the body, by means of operations that we are not aware of. On top of that human profiling is done 'automatically' to a very large extent. This automation or habit-formation is the result of a learning process that often starts with conscious attention shifting to implicit behaviour as soon as the habit is inscribed in our way of doing things. The competence to act on this basis is referred to as implicit or tacit knowledge (Polanyi, 1966). Machine profiling seems similar to organic profiling, in the sense that it does not involve conscious reflection, nor intentional action. However, organic profiling presumes an organic system that constitutes and sustains itself. Maturana and Varela (1991) have coined the term autopoiesis for this self-constitution.[23] Even if autonomic computing – as defined by IBM – can be successfully compared to the autonomous nervous system, we may have a problem in defining it as self-constituting as long as it needs an initial software architecture provided by human intervention.

In other words, machine profiling is like organic profiling to the extent that it is part of autonomic behaviour and like human profiling to the extent that human profiling is done implicitly. At the same time, machine profiling differs from human profiling in two salient ways: (1) other than human and organic profiling machine profiling is not part of an autopeiotic system that constitutes itself, (2) other than human profiling machine profiling does not integrate conscious reflection or intentional action.

2.5   Conclusions: From Noise to Information, From Information to Knowledge

As they say, we live in an information society and in a knowledge society. One of the challenges of the present age is how to deal with the overload of information, or rather, how to discriminate noise from information. Another challenge is how to

---

[23] The term has been introduced into sociology by Luhmann and Teubner, who also build on Heinz von Foerster (cybernetics), implying that not only individual cells or metacellular organisms form autopoietic systems, but also social systems. However, system theory and other sociological schools that claim that individuals are determined by the social system or the underlying structure do not seem to build on Maturana and Varela, who explicitly claim that *social* systems amplify the individual creativity of its components, arguing that the social system actually exists for these components (and not the other way round, as is the case in metacellular organisms, cf. Maturana and Varela (1998:199).

(re)construct knowledge out of the flows of noise and information, how to deal with the growing complexities of our scientific knowledge constructs and with the emerging unpredictability of the complex technological infrastructures built to face the increasing mobility of human and nonhuman imbroglios.

One of the answers to both questions is the use and further development of profiling technologies. They may incorporate the only way to reduce the overload of information, to make it 'manageable', to make sense out of it and to regain control of the effects of one's actions. In other words, they may provide the only way to adequately anticipate the consequences of alternative courses of action. If freedom presumes anything, it is precisely this: a reliable anticipation of the results of the choices we have. This is why legal certainty and scientific experiment create the freedom to act, allowing citizens to adapt their position in the world to the realities it contains. At this point in time scientific experiment already makes widespread use of profiling technologies and it may be the case that legal certainty will need profiling technologies to interpret the overload of legal cases and decisions[24] and to regain some control over the way one's personal data are put to use.[25]

The biggest challenge however may be how to constrain profiling practices in order to prevent the coming-of-age of a technological infrastructure that is entirely geared for dataveillance, normalisation and customisation – practically destroying the effectiveness of our rights to privacy, fairness and due process (Leenes and Koops, 2005: 329-340). It would be unwise to wait for such an infrastructure to be in place, before establishing constraints, as this may render effective restraint an illusion. In chapter 15 these issues will be discussed, in order to assess the implications of profiling for the identity of the European citizen.

2.6   Reply: Further Implications?

Thierry Nabeth*

> In her essay, Mireille Hildebrandt raises the important issue of considering profiles as knowledge itself, and not as mere information. This implies a new way of considering profiles and profiling, as knowledge is subject to interpretation and meaning and inseparable from the rich social contexts in which it is embedded.
>
> This perspective has some profound implications in the way the information society is going to extract, manipulate and exploit data of human beings, or shall we say knowledge and apply it to the design of new categories of applications and services. In the new information society, applications "know" the people and not the other way around.

* Institut Européen D'Administration Des Affaires (INSEAD)

[24] The sheer volume of case law that is published (online) would in the end destroy legal certainty, because no human individual would be able to find her way in the proliferating decisions.

[25] For example, by the use of private Identity Management Devices that enable tracking of one's data and can be used to restrict the leaking of personal data. To regain control written law in itself will not suffice; the right to hide certain data must be inscribed into the technologies that would otherwise threaten one's personal autonomy.

In our reply to Mireille Hildebrandt, we will further explore the implications of this shifting of conceptualisation of profiles from data to knowledge and the ensuing consequences of almost intimate understanding of people and groups. We will in particular try to understand in which cases profile-informed applications will be used to better serve people and groups, or will - on the contrary - be used to alienate them.

2.6.1 Introduction

The essay of Mireille Hildebrandt on the subject of "defining profiling" comes very much as a surprise but a pleasant one. One would initially expect a formal definition, some descriptions of algorithms, some indication of security issues and a series of illustrative examples, providing finally more of a description than an explanation of the concept of profiling. What she provides though is a much more profound attempt to understand the concept of "profiling" that borrows ideas from many different fields and areas such as philosophy, complexity, anthropology and cognition (theory of action). This perspective is particularly useful in providing readers with the conceptual tools that will help them to articulate the different parts of this volume: the description of profiling, including an in-depth discussion of algorithms and a first indication of risks in part I; a series of illustrative examples (applications) that were presented in part II and the wider implications for democracy and rule of law in part III.

2.6.2 Profiling as Knowledge

In the first part of her chapter, Mireille Hildebrandt engages the discussion on the nature of the knowledge generated by the profiling process. This "profile" knowledge originates from the automatic extraction from an important amount of information aiming at discovering patterns that will have some predictive capabilities. Indeed, the underlying assumption is that the function of profiling is to help to reveal some hidden "order of things" and therefore to provide an oracle that will predict how people will behave in the future. Indeed, if they have behaved in a certain way in the past, they will most probably behave the very same way in the future. Mireille Hildebrandt also very rightly points to one of the main limitations of this form of knowledge: profiling "knowledge" does not explain things, as it is of a more inductive nature. It is then suggested that profiling should therefore be complemented by well thought out profiling practices.

Mireille Hildebrandt then indicates what the different stakeholders of profiling are: the subject (human or nonhuman, group or category) to which a profile refers (referred to as the data subject), the entity of which data are used to generate profiles and to which a profile is applied (referred to as the subject) and the actor that is the initiator of the profiling and the exploiter of the profiling data (referred to as the data controller). This distinction is very important, since it raises the question of different actors that may have conflicting objectives.

If Mireille Hildebrandt presents profiling at the individual level via the concept of personalised profiling, we have to admit that profiling at the group level receives a much higher level of attention in this chapter. Indeed, even if she acknowledges the importance of personalised profiling, she does it principally for an application in an Ambient Intelligent (AmI) context. We personally believe that it would have been useful to generalise the reflection to a much broader context, such as the domain of e-learning or e-commerce to cite a few.[26] At the group level, one should distinguish between characteristics that belong to all the members of a group (referred to as distributive attributes) and from characteristics that only statistically belong to this group (referred to as non distributive attributes). It is of particular importance to identify the non-distributive nature of the knowledge (also known as non-monotonic logic[27] in artificial intelligence), since it can be at the origin of errors in segregating people due to the merely probabilistic nature of some characteristics.

Moreover, we should point out the danger of the segregating function of profiling. Even in the case where the characteristic is distributive and no error is made, how should we deal with using profiling, which usage can be directly associated to segregation? The answer to this question follows an interesting angle: profiling did not have to wait for the advent of the computer to appear, since society, and for instance the social process, can be considered as a big *profiling machine*. Societies use categorisation and generalisation to function better, since it allows anticipation. To answer the question of whether generalisation is a good or bad thing, we will follow the reasoning of Mireille Hildebrandt by excluding generalisations that do not have a statistical or a factual basis. We also agree with the idea that some ethical issues may apply, depending on the context and for instance, taking the example of the "presumption of innocence", the role of society should help to erase the inequality that originates from circumstance. Even if it is proved that someone who only has one parent is more likely to become a criminal, such knowledge should not be used as a tool to segregate this category of persons; for instance by reducing the level of protection provided by the presumption of innocence or by removing some of their rights.

2.6.3   *A Knowledge Ecology Perspective*

The second part of this chapter is very interesting since it situates profiling according to a systemic and knowledge ecology perspective (the term organic profiling is used in this chapter). This part in particular relates to all the theories of complexity

---

[26] See on this chapter 10.

[27] See http://plato.stanford.edu/entries/logic-nonmonotonic/ for a description of the non-monitonic logic concept.

and collective intelligence that have emerged during the last decades, e.g., with the work of Varela and others (those involved in the Santa Fe movement). Applied to the context of ambient intelligence, it draws a vision that is not far from the 'Universe' of the great Sci-Fi author Philip K. Dick, for which the separation between the real word and the virtual word tends to blur. In particular, with the advent of RFID and other similar devices, this vision proposes to dissolve the frontier between human and machine and in our belief, introduces the concept of the trans-humanity that will merge the human and the machine. Indeed, RFID represents the typical device helping to create the bridge between the physical and the digital world (with RFID, the virtual world has access to "sensors" relating what happens in the physical world).

The consequences of this vision of seeing the world as a system closely integrated in society rather than as a well identified "machine" are many. First, and as previously indicated, the distinction between the physical world and the virtual world becomes artificial and should no longer be made, since we are talking about the same world. Second, profiling the environment does not necessary "involve a conscious mind" that is controlled by a central body (such as a government) but can also happen quasi spontaneously in society by a variety of actors. Let us also add that the existence of technology, even if it is not a mandatory condition for profiling to happen, can have tremendous consequences. For instance, the combination of autonomy and profiling can lead to the concept of autonomic profiling, for which the profiling processes do not need to have the "man in the loop" and as a consequence risk the loss of control by humanity. Even if we do not believe in the taking over of society by machines – a doom scenario popular in Sci-Fi literature - a real risk exists that people will lose the ability to control what is happening because of the complexity (in particular if machines gain the capabilities to learn and adapt). As a consequence, humanity may very well become dependant on profiling processes (typically in ambient intelligence) as is the case with an addiction: being aware of the dangers but having no capabilities to act.

However, we do not believe that the consequences need to be apocalyptic. The systemic vision may also mean a shift from the idea of very "controlled" profiling systems counceived by engineers, to systems that are more "self-regulated" and for which the designers also include people from the social sciences or law field who know how to deal with less mechanical and less deterministic approaches. In this later case, engineering systems involving profiling would mean working on the level of the different feedback loops helping to regulate the systems that continuously evolve (and deciding which ones are acceptable), rather than very supervised systems in which profiling represents one of the critical parts of an effective mechanism. To conclude, it would be the responsibility of this new category of designers, able to reason in a more holistic way, to ensure that the profiling mechanisms are put in place to service the good of society and individuals (for instance profiling can enable better personalisation, or can help to reduce inequalities by exposing them), rather than a tool of which the role is only to enforce social control (and typically used to maintain people in their initial condition).

2.6.4   What to Conclude About This Chapter From Mireille Hildebrandt?

We feel there exists a risk, every time we enter into an epistemological, philosophical or complex discussion, to detach too much from reality. Many discourses about the nature of knowledge and complexity easily become very abstract and tend to lose their readers in abstractions with little possibility to apply in reality.However, in this case Mireille Hildebrandt was able to avoid this trap by providing an illustration of what may be the concrete consequences for reality, for instance when applying it to ambient intelligence environments. Her chapter is therefore successful in proposing a global picture of how to conceptualise profiling at a higher level without losing the ground of reality.

If we could add something to this chapter, it would probably consist first in incorporating research linking cognition and profiling and second in investigating the consequences and impact of technology on the evolution of "profiled" environments. In the first case we will refer to the work that we will call instant cognition, consisting in the unconscious perception / classification / generalisation that people perform in their everyday life, which leads to very effective results but is also subject to bias and is at the origin of many dysfunctions in society, such as racism without real intention (the reader is invited to read the book from Malcolm Gladwell for information on this subject).[28] In particular, it could be interesting to explore how the new profiling approaches can be used to counterbalance the biases we have indicated (making them more visible). In the second case, it would be interesting to investigate very futuristic scenarios exploring the limits of extreme profiling. For instance, what would be the consequences of very "efficient" profiling done by the society? The movie industry has already given us some food for the thought with movies such as *Gattaca*[29] or the *Minority report*[30] that explore the less positive consequences of profiling but we do not doubt that similar work can be conducted exploring the more positive side, such as improving the effectiveness of education or work via a better personalisation that profiling would authorise.

2.7   Reply: Direct and Indirect Profiling in the Light of Virtual Persons

David-Olivier Jaquet-Chiffelle*

In our reply, we elaborate the difference between individual and group profiling in a slightly different manner, by distinguishing and defining direct and indirect profiling. We study these two types of profiling in the light of virtual persons.

* VIP, Berne University of Applied Sciences and ESC, University of Lausanne, Switzerland

[28]Gladwell, M. 2005.

[29]Gattaca is a 1997 science fiction drama film that describes the vision of a society driven by liberal eugenics.

[30]Minority report describes a society able to predict the crimes before they happen and imprison people for crimes that they have not yet committed but intended to.

In direct profiling, data is typically collected for one single subject or a small group of subjects. Knowledge built on this data then only applies to this specific subject or this small group of subjects.

Direct profiling can be used to uniquely characterise a person within a population or to infer, for example, future behaviour, needs or habits of a specific target.

In indirect profiling, data is collected from a large population. Groups and categories of subjects with similar properties emerge from the collected data. Each group has its own identity defined through a small amount of information. The typical member of one group can be modelled using the concept of virtual persons. It is then sufficient to identify a subject as a member of the group, i.e., with the corresponding virtual person to be able to infer, for this subject, knowledge inherited from the group itself: probable behaviour, attributes, risks, etc.

2.7.1 Introduction

In this chapter, Mireille Hildebrandt presents three key concepts related to profiling, namely the *data subject*, the *subject* and the *data user*. First, we want to enlighten these concepts using the concept of virtual persons. Then we will refine the concepts of individual and group profiling by distinguishing direct and indirect profiling. The different types of profiling will be illustrated using the generic model based on the concept of virtual persons.

2.7.2 Individual and Group Profiling

Individual profiling is used either to identify an individual within a community or just to infer its habits, behaviour, preferences, knowledge, risks, potential or other social and economic characteristics. Forensic individual profiling, for example, covers both aspects. Commercial individual profiling on the other hand is more interested in the latter, the inference of knowledge or rules about the individual.

Group profiling is used either to find shared features between members of a predefined community or to define categories of individuals sharing some properties. Forensic group profiling could, for example, find common characteristics in the community of convicted murderers or define risk categories of individuals. More generally, group profiling often raises ethical issues as it can lead very quickly, for example, to discrimination.

Several techniques can be used together or separately to define a direct profile:

- Information collected about an individual may directly give some important attributes of his profile (age, gender, etc).
- Data mining techniques applied to the data collected about an individual may help to induce his habits, his preferences, etc.
- Data mining techniques also help to find correlations between large sets of data collected about groups of people. These correlations might allow in turn the creation of categories: for example individuals sharing some attributes, living downtown, earning more than €100,000 a year, etc. Profiles are defined by associating knowledge with each category.

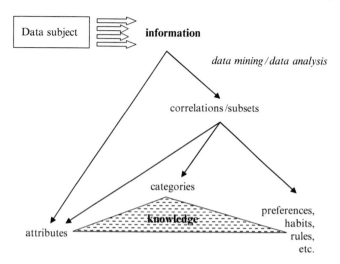

Fig. 2.1 From information to knowledge

Subsets are defined as elements sharing some properties. With each subset found in this process is associated its profile: attributes, rules, preferences, etc.

A *category* results from a process of generalisation. Each defined subset can be virtualised in a generalised subset or category, defined by the properties identifying the original subset; it inherits the profile of the original subset. The generalised subset may then exist independently of the original data subject.

2.7.3 Virtual Persons

We have elaborated the concept of *virtual persons* within the second work package of FIDIS *Identity of Identity*.[31] Virtual persons create an abstract layer allowing a more faithful description of many real-life scenarios appearing in our modern society. We want to apply this generic model to data mining and profiling, in particular to the data subject, the end user and the categories.

Virtual persons traditionally refer to characters in a MUD (Multi User Dungeon), MMORPG (Massively Multiplayer Online Role Playing Games) or other computer games.[32] These characters interact in a game; some of them rely on human beings (players) for their actions and/or behaviour, while others

[31] Jaquet–Chiffelle D.-O., Benoist, E., Anrig, B., Chapter 3 of Nabeth, T. et al. (eds), 2006a and Jaquet–Chiffelle D.-O., Benoist, E., Anrig B, in Jaquet – Chiffelle D.-O., Benoist, E., Anrig B. (eds.), 2006b: 6-7.

[32] http://dud.inf.tu-dresden.de/Anon_Terminology.html (Version 0.28; May 29, 2006).

might be directed by the game itself. For an external observer, it may be impossible to decide whether the subject behind a specific virtual person is a real player or just a computer programme. We see these virtual persons (characters) as masks used by subjects (human players, computer programmes) to act and/or interact within the game.

Laws also create a virtual world by associating rights, duties and/or responsibilities with virtual persons.[33] The one who is older than 18, the one who is married, the one who is president of a company, the person legally responsible... are typical examples of virtual persons living in the virtual legal world. These virtual persons are not linked to any physical or legal entity until the given conditions described in the law are fulfilled. Several physical or legal entities can be linked to these virtual persons as actions and/or transactions take place. Moreover, a single physical or legal entity may be linked to several virtual persons. These links are very often time dependant.

As an example, we consider *the person legally responsible* in a given transaction. The subject, i.e., the physical or legal entity behind this virtual person, could be the person executing the transaction himself; but it could be someone else, not necessarily visible: a tutor or the parents of a child – it could even be a company.

Such analogies between multiplayer games and real-life scenarios extend the field of application of virtual persons.

The concept of an abstract subject used by some authors is very close to our concept of virtual person. However, in using *virtual person*, we take advantage of the similarity between characters appearing in computer games and characters created in our daily life scenarios. Moreover, etymologically speaking, *person* comes from *personae* which means *mask*. Instead of adding a new theoretical term, we extend a well-known concept that is easy to imagine, even for non-specialists. Last but not least, in using two very distinct terms (subject and virtual persons), we avoid a possible confusion between both concepts and emphasise their differences: the virtual person is like a mask, the subject is the entity behind this mask.

In order to better understand the concept of virtual persons, we need a few core definitions. A *subject* is any physical or legal entity having – in a given context – some analogy with a physical person. Here subject is not opposed to object. Indeed, physical objects may satisfy our definition of a subject. In our definition, subjects typically act or play a role. Our subjects *are*, they *have*, they *do* or they *know* something just like physical persons.[34] Typical subjects are persons or groups of persons but can also be animals or computer programmes for example. A subject can be alive or not, can exist or not.

---

[33] In her article, Danièle Bourcier (2001: 847-871) introduces the concept of virtual persons in the context of artificial intelligence (intelligent programmes, software-agents, etc). She also refers to previous uses of this term in similar contexts. Our concept of virtual persons covers this approach while being more general and more adaptable to a wide variety of real-life scenarios.

[34] Our subjects look like the grammatical «subject» in a sentence as pointed out by Sarah Thatcher, London School of Economics, during the FIDIS WP2 workshop in Fontainebleau (December 2004).

A *virtual person* is a mask for a subject. In the context of individual authentication and/or identification, a *virtual person* is usually defined by what it *is* and/or what it *has* and/or what it *does* and/or what it *knows*.

The *one who knows your credit card PIN code* is a virtual person defined by what it knows. The subject behind this mask should be yourself and yourself only. However, the subject can be a group of persons (e.g., you gave the PIN code to other members of your family) or there might be no subject at all (e.g., you do not remember the PIN code).

More generally, a virtual person can also be defined by its *attribute(s)* and/or its *role(s)* and/or its *ability(-ies)* and/or its *acquisition(s)* and/or its *preference(s)* and/or its *habit(s)*, etc.

The *President of the United States* is a virtual person defined through its role; the subject linked to this virtual person might change after each Presidential election. However, rights, duties and responsibilities described in the law and associated with this role, i.e., with this virtual person, do not depend on who is elected.

Actually, a virtual person acquires its own existence, which is not necessarily correlated with the existence of any real subject behind it.

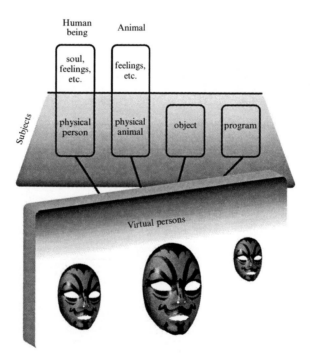

Fig. 2.2 Virtual persons

2.7.3.1 Virtual Persons Applied to Profiling

In her contribution, Mireille Hildebrandt gives the following definition for the *data subject*: "subject (human or non-human, individual or group) that data refer to." Her concept of *subject* is covered by our own definition of this term and is therefore compatible with our approach.

Using data mining techniques, subsets of elements sharing some properties can be defined. Virtual persons allow representation of the corresponding categories.

With each category, i.e., with each virtual person, is associated the inherited profile.

Indeed, with each virtual person is associated attributes, rules, preferences, etc. deduced from the correlations found via the data mining techniques: its *profile*. For example, people living downtown and earning more than €100,000 a year are likely to be more than 30 years old and not retired.

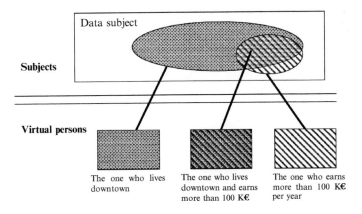

Fig. 2.3 Subsets of data subjects with their corresponding virtual persons (categories)

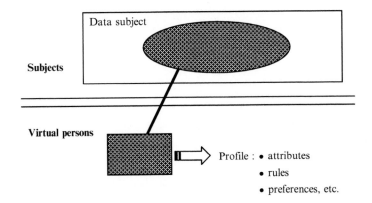

Fig. 2.4 Profile associated with a virtual person

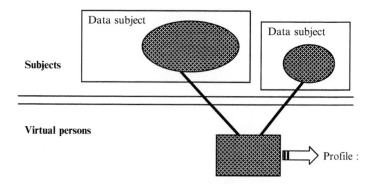

Fig. 2.5 Equivalent subsets defining the same category

At a later point, this knowledge may be used to infer probabilistic characteristics about what Mireille Hildebrandt calls the "end user" or the "profiled data subject."

Virtual persons acquire their own existence, which no longer depends on any specific, original subset of data subjects. Different data subjects can lead to equivalent subsets that define the same category, i.e., the same virtual person

2.7.4 Direct and Indirect Profiling

Profiling an end user consists in finding his profile by linking the end user to virtual persons.[35] Information gathered about the end user enables the data controller to find virtual persons linkable to this end user and to use the corresponding profiles for this end user. We consider that the classical distinction between individual and group profiling is not precise enough. We want to refine these concepts using direct and indirect profiling. *Direct profiling* occurs when the end user and the original data subject used to define the virtual person with its profile are the same. *Indirect profiling* aims at applying profiles deduced from other data subjects to an end user.

2.7.4.1 Direct Group Profiling

In the first chapter, Mireille Hildebrandt gives two examples of group profiling. In the case of a pre-existing community (members of a local church, students living in a certain dormitory) data are "collected, aggregated, stored and processed, in order

---

[35] In case of a direct profiling, it is essentially a direct construction of the profile. In case of an indirect profiling, it is the construction of the profile by applying a typical profile of a category.

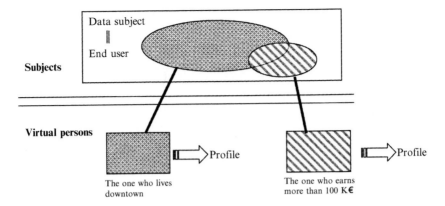

Fig. 2.6 Direct group profiling

to find shared features". Knowledge about this community (data subject) is established as the profile of the virtual person defined by this group.

When the end user is later the community itself, we have a typical example of a *direct group profiling*.

2.7.4.2 Indirect Group Profiling

Another example of group profiling given by Mireille Hildebrandt explains how data mining techniques find subsets of individuals in the group, who share certain attributes. This case illustrates the analogy between group profiling and the natural process of categorisation and generalisation of Schauer also described in the first chapter.

Each category defines a corresponding virtual person. The profile of this virtual person can then be applied (successfully or not) to any group (end user) linked to this virtual person. This gives a typical example for an *indirect group profiling*.

2.7.4.3 Direct Individual Profiling

In the case of individual profiling, the data subject contains one single element, the individual himself. Information is gathered about this individual and processed using data mining techniques, for example, in order to define his profile.

Knowledge in this profile derives directly and exclusively from the information about this individual. Such a profile will typically describe his habits and preferences, directly deduced from the observation of him.

This profile is then used for the individual himself in order to anticipate, for example, his actions, his behaviour or his preferences. This is what we call *direct individual profiling*.

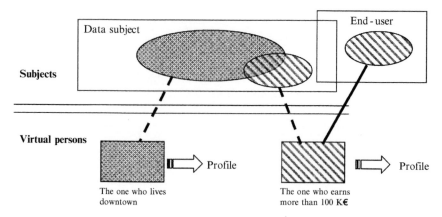

Fig. 2.7 Indirect group profiling

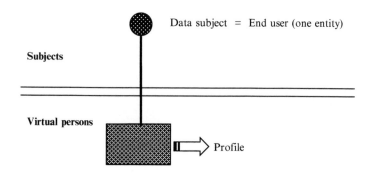

Fig. 2.8 Direct individual profiling

2.7.4.4 Indirect Individual Profiling

Direct individual profiling produces knowledge. This knowledge can in turn be mapped to pre-existing compatible virtual persons in order to infer probable profiles for this individual. These probable profiles come from pre-existing group profiles. This is what we call *indirect individual profiling*.

As an example, an insurance company might use group profiles in order to estimate risks associated with a potential client. If the person smokes, the group profile associated with the virtual person *the one who smokes* is used to infer probable characteristics of the potential client.

In a recent paper,[36] the authors explain how the knowledge of what a consumer watches on television (direct individual profiling) allows us to infer demographic characteristics about this consumer, such as his age or gender (indirect individual profiling).

---

[36] Spangler, W.E., Hartzel: K.S. and Gal-Or, M., 2006: 119-123.

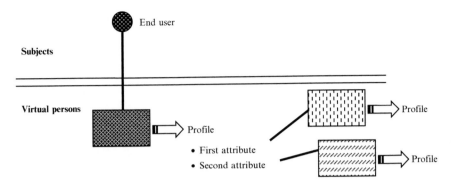

Fig. 2.9 Indirect individual profiling

The online bookstore *Amazon* gives personalised advice such as "people who have bought this book have also bought these others". Furthermore, it proposes personalised offers when the client is recognised through a cookie or when he enters his personal account. Those are typical examples of indirect individual profiling.

Real-time adaptive indirect individual profiling is part of the vision of the future AmI space, where the environment interacts with the individual in order, for example, to anticipate his needs.

2.7.5 Conclusion

Individual and group profiling have been refined using the new concept of direct and indirect profiling. While direct profiling is expected to be more reliable, indirect profiling uses the full potential of knowledge based on categorisation and generalisation.

We have shown how the generic model of virtual persons helps to describe profiling types. The four combined types of profiling have been illustrated using this model: direct group profiling, indirect group profiling, direct individual profiling and indirect group profiling.

2.8 Bibliography

Aarts, E. and Marzano, S., (eds.), *The New Everyday. Views on Ambient Intelligence.* 010 Publishers, Rotterdam, 2003.

Bourcier, D., 'De l'intelligence artificielle à la personne virtuelle: émergence d'une entité juridique?', *Droit et Société*, Vol. 49, l'Association française Droit et Société, Paris, 2001, pp. 847-871.

Custers, B., *The Power of Knowledge. Ethical, Legal, and Technological Aspects of Data Mining and Group Profiling in Epidemiology*, Wolf Legal Publishers, Nijmegen, 2004.

de Waal, F.B.M., *The Ape and the Sushi Master: Cultural Reflections of a Primatologist*, Basis Books, New York, 2001.

Edens, J.R., 'Misuses of the Hare Psychopathy Checklist-Revised in Court', *Journal of Interpersonal Violence*, Vol. 16, No. 10, Sage publications, London, 2001, pp. 1082-1094.

Gladwell, M., *Blink: The Power of Thinking Without Thinking*, Little, Brown and Company, Boston, 2005.

International Telecommunications Union (ITU), *The Internet of Things*, 7th Internet ITU report, 2005. Available (for purchase) at: http://www.itu.int/osg/ spu/publications/internetofthings/.

ISTAG (Information Society Technology Advisory Group), *Scenarios for Ambient Intelligence in 2010*, IST – IPTS report, EC, 2001. Available at: http://www.cordis.lu/ist/istag-reports.htm.

Jaquet – Chiffelle D.-O., Benoist, E., Anrig, B., 'Virtual? Identity', Chapter 3 of Nabeth, T. et al. (eds), *Set of use cases and scenarios, FIDIS Deliverable 2.2*, European Union IST FIDIS Project, 2006a. Available at: http://www.fidis.net/fileadmin/fidis/deliverables/fidis-wp2-del2.2_Cases__stories_and_Scenario.pdf

Jaquet – Chiffelle D.-O., Benoist, E., Anrig B,, 'Virtual persons applied to authorization, individual authenticatinon and identification', Jaquet – Chiffelle D.-O., Benoist, E., Anrig B. (eds.) *FIDIS brochure Deliverable 2.6*, '*Identity in a Networked World: Use Cases and Scenarios*', 2006b, pp. 6 and 7. Avalable at www.Vip.Ch

Kephart, J.O., Chess, D.M., 'The Vision of Autonomic Computing', *Computer*, Vol. 36, No. 1, IEEE Computer Society, Washington DC, 2003, pp. 41 - 50.

Lawton, G., 'Machine-to-Machine Technology Gears Up for Growth', *Computer*, Vol. 37, No. 9, IEEE Computer Society, Washington DC, Sept. 2004, pp. 12-15.

Leenes, R. and Koops, B.J., ' 'Code': Privacy's Death or Saviour?', *International Review of Law Computers & Technology*, Vol. 19, No. 3, Routledge, Oxford, 2005, pp. 329-340.

Maturana, H.R. and Varela, F.J., *Autopoiesis and Cognition: The Realization of the Living*, Reidel, Dordrecht, 1991.

Maturana, H. R., Varela, F.J., *The Tree of Knowledge. The Biological Roots of Human Understanding*, Shambala, Boston and London, 1998 (revised edition).

Peirce, Ch.S., *Pragmatism as a Principle and Method of Right Thinking. The 1903 Harvard Lectures on Pragmatism*, edited and introduced with a commentary by Patricia Ann Turrisi, State University of New York Press, Albany,1997.

Peppers, D., Rogers, M., *The One to One Future*, Currency, New York, 1993.

Plessner, H, *Die Stufen des Organischen under der Mensch. Einleitung in die philosophische Anthropologie*, Suhrkamp, Frankfurt, 1975.

Polanyi, M., *The Tacit Dimension*, Anchor Books, Garden City, New York, 1966.

Rafter, R. and Smyth, B., 'Passive Profiling from Server Logs in an Online Recruitment Environment', paper presented at *the IJCAI's Workshop on Intelligent Techniques for Web Personalization*, Seattle, Washington 4-6 August 2001. Available at http://maya.cs.depaul.edu/~mobasher/itwp01/papers/rafter.pdf.

Rasch, G., *Probabilistic Models for Some Intelligence and Attainment Tests*, University of Chicago Press, Chicago, Illinois, 1980.

Schauer, F., *Profiles Probabilities and Stereotypes*, Belknap Press of Harvard University Press, Cambridge, Mass. London, England, 2003.

Spangler, W. E., Hartzel K. S. and Gal-Or M., 'Exploring the Privacy Implications of Addressable Advertising and Viewer Profiling', *Communications of the ACM*, Vol. 49, No. 5, ACM Press, New York, 2006, pp. 119-123.

Stergiou, C. and Siganos, D., 'Neural Networks and their Users', *Surprise 96 Journal*, Vol. 4, Department of Science Technology and Medicin, Imperial College London, London, 1996. Available at: http://www.doc.ic.ac.uk/~nd/surprise_96/journal/vol4/cs11/report.html # Why%20use%20neural%20networks.

Thorndike, R.L. (ed.), *Educational Measurement*, American Council on Education, Washington, D. C., 2nd edition, 1971.

Turvey, B., *Criminal profiling: An introduction to behavioral evidence analysis*, Academic Press, New York, 1999.

Van Brakel, J., 'Telematic Life Forms', *Techné: Journal of the Society for Philosophy and Technology*, Vol. 4, No. 3, DLA, Blacksburg, 1999. Available at http://scholar.lib.vt.edu/ejournals/SPT/v4_n3html/VANBRAKE.html.

Vedder, A., "KDD: The challenge to individualism." *Ethics and Information Technology*, Volume 1, Number 4, Springer, 1999, pp. 275-281.

Weiser, M., 'The Computer for the Twenty-First Century', *Scientific American*, 265, 3, Scientific American Inc, New York, 1991, pp. 94-104.

Wilkie, William L. and Moore, E.S., 'Scholarly Research in Marketing: Exploring the "4 Eras" of Thought Development', *Journal of Public Policy & Marketing*, Vol. 22, No. 2, AMA Publications, Chicago, 2003, pp. 116-146.

Zarsky, Tal Z., '"Mine Your Own Business!": Making the Case for the Implications of the Data Mining of Personal Information in the Forum of Public Opinion', *Yale Journal of Law & Technology*, Vol. 5, 2002-2003. Available at: http://research.yale.edu/lawmeme/yjolt/files/20022003Issue/Zarsky.pdf

Chapter 3
General Description of the Process of Behavioural Profiling

Ana Canhoto and James Backhouse

The study of patterns of behaviour and the grouping of users according to exhibited behaviour is called behavioural profiling. Behavioural profiling uses detailed records of the relationship between the organisation and the user, such as records on product usage, account balance or transaction history. Beyond just knowing that someone did something, behavioural profiling involves capturing records of events and actions over time and using these stored records of interactions to model typical behaviour and deviations from that behaviour. Sometimes, this is augmented with data from outside databases, such as census data.

Behavioural profiling is performed through data mining, a process that ranges from data selection and preparation to post processing and includes the interpretation of the emerging results. This chapter provides an overview of the process of data mining, including a discussion of the main models and algorithms used and a reflection on the relationship between these and the objectives of the data mining exercise – e.g., an inductive process that aims to uncover patterns or relationships previously unknown versus a deductive process that looks for confirmation, or indeed departures, from accepted patterns or models of behaviour.

Data mining has its origins in quantitative disciplines, including the artificial intelligence community (e.g., machine learning and pattern recognition) and the mathematical community (e.g., statistics and uncertainty processing). However, human cognitive factors can deeply affect the results of a data mining effort. This chapter concludes with a discussion of how the data mining user can influence the outcomes of data mining.

3.1 Introduction

The study of patterns of behaviour and the grouping of users according to exhibited behaviour is called 'behavioural profiling'. Behavioural profiling uses detailed records of the relationship between the organisation and the data subject, such as evidence of product usage, account balance, preferred method of payment or transaction history. Sometimes, the profile is augmented with data from outside databases, such as census or credit bureau data. Beyond just capturing and storing records of events and actions over time in order to know that someone did something, behavioural profiling involves using such records to model typical behaviour and detect deviations from that behaviour. Additionally, the actual profiling exercise

Henley Management College, London School of Economics (LSE)

M. Hildebrandt and S. Gutwirth (eds.), *Profiling the European Citizen:*
Cross-Disciplinary Perspectives.
© Springer Science + Business Media B.V. 2008

may aim at either identifying individual patterns of behaviour or allocating observed behaviour to a pre-existing category. This section analyses the process through which data records are transformed into information about behaviour.

Profiling is an attempt to deal with the diversity and complexity of reality, through categorisation. Society is complex and, therefore, individuals often need to make decisions and judgements very quickly, which is made possible only through the identification and understanding of underlying patterns in particular situations. In their lives, people classify behaviours and occurrences into categories by identifying similar characteristics between a given exemplar and stored representations – for instance, a tax analyst may learn about the average income levels of particular professional occupations. Once categories are established in the analyst's mind, he or she can use them to draw inferences in a new situation – for instance, if someone reports that he or she works as a parking attendant, the analyst infers that such person will have a monthly income within a certain bracket. Similarly, organisations try to make sense of the complex reality in which they operate by categorising interactions between the organisation and its users. Traditionally, the strategic level of the organisation defines the management information needs such as which customers buy which products. The operational level collects and manipulates the data, mechanically. The data being collected refers to human behaviour which is of an informal nature.

At this stage, it is important to distinguish between the terms 'data' and 'information'. Liebenau and Backhouse (1990) define data as *'symbolic surrogates which are generally agreed upon to represent people, objects, events and concepts'* whereas *'information is the result of modelling, formatting, organising or converting data in a way that increases the level of knowledge for its recipient'*. That is, *'information is data arranged in a meaningful way for some perceived purpose'* (Liebenau and Backhouse, 1990). The different natures of data and information, in turn, imply that capturing more data does not necessarily lead to better information. Furthermore, the skills necessary to collect and transmit data, are not necessarily the same as those needed to identify and understand information. We propose that the ability to identify the relevant data inputs and to understand their meaning is a key skill in profiling. The remainder of this chapter examines both the technical and the social aspects of profiling. The chapter concludes with a discussion of how the data mining user can influence the outcomes of data mining.

3.2   The Technical Process

The technical process of profiling refers to the mechanical manipulation of the data. The analysis of the technical process is primarily focused on issues of efficiency, such as reducing uncertainty or avoiding errors caused by noise or distortion inherent in the tools being used. The process can develop in two ways (Table 3.1).

On the one hand, profiling may follow an inductive logic that actively explores raw facts and looks for connections in the data. Performed in this way, profiling

Table 3.1 Elements of the inductive and deductive approaches to profiling

	Inductive process	Deductive process
Input:	Data	Known pattern + data
Search for:	Pattern in the data (directed or undirected)	*Confirmation or departure from pattern*
Output:	Explanation of observed behaviour	*Monitoring of behaviour*

aims to uncover patterns or relationships previously unknown and, thus, assist the analyst in explaining the behaviour observed. The inductive approach may be undertaken with the support of a domain expert who will suggest which attributes are the most informative, in which case profiling is referred to as 'directed'. Or, at the other extreme, the 'undirected' approach, where the exercise is measuring everything available. Pure 'undirected' exercises are rare, though. As Clive Humby (2003), a renowned market research expert, notes '*Trying to achieve perfection with transactional data is next to impossible: far better to have a good idea based on experience and instinct, then to go looking for the data to prove it, or at least strongly support it*' (Humby, 2003, 97).

Alternatively, profiling may follow a deductive logic that looks for confirmation, or refutation, of accepted patterns or models of behaviour. In this case, profiling is performed in order to test hypotheses, fit models to a dataset or to identify behaviours that depart from the norm: while the inductive approach aims to identify behaviour of the data subjects, the deductive approach aims to monitor behaviour.

In practice, the two goals are often interrelated and it is very common that following a deductive approach, in which the analyst identifies an outlier of an existing model of expected behaviour, an inductive process will take place in order to refine the model and eventually, inform future deductive profiling efforts. For example, an economist using a model to predict the risk of corporate bankruptcy *vis a vis* certain environmental factors, may realise that the accuracy of the model declines significantly in periods of sustained economic recession. Such a finding, in turn, may prompt the analyst to develop a new profile to be applied specifically under economic crisis conditions.

The traditional method of processing behavioural data and classifying the data subjects relied on manual analysis and interpretation. Nowadays, however, the process is highly automated and dependent on computer technology. This dependency is justified by the increase in size of the typical database as well as by a desire to keep costs under control. In particular, organisations routinely use data mining technology and techniques to analyse the vast amounts of data available.

The process of data mining will vary according to whether it is aimed at identifying (inductive) or monitoring (deductive) behaviour. Nonetheless, it usually starts with a specification of the problem domain, as well as an understanding of the goals of the project. Such a specification is usually undertaken by the business users of the profile who, in this way, impart domain knowledge to the exercise. For instance, in a supermarket located in a busy office area, a directed inductive approach may seek to answer a question such as 'What items sell with sandwiches?' in order to maximise the supermarket's appeal to lunchtime customers. If the exercise is undirected, however, the question would be something like 'What items sell together?'. If profiling follows a deductive approach, however, it will look for early signs that lunchtime customers are changing their preferences or preparing to switch to a competitor. Clive Humby reports that '*if we can't answer that question, how can we redefine the question so that we can answer it? There is always a solution*' (Humby, 2003, 143).

The following stage comprises the selection of the relevant data to be used in the profiling exercise. This stage includes an assessment of the existing knowledge and data, as well as an appraisal of the data that needs to be collected. In order for the analyst to be able to select the relevant input variables, it is imperative that he or she has a good knowledge of the business problem being addressed. A common problem at this stage is that the inputs which the domain expert considers important, based on his or her experience, are not represented in the raw input data, or are represented but not in a way that the data mining tools can recognise. In this case, the analyst uses proxies, that is, data fields or sources that represent, albeit incompletely, the data needed. The output of this stage is a target dataset that will be used for the data mining exercise.

Before the actual mining starts, it is necessary to pre-process the target dataset in order to minimise some of the problems usually encountered in datasets. A common problem is that the existence of too many attributes, i.e., too much detail. In this case, it is necessary to reduce the number of attributes, using dimensionality reduction or transformation methods to detect variant representations of the same data. Additionally, the analyst can use attribute mining to isolate from the remaining ones those attributes that are particularly informative. Another common problem is the incompatibility of different computer architectures. This problem requires the data to be 'translated' between platforms. Yet another issue is the inconsistency of data encoding and the possibility of missing data fields such as questions that were not answered in a questionnaire or attributes not applicable to a given object. Finally, the datasets need to be cleansed of existing 'noise', such as random events that have no perceivable causality.

In the following stage, the analyst analyses the data with the purpose, in the inductive case, of finding useful patterns or, in the deductive case, of fitting an existing model to the data in order to test its suitability and detect outliers. A key component of this stage is the choice of the algorithm to search the data. As discussed above, the choice is influenced by the data available, the model that informs the process and the preference criterion of one model or set of parameters over another. The model informing the process, in turn, reflects the function to be performed, as well as the representational form chosen. Figure 3.1 illustrates this relationship.

A *classification* model emerges after examining the features of a newly presented object and assigning it to one of a predefined set of classes. This task has a discrete outcome and the analyst expects to be able to assign any record into one or another of the predefined classes. An *estimation* model is similar to the classification

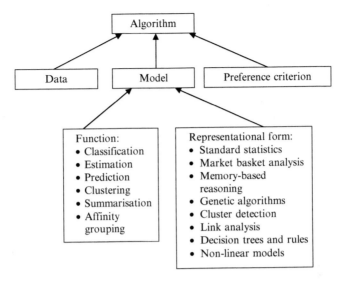

Fig. 3.1 Factors influencing the choice of algorithm

one, except that it deals with continuous variables. Furthermore, the resulting records may be ranked in order. A *prediction* model, also referred to in the data mining literature as 'regression' (e.g., (Chan and Lewis, 2002)), also has similarities to the classification and estimation models, except for the fact that it refers to the future whereas the other two refer to past events. A *clustering* model, also referred to as 'segmentation', assigns an object to a class. These classes are determined from the data by finding natural groupings of data items. It is up to the analyst to determine what meaning to attach to the clusters resulting from the grouping exercise. A *summarisation* model, also known as 'description', provides a compact description for a subset of the data in a way that increases the understanding of the processes that produced the data in the first place. Finally, an *affinity grouping* model, also known as 'dependency analysis', 'link analysis' and 'sequence analysis', generates rules from the data that describe significant relations between fields in the database. These relations can either occur together or in a sequence.

Models, in turn, may be represented in many forms. The choice of model representation is, in fact, very important because it determines both the robustness of the model and its interpretability. Popular model representations are standard statistics, market basket analysis, memory-based reasoning (also known as example-based models), genetic algorithms, cluster detection, link analysis, decision trees and rules and non-linear models (e.g., neural networks). The choice of model representation and the specific parameters of the model are partially influenced by the type of data available (Table 3.2). For instance, complex models such as decision trees are particularly useful for finding structure in high-dimensional problems, such as classification or prediction.

Table 3.2 Correspondence between model representational forms and model functions

		Function				
		Clustering	Classification	Prediction	Affinity	...
Representational form	Cluster detection	▓▓▓				
	Neural networks	▓▓▓	▓▓▓	▓▓▓		
	Memory-based reasoning				▓▓▓	
	Decision trees		▓▓▓	▓▓▓		

However, models with increased complexity may also be more difficult to understand by users other than the initial developers. Therefore, what tends to happen, according to Fayyad *et al.* (1996), is that while researchers develop and advocate rather complex models, practitioners often use simple models that provide ease of interpretability while guaranteeing a reasonable robustness. Ultimately, the choice of the model is subject to the analyst's judgement and tends to be heavily influenced by the data analyst's experience, the model robustness and its interpretability and the total cost of implementing the analytical solution.

Finally, the preference criterion reflects the objective of avoiding over- or under-fitting of the model. Over-fitting is when the model memorises the data and predicts results based on idiosyncrasies in the particular data used for training. It tends to occur when the data set is too small, or when the predicted field is redundant. Under-fitting is when the resulting model fails to match patterns of interest in the data. It tends to occur when variables with predictive power are not included in the model, or if the technique does not work well for the data in question.

The final stage of the profiling process consists of examining the outcomes of the data mining exercise and interpreting and using the resulting information. A major problem at this stage is the gap between the volume of output generated in the previous step and the capacity to inspect such output manually in order to gain insight from the data mining exercise. A number of studies present measures of 'interestingness' of the patterns identified (e.g., (Silberschatz and Tuzhilin, 1996)). These measures can be classified as objective when they depend solely on the structure of the pattern and the underlying data used in the data mining effort and are classified as subjective when they also depend on the analysts examining the data mining output. Another important issue at this stage is that the analyst has to judge whether the outcomes are possible, internally consistent and plausible. The statistical results need to be critically interpreted or they may lead to ridiculous conclusions, such as the finding of strong positive correlation between the number of buildings destroyed in fires and the number of water tanks involved in fire fighting, the occurrence of stillbirths and the presence of a doctor during labour or the number of births and the number of storks. These results will typically raise further questions, sometimes in

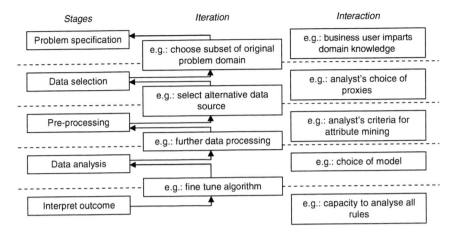

Fig. 3.2 Iterative and interactive nature of profiling
Source: (Canhoto 2007)

conflict with previously believed knowledge therefore leading to the generation of new hypotheses and the start of a new data mining cycle.

It is important to highlight that the process is both iterative and interactive (Fig. 3.2). It is iterative in the sense it often requires feedback loops, with the information feeding back to inform the iteration of prior steps in the process. It is interactive in the sense that the analyst needs to make several decisions and take actions throughout the process. The iteration of the process is discussed in chapter 3.4, with reference to the CRISP-DM model. The next section examines the role of the analyst in the profiling exercise.

3.3 The Social Process

Given that data mining follows an interactive process where the analyst makes several decisions and takes actions, it is critical to understand the impact that the user has on the whole process. The social process of profiling refers to the issues concerning cognition and communication between those involved in the collection, processing and analysis of data. The analysis of the social process addresses issues of effectiveness, such as whether the algorithm chosen fits the business user's intentions. The profiling and, in particular, the data mining literature identify two ways in which the user influences the data mining tool: domain knowledge and bias information. The former refers to the information available at the beginning of the data mining process. The later refers to the syntactic and support constraints introduced during the process regarding the search space, the rules to apply and, ultimately, which patterns in the data are deemed useful or interesting. Hence, even though profiling is largely a quantitative and automated process, it is important to understand how the analyst plays a crucial role in the several steps and, therefore, how social and cognitive factors can affect the profiling exercise.

We compare profile development to a process of deriving information (*variable z*) from specific data inputs (*variable x*) through cognition (*variable y*). Different analysts may reach diverse conclusions because they focus on different data or because they interpret the same data input differently as a result of disparities in what the analysts are afforded with (*variable y_1*) or the norms that guide the analysts' behaviour (*variable y_2*). This understanding is illustrated in Fig 3.3, below.

'Data', as discussed above, includes records collected by the organisation as well as by external sources. Examples are identity data such as the customer's date of birth, name and address, as well as activity data such as the customer's spending patterns or product acquisition. 'Cognition' refers to the mental process of recognising patterns in the data, or its usefulness and is influenced by affordances and norms. The concept of 'affordance' is borrowed from direct perception psychology (see (Gibson, 1979)), and refers to the patterns of behaviour made possible by some combination of the structure of the organism and its environment. In the case of profiling, affordances are the possible actions that the organisation's technical artefacts and its employees can perform, such as manipulation of data and dissemination of information. The concept of 'norm' is the social equivalent of the affordance in the sense that norms provide the socially acceptable repertoire of behaviour but are realised by groups of agents rather than single agents as with affordances. Of particular importance to the study of behaviour in organisations is the distinction between technical, formal and informal norms.

Technical norm is a term that implies the operands are clearly identified and the operators can always be applied to them – for instance, a customer with an overdraft that is more than what is authorised will be charged a fee of £25 plus for each day outstanding a higher rate of interest. Additionally, technical norms are so exactly specified that they can be automated and executed by a computer and there is no scope for ambiguity in interpretation.

Formal norms are those that have been officially documented, such as national laws, industry regulations or organisational policies. Formal norms are specified at a higher, more abstract level than the technical ones and, therefore, have to be interpreted (by humans) – for instance, the legal norm stating that 'data should only be collected

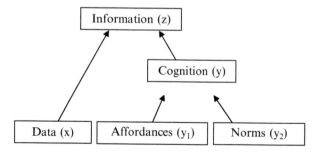

Fig 3.3 Factors impacting on profiling

with the consent of the data subject and used for the purposes stated' still requires assistance from a legal professional in interpreting 'consent', 'used' and 'purposes'.

Informal norms are habits and unofficial conventions that may have been verbally agreed or even never verbally mentioned but that people nonetheless follow. For instance, the generally accepted convention that investment bankers may wear casual clothing on Fridays but are not to do so on any other day of the week. Informal norms may or may not have the power of the law associated with them[37] but will always have the power of social forces behind them. Traditionally, we are talking about informal expectations such as 'a person who earns less than the national average will be unlikely to own a yacht', or even more informally 'a mother who abandons her child to another person is beneath contempt'.

In the context of profiling, technical norms may regard which employees are given user names and passwords that grant them access to particular databases, formal norms may include the organisation's policy for development of algorithms and informal norms may refer to the *ad hoc* discussion of relevant snippets of news among colleagues.

The role of these factors in profiling is discussed next, illustrated with the findings from a case study developed in a UK financial institution, to be referred to as 'FI'. In order to protect the organisation's security and operational interests, all names and figures have been disguised. The particular profiling application studied is the development of profiles of behaviour to detect instances of financial crime.

The inputs that FI considers for the profiling process are drawn from a pool of external and internal sources (Table 3.3). Some sources are considered more valuable than others: the knowledge that another bank, widely regarded as a leader in anti money laundering monitoring, was targeting certain geographical areas and commercial organisations quickly prompted FI to develop similar rules. By contrast, the information that another institution monitors a specific age group did not prompt FI to apply the same rule, which was justified by the fact that the given organisation faced a different type of money launderer.

Similarly, some data are considered more relevant than others. In particular, FI is interested in data concerning the crimes that it considers more likely to be perpetrated by its client base. For instance, given that it has branches in areas where

Table 3.3 Data considered in the profile building process

	Internal to the organisation	
External to the organisation	Outside the profiling team	Inside the profiling team
Financial intelligence unit	Fraud department	Reports of success stories
Law enforcement agencies		
Other banks		
Research bodies		
Press		

---

[37] Although it may be used in common law to support a "custom and practice" defence.

terrorist cells are suspected of being active, it has devoted considerable resources to the development of profiles of terrorist financing activity.

Some of the data obtained by the profiling team has a factual, denotative[38] nature, demonstrating that specific behaviour is or was pursued by known money launderers, as illustrated in the quote below:

> *"We had a couple of cases where we had good hits - for instance, a human trafficker that we helped to get arrested coming out of the branch. It was a huge success and it is good feedback to the team. Because we don't get a huge feedback..."*

Information of this nature is the most valued by the team because it clearly establishes the relationship between banking and criminal behaviour:

> *'I told them of the stolen vehicles that went to [country x] and other countries that [have particular characteristic in common]. I told them about the scam and the referral we had. When we investigated, it was a [specific type of commercial organisation], and the only thing that was happening was [particular type of transactions]...'*

However, instances of denotative information do not occur systematically. Moreover, such information tends to refer to unique, unrepeatable events upon which a judgement must still be made regarding the application of that knowledge to other situations.

Most descriptive information available at FI is of an affective[39] nature, embodying value judgements about which transactions are likely to reflect money laundering activity, or which businesses or post codes are particularly risky. One example was the development of an algorithm to monitor the business accounts linked to a specific type of commercial organisation and whose postal code indicated that they were located along the border of two particular countries. Such a rule was developed following news that, in order to fund its terrorist activity, a known terrorist group smuggled items traditionally traded by such organisations. The accounts flagged by this rule were subsequently investigated by the analysts who, in the absence of intelligence regarding which commercial organisations were under the control of the terrorist group or which were the specific patterns of transactions of a 'legitimate' organisation of that type as opposed to one controlled by the terrorist group, could only guess which outlets were engaged in suspicious activity.

The transformation of data (variable x) into information (variable z), is performed by the profiling team. That is, it is an affordance (variable y_1) of the individual members of the team, while employees of FI. But there are also other affordances that are specific to each role in the team and that emerge from the team members' different positions in the organisation. For instance, one team member participates in several executive committees and steering groups which grants him a wide view of the operations of the organisation but also exposes him directly to cost-control pressures. Another member assists marketing department colleagues in

---

[38] I.e., Objective information, specificly and directly referring to a particular instance of money laundering activity.

[39] I.e., Information resulting from, or influenced by, the interpretation of the analyst.

their profiling efforts and hence, obtains insights regarding the typical revenue and spending patterns of particular types of business, or the socio-demographic profile of residents in selected postal codes.

Of further interest is the study of the behaviours allowed to FI's employees by force of the informal, formal and technical norms (y_2), as illustrated by the following case of development of a profile to monitor possible tax evasion. The patterns of banking behaviour that are deemed suspicious of representing this crime are described at decreasing levels of abstraction and *translated* into the machine language until specific unambiguous criteria are reached. The process aims to connect otherwise disparate pieces of personal, product and transaction data into a complex formula. The descent from the most abstract level to more concrete ones requires decisions between various possible alternative solutions, focusing the attention on a few specific concrete paths.

The decision between specific paths is determined by technical norms, such as the maximum number of algorithms that can run on the system at any moment. As a result, the system's administrator switches rules on and off according to external events (e.g., a terrorist attack), internal priorities (e.g., suspicion that FI has been targeted by a fraud ring) or the lack of activity from a given rule (e.g., if the number of alerts from a rule falls below a given threshold). The choice between paths is also affected by formal norms such as the rule that personal accounts cannot be used for business purposes. This is because of internal policies such as different fees charged for the two types of accounts, as well as external regulations. Finally, there are informal norms such as the desired level of output. In order to keep the number of alerts within a level that can be analysed by the team of analysts within a given period, the rules are often fine-tuned and narrowed down.

In summary, profiling is not only a technical process but also a social one. Far from being the discovery of an objective truth, in which the methods comprise neutral techniques, separated from the value system of the analyst, profiling is an activity where subjectivity matters. The definition of behavioural patterns is achieved by way of definition by context – that is, it is done in the context of normal behaviour for a given type of customer, product or activity which enable the analysts to advance some general laws about how certain data subjects behave and why. However, when the information circulating in the organisation is of an affective, rather than denotative, nature, such profiles embody more values than facts. That does not mean that the profiles should be dismissed but rather that their nature and limitations must be recognised, namely the permeability to the cognitive and task constraints of those in charge of construing the definition. What is essential is that those involved in developing and applying profiles be aware of the tensions herewith described and periodically check the quality of the information being circulated.

Similarly, holding specific positions in the organisation gives employees access to different pieces of information and also puts them under different pressures, thus possibly leading to differences in terms of point of view and knowledge. As Berger and Luckmann (1966) explained, a society's body of knowledge is structured in terms of relevance and the areas of knowledge that are likely to be relevant to the members of a social group are determined by the members' pragmatic interests and situation in society.

The technical norms limit not only the content of the rules that can be developed but also the variety of behaviours that can be monitored at any time. The formal norms may provide explicit guidance but, ultimately, the use of specific formulae is determined by pragmatic interests. Individuals draw on a flexible set of tools or *repertoire* of habits and techniques that are actively deployed by the individuals in order to pursue valued ends. It is important for those engaged in profiling to investigate the ways in which differing environmental cues situate particular cultural frames and, therefore, profiles. Until the emerging profiles are crystallised in the organisation's procedures, it is essential that the existing sources of bias be identified and corrected as soon as possible.

3.4   Reply: Towards a Data Mining De Facto Standard

Mark Gasson, Will Browne*

Profiling is undoubtedly a powerful tool and is evidently being enabled by advances in data mining technologies. Yet, for exactly the reason that it is 'powerful', we have to be vigilant during its deployment into the mass of disparate applications. Despite this, we continue to develop software tools, whose misuse have great potential consequences, which we place into the hands of the masses with little guidance or suggestion and with little idea how to assess the results. Consider the analogy of electrical power-tools. It is because of the acute awareness of the consequences of their misuse that we are guided at each step by the manufacturer's instructions. We are not expected to adopt the 'suck it and see' approach in the hope that what results will be sufficient. The same degree of support should be realised for software tools whose apparent risk is far outweighed by the consequences of its inappropriate usage. As such, here we discuss the relevance of developing models of best practise for data mining applications, such as CRISP-DM, which will enable a reasonable level of assurance that the involved, complex and esoteric data mining process will ultimately render useful, repeatable and, most importantly, valid results.

"*Profiling is an attempt to deal with the diversity and complexity of reality, through categorisation*".

We chose this statement as our starting point for two reasons. Firstly because it goes a long way to revealing profiling's raison d'être and secondly because of something that is does not say. Profiling is not an activity that is restricted to the domain of computer technology - it is an activity that takes many forms. Indeed, we actively profile, be it consciously or sub-consciously, everyday of our lives. We may know it by other names: 'intuition', 'gut-feeling' or simply rational reasoning, yet when we cross the street to avoid that unsavoury looking character or conclude that the man sporting both a beret *and* a goatee probably owns a vast collection of works by Voltaire, we are making an 'educated' guess based on our experiences, we are profiling. This is certainly not to say that profiling is inherently wrong and

---

* University of Reading

that we are unjustly stereotyping. Indeed as discussed in Chapter 2, many authors such as Schauer claim that profiling is a form of dimensionality reduction which is simply necessary for us to cope with everyday life.

The act of profiling, in what ever form it takes, is the *art* of generalisation through simplification. Being scientists, 'art' is not a term that we tend to use – however, profiling is a process that is learnt through practise and observation and one which we continue to hone over time. This is rightly reflected in the quote above: profiling is an 'attempt', an estimation, an approximation. It falls short of being an 'exact science' in the literal sense. It is because people can adapt, improvise and above all be creative, that we are in good stead for being able to profile. We are not 'perfect'. We do not operate using rigid or stoic rules. Yet, in a way, this serves to enable us.

However, as we become increasingly swamped by information we turn to technology to remove from us the burden of utilising it to full effect. Indeed, as discussed in this chapter, with the advent of new technologies to both capture, store and analyse data 'the process' in a commercial context has become "... *highly automated and dependent on computer technology.*" The interesting irony here is that computers are renowned for having the opposite of some of the attributes that perhaps make us proficient profilers. They will repeatedly do exactly what we programme them to do, line for line, word for word, regardless of how (to us) obviously wrong this may be. Perhaps we can say that they simply lack common sense? They are emotionless number-crunchers. Yet it is because of this that we tend to have unwavering, albeit misplaced, faith in them, a way of thinking that seems to have become entrenched in the public consciousness. The roots of this logic can perhaps even be traced back to the conception of the very first 'programmable machine' - whilst seeking funding for its development, members of the UK parliament queried its creator, "*Pray, Mr. Babbage, if you put into the machine wrong figures, will the right answers come out?*"

This is not to say that the casual user cannot adopt new technological innovations, this is clearly not the case. The onus is however on the scientists, as we develop tools for use within the mass-markets, to be aware that the underlying technologies will remain esoteric. Automated profiling is undoubtedly a powerful tool but there are consequences for using it inappropriately or for drawing ill-informed conclusions from it and these issues serve to fan the flames of the technophobes.

For many, automated profiling marks a shift in thinking from the traditional social science approach, which typically starts with a hypothesis that is then tested by researching a sample of a population. In this case, the research aims at explaining phenomena in terms of causal relationships, with intuition and professional experience playing a crucial role but not actually to construct hypotheses or predict future behaviour as is the case with data mining techniques. In this sense the knowledge or 'correlations' produced by profiling technologies are different in several ways

One of the key considerations is that the existence of a correlation, as revealed by the technological process *does not* necessarily imply that there is an underlying causal relationship. Even if it does, it may be meaningless because it is dependent on one or more other factors. These issues are further compounded because, although typically perceived as a wholly quantitative and automated process, one cannot simply ignore that the human user is an integral part of the loop '... *the data mining user can influence the outcomes of data mining.*' As discussed in the chapter, the effects of 'domain knowledge' and 'bias information', i.e., social and cognitive factors, cannot be discounted.

Given the inevitability of spurious correlations and the inherent user bias within the process, misinterpretation is not uncommon – most notably, this is where the flawed axiom of machine infallibility comes into play and highlights the importance of evolving a data mining *de facto* standard model, which can guide some of the data mining processes for multiple and diverse data mining objectives. Such an application and industry neutral model will enable a reasonable level of assurance that the involved, complex and esoteric data mining process will ultimately render useful, repeatable and valid results for any given application.

Although several such models have been proposed, the non-proprietary and freely available CRoss-Industry Standard Process for Data Mining (CRISP-DM) [40] has been widely adopted. CRISP-DM provides a uniform framework of guidelines and methodology specifically designed to help guide the overall process and is analogous in many ways to the social science borne semiotic analysis of knowledge discovery in databases model.[41]

However, partly funded by the European Commission,[42] the CRISP-DM methodology was created in conjunction with practitioners and vendors to supply checklists, guidelines, tasks and objectives for every stage of the data mining process. In this way, CRISP-DM aims to ensure the quality of the results while reducing the core skills necessary to perform the process and ultimately reduce the time and costs involved.

The CRISP-DM model focuses on six key phases of the overall process, shown in Fig. 3.4 of this chapter. The order of the phases is not strict since the results of one phase may show that more effort is required in a previous one. However, the general dependencies between each phase are shown. The surrounding circle illustrates that the process itself is indeed continuous in that information gathered throughout the process and especially during deployment may well be used to feed back into earlier phases.

The six key phases in the CRISP-DM model are specific areas in which the user needs to have a good understanding in order to ensure valid results from the data mining endeavour. However, arguably the aspect of most importance is that of *Business*

---

[40] An electronic copy of the CRISP-DM Version 1.0 Process Guide and User Manual is available free of charge at: http://www.crisp-dm.org/.

[41] Canhoto, I. A., and Backhouse, J. (2004).

[42] Partially funded by the European Commission under the ESPRIT Programme, project number 24.959. http://cordis.europa.eu/esprit/.

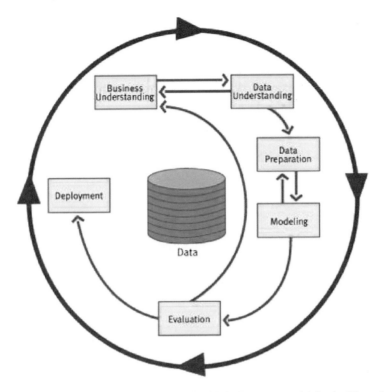

Fig. 3.4 A facsimile of the key phases of the CRISP-DM process model for the life cycle of a data mining project from the CRISP-DM Process Guide and User Manual[43]

Understanding. This is because it is essential that the data mining user appreciates the business for which the analysis is being performed. Without this understanding it is not guaranteed that the correct data is being used or indeed that it is being used in an appropriate manner. As such, it is suggested in the model that objectives and requirements of any data mining task are first conceived from the business perspective and from this an initial framework to achieve these objectives is evolved.

The *Data Understanding* phase is closely linked with business understanding but it is more concerned with increasing familiarity with the data. Through this familiarity the analyst will be able to form initial hypotheses about relationships in the data or equally importantly be able to observe weaknesses in the data collection such as missing data or issues with quality. Once the data is deemed appropriate, it

[43] © CRISP-DM consortium: NCR Systems Engineering Copenhagen (USA and Denmark), DaimlerChrysler AG (Germany), SPSS Inc. (USA) and OHRA Verzekeringen en Bank Groep B.V (The Netherlands), see http://www.crisp-dm.org/.

needs to be transformed from raw data into the data sets which can then be applied to the data modelling phase. This is likely to include multiple iterations of data cleaning, choice of important attributes for usage and other transformations. Because of the data manipulation involved this *Data Preparation* phase is notorious for being a key cause of user generated bias in the data, so a good understanding of the potential consequences this stage inherently involves is important. Once the data sets are constructed a range of modelling techniques are applied and opti-mised. This is the actual data mining phase and known in the literature as *Modelling*. Because there are many modelling tools that have been developed, which may pro-duce varied results depending on the nuances of the data, it is usual to go back to the data preparation stage to transform the data into a form more suited to each technique in order to test them.

With any modelling process it is necessary to assess whether or not the model actually fulfils the objectives set at the beginning. This *Evaluation* stage will usu-ally lead to subsequent modification of previous stages in the data mining process to improve the results before they are deployed. The *Deployment* phase can be any-thing from documenting knowledge gathered through the process or implementing real-time versions of the model depending on the specific application.

Each of these phases has a hierarchical structure which incorporates four further layers of abstraction. These serve to expand the simple model into a comprehensive guide for implementing any given application, helping to ensure the validity, effi-ciency and repeatability of the data mining process. A more detailed description of CRISP-DM can be found in [Shearer 2000][44].

Over the past few years, since CRISP-DM was originally conceptualised and developed, the needs of data mining users, technologies available, types of data harvested and types of deployment required have all evolved. To address these and other emerging issues, the CRISP-DM 2.0 Special Interest Group has been created which aims to harness the knowledge and experience of users, vendors, developers and service providers to further develop this data mining methodology and make it even more relevant to today's applications.

Whilst such developments in structured approaches to data mining are evidently invaluable, they must not be considered a panacea for the increasingly overwhelm-ing volume of data, from every aspect of our daily lives, which is being captured and stored. Irrefutably, intelligently analysed data is a valuable resource but '... *the ability to identify the relevant data inputs and to understand their meaning is a key skill* ...' In this vein, perhaps the most pertinent point to take from this chapter is that the thesis 'more data will inevitably lead to better information' simply *does not hold true*. However, any data mining user who is properly informed by methodolo-gies such as those discussed here will, in any case, be able to intelligently approach any given data mining endeavour.

---

[44] Shearer, C. 2000:13–23.

3.5 Bibliography

Canhoto, I.A. and Backhouse, J., 'Constructing categories, Construing signs – analysing differences in Suspicious Transaction Reporting practice', IS-CORE 2004 - 4th Annual SIG IS Cognitive Research Workshop, 2004.

Canhoto, A.I., 'Ontology-based interpretation and validation of mined knowledge: Normative and cognitive factors in data mining', in Nigro, H. O., Cisaro, S. E. G. and Xodo, D. H., *Data mining with ontologies: implementations, findings, and frameworks,*. Hershey, NY, Information Science Reference, 2007, pp. 84-105.

Chan, C. and Lewis, B., 'A Basic Primer on Data Mining', *Information Systems Management*, Vol. 19, No. 4, Taylor & Francis, Inc. Philadelphia, 2002, pp. 56-60.

Fayyad, U., Piatetsky-Shapiro, G. and Smyth, P., 'The Kdd Process for Extracting Useful Knowledge from Volumes of Data', *Communications of the ACM*, Vol. 39, No. 11, ACM Press, New York, 1996, pp. 27-34.

Gibson, J.J., *The Ecological Approach to Visual Perception*, Houghton Mifflin Co, Boston, 1979.

Humby, C., Hunt, T. and Phillips, T., *Scoring Points: How Tesco Is Winning Customer Loyalty*, Kogan Page, London, 2003.

Liebenau, J. and Backhouse, J., *Understanding Information: An Introduction*, Macmillan, London, 1990.

Shearer, C. 'CRISP-DM Model: The New Blueprint for Data Mining', *Journal of Data Warehousing*, Vol. 5, No. 4, The Data Warehousing Institute. 1105 Media, Inc, Chatsworth, CA, 2000, pp. 13-23.

Silberschatz, A. and Tuzhilin, A. 'What Makes Patterns Interesting in Knowledge Discovery Systems', *IEEE Transactions on Knowledge and Data Engineering*, Vol.8, No. 6, IEEE Computer Society, Washington D.C, 1996, pp. 970-974.

Chapter 4
The Role of Algorithms in Profiling

Bernhard Anrig, Will Browne, and Mark Gasson

Algorithms can be utilised to play two essential roles in the data mining endeavour. Firstly, in the form of procedures, they may determine how profiling is conducted by controlling the profiling process itself. For example, methodologies such as CRISP-DM have been designed to control the process of extracting information from the large quantities of data that have become readily available in our modern, data rich society. In this situation, algorithms can be tuned to assist in the capture, verification and validation of data, as discussed in the reply to Chapter 3.

Secondly, algorithms, dominantly as mathematical procedures, can be used as the profiling engine to identify trends, relationships and hidden patterns in disparate groups of data. The use of algorithms in this way often means that more effective profiles can ultimately be computed than would be possible manually. In this chapter we show how algorithms find a natural home at the very heart of the profiling process and how such machine learning can actually be used to address the task of knowledge discovery.

4.1 Algorithms as the Engine of Profiling

Data mining techniques and algorithms can be considered as the main ingredient for profiling. In this chapter we will consider the respective algorithms[45] as the engine of the profiling process and discuss the general notions and techniques as well as the types of data mining. The introduction to the basics of data mining is based on the assumptions that the reader has limited statistical background and some previous exposure to data mining techniques, thus the text is intended as an overview and not considered as a technical documentation of algorithms. It should be noted that the domain of data mining is immense and ever growing, so this chapter does not attempt to be exhaustive in its scope.

Bernhard Anrig (VIP, Berne University of Applied Science), Will Browne and Mark Gasson (University of Reading)

[45] An alorithm is like a recipe: given some input it describes the steps to be performed in order to generate the output. These steps may be very complex, include loops and decisions. For different definitions and further information see Wikipedia http://en.wikipedia.org/wiki/Algorithm.

M. Hildebrandt and S. Gutwirth (eds.), *Profiling the European Citizen:*
Cross-Disciplinary Perspectives.
© Springer Science + Business Media B.V. 2008

4.1.1   Types of Output

In general, common data mining techniques provide one of two possible outcomes: either a human readable, structured decision process or just a black box that computes a result. The type of outcome is determined by the method used for data mining, although any method providing the first type of result implicitly can provide the second (but not vice versa). Some methods, such as neural networks only allow for a black box approach which, in its simplest case, provides us with a real number output. This number will be associated with a specific class in a predefined set of classes in which all items of interest will be assigned. This is usually enough information for automatic post-processing and hence adequate for many applications. However, typically for a human decision maker and also partly for profiling issues, especially the non-automatic parts, this is not sufficient. Preferably, one would have some meaningful, structured decision process explaining how the result is computed. Furthermore, arguments with respect to the process, for and against the result and some explanation linking the result to the item of interest would be provided. A common situation where this is preferable is in the banking domain where the banker wishes to explain the reason why a new customer is refused credit. Methods for representing output such as decision rules, decision tables, decision trees, etc. will be discussed later.

4.1.2   Structure Testing Versus Structure Exploring Methods

Data mining techniques can be split into two broad types: structure testing methods and structure examining methods.[46] The choice of which to use is mainly dependent on the application, although in practice the choice may not be clear and a combination of both types may be the optimum option.

If searching for an unknown structure in a dataset, i.e., the user has no idea (or assumes not to have) about the structure to be found in the data, then a structure exploring method can be used. There are many types of these, for example, factor analysis, cluster analysis, neuronal network, naive Bayes and divide and conquer amongst others. In the worst case, no or only uninteresting structures are found by the algorithms. For example, it may find that there is a strong connection between the postal code and the name of the town which is obvious and uninteresting. Some sort of post-processing must then be applied to choose the "interesting" structures from the others. Structure exploring algorithms are therefore only useful in profiling when no predefined structure is to be used to classify people, i.e., when classes of behaviour are to be created. This may be as simple as "shoppers who buy this also buy that".

---

[46] Note that these types correspond to inductive and deductive process of Chapter 3 respectively. The terminology used is motivated by the central aspect of the algorithms themselves in this chapter.

If a structure is provided (or assumed by the user), structure testing methods can be applied i.e, regression analysis, variance analysis and discriminance analysis (see below). These methods do not discover new structures in the data but check to see if the structure provided is reflected by the data and to what extent. A typical example is the test of how strong some commercials influence the number of items bought at a given supermarket. Typically, these methods assume that the variables being considered can be classified as dependant or independent and afterwards try to compute the strength of the dependence. The main problem for this type of method is that the user rarely has a clear and precise idea about the structure and in turn can actually formulate it.

4.1.3   Supervised and Unsupervised Methods

Reinforcement learning, also known as supervised learning, can be used when the objective function is known but the exact relationship is not clearly determined. A supervisor i.e, a human being, supervises the learning process and qualifies the results. This feedback is utilised by the data mining algorithm which tries to adapt its behaviour in order to better fulfil the supervisor's expectations. Its goal is to learn the expected behaviour implicitly expressed by the feedback such that changes from the supervisor become insignificantly minimal. As an example, consider a student trying to solve a problem in an exam. His attempt to find a solution is based on his prior knowledge. The solution is subsequently corrected or improved by the teacher and this feedback is given to the student which, possibly in a later exam, will be taken into consideration in order to better solve similar problems (Backhouse et al., 2000:754). If there is a computer instead of the student mentioned above, we are in the context of supervised computer learning if this computer is able to use the feedback from the supervisor to eventually improve its abilities to solve "similar" problems. Another typical application of supervised computer learning is the recognition of handwriting on e.g., handheld computers. In this case, the user has to provide, typically over many iterations, samples of his handwriting to the handheld device, after which the device can recognise subsequent written characters.

Unsupervised learning on the other hand is used for clustering, computing relations between inputs, etc., so does not need extra supervisor input, which may be an advantage in automatic data processing.

4.2   Preparing the Input

Usually, a significant amount of work must be done in the beginning phase of any profiling and data mining process in order to "clean" the raw data. Parts of this can be performed automatically, yet the initial analysis of what needs to be done usually requires human intervention. To understand this process we must first look at the various forms the input could take.

4.2.1 Instances and Attributes

Following Witten and Frank (2005: 42ff) we will hereafter discuss concepts, instances and attributes, terms generally used in data mining which are also applicable to profiling.

The *concept* is what we want to have as the output of our data mining process. This may be the (textual) description of how to determine the favoured brand of coffee of a new person "entering the system", i.e., depending on the set of data available.

Attributes are the members of a pre-defined set of 'features'. Each attribute has a known set of possible values, which is not necessarily finite or bounded. An *instance* (often also called an example) is defined by its values on (all) attributes; in a simplified view, an instance is a row in a table whose columns are labelled by the attributes. The whole table consists of the set of data available for the data mining process, structured in instances which are characterised by their values on the attributes. Clearly, this is only a conceptual view. In concrete implementations further techniques have to be used to efficiently work with those instances.

As an example, consider entering into your favourite shop with your frequent shopper card in your pocket. Assuming an RFID (Radio Frequency Identification) tag is on this card (i.e., non-contact reading of the card data), an instance, from the point of view of the shop, may be the customer number (as on the card), the time of entering the shop, the time of leaving the shop, the amount paid, the payment method, information regarding the items and quantities bought, etc.

Generally speaking, there is no restriction on the possible values of the attributes: usually we distinguish between numeric attributes whose values can be integer numbers, real numbers, etc. and nominal attributes who usually take their values from a predefined set. There are other possibilities such as ordinal, ratio and interval attributes, which are usually imposed by the type of data available.

4.2.2 Denormalisation

It is normally the case that data used for data mining is not available as a set of instances but stored in some other form in a database. The first task is then to extract all the data necessary from the database and then to build a set of instances which will subsequently be used as input for the data mining process. This extraction is essentially the opposite of what is known as 'normalisation' in database terminology (cf. normal forms (Codd, 1970)). In the context of a relational database, where data is organised and accessed according to the relationships between data items, this involves denormalising the relations that are of interest to us by joining them together. In general, this process of extracting information from a database as a set of instances will produce data which inherently contains multiple occurrences of the same parts. As an example, consider a database which contains the details of a company's employees, i.e., their surname, first name, address, postal code, city, etc. In a normalised database the connection between city and postal code will be stored independently of any data regarding the real employees (inspired by the normal forms for relational database theory). For every employee only the postal code is stored in this instance and not the city. However, some algorithms will perform better using the postal code, some using the city and some might even profit from the occurrence of both of them. For this reason, the resulting instances for data mining should contain both city and postal code in order to have the maximum data available for the data mining process.

4.2.3 Problematic Values

There are several problems which arise when considering actual data: some values can be missing, omitted, declared as being unknown or unrecorded. There may also be attributes which only make sense if other attributes have some special values, for example, the 'husband's name' field is only useful if the person is married. On the other hand, data may be missing because of faulty equipment which perhaps did not measure some variables. These issues are especially evident in profiling where data is drawn from different sources whose attributes may not completely overlap.

In some cases, several values may be used for the same thing, e.g., the name of a product and one or more of its abbreviations. In this case, pre-processing of the data must take care of this and eliminate the duplicates. Sometimes, these different values simply come from incorrect spelling or typing errors, although techniques for eliminating such occurrences do exist.

In general, much care has to be taken because of these problematic values, most often they are handled in the pre-processing phase. Consider, for example, the situation where missing values of an integer attribute are denoted by the value '−1' (assuming only positive values are present otherwise). Any data mining algorithm should be aware of the special meaning of this value, which may be useful for some applications but omitted for others.

Many algorithms used for data mining can deal with missing values, either by taking special actions for them or assuming some default value.

Further issues are caused by duplicate instances occurring in a data set. This may be caused by a real event, such as something occurring in exactly the same way several times or it may simply be caused by errors. During the pre-processing, this issue must be resolved and ultimately duplicates must be removed. This is essential since (unmotivated) duplicates can have an impact on the results and will in the worst cases make them useless, hazardous or even damaging.

4.2.4   Training and Tests

Learning algorithms require training using a training set and then testing using a test set which must be different from the original training set. This process is known as 'cross-validation'. Data available for cross-validation is usually restricted, i.e., typically only a set of limited size (which nevertheless may be large) will be available. Commonly, less than one third of the data available is reserved as a 'blind' set for testing while the rest is used for training.

However, it may be that the instances become unequally distributed between the two sets with regard to the classes, i.e., one class occurring in the test set may not be present in the training set. This may be the case when using the simplest form of splitting up the data, 'Holdout Cross-Validation', whereby data is simply randomly selected for the validation set. Clearly the resulting algorithm cannot be expected to function well in this case.

Because of this, stratification is utilised, i.e., one splits the initial set while assuring that all resulting sets contain approximately the same proportion of each class. However, even using stratification there may be some problems with the distribution of the instances. A further technique for avoiding some of these disturbances is called 'k-Fold Cross-Validation' where the initial data is sub-divided into k parts. The cross-validation process is then performed k times with each of the parts being used once as the validation set. A commonly used version of this is three-fold stratified cross-validation where the initial set is split into three parts of equal size. One of the parts is firstly used for testing and the other two for training. This is then repeated twice more, every set being used once for testing and twice as a part of the training set.

In general, testing the quality of what has been learned is crucial to any data mining process and especially to profiling. Different techniques besides those mentioned above exist, see Witten and Franke (2005: 143ff) for an excellent introduction. Nevertheless, here we want to focus on one specific and important aspect - any testing scheme should encapsulate the errors which can occur when applying the algorithms. In the simplest case, with two available classes to be assigned, there are two errors possible: assigning class A to an instance which is actually more suited to class B, and, vice versa, assigning class B to an instance which is actually more suited to class A. While these two errors may appear symmetrical, the consequences in general are not! Consider the case where class A stands for an event which potentially causes some personal hazard and B for the normal situation. Here, the first case of error "only" induces some additional cost for protecting people from a hazard which is not present, while the converse, i.e., not protecting people from a hazard because a normal situation is indicated, potentially leads to tragedy. Often these two errors are visualised using the confusion matrix, which for the example above could be as follows:

	Actual class is A	Actual class is B
Predicted class is A	100	15
Predicted class is B	2	20

Hence in this example, the prediction of instances being A when they are actually B is quite good (only 2 errors out of 102 instances) whereas the prediction of instances being B when they really are A is quite bad (i.e., 15 out of 35 are misclassified).

4.3 Representing the Output

The algorithms that are designed for structure *testing* basically provide the user with an output representing the strength to which the structure is actually found in the data being processed. This output can be very detailed with many different aspects, since there are many statistical methods that can be used for this testing (Backhouse et al., 2000: 78ff; Witten and Franke, 2005). However, we will not focus on this type of output here and instead will describe the different output representations of the algorithms that do structure *exploring*.

The typical output for structure exploring algorithms is a decision procedure which is used to select an appropriate class for the new instance being analysed. The representation itself is of main interest as it allows, in general, not only the computation of a result, i.e., a class but also an explanation of how or why this result is computed.

4.3.1 Decision Tables

Decision tables are the simplest structures for describing the output of a data mining process. As the name indicates, it mainly consists of a tabular representation of all possible cases of inputs and their respective classes. For generating such tables, we may copy the input, i.e., the set of instances and their assumed class, as is, which gives a "trivial" decision table. Further processing may consist in merging instances with (partly) the same values for attributes; when the set of instances to be merged does not belong to the same class, some criteria is needed to compute the class of the merged instance itself. As a first approach, a majority argument is possible, further more "intelligent" reasoning is possible, for example based on the expected frequency of the instances. If irrelevant attributes (with respect to the classification) occur, the respective columns in the table may be deleted in order to get a more compact table.

Clearly, this type of output is feasible only in very restricted cases where either the set of possible instances is very small or most attributes are irrelevant ones and can be removed from the table and hence the decision table is very small.

4.3.2 Decision Trees

Starting from the disadvantages of decision tables, decision trees allow for a more compact representation. Decision trees are read from their 'root node'. In every 'internal node' of the tree, a decision is reached and according to its result one of the finite number of children nodes is processed and so on, until a conclusion is reached. Every external node (also called leaf node) contains a class (where different external nodes may contain the same class). For example, consider an instance arriving, we start at the root node which contains the test: "value of attribute colour?" and according to the three possible answers "red", "blue" and "green" the respectively labelled path to a child node is followed. If that one is an internal node, the same process happens again and so on until an external node is reached and the class of the instance is resolved.

The tests in the nodes can be binary, i.e., testing for a value of an attribute, testing the possible values of an argument as in the example above or more generally testing if the value of the attribute is larger than some constant. In its simplest form, decision trees only allow for comparisons of one attribute value to some constant value in every node and on any path from the root node to an external node, every attribute is tested at most once. More general versions allow for comparing attributes to other attributes, which generally allows for more compact representation, yet it requires more work to compute the final result.

An interesting feature of decision trees is that they can easily be 'pruned' to simplify them, although this introduces approximations, i.e., errors in some cases. Consider for example the situation that in some sub-tree, statistically speaking 99% of the instance being processed therein will have class A and only 1% of them class B. In this case the whole sub-tree can be replaced by just one leaf node containing the class A and this whole pruning process only introduces 1% more false class values (in this sub-tree).

4.3.3   Classification Rules

Starting from decision tables, another approach to simplify their structure is to build so-called classification rules[47], which are a set of rules interpreted in a specified manner. Each rule consists of an antecedent being a set of conjunctively interpreted tests and a conclusion being a class. For a new instance, the tests of the first rule are considered and if all of them are true, the rule's respective conclusion, i.e., the class, is taken as the result. Otherwise the second rule of the set is considered and so on, until eventually a final (default) rule is used. Classification rules are very similar to decision trees, in fact any decision tree can simply be translated into a set of classification rules by considering each path from the root to a leaf node as a rule. The converse is not as straightforward but can be done as well. Classification rules, in general allow for more compact representation than decision trees but there is often no tree-like representation that is visually appealing for humans to use.

---

[47] Classification rules are similar to so-called production rules known from knowledge representation, i.e., rules of the form "if condition then conclusion".

4.3.4 Association Rules

Association rules are a much more general concept than those introduced above. Decision trees and the like only allow us to deduce the class from the given attributes. Hence, in the beginning of the profiling process it must already be clear which one is to be focused on as the class value. In contrast, given all values but one of a new instance, association rules allow us to deduce the value of the remaining attribute. Here we do not speak of a class as in this general context, all attributes are considered to be of equal importance. Clearly, classification rules are a special case of association rules where only one special attribute can be deduced. The effort needed to deduce association rules from input data is much higher than the other types described above.

4.3.5 Remarks

There is no perfect representation of results from a profiling process or data mining as, almost always, information is lost in building a representation. As such, several different possibilities must be considered and the best one used for a concrete application. Clearly these structures are only needed if more information than a simple result, i.e., the class of a new instance, must be provided. Furthermore, there is usually a trade off between more information in the resulting structures and computing time and thus between quality of information and processing speed. Hence, efficient and effective pruning techniques are of major interest but on the other hand it is crucial to compute the effect of any pruning to the overall error rate in order to decide if the trade-off is favourable.

4.4 Deterministic Algorithms

In this section, we will informally introduce the main concepts of deterministic algorithms - algorithms which will always produce the same result when applied to the same data, which are used in the field of data mining and profiling. Although there will not be detailed descriptions on all issues, here we aim to introduce the key elements of this type of processing technique. More detailed information can be found in the literature, e.g., (Han and Kamber, 2000; Witten and Franke, 2005; Backhouse et al., 2000).

4.4.1 Regression, Analysis of Variance and Factor Analysis

We first look at the simplest variant, the linear regression analysis. The underlying assumption when applying linear regression analysis to a set of instances is that the respective class values (in this case a number) can be determined by a linear combination of the values of the attributes which usually have numerical values, i.e., class = weight0 + attribute1*weight1 + attribute2*weight2 + ... The main problem is to estimate the respective weights, which can be done by ordinary least squares estimation, a common technique from statistics. This technique has strong theoretical justifications when some assumptions are made, for example that the independent variables, i.e., the attribute values are linearly independent (Backhouse et al., 2000: 119ff; Witten and Franke, 2005: 46ff).

Generalisations are 1) quadratic regression, where besides linear terms quadratic ones occur 2) multivariate regression, where besides linear terms attribute values can be multiplied by each other 3) exponentiation regression, etc. (Backhouse et al., 2000:81ff). While, on one hand these generalisations extend the power of the regression and move away from the restriction of linearity, on the other hand the need for computation time will in general "explode". One main problem is also to determine the type of regression to be used for a set of instances, which in itself is not a simple problem if the type is not easily deducible from the input.

Related to regression is the analysis of variance, which looks at the extent to which some independent variables influence the dependant ones, i.e., tries to explain the variance of the dependant variables by independent ones (Fisher, 1918; Backhouse et al., 2000: 120ff).

Another interesting tool is factor analysis, also a standard tool of data mining. It is very different from the ones above, as it studies relationships between values of attributes by trying to discover independent variables that influence these values. Note that here, these independent variables are not measured directly and hence go beyond the actual set of instances. Factor analysis tries, first of all, to determine the (minimal number of) different factors which can explain the relationships between the attributes as well as the quality of this explanation. Due to this open approach, the results of factor analysis are to be considered with care, as much hypothetical reasoning is contained therein.

4.4.2   1R and Divide & Conquer

There are two quite simple algorithms which in general allow for good results on reasonably sized data collections. The first one, called 1R (Holte 1993; Witten and Franke, 2005: 84), is probably the simplest one for data mining, nevertheless it can give quite reasonable results and can be implemented quite efficiently. The basic idea is to construct a decision tree with only one decision node or in other words just test the values of one attribute of the instance to be processed and decide at that point the class to be assigned to this instance. The question is then how to select the attribute to be used. The simple answer: try out all of them and select the best one! So for example, given a data set of 100 instances, we select the first attribute and - assuming it has three possible values - we select all those instances in which the first value occurs and count the respective classes. Then, the class with the maximal occurrence is selected as the class for this whole subset of instances and we count the number of errors made by using this reasoning in this subset. The errors for the different values of the attribute are then added and the result is the number of errors occurring when selecting this attribute for choosing the class. The same process is then done with the second attribute and so on. Finally, the attribute with the smallest number of errors is the one to be used.

The algorithm 1R gives a small and neat result, just one decision node. Nevertheless, there is some computing effort since every attribute has to be considered as a potential candidate and for every one of these attributes, all instances have to be considered.

The idea of counting the number of errors in 1R is a very simple one. Generalising this idea and allowing a recursive procedure based on 1R, we come to the Divide & Conquer method for constructing decision trees (Quinlan 1986; Witten and Franke, 2005: 97ff). As in 1R, we have to test each attribute and select the "best one" for the test at the actual node. Then, we apply the same idea to each branch starting from this node, where at each branch only the instances satisfying the respective test are considered and further testing on the same attribute can in general not occur. Note that on different branches, different attributes may be tested next as the processes are done independently after the branching (hence the name divide & conquer). The recursive processes stop if either there is no attribute left which can be tested or if all instances present at the node belong to the same class in which case no further testing is needed to differentiate between different classes. The remaining question is how to select the "best attribute" at each node? For that purpose, a measure of information is introduced based on the concept of entropy. Consider a node and assume that an attribute with three possible values must be qualified. As in the case of 1R, the instances are separated according to the values of the attribute, e.g, the first branch gets 10 instances, the second 20 and the third one 30. For simplicity's sake, let us assume that there are only two classes, A and B. Now, considering the first branch, assume that there are 2 instances (out of the 10) of class A and the other 8 of class B. Using the formula of the entropy we obtain:

$$\text{info}(2,8) = \text{entropy}(2/10, 8/10) = -2/10 \log(2/10) - 8/10 \log(8/10)$$

and the respective values for both the other branches are computed similarly. A mean of the three information values weighted by the number of instances in each branch is then computed and used as a qualification of using the first attribute for a test at that node. This qualifying value is then compared to the values computed analogously for the other attributes. The attribute with the smallest qualifying value is then selected as the attribute to be tested at this node (Witten and Franke, 2005: 99).

But why are entropy and information important here? While building a decision tree we want to reduce in some sense the uncertainty contained in the subsets of instances after each branching and optimally obtain subsets of only one class each. In finding an "optimal" ordering of the test, i.e., minimising the size of the tree, we try to maximise the information gained from a test.

Constructing a decision tree, as introduced above, requires substantial computational power as at each node, any "remaining" attribute to be tested must be qualified, hence the quantity of attributes to be considered is crucial. On the other hand, once a branch has been made, the computation on the branches can be done independently, i.e., in parallel. Pruning with estimated error, as described in the decision tree section above, can be done automatically as well.

4.4.3   Clustering

Given a set of instances, clustering algorithms try to generate a set of clusters which are in general mutually disjoint and exhaustive, such that each cluster contains a set of instances which are in some sense related to each other. Each cluster therefore defines implicitly the class of the instances therein. Different distance measures can be used for defining "close", however usually three axioms must be satisfied, namely the distance of an object from itself must be zero, the distance from A to B must be the same as from B to A and finally the 'triangle inequality'. The usual distance we use (the length of a direct line) satisfies this. The 'Manhattan distance' is also famous but there are many others. These distance functions must be generalised to a higher dimensional space as we are measuring the distance between two instances each having a large number of attributes. Technically, this is not a problem, however visualisation is not made easier when many dimensions are used.

Here we will not go into details of clustering algorithms, although there are many good and interesting algorithms available. For further reference see (Jain et al., 1999; KacKay, 2003).

Nevertheless, consider the problems of clustering in general: usually a quality measure for the result is needed which must incorporate the number of clusters computed and the quality of their discernment. Trivial clustering, i.e., every instance has its own cluster or just one cluster containing every instance, is usually not the optimal answer we are interested in. Hence, in between these two extreme cases there is a trade off and an "optimal" solution to be found.

4.4.4   Remarks

The algorithms introduced above have shown their efficiency and worth over years of use in actual data mining applications. Certainly there are many instances where these techniques have been applied to very large problems but the application may be costly in terms of time and properties of the data such as noise, inconsistencies and discontinuities which may cause these techniques to fail. Typically in these cases heuristics have been utilised where a heuristic is a "rule of thumb" and so is distinct from the finite set of well-defined instructions that makes up an algorithm. However, although the use of additional input or in some cases random processes can improve results, it still does not guarantee always finding the optimal solution. Such techniques are non-deterministic and will be further discussed in the next section.

4.5   Probabilistic Algorithms

There are many different approaches using probabilistic algorithms in the field of data mining and profiling. Introducing Divide & Conquer algorithms above, we have already seen some application in the computation of the information contained in a decision which is also pertinent here.

Naive Bayes classifiers are a simple and powerful instrument for data mining. The idea is to build a tree with one node and as many children as there are attributes. The root node contains a variable ranging over the possible classes. Using the instances available, one can then estimate the probabilities to be contained in this structure, that is on one hand the a priori probabilities of the classes estimated by the fraction of instances of the respective class in the root node and on the other hand the conditional probabilities of attribute x having value y given that the instance is of class A, which can also be estimated using the set of instances. This structure then allows us (using mainly Bayes' formula) to compute the class of a newly arriving unclassified instance. The advantage of this approach is its simplicity, the disadvantage is the assumption of all attributes being independent, an assumption which may influence quite drastically the quality of the results.

More general Bayesian Networks (Pearl, 1998) can be used in data mining as well. Bayesian Networks are a framework for expressing probabilistic dependence and independence of variables locally. In data mining, a set of instances is used as learning input for the Bayesian Network. Much work has been done in this field and many techniques for computing the "best" fitting Bayesian networks have been presented (Witten, 2005: 271ff, 283). Once the Bayesian Network is constructed, an analysis of a new arriving instance to be classified is quite simple and can be executed by computing locally in the network. In the case where the size of the nodes (i.e., the number of predecessors) in the network is small, this computation can be performed rapidly.

However, one can go further and even use non-numeric argumentation systems - with or even without probabilistic information available - for data mining (Picard, 1998).

4.5.1   Neural Networks

Neural networks have initially borrowed the ideas of computation from the human brain, yet in data mining this is not of importance, as they are just used as a framework that can learn structures. In fact, neural networks can learn to distinguish classes of objects by, in simple terms, making a high dimensional regression (see above). Concretely, a neural network consists of an input layer consisting typically of one node per attribute to be considered. This input layer is connected to one or several 'hidden layers', which are neither output nor input nodes. Finally, there is one (or several) output nodes. There are typically different types of neural networks, mainly influenced by the types of connections between the different layers. In the case of data mining, we might think of one output node (real valued) which determines the class of the instance (Banks et al., 2004: 141; Backhouse, 2000: 750ff).

In the learning phase, the instances of the learning set are presented to the neural net and (using also the known classes) it learns its expected behaviour using, for example, back-propagation. If the neural net has learned its behaviour, newly arriving instances are then given as input and the output determines its class.

Several interesting problems arise when using neural networks: what is the size of the network? what is its structure? where are connections? what is the learning rate? And so on. However, some conceptual ideas for selecting "good" choices exist. Once the time-consuming learning phase is finished, an output can be computed very rapidly.

A disadvantage and often cited criticism of neural networks is that the information "learned" from the data is somewhat hidden in the network and cannot be used as evidence for the result. Data mining techniques, in general, provide a way to gain information about the data, i.e., the knowledge discovered can be understood and used. Neural networks on the other hand work as black boxes. There is no easy way to understand how a pattern has been learnt or what sort of deduction has been done, i.e., the translation into a humanly understandable language is typically not possible although post-processing can shed some light on the inner workings of the network. Additionally, in order to "learn" a way to answer a new question, a neural network requires a huge training set, which might not be available.

A further problem is "overfitting", which is often mentioned in the specific context of neural networks but can, in principle, also appear when using other methods. The typical example is a neural network that is trained to recognise hand-written numbers from 0 to 9. Often, the quality of correct recognition (measured using a test set) grows when more time is available for learning with the specified learning set. After some maximal point however, the actually quality decreases because the neural net has begun to "learn the learning set by heart" and therefore is losing its key ability to generalise and recognise the handwriting of the other person. This problem can be countered using so-called validation sets of instances (which is disjoint from the learning set, cf. cross-validation) for determining the quality of the learning process (Backhouse et al., 2005: 781).

4.5.2 Fuzzy Rule Induction

An application of fuzzy sets on problems of profiling is called fuzzy rule induction. It consists of three phases: first, the initial data, i.e., the set of instances is fuzzified, which means that the crisp attributes are transformed into a set of variables that are associated to linguistic interpretations, as in general fuzzy sets. Second, fuzzy rules are then deduced from this data using standard fuzzy set techniques. Third, if necessary, de-fuzzification of the output is performed in order to obtain a result in the given output space, i.e., a class value. A major advantage of this approach is that fuzzy rules have a human readable form (usually they are coded as "if-then" statements) and can therefore be interpreted or changed. See for example (Müller and Lemke, 2000: 131ff) for details.

4.5.3 Support-Vector-Machines

The comparatively new concept of Support-Vector-Machines (SVM) describes a set of unsupervised learning methods. The original instances are considered as data points in a high-dimensional space, which is then transformed to a so-called feature space for applying a linear classifier, i.e., a hyperplane, which is usually non-linear in the original space. Since SVMs use linear classifiers they can be very efficient and tend to produce simple results. See (Cristianini and Shawe-Taylor, 2004; Schölkopf and Smola, 2002) for more information.

4.6   Conclusions

Here we have discussed standard techniques that are commonly used in data mining applications. In particular, these include deterministic algorithms which are based on interpretable mathematical procedures and which are well understood in terms of their operation. In moderately complex domains these techniques perform well. However, where the environment is more complex it is not uncommon for them to fail to reach their goal.

Improved results can be achieved by moving away from deterministic algorithms, e.g., through additional human knowledge which can be integrated into the process through supervised learning or 'human in the loop' learning. Reinforcement learning is especially useful where the objective function is known, but exact output is not.

A wide range of algorithms and techniques for data mining exists and can be applied to profiling. The problem is how to select the "best" technique for a given situation (cf. also Chapter 3). This depends greatly on the size of the data sets considered, the amount of data usable for learning or determining the decision structure, the available computing time (for computing the decision structure itself or for determining a class value), the type of attributes (numeric, nominal, ...), etc. This problem is not easily solvable and although some guidelines have been developed there is no simple "rule of thumb" solution. Often, different methods are used and the quality of their results compared in order to select the "best one". Such ensemble methods may ultimately produce better results but are more expensive in terms of complexity and time.

Despite the improved effectiveness of data mining techniques, there is often an underlying assumption that the profile can actually be characterised in terms of the constituent variables, i.e., there is actually something of worth to be discovered.

This is not always the case. Equally, profiles discovered by these techniques may not be desirable or politically correct but modern algorithms do not have the functionality to care about such issues. As such, profiles that are generated using automated techniques should only be used with these issues in mind.

Note: a good starting point for further investigation is Witten and Franke (2005) and as an accompanying tool, the use of Weka[48], a powerful open source data mining programme.

4.7   Reply: Neat Algorithms in Messy Environments

Jean Paul van Bendegem*

In this reply we wish to focus on issues of complexity as they emerge in the use of algorithms. More specifically, three topics are addressed: (a) the deep, irreducible problem of dealing with conflicting data and inconsistencies, (b) the nearly intractable problem of verifying programmes to ensure correctness and (c) the limitations and negative effects of all methods for extracting information from a database. This reply is not meant as a criticism as such but rather as a series of warnings.

4.7.1   Introduction

When writing a reply, an author has basically two options: to address (a selection of) the separate issues in as much detail as possible or to discuss a more general underlying theme. As there are many topics dealt with in this chapter, I will explore the alternative route and present here some thoughts and reflections on the theme "How badly can things go wrong?". The authors are fully aware of the wide range of problems that can and do occur. However, my point here will be that the situation is far more serious than one can imagine.

4.7.2   A First Issue: How to Deal With Inconsistencies

The problem is very well known: a database can contain and in most cases does contain, contradictory, conflicting data or, to use the authors' words, problematic values. It is clear something should be done but what are the options?. "Wait and see" is, of course, a possibility: when an inconsistency occurs, deal with it immediately,

---

* Vrije Universiteit Brussel (VUB)

---

[48] Weka 3: Data Mining Software in Java, see http://www.cs.waikato.ac.nz/~ml/weka/.

e.g., by selecting one of the values and deleting the others. This, of course, is a lazy strategy; a far better approach would be to check the database for possible inconsistencies or, in other terms, to *prove* that the database is consistent. Logicians will immediately claim that this problem is unsolvable - in more precise terms: if T is a theory, formulated in a language La and based on an underlying logic Lo, then, if T is sufficiently expressive, T cannot prove itself consistent (assuming, of course, that it is consistent). The phrase "sufficiently expressive" means that the language must permit one to map statements about T to statements in T, which, in most cases, is guaranteed if elementary arithmetic is a part of T. (In short, I am repeating here the conditions under which Gödel's second incompleteness theorem is applicable, see Franzén (2005) for an excellent introduction). It follows that if there were an algorithm to check whether a database is consistent or free of contradictory information, then, if the algorithm can be formulated within T, we could prove the consistency of T. But as we cannot, such an algorithm cannot exist. This implies that, if databases are sufficiently rich in data and we want to reason about these data, then we will never obtain certainty as to the consistency of the database.

This problem cannot be underestimated. Perhaps one thinks that if information is added step-wise, one keeps sufficient control over what is happening. But that is definitely not the case. Take the following quite simple and straightforward example: a database consisting of two data, viz. "if p then q" and "if p then not-q". As long as p is not added there is no problem but the simple addition of p, makes this elementary database inconsistent. As soon as things become a bit more complex, it becomes a really difficult thing to detect whether a set of statements or values is indeed consistent. Take a simple example: suppose we have a set S and a relation R in S and we have the following four statements:

(a) R is irreflexive, i.e., there is no $x \varepsilon S$, such that xRx
(b) Every element has a next element, i.e., for every $x \varepsilon S$, there is a $y \varepsilon S$, such that xRy
(c) R is transitive, i.e., given xRy and yRz, then we have xRz
(d) S is finite.

Do (a), (b), (c) and (d) form a consistent set? I presume that a trained logician or mathematician will quickly see the negative answer but no matter how fast one performs the task, one has to *reason* about the four statements. Imagine the complexity issue if the database contains millions of pieces of information.

To further complicate matters, one should note that as the database becomes larger, the number of problematic values will increase. A simple probability argument can support this claim. Suppose there is a non-zero probability p which, if an item is added to a database, it produces an inconsistency or a conflict. If the database consists of N items, then on average, $p.N$ items will cause problems. If N increases, so does $p.N$. To see how serious this problem is, let us do a quick realistic calculation to make things more tangible. Suppose that $N = 1,000,000$ and that p is 0.001 – which is *really* good, as it says that only one-tenth of a percent of the data goes wrong – then $N.p = 1,000$. Approximately, one thousand data in the base are potential troublemakers.

4.7.3   A Second Issue: Proving the Correctness of Programmes

Is there an "escape" route? Actually, there is. I did suppose that the consistency of the theory T could be shown within T itself. Of course, one could relax this requirement and ask for a proof of the consistency of T in another, more expressive theory T^*. Example: to show that propositional logic is consistent, one can use the method of the truth tables, which is more expressive. These considerations lead us straightaway into the domain of programme correctness, an issue that is addressed by the authors in several places. What is the main issue? Quite simply the fact that such proofs of correctness, on average, turn out to be far more complex than the programme itself. This of course leads to the problem of why one should believe or accept such a proof. In fact, in many cases, programmes are not shown to be correct by proof but rather by checking fragments here and there and by evaluating the programme's performance. In short, one has to rely on heuristics rather than on algorithms. Heuristics, as we all know, guide us towards a solution but without a guarantee that we will ever reach it.

This is not just a logical, mathematical, theoretical or philosophical problem. It has a direct societal importance, as there have been trials in courtrooms to decide whether a (commercially available) programme was indeed sufficiently verified, as the programme malfunctioned and a "guilty" party had to be identified, see MacKenzie (2001) for an excellent report of this affair.

4.7.4   A Third Issue: The Worst is Yet to Come

Let me complicate matters even further. Apart from the problem of finding the inconsistencies or conflicting data and the problem of what to do when such cases have been identified – how do we reason with inconsistent data? How much information is lost by deleting data? Besides the problem of solving this, even if consistent, will the programmes that extract the information from the data do what they are supposed to do? Additionally, there still remains the problem that all of the methods presented have their limitations and negative effects. How well are these taken care of? Let us consider two simple examples (with no specific reason for this particular choice):

(a) The authors mention the Bayesian method, an indeed very powerful method. However, one of the most famous drawbacks of this method is that in many cases to increase the size of the sample to be checked means to increase the number of false positives and negatives. A classic example: consider a population of 1,000 people. Suppose one wants to check whether some disease is present in the population. Suppose further that the probability p to have the disease is 1 in 50. Suppose finally that there is a test with success rate q, say, 99 per cent. What will happen? One expects approximately 20 people to have the disease, nearly all identified correctly. But there are 980 people remaining and a 1 per cent chance of a mistake, thus about 10 people will be wrongly identified as having the disease. It is easy to see that as the population grows, the number of false positives will increase as well. What applies to diseases also applies to profiles.

(b) The authors discuss the problem of metrics on data sets, i.e., distance functions that allow one to define clusters and/or classes. In this case, one has to take into account the curious properties that mathematics brings into play. A well-known problem is, of course, the fact that different distance functions or metrics lead to often totally different classifications. But perhaps less well known is the curious property known as "the curse of high dimensionality" (see, e.g., Aggarwal et al. (2001)). If there are too many features involved to define the metric, then it can be shown mathematically that distance functions cease to be effective. A simple probability argument may (once again) serve as an illustration. Suppose there are k features or dimensions and suppose, for simplicity's sake, that for each feature the probability is 60 per cent to be equal and thus 40 per cent to be different. If there are k features then the probability that two individuals are totally different is $(0.40)^k$. For $k = 10$, this is about 0.0001. This means that any two individuals will share at least one feature with a probability of 0.9999. In short, if there are too many features, individual ones tend to become indistinguishable. However, a complete description requires many features. Indeed a curse!

4.7.5 Afterthought

A separate issue, far too complex to deal with in this limited space, is that, quoting the authors, "the profiles discovered by these techniques may not be anticipated, desired or politically correct but modern algorithms do not yet have the power to care". Let me just remark that this perhaps innocent quote expresses a division of labour that is quite debatable: on the one hand, the designers of algorithms, mainly driven by practical-computational concerns and problems and on the other hand, the ethicists, politicians and basically we ordinary citizens, who will have to worry about what the first group has done. True, the algorithms are not supposed to care but their creators should, since, apart from being scientists, they too are at the end of the day ordinary citizens.

4.8   Reply: Privacy Preserving Data Mining

Martin Meints*

In this reply the focus is put on a special discipline of profiling: Privacy Preserving Data Mining (PPDM). PPDM has been an area of research since the 1990s. In this reply the main objectives of PPDM and state-of-the-art methods will be described and analysed. PPDM is based on data modification techniques. For this purpose, mainly data mining algorithms

* Unabhängiges Landeszentrum für Datenschutz Schleswig-Holstein, Germany (ICPP)

and cryptography-based techniques are used in a specific way. Possibilities, technical limitations and trends in research such as the further development of PPDM algorithms and developments towards standardisation in PPDM will be described.

Privacy Preserving Data Mining (PPDM) has been an area of research since 1995[49] both in the public and private[50] sector and has already found applications such as in medical research to protect patients' privacy[51]. In this chapter, a brief overview of the state-of-the-art in privacy preserving data mining will be given, followed by a summary of current topics in research and suggestions for future steps that should be taken towards standardisation in PPDM.

Oliveira and Zaïane (2004) define PPDM as data mining methods that have to meet two targets: (1) meeting privacy requirements and (2) providing valid data mining results. These targets are in some cases – depending on the type of data mining results and the attributes in the basic data – antagonistic. In these cases the use of PPDM offers a compromise between these two targets.

Privacy preserving data mining typically uses various techniques to modify either the original data or the data generated (calculated, derived) using data mining. To achieve optimised results while preserving the privacy of the data subjects efficiently, five aspects, so-called dimensions, have to be taken into account. These dimensions and the corresponding relevant factors or methods are as follows (Verykios et al. 2004):

1. Data distribution: Possible methods to preserve privacy depend on the data source: are the data stored in a central database or are they distributed among different databases? If they are distributed, how is this done? Is it by data record (horizontal) or by attribute (vertical)?
2. Data modification: how are data modified? Typically five ways are used to modify data:

    a. Perturbation by altering attributes, for example, by adding noise to them.
    b. Blocking by replacing them, for example by using "?".
    c. Aggregation or merging of attributes.
    d. Swapping of attributes.
    e. Sampling, i.e., releasing attributes to a sample of datasets only.

3. The data mining method (association rules, classification, clustering etc.) and corresponding data mining algorithm (for example regression algorithms, Kohonen networks etc.).
4. Data or rule hiding: what is to be hidden, basic data or calculated data (requiring rule hiding within the data mining algorithms)?

---

[49] See overview of articles by S. Oliveira at http://www.cs.ualberta.ca/%7Eoliveira/psdm/pub_by_year.html.

[50] For example research carried out by IBM, see http://www.almaden.ibm.com/software/disciplines/iis/.

[51] See for example http://e-hrc.net/media/ExtHealthNetworksMuscle02Feb2005.htm.

5. Privacy preservation: what specialised methods are used to achieve privacy preservation? In this context mainly three methods have been the subject of recent
   research:

   a. Heuristic-based techniques to selectively modify attributes with the objective
      of preserving a maximum utility of the overall data mining process.
   b. Cryptography-based techniques such as secure multiparty computation that
      are used with distributed data. The target of these techniques in most cases is
      to achieve optimised mining process results whilst hiding the data of one
      participating party against all other participating parties.
   c. Reconstruction-based techniques. In this case, the first step is to modify
      attributes by adding noise, in the second step they are reconstructed using
      specific algorithms and in the third step data mining is performed using these
      modified data.

This overview shows, from a technical perspective, how complex the undertaking
of optimised PPDM is.

Oliveira and Zaïane (2004) observed an extensive and rapidly increasing variety
of different methods and tools that are available to perform PPDM. These
approaches, in most cases, seem to be limited to one data mining method or algorithm. In addition, they concluded that there is no common understanding of privacy in the context of PPDM. Areas of application of PPDM cover confidentiality
of basic data or mined rules among organisations (protection of trade secrets) as
well as the implementation of data protection principles, such as the data minimisation principle, by anonymising personal data.

As a result, there are currently no common metrics for (1) the quality of different
methods and algorithms in meeting privacy requirements and (2) the loss of quality
in the data mining results compared to today's standard data mining systems.

Oliveira and Zaïane (2004) developed a three-step model for the success in
PPDM research. They observed the following steps (so-called landmarks):

1. Conceptive landmark: since 1995 it was understood that data mining raises specific privacy issues that need to be addressed.
2. Deployment landmark: this landmark described where we are today. We observe
   a number of solutions for different methods and algorithms used in PPDM. The
   results achieved in PPDM research and development so far are promising and
   suggest that PPDM will reach the target it has been set up for.
3. Prospective landmark: future research and development in PPDM will increasingly
   lead to directed efforts towards standardisation. This is required in order to overcome the observed confusion among developers, practitioners and others interested
   in this technology caused by the excessive number of different PPDM techniques.

For the standardisation process with respect to privacy they suggest using the
OECD Privacy Guidelines[52] from 1980, which are accepted worldwide. Based on

---

[52] See http://www.oecd.org/dataoecd/33/43/2096272.pdf.

the principles stated there and their enforceability in the context of PPDM, they suggest a set of four policies that should be defined when applying PPDM:

- Awareness Policy: the target is to define a policy regarding how the data subject is informed.
- Limit Retention Policy: the target of this policy is the deletion of data that is not up-to-date to avoid unnecessary risks.
- Forthcoming Policy: this policy contains the information regarding which data is processed for what purpose and how the results are to be used and with whom they are shared.
- Disclosure Policy: this policy specifies that discovered knowledge is disclosed only for purposes for which the data subject has given his or her consent.

In addition, Oliveira and Zaïane (2004) identify a set of requirements that future PPDM solutions should meet. This includes (1) independence of the PPDM solution from a single algorithm, (2) accuracy, (3) an acceptable privacy level, (4) the ability to handle heterogeneous attributes (e.g., categorical or numerical attributes), (5) versatility (independence from the way data are stored in repositories) and (6) low communicational costs (especially in cases where data are stored in a distributed way). Today's PPDM solutions do not typically meet these requirements.

For the deployment of PPDM, additional requirements have to be met. These are (1) the identification of private information that is to be protected, (2) the compliance with international instruments to state and enforce privacy rules, (3) logging of steps taken in PPDM in order to allow for transparency, (4) limitation of disclosure of private information and (5) matching of the solution with privacy principles and policies especially in cases where policies or technical solutions (for example the data mining algorithm or its parameters) are updated.

These suggested requirements are of relevance for today's profiling techniques, even in cases where no PPDM can be applied. For the enforcement of these principles organisational measures have to be taken by the data controller and data user where no technical solutions are available.

4.9   Bibliography

Aggarwal, C. C., Hinneburg, A., Keim, D.A., 'On the Surprising Behavior of Distance Metrics in High Dimensional Spaces', *Proceedings of the 8th International Conference on Database Theory 2001*, Springer Verlag GmbH 2006, pp. 420-434,

Agrawal, R., Imielinski, T., Swami, A., 'Mining Association Rules between Sets of Items in Large Databases', *Proceedings of the ACM SIGMOD Conference* Washington DC, USA, May 1993, ACM Press, New York,, 1993, pp. 207-216.

Banks, D., et al., *Classification, Clustering, and Data Mining Applications*, Springer, Berlin, 2004.

Backhaus, K., et al., *Multivariate Analysemethoden - Eine anwendungsorientierte Einführung*, Springer, Berlin, 2000.

Cristianini N., Shawe-Taylor J., *Kernel Methods for Pattern Analysis*, Cambridge University Press, Cambridge, 2004.

Codd, E. F., 'A Relational Model of Data for Large Shared Data Banks', *Communications of the ACM*, Vol.13, No 6, ACM Press, New York, pp. 377–387, 1970.

Fisher, R., 'The correlation between relatives on the supposition of Mendelian inheritance', *Philosophical Transactions of the Royal Society of Edinburgh*, Vol. 52, Royal Society of Edinburgh, Scotland, 1918, pp. 399-433.

Fisher, R., 'On the mathematical foundations of theoretical statistics', *Philosophical Transactions of the Royal Society*, Royal Society of Edinburgh, Scotland, Vol. 222, 1922, pp. 309-368.

Franzén, T., *Gödel's Theorem. An Incomplete Guide to its Use and Abuse*, Wellesley, Mass.: A. K. Peters, 2005.

Han, J., Kamber, M., *Data Mining: Concepts and Techniques*, Morgan Kaufmann Publishers, 2000.

Holte R., 'Very simple classification rules perform well on most commonly used datasets', *Machine Learning*, Vol. 11, No. 1, Springer, Netherlands, 1993, pp. 63-91.

Jain, A. K., Murty, M. N., Flynn P. J., 'Data Clustering: A Review', *ACM Computing Surveys*, Vol. 31, No. 3, ACM Press, New York, 1999, pp. 264-323.

Lusti, M., *Data Warehousing and Data Mining*, Springer, Berlin, 2001.

MacKay, D. J. C., *Information Theory, Inference and Learning Algorithms*, Cambridge University Press, Cambrigde, 2003

Mackenzie, D., *Mechanizing Proof. Computing, Risk, and Trust*. Cambridge, Mass.: MIT, 2001.

Müller, J. A., Lemke, F., *Self-Organising Data Mining*, BoD GmbH, Norderstedt, 2000.

Oliveira, S. R. M., Zaïane, O. R., 'Towards Standardization in Privacy-Preserving Data Mining', *Proceeding of the 3rd. Workshop on Data Mining Standards (DM-SSP 2004)*, in conjunction with KDD 2004, Seattle, WA, USA, August, 2004. Available at: http://www.cs.ualberta.ca/%7Ezaiane/postscript/dm-ssp04.pdf

Pearl, J., *Probabilistic reasoning in plausible inference*, Morgan Kaufmann, 1988.

Picard, J., 'Modeling and Combining Evidence Provided by Document Relationships Using Probabilistic Argumentation Systems', *Proceedings of the ACM SIGIR'98 Conference*, ACM Press, New York, 1998, pp. 182 - 189.

Quinlan, J. R., 'Inductive Learning of Decision Trees', *Machine Learning*, Vol 1, No. 1, Springer, Netherlands, 1986, pp. 81-106.

Schölkopf, B., Smola, A., *Learning with Kernels: Support Vector Machines, Regularization, Optimization, and Beyond (Adaptive Computation and Machine Learning)*, MIT Press, Cambridge, MA, 2002.

Verykios, V. S., Bertino, E., Fovino, I. N., Provenza, L. P., Saygin, Y., Theodoridis, Y., 'State-of-the-art in Privacy Preserving Data Mining', *SIGMOD Record*, Vol. 33, No. 1, New York, March 2004, pp. 50-57. Available at: http://dke.cti.gr/CODMINE/SIGREC_Verykios-et-al.pdf

Witten, I. H., Frank, E., *Data Mining: Practical machine learning tools and techniques*, Morgan Kaufmann, San Francisco, 2005.

Chapter 5
Behavioural Biometric Profiling and Ambient Intelligence

Angelos Yannopoulos, Vassiliki Andronikou, and Theodora Varvarigou

In many applications, the most interesting features that we may wish to discover, store and/ or exploit in decision making, concerning a human subject, involve the psychology at a variety of levels, of this subject. Parameters, ranging from enjoyment to honesty, important to applications such as adaptive entertainment, through to intrusion detection, are commonly but subtly manifested in an individual's behaviour. As humans, we systematically exploit information gleaned from the observation of others' behaviour, often with astounding levels of success, proving the existence of immensely descriptive data in such observations. Technical attempts to exploit the exact same information have been successful in much more focused and limited applications, demonstrating that at least an initial level of access to this information lies within the capabilities of technology. As a core problem, extraction of useful features from measurements of human behaviour is approached as a pattern recognition problem. Behavioural biometrics may be used for verification, identification or miscellaneous types of classification, without the difference between these applications amounting to a paradigm shift, although the technical difficulty of the problem and the technological sophistication required may change significantly. A critical issue, however, is that such input data cannot, in the general case, be filtered to support one application but not another, which raises even deeper ethical concerns than usual. The total information that can be extracted from behavioural biometric measurements forms an especially rich profile for the subject of the analysis. Since behaviour is easy to observe, many of these techniques are non-intrusive, i.e., the subject may not even be aware of them. This leads us to a major current limitation of practical behavioural biometric systems: their sensing capabilities. This is actually a volatile research issue: from camera and microphone installations to monitoring PC users' input device usage rhythms, better measuring capabilities can lead to much improved behavioural biometric systems. There exists therefore a strong connection with the ambient intelligence vision, which creates the potential for highly advanced applications – but also much more subversive threats.

5.1 Introduction

The term *biometrics* refers to the scientific and technological measurement of either physiological or behavioural human characteristics. Biometrics is a rapidly developing area of research that encapsulates knowledge and co-ordinated efforts from

Institute of Communication and Computer Systems, National Technical University Athens (ICCS)

M. Hildebrandt and S. Gutwirth (eds.), *Profiling the European Citizen:*
Cross-Disciplinary Perspectives.
© Springer Science + Business Media B.V. 2008

various scientific and technological fields, such as psychology, computer science, engineering and medicine. *Behavioural biometrics*, in particular, is a set of technologies that "measure" human characteristics related to a person's conscious or unconscious behaviour, actions or skills - and not his/her physical features. At the most basic level, behavioural biometrics focus on providing personal verification and identification. Additionally, behavioural biometrics can provide useful profiling information, such as a measure of a person's preferences or mood, while they can also link the individual to a non-biometric profile. These capabilities can be regarded as direct and indirect profiling, respectively, and constitute *behavioural biometric profiling*.

The measurement of behavioural biometrics requires the sensing of human subjects in great detail, using high-quality sensors including cameras, medical sensors measuring e.g., temperature or blood pressure, location sensors, inertial sensors for fine movement measurements and more. But even if the detection of such information is feasible, its representation in a computer remains a serious issue. Current representation approaches are generally ad hoc and oversimplifying, with real knowledge-based structuring of the raw data being rare. Most commonly the raw measurements are used directly in the final stage of such a system: pattern recognition. However, if the potential of behavioural biometric profiling is to be fulfilled, all three stages of sensing representation and pattern recognition need to be in interaction - a representation that reveals structure assists recognition, which in turn reveals more structure, while this process itself guides the acquisition of additional relevant data.

None of these enabling technologies are yet capable enough to support serious, industrial quality behavioural biometric profiling applications. Nevertheless, behavioural biometric profiling is a technology of the near-to-mid future with its progress being strongly dependent on the integration and cross-fertilisation of several technologies, in combination with serious yet realistically achievable improvements in each of these technologies. If a certain application seems unrealistic, we should first ask which additional scientific discipline is necessary to exploit in order to fill in the missing capabilities, rather than immediately dismiss it. In this chapter, we review the relevant state-of-the-art technology, as well as assess the future developments that the current situation points towards. The interaction between society and technology, however, forces us to extend the field of these future developments from upcoming improvements of low-level technical mechanisms to the resulting impact on people's lives.

More specifically, in this chapter we review existing behavioural biometric technologies and their capabilities for profiling applications (the first subsection) and we discuss how the current limitations of these technologies (discussed in the second subsection) can be overcome (in the third subsection) - not by endless research toiling away at the isolated problem of behavioural biometric profiling but by integrating with the emerging Ambient Intelligence environment. This is a technical issue but we do not intend to de-emphasise the human side of these impending developments and all the related risks and dangers. These are covered in other chapters of this book; for instance, in chapter 7, we discuss biometrics in general and their potential to violate privacy, promote discrimination, etc., while some of the most disquieting discussions in this book show, in chapter 15, how our very "sense of self" may be subverted by profiling technology. We argue that these risks should not be underestimated. A more thorough analysis of the lurking risks related to biometric profiling applications is provided in Chapter 7 in an effort to provide a broader view of biometric profiling taking into account the currently more widely applied and more heavily researched field of physiological biometrics. This analysis goes beyond the risks stemming from the current technical limitations of biometric systems, which are briefly presented in the current chapter, and identifies threats also accruing from the inherent capabilities of biometric profiling systems. The critic who thinks that such systems cannot ever seriously affect real life is imagining the systems of today running on faster computers, with better tweaked implementations but based on models and conceptions that have not improved. Hence, what we endeavour to show is that behavioural biometric profiling has a real potential to evolve into a radically better technology and can thus influence people's lives more than many would imagine.

5.2 Behavioural Biometrics State-of-the-art

The construction of an individual's profile with the use of behavioural biometrics can be achieved either by extracting profiling information from the measured biometric (e.g., determination of gender from a person's voice) or by performing identification or verification of the individual and using the person's identity to link current information to other data related to this person. An example of the latter case is identifying a person's signature in a financial transaction and using the result of this identification to monitor all of the person's financial transactions together. This section describes the state-of-the-art of behavioural biometric technologies that forms the basis for the evolution of behavioural biometric profiling.

5.2.1 Emotion Recognition

Emotion recognition is the task of processing a stream of data selected by the system designer with the understanding that it reveals the emotional state of its subject. The objective is to mechanically extract from it measurements which are simply and directly related to the classification of emotions according to a model of emotions accepted by the designer. As an oversimplified example, if we wanted to detect either extreme agitation or extreme boredom in the speech of a subject, we could record the speech signal, compute a measure of its speed, compare this to an acceptable measure of "average" or "normal" speech speed – which could be subject-dependent – and specify that fast speech is to be considered agitated and slow speech is to be considered as signifying boredom; the classification suggested is trivial but the actual measure suggested is a reasonable component of a real system, although of course many more measurements are required. A mature decision in many systems is to clearly isolate the process of measuring objective features from the process of their classification according to the chosen emotion model.

Most emotion recognition systems can be partitioned into three levels of operation (Fasel and Luettin, 2003; Scherer, 1999). The first level, *acquisition*, involves isolating input data that carry biometrically significant information from irrelevant data in the input stream. The second level, *class feature extraction*, involves fitting model parameters describing the first level's output; these features are not emotion classes themselves but can be correlated to emotions, for instance fundamental frequency movements in voice or eyebrow corner motions in face analysis. The third level, *interpretation*, involves determining an application-usable classification of these features by correlating them to modelled emotion classes. The boundaries of these levels of operation are not always extremely distinct: for instance, both of the first two levels are technically feature extraction tasks and the difference concerns the biometric depth of information accessed; both latter levels are technically pattern recognition tasks and the difference concerns the physical objectivity of the measurements.

In this paragraph we present some major facial and voice emotion recognition methods (Scherer et al. 2001; Scherer, 1984; Plutchik, 1994). The acquisition level is addressed in all methods and involves "background" technology such as human location followed by face location and noise removal and/or speaker isolation, respectively. Concerning the second level, in facial analysis, deformation extraction methods fit a facial model to each face image and their output is the parameter variation of this model over the images of the input stream, measuring deformation of facial features. Motion extraction methods follow another philosophy, identifying salient points or other low-level features of the face that are considered immutable and then measuring their motions as the face changes. In voice analysis, the standard features employed are statistics of fundamental frequency/formant frequencies, energy contour, timing parameters such as duration of silence, voice quality, frequency power coefficients, articulation features, etc.

In the interpretation level, the details of what features have been measured is not conceptually a point of focus but rather an implementation issue. A desired classification space is obtained with a psychological or application-determined motivation. It is then a pattern recognition task to map from features to classes. Often only rather basic or *archetypal* emotions are focused on, such as: joy, sadness, anger, fear, surprise and disgust (Ekman and Friesen, 1971; Muller, 1960).

5.2.2   Gesture

The concept of *gesture* is very general: in one definition "the notion of gesture is to embrace all kinds of instances where an individual engages in movements whose communicative intent is paramount, manifest and openly acknowledged"

(Nespoulous et al. 1986), encompassing, for example, gesticulation, where gestures accompany spoken communication (Lozano and Tversky, 2006) and autonomous gestures, where gestures intentionally convey an intended message as when somebody needs to be quiet and points at an object of interest; however, body language, unconscious gesticulation, etc., may also be considered to be gestures.

Current automatic gesture recognition systems rely on modelling a predetermined gesture structure so as to compare incoming video data with a code book of prototype sequence representations. Thus, the best performance is achieved in recognising gestures exhibiting systematic spatial variation (Oka et al. 2002; Patwardhan and Roy, 2006). The process begins with a typical feature extraction problem. A *model* of the human body or relevant part of it (e.g., for the arms and hands) must be fitted to input video so as to derive a measure of model parameter variations that best describes the input. Comparing extracted features to gesture models needs to be a flexible process due to the great degree of variability of possible gestures. Thus, the prototype sequences must be *parametric* and *classification* must involve an assessment of which prototype parameterisation represents the best fit to the measured features. Motion based approaches have also been experimented with that endeavour to classify gestures from their motion content only, without referring to a physical model of the human body (Polana and Nelson, 1994; Bobick and Davis, 2001; Ong et al. 2006): these systems are easier to implement as they avoid the high complexity of modelling the human body but lack the information richness to achieve a high performance in loosely constrained real-world problems. In Demordjian et al. (2005), the authors correlate gesture hypotheses based on visual data with speech hypotheses, thus combining correlated information to improve gesture recognition in their multimodal system, whereas in Licsár and Szirányi (2005) an interactive gesture recognition method is presented enriched by a user-controlled error-correction method in an effort to make the training set rather adaptive.

5.2.3 Gait

Human gait, as a result of various integrated synchronized movements of a great number of body joints and muscles (Murray, 1967), encapsulates a variety of features and properties - either static or variable - which depend both on various individual-dependent psychological and physiological factors and on external influences such as walking ground, person's health, clothes and mood. *Gait analysis* has shown that human gait encapsulates recognition capabilities and thus, it comprises rather new yet promising behavioural biometrics. The *non-intrusive* nature of this biometric – based on the potential of biometric data collection without the individual's consent - has turned it into a promising alternative for passive surveillance, while, being dependent on human characteristics such as height, gender and body build, it "hides" useful profiling information. Its low requirements in sensor devices and surrounding conditions - measurements can be taken even with captured images of low resolution or partial occlusion – is one of its greatest advantages.

Progress in the field of gait analysis and recognition is strongly connected to research in human detection, human motion detection, human tracking and activity recognition. As in most recognition problems, gait recognition involves two main phases: a *feature extraction phase* in which motion information is extracted from the captured data and described in a defined form and a *matching phase* that involves the classification of the motion patterns produced in the first phase. The extracted features can be either *appearance-based* or *motion descriptors*. In the first approach, either the whole silhouette is used (Philips et al. 2002; Collins et al. 2002) or these data are reduced (Hayfron-Acquah, 2001; Niyogi and Adelson, 1994; He and Debrunner, 2000) through, e.g., data projection, whereas in the second approach the motion descriptors are the combination of parameters such as stride length and limb angles, as well as body parameters that determine motion (e.g., height, limb length, etc.). These parameters could also be regarded as *profiling parameters*. During the matching phase a pattern classification method is applied, such as Hidden Markov Models (HMM) (Kale at al. 2002). Taking advantage of the distinct symmetrical properties of human motion patterns suggested by (Cutting et al. 1978; Hayfron-Acquah et al. 2003) a method was proposed for gait recognition with greater sustainability in noise and occlusion. Liang Wang (Wang et al. 2003) presented a visual recognition method that integrates both static and dynamic body biometrics in gait recognition, aiming at enriching extracted motion features with more human information already included in the captured images. Most of these approaches, however, have mainly been tested on small and/or non-realistic (trivial) databases and face limitations due to noise, missing spatial data, precision of extracted motion parameters, etc.

5.2.4 Voice

As *human voice* comprises a biometric richness in identification, verification and profiling information that can be collected and extracted through an "eyes-free" operation, active research has been taking place over the past decades. Generally, a recorded test signal "produced" by the person to be authenticated (or identified) is compared to one (or a set of) stored *reference signals*. Nevertheless, due to the sensitivity of human voice to a variety of factors, including the speaker's psychological and physical condition or aging, etc., current implementations of speech identification or verification systems are limited to small-scale applications of low security requirements. This sensitivity, however, is also a *proof* that human voice includes profiling information, such as age (Ptacek, 1966), gender (Harb and Chen, 2005), emotional state (Banse and Sherer, 1996; Sherer, 2003; Sherer, 1995; Cauldwell, 2000) and physical state (fatigue, pain, etc.), and others. An interesting remark is that this biometric is one of the few biometrics that do not require installed specialised hardware at the point of monitoring, since mobile phones and microphones are technologies that are widespread and easily installed.

Voice verification systems can follow a *challenge/response* protocol or be *text-independent*. The first type of voice verification systems offers interactive authentication and in parallel provides an anti-spoofing technique; biometrics provided by artificial equipment are rejected. Such a system asks the individual to speak a series of words or numbers, so that not only voice features but also the order of the words/numbers is checked (Markowitz, 2005). Text-independent voice recognition/verification systems (Ganchev et al. 2003) are much more challenging due to the variety of sounds and words spoken by the person. For this reason, the selection of the set of features (Lung, 2005; Nathan and Silverman, 1994; Haydar et al. 1998; Ji and Bang, 2000) that will be used is crucial for the performance and thus the reliability of the system.

Voice recognition techniques face great *challenges* due to the similarity of human voices and the distortion of human voices due to existing voice-capturing devices. Speech signals are characterised with high variability, with the major variations depending on the speaker himself/herself (his/her health, emotional state, education, intelligence, etc.), they are very vulnerable to noise handset type and thus their decoding so that the extraction of the features that will be used for identification/ verification is a quite difficult and heavy task. Hence, voice identification/recognition systems are still regarded to be rather inadequate for large-scale applications and mainly support existing systems or are part of multimodal biometric systems.

5.2.5 *Keystroke Pattern and Mouse Movements*

Keystroke dynamics (Bleha, 1990) typically utilise the unique rhythm generated when a person types on a computer keyboard to verify that individual's identity. Indeed, their prime application is in user verification and the generality of possible application to user identification amongst many individuals remains open. Still, the unique and unobtrusive method of timing key presses during computer usage offers a very interesting method to access information about a computer user (Peacock et al. 2004). Verification/identification of a user can be used to connect to a conventional profile. Obtaining deeper profiling information remains to be seriously experimented with - for instance, an agitated typing rhythm should be easily detectable assuming correct user identification has already been achieved, or perhaps women type in a detectably different manner as compared to men.

Most implementations are specifically intended to provide an additional layer of security for computer logon, over and above the standard password usage and specifically in conjunction with it. Thus, each keystroke is specifically known by its ordinal position within the password, so a fully appropriate feature can be constructed simply by placing each successive keystroke timing into an array/vector of measurements. This is then dealt with using any desired pattern recognition system, often with textbook-level directness. In (Gunetti and Picardi, 2005), users are re-authenticated based on their continuous typing; the keystroke analysis of free text engenders a much more sophisticated feature construction scheme, whereas in (Robinson and Liang, 1997) the authors conclude that the best inductive classifier is the combination of interkey and hold times.

Mouse movements have also been studied as a behavioural biometric for computer user authentication (Ahmed and Traore, 2005; Pusara and Brodley, 2004; Ahmed and Traore, 2003). Several features are experimented with, such as the average mouse speed against the travelled distance, or calculating the average speed against the movement direction. Mouse clicks are also measured as useful features. The performance of these experimental systems does not indicate that mouse actions can be used alone as a user authentication mechanism. Rather, they can be used in conjunction with other authentication mechanisms in order to provide additional discriminative capability, thus creating an overall system with good performance. Finally, it remains to be tested whether deeper profiling information can be extracted from mouse actions – it is possible that they do indeed manifest at least *some* emotions, or offer discriminative information as to whether a subject is an experienced computer user, or tired, or is acting hurriedly.

5.2.6   Signature

Handwritten signatures comprise a broadly accepted means of individual verification in civilian applications, document authenticity checks, financial transactions, etc. People are able to recognize their signature at a glance, whereas signature verification is usually done under surveillance. Nevertheless, due to the amount of time and effort required, signature verification is quite often skipped leading to regular instances of undetected forgery, concerning formal agreements, contracts, etc. Hence, automatic signature verification is required. Such a system is able to verify a person's identity by examining the person's signature and/or the way the person writes it and comparing this data to the person's enrolled signature samples.

Automatic signature verification systems are divided into *off-line systems* which examine only the handwritten signature itself and *on-line systems* which collect and process additional information during the signing process such as the time taken by the person to sign, the speed and acceleration of hand movements, etc, with the aid of proper devices. Off-line signature verification systems collect less information than on-line signature verification systems due to the dynamic aspect of the signing action being captured in a much more difficult way, if possible at all and is of a much lower quality. In the first case, a set of (considered to be) invariant features is extracted from the signature image (Deng et al. 1999; Santos et al. 2004; Huang and Yan, 2002), such as the number of closed contours, ratios of tall letter height to small letter height and distance between the letters. On-line signature verification systems (Jain et al. 2002; Kholmatov and Yanikoglu, 2005) require special equipment (e.g., pressure-sensitive tablets) in order to extract the dynamic properties of a signature in addition to its shape (Lei and Govindaraju, 2004); the time taken by the person to sign, the pen pressure, the number of times the pen is lifted from the paper, the number of times this happens, the directions, etc. Regardless of the system being on-line or off-line, in case of signature verification, the extracted feature set is classified into one of two classes; genuine or forgery. The most common classifiers used are Support Vector Machines (SVM) (Lu et al. 2005) and Hidden Markov Models (HMM) (Igarza et al. 2003; Justino et al. 2005; Muramatso and Matsunoto, 2003).

Apart from the limitations deriving from the actual performance of current pattern recognition and feature extraction algorithms, signature verification systems also face the problems due to the *variations in a person's way of signing through time*. For this reason, periodical updates of the enrolled signatures are required with their automation making them a less uncomfortable process for the users. Furthermore, reliable forgery checks require reliable input, i.e., forged signatures produced by experts, with such data, however, not being available to researchers most of the times.

5.3   Current Limitations

5.3.1   *Technological Limitations*

Many of the *technical limitations* suffered by existing behavioural biometrics have already been mentioned in the previous paragraphs. Small or even trivial *databases* with training and test data, insufficient sensitivity of *sensor devices, noise* that distorts the useful information included in the processed signal and sets of extracted features that still fail to capture the *richness* of the biometric information included in the processed signal – are just a few. An important factor which strongly affects the performance of biometric systems is the sensitivity of these systems to *external conditions*. Hence, for example, for a video signal, changing weather conditions, illumination variations, complex and/or moving background, complex foreground and occlusions significantly affect the output of the biometric system (Lerdsudwichai et al. 2005; Zhang and Kambhamettu, 2002). However, much research is being carried out to enable these systems to operate under adverse conditions, e.g., *outdoors*, their performance is rather poor or still inadequate for large-scale applications.

Even though the performance of biometric systems is constantly improving through the use of faster and more robust feature extraction algorithms, improved learning and classification techniques and computational resources of higher capabilities, their successful application is still limited to *specialised* or at least *highly constrained* problems. Success rates, though sometimes described with numbers higher than "90%", still require explicit attention to be given to error handling, while a trade-off exists between system security and convenience (Gibbons et al. 2005). In an application with millions of users, an error rate of just a few per cent may well be totally unacceptable, depending on what each error actually implies (e.g., service denial or incorrect service, or perhaps just a manual correction by the individual concerned) and the application-dependent performance requirements of this system. In practice, though, increasing the number of users causes performance to degrade, so the challenge of scale remains a first priority. Apart from that, large-scale biometric systems require a huge amount of *computational resources* in order to operate, whereas the *maintenance* of such systems with very large *geographical dispersion* and supporting *a great number of users* may prove to be an extremely difficult task.

The reduction of the cost and size of biometric sensors and the popular notion that biometrics is actually an effective strategy for *protection of privacy* and from fraud (Tomko, 1998), has led to this technology likely being used in almost every transaction needing authentication of personal identity. However, in order for a significant variety of commercial applications to become feasible, it will be required that biometric sensors are deployed much more broadly than is required by high-risk verification/identification needs. Multiple interconnected sensors will be needed in every room, at home, in shops, in public buildings, in every street, in public transportation and even worn by individuals when embedded in clothing, etc. The *cost* of such coverage is still far greater than current applications could support.

5.3.2   Other Limitations

Not only the technological vulnerabilities but also the capabilities of biometric profiling systems have been subjects of strong debate and have given rise to multiple legal and social concerns. Such concerns involve amongst others the *systematic unnecessary and/or unauthorised collection* (Cavoukian, 1999) and use of biometric data and biometric data disclosure to other parties without the individual's consent, which composes a threat to the individual's right to control his/her own personal data and constitutes a serious threat to the person's privacy and civil liberties. Furthermore, *identity fraud* (Tiné, 2004), as the action taken by a person when he/she 'with malicious intent consciously creates the semblance of an identity that does not belong to him, using the identity of someone else or of a non-existing person' (Grijpink, 2003),[53] still remains an open issue (Leenes, 2006).

As biometric systems are gradually incorporated into governmental and commercial applications, necessary actions are being taken so that a legal framework is built covering issues deriving from the new technologies. Still, the fleeting nature of behavioural biometrics may make it harder to apply law to and manage them. Many of these measures, on a purely technical level, impose serious restrictions on the research efforts in the field of biometrics. For example, the storing of captured raw data (e.g., a person's image or videos from cameras monitoring public areas) in databases poses a threat to the subject's privacy, since post-processing and extraction of additional information, including age, gender and ethnicity, on this data is possible. Nevertheless, the mere collection and storing of only the features extracted by the biometric system comprises a bottleneck for a future automatic update of the system (e.g., use of a better set of extracted features) by requiring data

---

[53] Quoting from Leenes, 2006: 11, in a translation from Bert-Jaap Koops.

re-collection from enrolled people, whereas the possibility of using this data to enrich the training and test databases used in research is eliminated.

5.4 The Future of Behavioural Biometric Profiling Technology and Applications

The integration, convergence and cross-fertilisation of previously unrelated technologies is an important pattern in scientific evolution and often comprises the reason behind true non-incremental innovations and paradigm shifts. In this section, we discuss existing technologies which, for the most part, are not a part of biometric technology but are nonetheless of critical importance due to the explosive synergies that can be achieved by combining them with biometrics. The relation to behavioural biometric profiling is especially pronounced because this is one of the most challenging and multifaceted amongst both biometric and profiling technologies.

This section proceeds from considering *necessary infrastructure* (in the first subsection) through discussing how the fundamental performance limitations of today's behavioural biometric profiling systems can be transcended in the future (in the second and third subsections) to seeing behavioural biometric profiling in the broader scope of the overall future technology landscape (in the third and fourth subsections).

5.4.1 Part One: The Grid

Feverish research is taking place all over the world on providing a solution to the advanced need for *computational* and *communicational resources, data* and their *secure access* and *management* deriving from the increasing complexity of problems that science, engineering and commerce are dealing with and working on. New computing technologies involving provisioning, synchronisation of a huge number of simple or complex tasks and visualisation are followed by strict requirements on accuracy and robustness. The advent of *Grid computing* is the result of such consistent and systematic research efforts initially focusing on taking advantage of the huge, unused computing capacity which is widely distributed within heterogeneous Information Technology (IT) environments. The Grid is defined to be a system that '*coordinates resources that are not subject to centralised control using standard, open, general-purpose protocols and interfaces to deliver non-trivial qualities of services*' (Foster, 2002). It is actually a new wave of technology offering a look beyond the current capabilities.

A fundamental requirement for a successful large-scale Grid deployment is one of *transparency*. A Grid application commonly runs in a highly distributed fashion, executing on distributed CPUs, accessing data from distributed storage, crossing organisational borders, regularly recovering from a variety of faults, ensuring security and protection of application data whatever physical infrastructure (Litke, 2004) is being relied on, providing agreed-upon Quality of Service (QoS) (Malamos et al. 2002; Litke et al. 2005) and so forth. Clearly, the application programmers cannot implement the functionality to satisfy all these requirements every time. Rather, the Grid infrastructure itself is designed to solve these problems for the application automatically. The application is aware merely of a service model: it negotiates the specifications of an appropriate environment to run in and then perceives that it is running in just such an environment.

Our discussion in the previous section stressed that *a large-scale behavioural biometric profiling system* is a system highly demanding in computational and communication resources, security and data access, whereas its management is of particularly high complexity. Mobile individuals must be handled, complex and computationally expensive algorithms must be applied, distributed databases must be accessed, privacy of profiling data must be ensured by trusted organisations, service providers will need dynamically regulated access to such profiling data as their services depend on, communications in dynamic environments may well be provided by third parties which should not be able to access sensitive content etc. Creating the appropriate infrastructure for a behavioural biometric profiling application is, thus, in many ways harder or as hard as creating the behavioural biometric technology itself. As the Grid research and development community is pursuing a very concrete agenda with the goal of bringing the infrastructure described into practical usage, the implementation of large-scale behavioural biometric systems becomes a lot less distant: the required infrastructure is actually on the way.

5.4.2   Part Two: Semantics and Pattern Recognition

The preceding discussion addressed necessary infrastructure constraints that must be satisfied before behavioural biometric profiling can become practicable in applications with extensive impact. In this section, we consider the performance and usability of the core biometric technologies themselves (Ripley, 1994; Uschold, 1996).

It is always possible, and often desirable, in an application with a pattern recognition component, to isolate this component and try to optimise it out of context. Behavioural biometric profiling is such an application: processing collected data from biometric sensors to extract behavioural verification, identification or profiling classifications is, by definition of the term in its technical sense, a *pattern recognition problem*.[54] Much of the related literature, including the references we provided in our survey in section 2, focuses to a large extent on this approach, achieving a regular flow of incremental performance improvements.

---

[54] Pattern recognition. In *Wikipedia, The Free Encyclopedia*. Retrieved September 2006, from http://en.wikipedia.org/w/index.php?title=Pattern_recognition&oldid=73293380.

This is technically desirable but can obscure long-term trends. Today's methods will reach bottlenecks and then the motivation for disruptive improvements will grow.

Speech recognition provides a useful example here, as its technical aspects are similar to behavioural biometric profiling while its high commercial value makes it a rather heavily researched area; the combination of the audio speech recording with a camera's view of the speaker's lips and with natural language processing technology is able to lead to much-improved performance. In this example, the system attempts lip reading in the captured video, supplying in this way additional features for recognition, whereas the natural language processing assesses the grammar and syntax of the various possible interpretations of the recorded utterances in order to choose one that makes linguistic sense - just as humans do when they talk and listen to each other. In addition, communication not only produces but also constantly relies on *interpretation*: situational knowledge combined with an understanding of communication content is exploited for the achievement of the interpretation of further communication, while new information may trigger a re-interpretation of the already processed stream (e.g., note how we sometimes miss a word in a conversation but, a second or two later we "hear" the entire utterance, having filled in the missing sound by understanding its meaning).

Taking this example further, a behavioural biometric profiling application relying on emotion recognition from speech could incorporate an entire speech recognition application. Take, for instance, a cool tone of voice uttering a phrase that could be classified as passionate when written down. This might then be irony - the emotion is more likely to be say, "bitterness" rather than, say "indifference".

There are serious technical challenges that arise when trying to implement such an integrated system. In simple terms, in traditional pattern recognition we can build an entirely mathematical solution: the output is a statistic of the input. In contrast, for these systems we need to model *knowledge*: they need to be able to *reason* about the interdependencies between different types of available data. How do we model the influence of the linguistic meaning of an utterance on how we interpret the emotion that we detect from the tone of the voice? The necessary knowledge technologies have been under development since the early days of computer science but ontological modelling, including *rule and reasoning systems*, is currently in a phase of explosive evolution in the context of the Semantic Web.

Exploiting this technological synergy is still at an experimental stage (e.g., (Voisine et al. 2005)), while it needs sound theoretical foundations and industrial-quality implementations before behavioural biometric profiling can rely on it.

An interesting barrier preventing the creation of a practical system of the type we are discussing is that the integration we require complicates the underlying *machine learning* task considerably. The output is a statistic of the input, biased by context. Firstly, this makes the mathematical challenge much greater, hence, a great deal of ingenious research is required. Secondly, and harder by today's standards, the sheer amount of data required by an application will be much greater. Today's sensor capabilities are insufficient. This leads us to the topic of the following subsection.

5.4.3   Part Three: Sensing/Input/Data Collection

Machine learning technologies (which include pattern recognition) are in general, data driven. This means that system designers must collect a dataset that clearly demonstrates the patterns that are to be recognised. *Learning algorithms* are then used to infer/calculate a model of this data with the critically important feature of *generalisation* capability: data not previously examined but exhibiting the same patterns as the training data, is classified (or otherwise processed) correctly according to the model.

In practice, correct experimental design remains a challenge: just as a poll collecting 10 answers is an insignificant predictor for election results, so recording the voice of 10 volunteers for 5 minutes each is almost surely useless for building an emotion recognition system. Of course, many more issues exist. In the poll example, even if the sample is large, we need to choose people from different areas, backgrounds, etc. How do we collect voice recordings that manifest all the emotions we intend to recognise? Compiling good datasets is very difficult today, so it is reasonable to consider whether future sensor deployment and exploitation might make this task easier and more natural. This is indeed the case: with technologies such as pervasive networking, streaming media, semantic integration of heterogeneous resources (Tseng and Chen, 2005), etc., the *isolation of electronic devices* from each other is gradually disappearing. Currently many Internet sites host real-time videos streamed by cameras installed inside or outside buildings around the globe. Soon, the kind of *sensors* that people are already buying anyway - microphones in mobiles and land phones, digital cameras, video cameras and webcams, surveillance equipment ranging from (more) cameras to location/motion detecting devices, non-intrusive medical sensors measuring e.g., heartbeat for sports or health applications, devices with mobile location estimation capabilities such as GPS, environment monitoring sensors such as thermometers in buildings or cars - will all be *online* and thus globally accessible, barring only policy constraints.

This creates more than a huge quantity of useful data; it also introduces synergies that increase the data value. Today we would have to hand-label emotions in speech recordings. In the future, sensor networks will be automatically collecting, in large volumes, parallel recordings of voice, facial expression, pulse, temperature and much more, possibly also including (synchronised) data about credit card transactions, RFID data about products purchased or even just examined, etc.

Current behavioural biometric systems are implemented based on simplifying design assumptions. A major limitation of the systems is that they only consider a single modality of input. Their relatively poor performance (in the sense that acceptably high performance is being achieved only in a highly constrained environment) indicates, and our own intuitive understanding of how we communicate information to each other highlights, that in order to decode the information stream produced by a (consciously or unconsciously) communicating (or "behaving") human, multiple modalities are essential.

In the speech recognition example of the previous subsection, it is clearly seen that lip -reading combined with listening to speech reveals more information and, thus, offers greater potential for better understanding. The proliferation of sensors that we have been discussing will lead to a plethora of such techniques, boosting behavioural biometric profiling systems' performance beyond what is possible when relying on a single modality.

5.4.4 Behavioural Biometric Profiling and Ambient Intelligence

We have built up a forecast of technological trends which constitutes *ambient behavioural biometric profiling intelligence*. The technologies we described provide transparent support for the "non-functional" requirements, such as security, that must be satisfied in addition to the main functional requirements of a behavioural biometric profiling application, if it is to be used freely in the consumer environment rather than in specialised and closely monitored situations; they provide the means to improve pattern recognition performance, not only in a low-level technical manner but also by guiding the recognition process with effective application-specific strategies even in complex, real-world applications and they take these improved biometrics, which are now more promising to be capable of functioning with real world conditions and actually put them in the real world, potentially operating in every building, vehicle, outdoor space or other area. This pervasive infusion of our environment with transparently operating biometric systems will be an important facet of the ambient intelligence technology of the future.

5.5 Conclusions

This chapter pursued a dual goal. We first overviewed the state of the art in behavioural biometric profiling. This showed that many interesting and useful applications are already possible – but they need to be quite specialised, clearly focused and even adapted to the technology that supports them. We next examined the barriers for improvement of behavioural biometric profiling. These barriers are immense but it is not up to behavioural biometric profiling researchers alone to overcome them. As technology progresses, many useful synergies between behavioural biometric profiling and other technologies will appear. Therefore, we can reasonably expect ground-breaking improvements to behavioural biometric profiling in the foreseeable future.

5.6   Reply: Old Metaphorical Wine – New
Behavioural Bottles

James Backhouse*

> While technocrats might admire the amazing capacity of algorithms and automated
> processing to identify useful trends and patterns in large volumes of data, they overestimate
> the capacity of formal systems to capture and represent human behaviour. Humans are able
> to manifest myriad behaviours that can never be modelled and reproduced satisfactorily in
> a computer-based system. Honesty, trust and pleasure undoubtedly exist in human systems
> at many different levels but it is moot whether they can be captured and adequately repre-
> sented in a technical one. Parameters are constructs of a formal logic, they do not exist in
> the wild but must be actively and continually associated with living specimens of human
> behaviour. This work of association becomes a relentless battle for the management of
> meaning that the system's sponsors are for ever cursed with. The automated creation of
> categories and the mechanical allocation of individuals to such categories may be accepta-
> ble when the data concerns purchases in a supermarket but when the data context is one in
> which these elaborations of personal information impact directly on the freedoms to pursue
> an unhindered private existence, then the question becomes far more serious.

Underpinning the shining new carapace of biometric behavioural profiling and ambient
intelligence is an extremely persistent old metaphor. Actually two. The first metaphor
has been integrated and reintegrated into the "science" of artificial intelligence, data
mining and now behavioural profiling such that it is no longer noticed. The metaphor is
the man as machine, sometimes transposing into the brain as computer metaphor but
generally identified where the signs that human social beings produce, are treated in the
same way as the signs that computer based information systems produce.

*Parameters ranging from enjoyment to honesty, important to applications such
as adaptive entertainment, through to intrusion detection are commonly but subtly
manifested in an individual's behaviour.*

This sentence encapsulates many of the problems. Instead of presenting the situation as one where behaviour is monitored and the signs that are captured are then categorised and parameters chosen, what is presented here is the reverse. The parameters
already have a prior existence and are merely demonstrated in the person's behaviour.
By contrast, parameters are quintessentially abstractions that are "discovered" in the
data in the process of analysis and mining. In this representation the abstractions, that
is the parameters, have taken on a concrete and material existence, becoming reified.
Instead of enjoyment or honesty being manifested in some signs that are captured into
data for mining, the parameters are to be found in real human activity. The parameters
are indistinguishable from the activity. They have become that activity – as far as the
information systems are concerned. The logic of the data miner and the behavioural
profiler has taken precedence over the behavioural logic of the humans being profiled.
This order of priority reflects a deeper problem of the precedence of the technical and
the subordination of the human and social. Furthermore, finding suitable parameters
for enjoyment and honesty does not strike one as a simple task.

---

*London School of Economics (LsE)

As humans, we ourselves systematically exploit information gleaned from the observation of others' behaviour, often with astounding levels of success, proving the existence of immensely descriptive data in such observations.

The use of the man as a machine metaphor is emphasised in this last sentence where a direct comparison is implied between humans exploiting, i.e., capturing and processing information from the environment and a computer based system doing likewise. The success of human information processing activities is given as proof of the existence of data. Because humans are able to observe the behaviour of others with success, this is deemed to prove the existence of descriptive data. Here, the reification is explained and reinforced. Humans perform various activities successfully following the observation of the behaviour of others, ergo the parameters and the descriptive data actually exist.

This upbeat, technologically-deterministic perspective thoroughly permeates the whole of Chapter 4. Afterwards, the authors inform readers that the Artificial Intelligence community is developing promising tools that the Semantic Web is about to deliver, that *"users must no longer worry about setting up the machine intelligence they require but rather find it already embedded in their environment"*. Again, the authors reassert the notion of machine intelligence. There will be many that reject the notion. What is artificial about intelligence? More importantly, how soon will users be assured that the machine intelligence which is taking decisions on their behalf is a) trustworthy, b) competent and c) safe. This institutionalisation of machine intelligence may be much further away than the authors believe.

For the parameters to be constructed in the recorded behaviour some very difficult decisions lie ahead. While it might be reasonable to discuss a measure of speech in the form of speed or the number of words spoken against time, a sweeping generalisation that deems *"fast speech is to be considered agitated and slow speech is to be considered as signifying boredom"* would be a hostage to fortune. Most important in behaviour is the notion of context and the significance of an outward semiotic manifestation, such as speech, will depend very largely upon the context in which it occurs. Slow speech might signify the need to make oneself understood to those who are hard of hearing, or who are not mother-tongue speakers. Simplistic assignation of such parameters ignores the subtlety of social behaviour, of rhetoric, of playfulness, or of mock-seriousness. Such shortcomings spring from the same well - the well of lost plots. Unless the technological determinism that underpins the proposed behavioural profiling and related technologies is tempered with important elements of social theory and practice, it is difficult to see these new initiatives not following their AI predecessor into the dustbin of history. Of course, the problem is that like Dracula, AI always rises again under a new identity – expert systems, data mining and so forth. This is beneficial for funding new research programmes and maintaining departments but rather short on real practical advances.

The second metaphor arises when the authors describe "emotion recognition systems" with three stages of operations – acquisition, extraction, interpretation. It is no surprise to find the term "extraction" here as it figured strongly in the halcyon days of Artificial Intelligence in the 1980s. It derives from the Chemical Engineering

Metaphor, a metaphor that is important to this perspective. It sees knowledge as something that is produced from raw materials that are mined (hence data mining) and then the value is extracted and used in an information system. It appears to be a value-free industrial life cycle but on the contrary, the parameterisation of the behavioural data will be used to apply important values to the population. Woe betide those who walk like some terrorist does, sport a beard like a freedom-fighter might or speak too fast on the phone. These behaviours might be classified and used as triggers for important governmental intervention and reaction. The intelligence in the machine will then be critical. If it has any, that is.

5.7   Bibliography

Ahmed, A.A.E., Traore, I. 'A New Biometrics Technology based on Mouse Dynamics', *Technical Report ECE-03-5*, University of Victoria, Department of Electrical and Computer Engineering, Victoria, Canada, September 2003.

Ahmed, A.A.E., Traore, I., 'Detecting Computer Intrusions Using Behavioral Biometrics', *Third Annual Conference on Privacy, Security and Trust*, October 2005.

Banse, R., Sherer, K.R., 'Acoustic profiles in vocal emotion expression', *Journal of Personality and Social Psychology*, Vol. 70, No. 3, APA Washington DC, 1996, pp. 614–636.

Bleha, S., 'Computer access security systems using keystroke dynamics', *IEEE Transactions on Pattern Analysis and Machine Intelligence*, Vol.12, No. 12, IEEE Computer Society, Washington DC, 990, pp. 1217-1222.

Bobick, A. F., and Davis, J. W., 'The recognition of human movement using temporal templates', *IEEE Transactions on Pattern Analysis and Machine Intelligence*, Vol. 23, No. 3, IEEE Computer Society, Washington DC, 2001, pp. 257–267.

Cauldwell, R., 'Where did the anger go? The role of context in interpreting emotions in speech', *ISCA Workshop on Speech and Emotion*, 2000.

Cavoukian, A., 'Consumer Biometric Applications: A Discussion Paper', 1999. Available at: http://www.ipc.on.ca.

Collins, R., Gross, R., and Shi, J., 'Silhouette-based human identification from body shape and gait', *IEEE International Conference on Automatic Face and Gesture Recognition*, Washington, DC, USA, May 2002, pp. 351–356.

Cutting, J., Proffitt, D., Kozlowski, L., 'A Biomechanical Invariant for Gait Perception', *Journal of Experimental Psychology: Human Perception and Performance*, Vol. 4, No. 3, APA Journals, Washington DC, 1978, pp. 357–372.

Demirdjian, D., Ko, T. and Darrell, T., 'Untethered Gesture Acquisition and Recognition for Virtual World Manipulation', *Virtual Reality*, Vol. 8, No. 4, Springer London, 2005, pp. 222-230.

Deng, P., Liao, H. M., Ho, C. W., Tyan, H. R., 'Wavelet-Based Off-Line Handwritten Signature Verification', *Computer Vision and Image Understanding*, Vol. 76, No. 3, Elsevier, Netherlands, December, 1999, pp. 173–190.

Ekman, P., Friesen, W.V., 'Constants across cultures in the face and emotion', *Journal of Personality and Social Psychology*, Vol. 17, No. 2, APA Washington DC, 1971, pp. 124–129.

Fasel, B., Luettin, J., 'Automatic facial expression analysis: A survey', *Pattern Recognition*, Vol. 36, No. 1, Elsevier B.V., Netherlands, 2003, pp. 259-275.

Foster, I., *'What is the Grid? A Three Point Checklist'*, 22 July 2002. Available at http://www.gridtoday.com/02/0722/ 100136.html

Ganchev, T., Fakotakis, N., Kokkinakis, G., 'Text-Independent Speaker Verification: The WCL-1 System', *6th International Conference on Text, Speech and Dialogue TSD 2003, Lecture Notes in Artificial Intelligence* (LNAI), Springer Verlag, Vol. 2807, September 2003, pp. 263-268.

Gibbons, M., Yoon, S., Cha, S.-H., Tappert C., 'Evaluation of Biometric Identification in Open Systems', *Lecture Notes in Computer Science*, Vol. 3546, Springer-Verlag Berlin Heidelberg, 2005, pp. 823-831.

Gunetti, D., Picardi, Cl., 'Keystroke analysis of free text', *ACM Transactions on Information and System Security*, Vol. 8, No. 3, ACM Press New York, August 2005, pp. 312–347.

Harb, H., Chen, L., 'Voice-based gender identification in multimedia applications', *Journal of Intelligent Information Systems*, Vol. 24, No. 2, Kluwer Academic Publishers, Netherlands, 2005, pp. 179-198.

Haydar, A., Demirekler, M., Yurtseven, M.K., 'Speaker identification through use of features selected using genetic algorithm', *Electronics Letters*, Vol. 34, IEEE Computer Society, Washington DC, 1998, pp. 39–40.

Hayfron-Acquah, J. B., Nixon, M. S. and Carter, J. N., 'Recognising human and animal movement by symmetry', *Proceedings IEEE International Conference on Image Processing (ICIP '01)*, Vol. 3, Thessaloniki, Greece, October 2001, pp. 290–293.

Hayfron-Acquah, J. B., Nixon, M. S., Carter, J. N., 'Automatic gait recognition by symmetry analysis', *Pattern Recognition Letters*, Vol. 24, No. 13, Elsevier, Netherlands, 2003, pp. 2175–2183.

He, Q., Debrunner, C., 'Individual recognition from periodic activity using hidden Markov models', *IEEE Workshop on Human Motion (HUMO '00)*, Austin, Tex, USA, December 2000, pp. 47–52.

Huang, K., Yan, H., 'Off-line signature verification using structural feature correspondence', *Pattern Recognition*, Vol. 35, No. 11, Elsevier, Netherlands, 2002, pp. 2467 – 2477.

Igarza, J. J., Goirizelaia, I., Espinosa, K., Hernáez, I., Méndez, R., Sánchez, J., 'Online Handwritten Signature Verification Using Hidden Markov Models', *Lecture Notes in Computer Science*, 2905, Springer Verlag Berlin Heidelberg, 2003, pp. 391-399.

Jain, A. K., Griess, F. D., Connell, S. D., 'On-line signature verification', *Pattern Recognition*, Vol. 35, No. 12, Elsevier, Netherlands, 2002, pp. 2963 – 2972.

Ji, H., Bang, S.Y., 'Feature selection for multi-class classification using pairwise class discriminatory measure and covering concept', *Electronics Letters*, Vol. 36, No. 6, IET Press, UK, 2000, pp. 524–525.

Justino, E. J. R., Bortolozzi, F., Sabourin, R., 'A comparison of SVM and HMM classifiers in the off-line signature verification', *Pattern Recognition Letters*, Vol. 26, No. 9, Elsevier, Netherlands, 2005, pp. 1377–1385.

Kale, A., Rajagopalan, A. N., Cuntoor, N., and Kruger, V., 'Gait based recognition of humans using continuous HMMs', *IEEE International Conference on Automatic Face and Gesture Recognition*, Washington, DC, USA, May 2002, pp. 336-341.

Kholmatov, A., Yanikoglu, B., 'Identity authentication using improved online signature verification method', *Pattern Recognition Letters*, Vol. 26, No. 15, Elsevier, Netherlands, 2005, pp. 2400–2408.

Leenes, R. (ed.), *ID-related Crime: Towards a Common Ground for Interdisciplinary Research, FIDIS Deliverable 5.2b*: European Union IST FIDIS Project, 2006, pp. 1-116.

Lei, H., and Govindaraju, V., 'A Study on the Consistency of Features for On-Line Signature Verification', *Pattern Recognition Letters*, Vol. 26, No. 15, Elsevier, Netherlands 2005, pp. 2483-2489.

Lerdsudwichai, C., Abdel-Mottaleb M., Ansari, A-N., 'Tracking multiple people with recovery from partial and total occlusion', *Pattern Recognition*, Vol. 38, No. 7, Elsevier Netherlands, 2005, pp. 1059-1070.

Licsár A., Szirányi, T., 'User-adaptive hand gesture recognition system with interactive training', *Image and Vision Computing*, Vol. 23, No. 12, Elsevier Science, 2005, pp. 1102-1114.

Litke, A., Panagakis, A., Doulamis, A., Doulamis, N., Varvarigou, T., Varvarigos, E., 'An Advanced Architecture for a Commercial Grid Infrastructure', *Lecture Notes in Computer Science*, No. 3165, Springer-Verlag Berlin Heidelberg, 2004, p. 32.

Litke A., Tserpes K., Varvarigou T., 'Computational workload prediction for grid oriented industrial applications: the case of 3D-image rendering', *IEEE International Symposium on Cluster Computing and the Grid, CCGrid 2005*, May 2005, Vol. 2, pp. 962–969.

Lozano, S. C., Tversky, B., 'Communicative gestures facilitate problem solving for both commu-nicators and recipients', *Journal of Memory and Language*, Vol. 55, No. 1, Elsevier, July 2006, pp. 47-63.

Lung, S.-Y., 'Wavelet feature selection using fuzzy approach to text independent speaker recogni-tion', *IEICE Transactions on Fundamentals of Electronics, Communications and Computer Sciences*, E-88-A, No. 3, IEICE, Oxford Journal Press, 2005, pp 779–781.

Lv, H., Wang, W., Wang, C., Zhuo, Q., 'Off-line Chinese signature verification based on support vector machines', *Pattern Recognition Letters*, Vol. 26, No. 15, Elsevier, Netherlands 2005, pp. 2390–2399.

Malamos, A.G., Malamas, E.N., Varvarigou T.A., and Ahuja, S.R., 'A Model for Availability of Quality of Service in Distributed Multimedia Systems', *Multimedia Tools and Applications*, Vol. 16, No. 3, Springer Netherlands, 2002, pp. 207-230.

Markowitz, J., 'Anti-spoofing techniques for Voice', *Biometric Consortium Conference BC*, 2005.

Muller, A., *Experimentelle Untersuchungen zur stimmlichen Darstellung von Gefuehlen*, Ph.D. dissertation, University Gottingen, Germany, 1960.

Muramatsu, D., and Matsumoto, T., 'An HMM On-line Signature Verification Algorithm', *Proceedings of International Conference on Audio- and Video-Based Biometric Person Authentication*, 2003.

Murray, M., 'Gait as a total pattern of movement', *American Journal of Physical Medicine*, Vol. 46, No 1, Lippincott Williams & Wilkins Published at: Baltimore, MA, 1967, pp. 290–332.

Nathan, K.S., Silverman, H.F., "Time-varying feature selection and classification of unvoiced stop consonants", *IEEE Transactions on Speech Audio Processing*, Vol. 2, No. 3, IEEE Signal Processing Society, Washington, 1994, pp. 395–405.

Nespoulous, J., Perron, P., Lecours, A., *The Biological Foundations of Gestures: Motor and Semiotic Aspects*, Lawrence Erlbaum Associates, Hillsdale, MJ, 1986.

Niyogi, S., and Adelson, E., 'Analyzing and recognizing walking figures in XYT', *IEEE Computer Society Conference on Computer Vision and Pattern Recognition (CVPR '94)*, Seattle, Wash, USA, June 1994, pp. 469–474.

Oka, K., Sato, Y., Koike, H., 'Real-time fingertip tracking and gesture recognition', *Computer Graphics and Applications*, Vol. 22, No. 6, IEEE, Nov.-Dec. 2002, pp. 64-71.

Ong, S. C.W., Ranganath S., Venkatesh, Y.V., 'Understanding gestures with systematic variations in movement dynamics', *Pattern Recognition*, Vol. 39, No. 9, Elsevier Netherlands, September 2006, pp. 1633-1648.

Patwardhan, K. S., Roy, S.D., 'Hand gesture modelling and recognition involving changing shapes and trajectories, using a Predictive EigenTracker', *Pattern Recognition Letters*, Elsevier Netherlands, preprint submitted on April 2006.

Peacock, A., Ke, X., Wilkerson, M., 'Typing patterns: a key to user identification', *IEEE Security & Privacy*, Vol. 2, No. 5, IEEE Computer Society, Wash, 2004, pp. 40-47.

Philips, P. J., Sarkar, S., Robledo, I., Grother, P., and Bowyer, K., 'Baseline results for the chal-lenge problem of human ID using gait analysis', *IEEE International Conference on AutomaticFace and Gesture Recognition*, Washington, DC, USA, May 2002, pp. 130–135.

Polana, R., Nelson, R. C., 'Detecting activities', *Journal of Visual Communication and Image Representation*, Vol. 5, Academic Press, June 1994, pp. 172-180.

Pusara, M., Brodley, C.E., 'User Re-Authentication via Mouse Movements', *Proceedings of the 2004 ACM workshop on Visualization and data mining for computer security*, ACM, 2004, pp. 1-8.

Plutchik, R., *The Psychology and Biology of Emotion*, Harper Collins College Publishers, New York, 1994.

Ptacek, PH, Sander, EK, 'Age recognition from voice', *Journal of Speech and. Hearing Research*, the American Speech-Language-Hearing Association, Vol. 9, 1996, pp. 273–277.

Ripley, B.D., 'Neural networks and related methods for classification (with discussion)', *Journal of the Royal Statistical Society Series B*, Vol. 56, Royal Statistical Society, Blackwell Publ., 1994, pp. 409-456.

Robinson, J.A., Liang, V.W., 'Computer user verification using login string keystroke dynamics', *IEEE Transactions on Systems, Man and Cybernetics*, Part A, Vol. 28, No. 2, IEEE System, man and cybernetics, New York, 1998, pp. 236-241.

Santos, C., Justino, E. J. R., Bortolozzi, F., Sabourin, R., 'An Off-Line Signature Verification Method based on the Questioned Document Expert's Approach and a Neural Network Classifier', *9th International IEEE Workshop on Frontiers in Handwriting Recognition*, 2004, pp. 498-502.

Scherer, K.R., 'Expression of Emotion in Voice and Music', *Journal of Voice*, Vol. 9, No. 3, Elsevier Medical Journals for The Voice Foundation and International Association of Phonosurgeons, 1995, pp. 235-248.

Scherer, K.R., 'On the nature and function of emotion: A component process approach', In Klaus R. Scherer and Paul Ekman (Ed.), *Approaches to emotion*, Hillsdale, NJ: Erlbaum,1984, pp. 293–317.

Scherer, K.R., 'Vocal effect expression: A review and a model for future research', *Psychol. Bull.*, Vol. 99, No. 2, American Psychological Association, Washington, DC, USA, 1986, pp.143-165.

Scherer, K.R., Banse, R., Wallbott, H.G., Emotion inferences from vocal expression correlate across languages and cultures', *Journal of Cross-Cultural Psychology.*, Vol. 32, No. 1, Sage Publ, Thousands Oaks, 2001, pp. 76–92.

Scherer, K.R., "Vocal communication of emotion: A review of research paradigms", *Speech Communication, Volume 40, Issues 1-2*, Elsevier, 2003, pp. 227–256.

Tiné, S., *Identity theft: a new threat for civil society*, Brussels, EU Forum for the Prevention of Organised Crime, 2 February 2004.

Tomko, G., 'Biometrics as a Privacy-Enhancing Technology: Friend or Foe of Privacy?' *Privacy Laws & Business*, 9th Privacy Commissioners/Data Protection Authorities Workshop, Spain, 1998.

Tseng, F. S.C., Chen, C.W., 'Integrating heterogeneous data warehouses using XML technologies', *Journal of Information Science*, Vol. 31, No 6, ACM 2005, pp. 209-229.

Uschold, M., Gruninger, M., 'Ontologies: Principles, Methods and Application', *Knowledge Engineering Review*, Vol. 11, No. 2, Cambridge University Press, 1996, pp. 93-155.

Voisine, N., Dasiopoulou, S., Precioso, F., Mezaris, V., Kompatsiaris I., Strintzis, M.G., 'A Genetic Algorithm-based Approach to Knowledge-assisted Video Analysis', *Proceedings of IEEE International Conference on Image Processing (ICIP 2005)*, Vol. 3, September 2005, pp.441-444.

Wang, L., Ning, H., Tan, T., Hu, W., 'Fusion of Static and Dynamic Body Biometrics for Gait Recognition', *Proceedings of the Ninth IEEE International Conference on Computer Vision (ICCV 2003)*, Vol. 2, 2003, pp. 1449.

Zhang, Y., Kambhamettu, C., '3D head tracking under partial occlusion', *Pattern Recognition*, Vol. 35, No. 7, Elsevier Netherlands, July 2002, pp. 1545-1557.

Chapter 6
Personalisation and its Influence
on Identities, Behaviour and Social Values

Simone van der Hof and Corien Prins

New ICTs support new ways of tailoring services to the individual needs and desires of customers. Increasingly, what is called personalisation of services is implemented particularly in Internet-based e-commerce applications but other kinds of technologies and services, such as location-based services, RFID, smartcards and biometrics are expected to follow closely and offer even better opportunities for personalised services. The growing popularity of personalisation requires an exploration of the broader and fundamental implications of this phenomenon. Issues related to the categorisation of people, the creation of identities, the (re)structuring of behaviour and the shaping of the overall movement of information and expression within society need consideration when implementing such techniques in organisational (e.g., e-Government) and business processes. More specifically, this chapter deals with privacy, transparency and the quality of personalisation processes, as well as inclusion, exclusion and control. It is argued that the phenomenon of personalisation must be deliberated in light of the broader developments in the area of ubiquitous computing.

6.1   Introduction

In our present-day society, *behaviour* is increasingly monitored, captured, stored, used and analysed to become knowledge about people, their habits and their social identity. We deliberately use the term behaviour here rather than personal data for it is not so much personal data that are used and processed anew and in isolation each time an organisation or company acquires a set of data. In contemporary society, "useful" information and knowledge goes beyond the individual exchange of a set of individual personal data. Data mining, pervasive or ubiquitous-computing techniques and other applications, often termed ambient intelligence, create a context-aware environment in which, by means of the coordinated use of databases, sensors, micro-devices and software agents, numerous systems spontaneously scan our environment and daily activities for data to be able to serve us with particular information and (inter)actions, based on certain notions about what is appropriate for us as unique individuals given the particulars of our daily life and context.

Tilburg University, Tilburg Institute for Law, Technology, and Society (TILT)

M. Hildebrandt and S. Gutwirth (eds.), *Profiling the European Citizen:*
Cross-Disciplinary Perspectives.
© Springer Science + Business Media B.V. 2008

In other words, the use and "value" of personal data cannot be separated from the specifics of the context (social, economic and institutional settings) within which these data are collected and used.

As such, the core theme of this book – profiling – has everything to do with monitoring and influencing human behaviour. One key ambition in using detailed knowledge about human behaviour is the rendering of personalised services. Both the public and the private sector have immense expectations of the opportunities that personalised services offer.

The growing popularity of personalisation warrants an exploration of the broader and fundamental implications of this phenomenon. This contribution chooses to focus on the issues related to the categorisation of people, the creation of identities, the (re)structuring of our behaviour and the shaping of the overall movement of information and expression within society. First, the concept of personalised services will be briefly outlined in section 2. It describes the ways in which user information is processed in personalisation techniques and, more specifically, the use of profiles in this respect. In section 3, the discussion is placed in the broader perspective of profiling and turns to possible concerns about the application of personalisation. Here, issues such as privacy, transparency, quality, inclusion, exclusion and control will be discussed. Finally, the chapter concludes with the argument that the phenomenon of personalisation must be discussed in light of the broader developments in the area of pervasive computing and the trend towards the use of our identities and behaviour. These developments necessitate a debate on the role of legislature in providing the necessary instruments to know and to control the ways in which our identities are created and shaped.

6.2   Setting the Stage: Personalisation and Profiling[55]

The beginning of the 20th century was characterised by industrial mass production. Industry thereby, to a large extent, determined the types and characteristics of goods to be produced and put on the market. Illustrative in this respect is the legendary remark by Henry Ford about the model T Ford: "[It] is available in every colour, on the condition that it is black." The production of goods focused on similarities rather than differences between customers and hardly took notice of the customer's wishes. In recent years, a remarkable trend from mass production to mass individualisation has emerged due to information and communication technologies (ICTs) supporting new ways of tailoring services to the individual needs and desires of customers. Increasingly therefore, what is termed personalisation of services is implemented. Prominent are Internet-based e-commerce applications

---

[55] This section is based on the results of a research project funded by the Netherlands Organisation for Scientific Research (NWO): Lips, van der Hof, Prins, Schudelaro, 2005.

but other kinds of technologies and services, such as location-based services (LBSs), radio frequency identification (RFID), smartcards and biometrics, are expected to follow closely and offer even better opportunities for such tailor-made or individualised services.

Although a uniform definition of this rather new phenomenon does not exist, personalisation can generally be perceived as an organisational strategy of companies, governments and other organisations to provide services by means of ICTs to a large number of individual customers worldwide on an individualised basis. When looking at the concept in more detail, it becomes clear that personalisation is a highly complex development. Numerous context-specific aims, ambitions, business models and conditions may determine the actual development and deployment of online personalisation services. Decisions on all these issues influence, to a large extent, the role and position of both the provider and the user of an online personalisation service. Here, the key aspects of the role that providers and users play in rendering personalised services will be briefly outlined.

In order to be able to personalise online services, service providers select, filter and classify user information. In essence, the *collection, management and use of user information* are at the heart of online personalisation strategies of organisations.[56] However, it should be noted that personalised services are not necessarily solely based on information of a particular *individual* user. The services can also be drawn from previous research with a predefined audience base.[57] As such, third-party data, such as demographic data, statistical profiles or data obtained from companies, can also be used to analyse user activity. Information can also be personalised by using specified rules-based session histories.[58] Illustrative are web-based personalised services, which can be based on any combination of different types of user data, such as profile data in a database or supplied in real time, clickstream data within the host site or from across a number of cooperative sites, collaborative filtering or choices based on what other people similar to the user have found desirable or useful.[59] When looking more closely at a broad range of user information, the following types of information can be distinguished.[60] First, users may actively provide information to service providers by, for instance, filling in forms (declared information). Second, users may be indirectly associated with information (inferred information) by, for example, identifying similar interests. Finally, user logins, cookies and/or server logs may passively record behavioural information.

---

[56] Cf. Paternoster, Searby, 2002.

[57] Bonnet, 2001.

[58] Mobasher et al., 2000: 143.

[59] An example of a service using collaborative filtering is Movielens, see <movielens.umn.edu>. See also: O'Looney, 2002.

[60] Crossley, Kings, Scott, 2004: 100.

In order to accommodate the need to know what (potential) individual customers want for personalisation purposes, (a combination of different kinds of) the above-mentioned types of user information are applied to create profiles. Although various techniques exist to create consumer profiles, three stages can generally be distinguished in the creation and use of such profiles. First, during the data preparation stage, customer data is collected and stored. Customer cards may, for example, be used to map customers' buying behaviour. On the Internet, what is termed click-stream data, i.e., data generated by users while surfing the Internet or a specific website, are collected. In order to obtain a profile of the needs of customers that is as complete as possible, suppliers collect user information from as many sources as possible. This process may require the identification of individual customers, since user information is generated across multiple channels and through multiple interactions and must be attributed continuously to that specific customer (for example, by using cookies).

Second, in the data analysis stage, the data collected and stored are analysed and processed. A way of analysing user information is by using vectors in a vector space when the user visits the website. Each vector represents, for instance, a hyperlink that has been followed by the user. Hyperlinks can be given different weighting factors as a result of previous analyses of how they impact the customer's buying behaviour. The website can accordingly be restructured to inform visitors about certain products or services at an early stage. If related pages are visited or related products and services are purchased, this too may be an indication of the interests of individual users. Such information can be used to suggest new products and services to other similar visitors or customers.

Finally, in the output stage, the aim is to actually tailor services to the needs of individual customers based on the results obtained during the data analysis stage, for instance, by supplying customers with personalised (commercial) information.

Various techniques can be used to make suggestions to existing and potential customers.[61] An example is so-called recommendation systems, in which case content-based filtering techniques and collaborative filtering are distinguished. When existing profiles indicate how a certain user values certain products or services, content-based filtering can be used to predict how this user will value new but similar products or services. Depending on the predicted value the user places on these products or services, they can either be offered to the customer or not. The most important drawback of this method is that new products or services that do not fit within a customer's current profile are not filtered. Potentially, a situation of overspecialisation can arise.[62] This problem can be circumvented with collaborative filtering. In that case, if two users have similar interests and one of them prefers a certain product, this product can also be suggested to the other user. Illustrative of this technique is the "customers who bought" feature of Amazon.com. Collaborative filtering requires input from users by making them value the products offered,

---

[61] For a more detailed discussion see, for instance, Van Barneveld, 2003: 5 *ff*.

[62] Smyth, Cotter, 2000: 108.

on the basis of which "nearest neighbour" algorithms can be applied to try and detect overlapping interests between users.[63] One of the drawbacks of collaborative filtering is scalability. As the number of users as well as products and services increases, the use of "nearest neighbours" algorithms becomes more and more laborious. Moreover, since products need to be valued to be used in suggestions, reserve on the part of users to do so may frustrate the system. Finally, collaborative filtering does not take into account the contents of products and services, since only the value that users put on them matters.[64] Combining content-based and collaborative filtering can solve some of these problems, since these techniques are, to some extent, complementary.[65]

6.3   The Dark Side of Personalisation and Profiling

The development and deployment of online personalised services raises a number of questions, dilemmas and fundamental issues. These issues partly relate to the ones that were discussed earlier in relation to profiling. Being a specific application of profiling,[66] personalisation may have similar far-reaching and sometimes unknown effects on a user's position and abilities in everyday life.[67] In light of this, the discussion on privacy and personalisation appears closely related to values such as autonomy, control, transparency and (digital) diversity. Issues related to these values will therefore be briefly discussed. Moreover, the discussion in this section will focus on what is believed to be a crucial issue for future deliberation: the wider societal and political consequences, when personalisation starts shaping the overall movement of information within society, for, in an ultimate scenario, personalisation services could even put cultural and social diversity at risk.

6.3.1   *Personal Data, Identities and Behaviour*

Privacy, or rather personal data protection, is generally conceived as one of the most prominent challenges with respect to personalisation and profiling processes. Personalisation techniques may be a threat to privacy because they provide the

---

[63] Shahabi, Chen, 2003: 3.

[64] Shahabi, Chen, 2003: 3.

[65] Smyth, Cotter, 2000: 109.

[66] Personalisation is seen here as a specific application in that it focuses on developing a relationship with the user based on profiling data, responsiveness to changes and adaptation to a (changing) context. Personalisation implies relationships between subjects which are mediated by technical interfaces, such as a website.

[67] For illustrations of this see the contributions in: Lyon (ed.), 2003.

companies and organisations using such techniques with a powerful instrument to know in detail what an individual wants, who he is, whether his behaviour shows certain patterns, et cetera. The potential for further use and sometimes abuse of the detailed and rich knowledge on individuals raises the first problem. Studies have shown that consumers and citizens are very particular about the types of information they are willing to provide in return for personalised content.[68] They also have strong opinions regarding personalisation services that share personal information with other companies: the majority feels that sharing personal information is an invasion of their privacy.[69] In addition, most consumers hardly understand how personalisation technologies actually work and thus have no opportunity to control the dissemination of their personal or behavioural information. Various personalisation services deploy hidden instruments to track and trace users and thus consumers are not aware of their data and preferences being collected and compiled into personal profiles.

We believe, however, that the core privacy challenge of personalisation lies in different types of implications, i.e., the implications for the way our lives are typified and our identities are constructed.[70] A key feature of personalisation is that individuals are given new ways to present and profile themselves – depending on the specifics of the context – in certain roles or "identities". They act as a certain type of citizen, consumer, patient, voter, et cetera. The growing importance of the context-specific concept of online identity raises challenging new questions with regard to the role as well as the status of identity and identification. To what extent does the concept of online identity have a different meaning compared to identity construction in offline relationships? Where exactly lie the boundaries between online identities and a person's "own" or "real" identity? When exactly, i.e., given what conditions, may a certain fragmented or segmented aspect of a person's identity be considered an adequate representation of the "real" person behind that identity? If online personalisation becomes in part tantamount to the online identity of a person, then this state of affairs may raise the question of who may control the use of the data behind this identity as well as the identity itself. Can an online identity be owned and, if so, in whom should such ownership be vested? Finally, new means of self-presentation also raises questions related to the reliability of identities and the implications of possible fraud with identities. To what extent can users "play" with their online identity or virtual reputation, use their online reputation as a certain type of commodity, mislead organisations with a claimed online identity, et cetera?

Another way to consider the relationship between privacy and personalisation is thus by focusing not so much on the individual data but on the *effects* of online personalisation instruments. In a sense, they require that we shift our attention from individual sets of personal data towards the statistical models, profiles and algorithms

---

[68] See e.g., Mably, 2000.

[69] See e.g., Mably, 2000.

[70] See also sections 15.2.4 and 15.4.

with which individuals are categorised in a certain group or "identity".[71] After all, these models and algorithms are privately owned and thus unavailable for public scrutiny. The interests of personal data protection however, seem to require that they are made known to the public and thus are part of the public domain. This point warrants discussion in more detail.

Our behaviour in the public domain is increasingly monitored, captured, stored, used and analysed, to become privately-owned knowledge about people, their habits and social identity. Indeed, the term *personal data* protection may lose its significance once we acknowledge this trend towards a commodification of *identities and behaviour.*[72] This trend is not sufficiently taken into account in the present debate on personal data protection. These data are not used and processed anew and in isolation each time a company acquires a set of personal data. In contemporary society, "useful" information and knowledge goes beyond the individual exchange of a set of personal data. In giving his or her personal data to a certain organisation, the individual does not provide these data for use in an objective context. With personalisation, the use and thus "value" of personal data cannot be separated from the specifics of the context within which these data are used. Processing of personal data occurs within and is often structured by, social, economic and institutional settings, as is shown, e.g., by Phillips in his analysis of the implications of ubiquitous-computing developments.[73]

To capture the essence of the new protection requirement, Helen Nissenbaum proposed the introduction of a concept called 'contextual integrity'. This alternative concept would tie adequate personal data protection to norms of specific contexts, "demanding that information gathering and dissemination be appropriate to that context and obey the governing norms of distribution within it."[74] Thus, the question is not so much *whether* personal data are processed. They always are and will be, whether for legitimate or unlawful purposes. The real problem is *how* personal data are processed, in what context and towards what end.[75] Therefore, the focus of the discussion should move away from entitlement to single data. What is needed are instruments to enhance the visibility of and knowledge about how personal data are used and combined, on the basis of what data individuals are typified, by whom and for what purposes.

In essence, the identity-related implications of personalisation must be put in the larger perspective of the development of ubiquitous-computing environments. Ubiquitous computing will create a context-aware environment in which, by means of the coordinated use of databases, sensors, micro-devices and software agents, numerous systems spontaneously scan our environment for data and serve us with

---

[71] For more detail on this argument see Prins, 2006.

[72] Prins, 2004.

[73] Phillips, 2005.

[74] Nissenbaum, 2004.

[75] See also section 15.7.

particular information and inter(actions), based on certain notions about what is appropriate for us as unique individuals, given the particulars of daily life and context. Some argue that ubiquitous systems will, to a large extent, structure and determine our daily lives, mediating our identity, social relations and social power.[76] As a result of the data collection involved, what happens within the four walls of our homes and working offices as well as our social identities may become public.

Given not only the development of personalisation but also the developments in the area of pervasive computing, the discussion about protecting personal data must become a discussion about how individuals are typified (upon what social ontology? with what goal?) and who has the instruments and power to do so.[77] In this sense, personal data protection has everything to do with position, social ordering, roles, individual status and freedom. Therefore, protection of personal data in our present-day society assumes the capability to know and to control the way in which our identities are constructed and used. It requires the availability of instruments to enable awareness of the context in which personal data are used and to monitor the data-impression that individuals disclose to others.[78] In other words, the discussion on the future of personal data protection in relation to personalisation must be a discussion on whether and to what extent, the statistical models, profiles and algorithms that are used to generate knowledge about individual behaviour, social and economic position, as well as personal interests, are transparent and controllable and based on certain quality standards.[79] In the end, it is precisely a discussion on the interests of transparency, quality and control that is essential – as will become clear below – in the interest of the broader societal values of autonomy and (digital) diversity. The discussion will now focus on these values and begins with the more or less 'practical' dimension of transparency and quality and will subsequently elaborate on the fundamental issues of control, autonomy and (digital) diversity.

6.3.2   Transparency and Quality

In general, transparency reveals itself in different and more aspects than merely with respect to the use of personal data and profiles. For example, a personalised service including transaction possibilities should inform users of the specifics of the transaction

---

[76] See e.g., the different papers presented at the workshop on the Socially-Informed Design of Privacy-Enhancing Solutions, 4th International Conference on Ubiquitous Computing (UBICOMP 02), Göteborg, Sweden, September 2002. Available at: <guir.berkeley.edu/pubs/ubicomp2002/privacyworkshop>.

[77] See Phillips, 2005.

[78] See Phillips, 2005. Also: Nguyen, Mynatt, 2002.

[79] Earlier, Vedder proposed the use of the concept of 'categorical privacy'. This concept is largely based on the concept of individual privacy but includes privacy as regards information that is no longer identifiable to persons because such information may still have negative consequences for group members. Vedder, 2000: 441 *ff.*

process, such as the price of the service (to prevent customer annoyance with respect to price discrimination),[80] general terms and conditions, payment methods, security of transaction and payment processes, et cetera. This information should be presented in such a way that customers are easily and comprehensively notified (although customers generally do not actually have to read the information).

Transparency also implies user awareness with respect to the way in which personalised profiles are created and used by the personalised service provider (e.g., what methods are used to create profiles and in what context(s) personal data are used and viewed). Users should also be informed of ways to access, review and update personal data and profiles and of the security of this process. Moreover, users should know whether and how (e.g., by sending an e-mail to a clearly specified address) they can restrict or object to (commercial) use of their personal and other data as well as whole profiles. In the case of web services, for instance, a privacy statement on the website of the service provider is a good instrument to provide such information. Privacy statements should be complete and easy to access and understand.

It seems obvious that, with ongoing ubiquitous-computing developments, transparency becomes even more critical and troublesome at the same time. When the technology itself is "transparent" it will be difficult to discern and control essential personal data processing activities. A related relevant issue is so-called function or functionality creep: (personal) data are used for different purposes than the one(s) they were originally collected for. Although functionality creep may further stimulate personalisation opportunities, transparency requires that users are informed of the purposes for which their (personal) data are used. Furthermore, Article 6 of Directive 95/46/EC states that personal data may only be collected for specified, explicit and legitimate purposes and not further processed in a way incompatible with those purposes.[81] Ubiquitous-computing environments may stimulate functionality creep even further.[82]

As with transparency, quality has more dimensions than those related to the use of personal data and consumer profiles. Quality of personalised service provision, for example, requires that user preferences are closely and adequately matched with the contents of the service, for example, information. Personalised service providers must also more generally guarantee adequate security in order to prevent fraud and abuse with respect to the personalised service and (personal) data involved. In general, it could be argued that many of the quality and security issues surrounding personalisation and profiling simply amount to matters of authentication and identification.

---

[80] For instance, travel agencies may want to inform customers about flexible price programmes where bookings become more expensive when demand increases (for example, see DFDS Seaways <www.dfdsseaways.co.uk>).

[81] OJ EC L281/40, 23 November 1995. It would, however, be naive to think such a rule will keep business or governments from using economically and strategically valuable personal data for other purposes than those originally stipulated, see also Friedewald, Lindner, Wright, 2006: 34.

[82] Friedewald et al., 2006: 34 *ff.*

Personalised services may be equipped with authentication mechanisms, which can provide verification of content of data or transactions of the connection between data/transactions and identifiers or attributes (i.e., characteristics associated with the individual)[83] and of the connection between individuals and identifiers.

Quality then implies that user information is correctly linked to services rendered. This requires adequate identification and authentication schemes. The identification of individuals for personalisation purposes can comprise different attributes, for example, personal data such as name, address, e-mail address, which are connected to the individual's preferences, location, behaviour, et cetera. Identifiers can be personal when attributes are used that are impossible or difficult to change (for example, date of birth or fingerprints) but identifiers can also be used in such a way as to allow pseudonymous (trans)actions by individuals.[84] In the latter case, identifiers are merely retraceable to non-personal identifiers, which are linked to certain attributes. Identifying an individual for the purpose of personalised service provision does not, therefore, necessarily have to mean that the person's real-life identity (for example, name, address or appearance) is used to provide the service. In a sense, it is sufficient to know that the service is provided to and individualised for the "right" person, i.e., the person to whom particular preferences and features, on which the personalisation is based "belong", and – if applicable – is paid for (in time). However, databases with personal data and profiles are valuable assets for businesses (for example, for marketing and market analysis purposes) and governments, such as for fraud detection, criminal investigations and national security, which is why the incentive to restrict the use of data that is retraceable to the actual identity of a particular individual is not particularly strong.

With the advent of ubiquitous computing, quality issues have become much more pressing. Increased personalisation in a ubiquitous-computing environment may provide greater quality of everyday life through the seamless implementation and anticipative workings of technology. At the same time, ubiquitous computing involves greater security risks, confidentiality, integrity and availability concerns and trust issues, due to the overall pervasiveness, invisibility and strong dependence upon technology.

6.3.3   Inclusion, Exclusion and Control

It has been contended that profiling may lead to "attribution of certain risks to certain categories of people, rather than to others, or it may lead to discrimination of certain categories of people because of the risks they are supposed to run."[85] A similar observation can be made in relation to personalised services. To the extent that

---

[83] On these terms, see Camp, 2003: 5.

[84] Camp, 2003: 5.

[85] Hildebrandt, Gutwirth (eds.), 2005.

personalisation allows users to be tracked closely, it is a simple matter to limit the scope of certain facilities to a specific group of consumers. Personalisation services may, for instance, facilitate the selected provision of access to certain services only to consumers who live in preferred postal codes, or have certain levels of income. Also, personalisation services seem well suited to choose who will be allowed to view or read a particular (copyrighted) work and who will not (what is termed digital rights management (DRM)). In other words, inclusion and exclusion of individuals is closely related to the phenomenon of personalisation and, more specifically, the use of consumer profiles. Apart from inclusion or exclusion of certain services, personalisation may also facilitate discrimination, for example, through dynamic pricing in which case service providers ask different consumers to pay different prices. In a ubiquitous-computing environment where profiling is an important requirement, exclusion and discrimination of people increases to disturbing levels.

Inclusion and exclusion, however, do not necessarily have to be perceived as detrimental. Inclusion or exclusion may be considered economically useful because it will do a better job of distributing the right information and services to the right people. Without personalisation and profiling techniques, organisations must make wasteful investments in distributing information of which it is unclear whether consumers appreciate it. Techniques that facilitate inclusion and exclusion may therefore be especially useful to accommodate the varying preferences of consumers. As such, personalisation is an effective tool to achieve an efficient market. By using personalisation techniques, content producers obtain control over the uses of a variety of legally protected works and the techniques will allow providers to manage access rights with respect to particular works. The control facilitated by personalisation techniques will increase the copyright owners' ability to uphold and enforce their copyrights.

By analysing the the phenomenon of inclusion and exclusion, it might be argued that this is essentially nothing new and, as such, there is nothing detrimental about it. Today, consumers' behaviour is also predetermined by their attachment to a group, their cultural or societal position or predisposition, et cetera Personalisation, however, provides a new dimension in that it may force individuals into restrictive two-dimensional models based on the criteria set by technology and of those who own and apply the technology. With commercial personalisation services, the myriad of individual differences is reduced to one or a few consuming categories, on the basis of which their preferences, character, life-style and so forth are determined for a specific context.

Because of its tendency to generalise, personalisation may lead to diminishing preferences, differences and values in a more provocative and, perhaps, exaggerated scenario. Exclusion of access to and the use of information and copyrighted works (music, books, films, etc.) may then put the values of free speech, free flow of information and consumer choice under pressure. The next step may go beyond these values, for personalisation may have even greater societal and political consequences if it shapes the overall movement of information within society. Free citizens are the cornerstones of democratic constitutional societies. In an ultimate scenario, personalisation services could put cultural and social diversity at risk: one political or religious message is to dominate the whole discourse.[86] In such a scenario, personalisation may have serious consequences because it could imply that behaviour is manipulated, freedom of self-determination and personal autonomy are limited and societal freedom is eroded. As noted above, personalisation as such is nothing new, since inclusion and exclusion are part of our daily lives. However, the control facilitated by personalisation services may potentially have (serious) consequences for the freedom of information as well as for the public interest of cultural and political diversity.

Of course, we should be careful in assuming that personalisation will indeed result in the above scenario before we begin to denounce personalisation as a threat to the freedoms and societal interests mentioned above. Opponents to this line of reasoning could argue that convincing qualitative examples and quantitative data of these negative effects of personalisation are required first.[87] However, once these examples are actually provided, it may be too late for an effective discussion. Hence, a discussion of the pros and cons of personalisation from the inclusion and exclusion perspective must be held with regard to the concepts of autonomy on the one hand and interference or even paternalism (based on the presumption that organisations or governments may decide for others what is in their best interest), on the other.[88] Finding a balance between the two concepts will be a key challenge in light of the new opportunities of personalisation. Furthermore, the search for this balance implies much more than just a discussion concerning personal data protection. It also requires a debate on the societal value of anti-discrimination and the rules we have outlined here.

On a more individual level, it is crucial that individuals be given the instruments to enhance the visibility of and their knowledge about how their personal data are used and combined, on the basis of what they are typified as, by whom and for what purposes – especially when information technology becomes more and more invisibly embedded in home and work environments. Consequently, to be able to make meaningful choices in the light of personalised services, an individual must be informed, i.e., have and understand the relevant information. In addition, control appears to be of crucial importance. Given that "the kernel of the idea of autonomy is the right to make choices and decisions",[89] freedom and respect in making choices is essential. Such freedom and respect implies that individuals have control over the use of their personal data, their identities and profiles. As we know, control can be built into business models so that individuals (in this case users of the personalised service) can manage personal data, identities and profiles within the

---

[86] See also section 15.2.3, which refers to Sunstein's Republic.com developing a similar argument.

[87] See section 15.7.

[88] On paternalism see Dworkin, 1988.

[89] Feinberg, 1986: 54.

system. As an example, privacy-enhancing technologies such as P3P[90] allow users to control what personal data are disclosed and under what identity and/or identifiers a particular service provider knows the user. Although still in their infancy, from an operational point of view, much is also expected from (privacy-enhanced) identity management systems (IMS).[91] These systems provide an infrastructure for the use and storage of personal information and authentication mechanisms. The public sector may play an important role in the administration of these systems because they themselves generate important tools for the identification of individuals (e.g., driver's licences, passports) that are often used in private sector identification and authentication processes as well, for example in banks.[92] IMS can use pseudonymous identification processes, meaning that personal identifiers are not disclosed in transactions and personal data may be more effectively protected depending on the amount of security provided. In a ubiquitous-computing environment where identification is based on passive authentication mechanisms (this means individuals are identified through presence or behaviour rather than through activities like typing a password or showing an ID) privacy-enhanced IMS may, however, be more problematic unless the system knows a user's preferences.[93]

6.4 Concluding Remarks

The proliferation of personalised services triggers various concerns. The development may also have profound effects on information and transaction relationships between individuals, organisations and communities in a society. At the heart of these concerns and effects is the very issue of user identification. It raises problems in the area of autonomy as well as concerns with respect to inclusion and exclusion and, as such, raises questions of anti-discrimination law. Moreover, personalisation may be a threat to personal data protection because it provides companies and organisations with a powerful instrument to know in detail what an individual wants, who he is, whether his conduct or behaviour shows certain tendencies and so forth. In a dark scenario, personalisation may become highly disturbing because it facilitates the selected provision to specific users only and may thus diminish certain differences and values. In a worst-case scenario, personalisation may have larger societal and political consequences if it could shape the overall movement of information within a society. A discussion on how to react to the emergence of online personalisation should therefore not be limited to how to protect individual

---

[90] See W3, <http://www.w3.org/P3P>. Critical notes on P3P: EPIC, Pretty Poor Privacy, An Assessment of P3P and Internet Privacy, June 2000, <www.epic.org/reports/prettypoorprivacy.html>.

[91] See also Bauer, Meints, 2006.

[92] Camp, 2003: 9.

[93] Friedewald, Lindner, Wright, 2006: 13.

data. Instead, discussion is required about essential interests such as autonomy, control, transparency, discrimination and (digital) diversity.

6.5 Reply: Online Personalisation. For the Bad or for the Good?

Thierry Nabeth*

Personalised profiling represents an important opportunity to better serve people by allowing the design of services that are truly able to take into account their specificity. However, as Simone van der Hof indicates, personalised profiling is not without risks, since it can also contribute to reinforce segregation in society.

This response further analyses the dual nature (positive or negative) of applications making use of personalised profiling. We explore the frontiers of personalisation and the consequences of personalisation such as: the risks associated with profiling errors (profiling techniques are not 100% reliable) or limitations (profiling is more like an oracle, which provides answers but few explanations); the increased level of transparency in society (profiling techniques can be used on a large scale); the increased stickiness (when people are constantly reminded of their past actions) and finally how to use personalisation in a way that brings the maximum benefit to the masses.

6.5.1   Online Personalisation: Dr Jekyll and Mr Hyde?

Online personalisation is considered by many as one of the "Holy Grails" of the information age: in an ideal future, people will only receive content and services tailored to their profile (implicit or declared) fulfilling their need to consume, entertain, learn, etc., leading to greater satisfaction. In particular, this customisation promises to offer to the masses what society has only offered so far to the powerful and the rich: the possibility to have their personal advisers, coaches, tutors …, optimising the way they conduct their lives. In this ideal vision, personalisation will be at the service of the citizens and will contribute to the construction of a better world, taking more account of personal identity and supporting individual aspirations.

This reasoning is not without flaws and other people believe the contrary, that profiling and personalisation is just a Pandora's box, which when opened, will authorise all kinds of abuses and will lead to a completely opposite result than the ideal vision that we have just described: people's actions will be monitored beyond their will and the personalisation will not be aimed at serving the individual but only as a tool used by governments and organisations to improve the controlling of people or by companies for enhanced reaching and influencing their customers.

---

*Institut Européen D'Administration Des Affaires (INSEAD)

Far from helping to construct a better society, personalisation will only reinforce individualism, segregation and conformism. In a dark scenario, profiling and personalisation only represents a key ingredient in the implementation of modern social control as depicted in the "Brave New World" of Aldous Huxley, or the setting in place of a society totally driven by consumerism.

6.5.2 van der Hof and Prins' Perspective

In their contribution, van der Hof and Prins help to clarify the reality of online personalisation, identifying the real issues of personalisation (versus the irrational ones), analysing them and determining their implications for people's lives in society. For instance, they acknowledge the complexity of profiling: the difficulty for people to truly appreciate what information is really used and they raise the question of ownership and control of the profile data. They also indicate the risk that personalisation puts on the person's autonomy, by reinforcing segregation and reducing the capacity for decision. They finally raise the issue of the reliability of this digital identity and the risks associated with the unlawful use of an identity.

Initially, van der Hof and Prins may appear to belong to the more "Pandora's box" or "paranoid" category of persons who consider profiling and personalisation as concealing many dangers: profiling and personalisation put society at risk by contributing to the invasion of privacy, increasing discrimination, diminishing autonomy and the faculty for decision making of individuals. Whilst their contribution is very useful for exploring the dark side of personalisation and profiling and at understanding the associated risks, the readers may initially wonder if their work is not biased by the desire to convince rather than the desire to understand. A second look shows that this is not the case and that the authors are clearly interested in a rigorous analysis of personalisation in the context of online environments with the objective of understanding the issues and proposing solutions. Indeed, far from rejecting profiling and personalisation altogether (although they actually seem to believe that the trend towards more personalisation is inevitable), they acknowledge its interest and they even propose solutions for addressing the different issues they have raised. For instance, they acknowledge that inclusion and exclusion should not necessarily be considered a bad thing since it allows a more effective distribution of information. More interestingly, they propose a solution aimed at addressing the personalisation issue, relying on the idea of providing more transparency in the way that personal data is collected and later used: "people should be aware of the way in which their personalised profile is created and used by the personalised service providers" and "individuals should be given the instruments to enhance their visibility of and the knowledge about how data are used and combined". How does one provide such transparency from an operational point of view? The authors suggest three elements for an answer: (1) the incorporation of the support of transparency into business models; (2) the use of identity-management systems (which are still considered to be in their infancy for applications in the real world); (3) the role of the public sector for administrating these systems (because they represent long time and critical users with the management of passports, driver's ID, etc.).

6.5.3 Our Comments on the Work of van der Hof and Colleagues

Firstly, we can only agree with their analysis: profiling and personalisation present important issues that should not be ignored, that are not always inevitable and should be the object of well-informed decisions by citizens and governments. In particular, we would like to emphasise that, as is the case of any technology, profiling and personalisation are neutral and that it is the responsibility of governments and citizens to decide how to use them in a way that we consider acceptable. Even if providing transparency of how profiling and personalisation is conducted appears important, in our opinion it is more difficult to answer the question of what level of profiling and personalisation should be acceptable and how to control it. For instance, the exploitation of personal data by companies should not necessarily be considered "evil" since it may allow them to deliver better products, services and experience to their customers. In the context of government, improved personalisation may help to enhance the quality that the public sector can offer citizens (for instance better learning) and this should be encouraged, since it can help to compensate the inequalities that exist in traditional society (the elite is already receiving more tailor-made solutions and personalised guidance than others, providing them with an advantage in life). However, personalisation can also represent the risk of reinforcing segregation amongst citizens if inappropriately used (even in the case of people having the "best intentions") and this may result in reducing social mobility (by creating social stickiness). Finally, one more issue worth investigating is the consequences of personalisation for the freedom of self-determination and the reproduction of behaviour: personalisation tends to hide the underlying complexity, leaving a minimum of necessary options for the users. Whilst the positive side is to reduce the cognitive load of the user by filtering the irrelevant details, this can result in reaffirming this user in pre-existing practices and hamper the adoption of new behaviours and new learning, that often occurs when people are confronted with unexpected situations. How can one be sure that personalisation will not filter elements favouring serendipity, thereby limiting the user's capacity to learn? What will happen to a person's capacity to decide in the case that the system provides a perfect personalisation (for instance selecting the optimal product to buy or the best course to attend) and in particular would this not result in a passive population having few initiatives? Finally, how do we obtain the maximum benefit from personalisation and use it in a way that benefits the masses?

6.6   Bibliography

van Barneveld, J., 'User Interfaces for Personalized Systems. State of the Art', Enschede: Telematica Instituut, 2003. Available at: https://doc.telin.nl/dscgi/ds.py/Get/File-28132

Bauer, M., and Meints, M. (eds.), *Structured Overview on Prototypes and Concepts of Identity Management Systems, FIDIS, Deliverable 3.1*, European Union IST FIDIS Project, August 2006. Available at: www.fidis.net.

Bonnet, M., 'Personalization of Web Services: Opportunities and Challenges', *Ariadne*, Issue 28, 2001. Available at: www.ariadne.ac.uk/issue28/personalization/intro.html

Crossly, M., Kings, N.J., Scott, J.R., 'Profiles – Analysis and Behaviour', *BT Technology Journal*, Vol. 21, No. 1, January 2003.

Camp, L.J., 'Identity in Digital Government', A Report of the 2003 Civic Scenario Workshop, Kennedy School of Government, Harvard University, Cambridge, MA., 2003.

Dworkin, G., *The Theory and Practice of Autonomy*, Cambridge University Press, Cambridge, 1988.

Feinberg, J., *Harm to Self*, Oxford University Press, Oxford, 1986.

Friedewald, M., Lindner, R., Wright, D., (eds.), 'Safeguards in a World of Ambient Intelligence (SWAMI), Threats, Vulnerabilities and Safeguards in Ambient Intelligence', Deliverable D3, July 2006. Available at: swami.jrc.es

Hildebrandt, M., Gutwirth, S. (eds.), *Profiling: Implications for Democracy and Rule of Law, FIDIS Deliverable 7.4*, European Union IST FIDIS Project, Brussels 2005. Available at: www.fidis.net

Lips, A.M.B., van der Hof, S. Prins, J.E.J, Schudelaro, A.A.P., *Issues of Online Personalisation in Commercial and Public Service Delivery*, Wolf Legal Publishers, Tilburg, 2005.

Lyon, D., (ed.), *Surveillance as Social Sorting. Privacy, Risk and Digital Discrimination*, Routledge, London/New York, 2003.

Mably, K., 'Privacy vs. Personalization', 2000, Cyber Dialogue Inc. Available at: www.cyberdialogue. com.

Mobasher, B. Cooley, R., Srivastava, J., 'Automatic Personalization Based on Web Usage Mining. Web usage mining can help improve the scalability, accuracy, and flexibility of recommender systems', *Communications of the ACM*, Association for Computing Machinery, August 2000, pp. 142 *ff*.

Nissenbaum, H., 'Privacy as Contextual Integrity', *Washington Law Review*, No. 79, 2004, pp. 101-139.

Nguyen, D.H., Mynatt, E.D., 'Privacy Mirrors: Understanding and Shaping Socio-technical Ubiquitous Computing Systems', *Georgia Institute of Technology Technical Report*, 2002. Available at: www.erstwhile.org/writings/PrivacyMirrors.pdf

O'Looney, J., 'Personalization of Government Internet Services', 2002. Available at: www. digitalgovernment.org/library/library/dgo2001/DGOMAC/MEDIA/OLOO.pdf

Prins, J.E.J., 'The Propertization of Personal Data and Identities', *Electronic Journal of Comparative Law*, Vol. 8, No. 3, 2004.

Prins, J.E.J., 'Property and Privacy: European Perspectives and the Commodification of our Identity', in: Guibault, Hugenholtz (eds), *The Future of the Public Domain*, Kluwer Law International, Alphen a.d. Rijn, The Hague, 2006, pp. 233-257.

Paternoster, C., Searby, S., 'Personalise or Perish?', White Paper BT Exact Technologies, 2002.

Phillips, David J., 'From Privacy to Visibility: Context, Identity, and Power in Ubiquitous Computing Environments', *Social Text*, Vol. 23, No. 2, Duke University Press, Durham, 2005.

Shahabi, S., Chen, Y. 'Web Information Personalization: Challenges and Approaches', 2003. Available at: infolab.usc.edu/DocsDemos/DNIS2003.pdf

Smyth, B., Cotter, P., 'A Personalized Television Listings Service. Mixing the Collaborative Recommendation Approach with Content-Based Filtering Seems to Bring Out the Best in Both Methods', *Communications of the ACM*, Vol. 43, No. 8, Association for Computing Machinery, Wash., August 2000, pp. 107-111.

Vedder, A., 'Medical Data, New Information Technologies and the Need for Normative Principles Other Than Privacy Rules', in Freeman, M., Lewis, A. (eds.), *Law and Medicine, Current Legal Issues*, Vol. 3, Oxford University Press, Oxford, 2000, pp. 441-459.

Part II
Applications of Profiling

In this part, some of the main fields of application will be dealt with: profiling web-use, e-learning or virtual community formation, employment and customer loyalty programmes.

Chapter 7
Biometric Profiling: Opportunities and Risks

Vassiliki Andronikou, Angelos Yannopoulos, and Theodora Varvarigou

During the past decades profiling has gained ground as both a technique and a technology providing automated knowledge construction of individuals or groups of people. This interest has been intensified by the use of biometrics serving as a source of profiling information, with the core capabilities of human verification and identification, as well as a variety of further characterisation possibilities. Biometric characteristics are often persistent and/or non-concealable traits, which therefore have the capability to function as unique linking information between other profiles for each given individual. Biometric profiling serves a wealth of applications, from medicine, statistics and crime prevention to e-commerce and service provision. This chapter seeks to review not only the promising opportunities but also the crucial risks and key concerns deriving from biometric profiling. Hence, we discuss risks that arise from the ability of an adversary to attack a biometric profiling system, as well as risks related to the dangerous functionality of such a system, which can be due to implementation problems or even a misguided conception that was correctly implemented.

7.1 Introduction

As already mentioned in Chapter 5, *biometrics* comprise both a science and a set of technologies that focus on the measurement of either physiological or behavioural human characteristics. A biometric trait is a human characteristic satisfying some requirements: sufficient inter-person variability for distinctiveness purposes, invariability over a period of time and thus a rather low intra-person variability, measurability and universality (Jain et al. 2004b). A broadly accepted categorisation of biometrics divides them into *physiological (or passive)* and *behavioural (or active)* biometrics. The first one concerns stable or fixed human characteristics strongly connected to the physiology of the human body such as iris patterns, face image, odour, hand and finger geometry, DNA and fingerprints, whereas the second one is based on "measurements" of characteristics represented by those actions, skills or functions performed by a person at a specific point of time for a specific reason (e.g., a person's typing patterns, signature or method of moving the computer mouse). Physiological biometrics comprise a heavily researched area with the main

---

Institute of Communication and Computer Systems, National Technical University Athens (ICCS)

M. Hildebrandt and S. Gutwirth (eds.), *Profiling the European Citizen:*
Cross-Disciplinary Perspectives.
© Springer Science + Business Media B.V. 2008

focus however, being on identification and verification applications. Nevertheless, as has been presented in Chapter 5, feverish research is currently taking place in the field of behavioural biometrics as well, in an effort to take advantage of their richness in profiling information. The term *soft biometrics* refers to measurable human characteristics that include information about the individual with no high inter-person variability and thus no human identification possibilities, due to its lack in distinctiveness and permanence (Jain et al. 2004a). Examples of soft biometrics comprise gender, ethnicity,[94] age and eye colour. Biometrics, as emerging technologies, promise to be the next step towards the establishment of end-to-end trust amongst all parties involved in financial transactions, e-commerce, access to restricted areas, etc. What makes biometric profiling powerful and reliable is the fact that it is based on human characteristics and, thus, includes more accurate information on what a person is and what a person does. By their nature, biometric traits cannot be forgotten, lost, shared, broken or stolen (unless surgery takes place), proving to be *advantageous* compared to other means of identification and verification, such as smart cards and passwords. While biometrics currently *can* be foiled by forgery (or "spoofed") (Kryszczuk and Drygajlo, 2005; Khan and Zhang, 2006), it remains an open research problem whether this threat can be eliminated, while alternatives such as smart cards are at least equally vulnerable. In Chapter 5, the main technical limitations of current behavioural biometric profiling systems have already been presented, followed however by a near-to-mid future technological view of the real potential of these systems thanks to not only the improvements of the profiling techniques but also the capabilities of the underlying infrastructure. This forecast of technological trends combined with the development of applications that are more tightly tied to identity, the automatic provision of personalised services as well as the increased failure of existing security systems, have increased the expectations placed on biometrics.

Although inherently related to identification and verification, biometrics also include data rich in *profiling information*. As profiling itself is not a well specified application such as identification and verification, there is also no clearly defined research corpus dealing explicitly with biometric profiling. Rather, an array of specific biometric challenges is independently tackled with; e.g., emotion recognition, ethnicity or gender classification, various types of medical diagnosis, etc. From the profiling perspective, biometric information can either directly characterise its subject,

---

[94] According to wikipedia (http://en.wikipedia.org/wiki/Ethnicity#_ref-EB_0) the term *ethnicity* refers to a population of human beings, the members of which identify with each other, usually on the basis of a presumed common genealogy or ancestry, or is recognised by others as a distinct group (Smith, 1987) and by common cultural, linguistic, religious, behavioural or biological traits (Encyclopaedia Britannica, 2007). Though anthropometrical studies suggest that racial and ethnic morphometric differences exist in the craniofacial complex (Farkas, 1994), we note that ethnicity does not imply physical or genetic similarity and the reader should take into account that the notion of different human races is highly controversial. The reasons for this are not only the potential abuse that categorisations like these make possible but also the questionable scientific evidence for such classification (e.g., Foster and Sharp, 2002).

in which case we have *explicit biometric profiling*, or it can be used for individual identification or verification and, thus, provide a *link* to an existing (and probably non-biometric) profile.

7.2   Opportunities

7.2.1   Current Biometric Systems

Existing biometric systems are mainly *small-scale systems* built on rather *limited requirements* and *assumptions*. For instance, camera-based smart (or active) surveillance systems that are used in indoor environments, such as a museum or a room with restricted access, are not expected to have to cope with great illumination variations, changing backgrounds or varying weather conditions, as an outdoor system would. Hence, these indoor *smart surveillance systems* (Hampapur, 2005; Foresti, 2005) use rather simpler and thus faster background subtraction and/or human detection algorithms compared to outdoor systems. The term 'smart (or active) surveillance systems' refers to systems that can automatically detect *suspicious* behaviour (in the sense that it deviates from the usual, expected one) in the area they are covering. Smart surveillance systems, however, strongly demand real-time processing of the stream of captured images and thus a proper balancing of the requirements is essential, with this balancing being mainly application-dependent.

When we consider emerging opportunities created by biometric profiling technology, we do not wish to restrict ourselves to mere improvements to the performance of applications such as the above. Such improvements are always taking place - both as enabling technologies improve, e.g., better human and action detection in the example above and as the biometric techniques themselves become more refined – and, as new performance thresholds are crossed, the methods achieve new levels of applicability – for instance, robustness against environmental variations could lead the above example application into a new outdoor era. However, such incremental evolution of applications is the norm in engineering today. Here, we will take a fair degree of incremental improvement to current biometric *technology* for granted and consider *new* possible *applications*. Thus, we focus on discussing realistic but non-obvious future applications as well as emphasising wide-impact rather than specialist applications.

7.2.2   Future Applications

A notable feature is that biometric data collection is closely related to the *person's location*. The devices installed (e.g., cameras or signature tablets) or carried by the individual (e.g., mobile phones) are either static and thus of known location, or mobile but with location detection capabilities (e.g., GSM). Hence, a system collecting biometric data for profiling (or other) purposes may also enrich the individual's profile with dynamic location information. This combination of information offers new potential to commercial applications, location-based services, law enforcement and surveillance, amongst others.

As already mentioned, simple biometric identification can be used to link an identified individual to his/her biometric and/or non-biometric profile. Biometric technology will quite possibly remain incapable of collecting very thorough profiling information in the near future due to a number of limitations it faces, which are not restricted to being purely technological (see Chapter 5), so this approach makes a great deal of sense. A quite interesting compromise, hence, appears to be the creation of non-biometric profiles which are, however, parameterised in terms of biometric readings or enriched with partial biometric profiling.

This is especially applicable to *group profiling*.[95] By its nature, group profiling is powerful because it allows *generalisation*: simply identifying that an individual can be classified as belonging to a given group allows us to use a complex group model to describe that individual, even if, in fact, we do not have all that much information about him/her. Obviously, the main weakness of group profiling arises from exactly the same idea: generalisation will never be perfect and our system is going to treat each given individual in a way that we have designated as appropriate for a group to the traits of which he/she only *partially* conforms (Hildebrandt, Backhouse, 2005). Thus, it makes excellent sense to parameterise a group profile in terms of additional information that can be gathered for each specific individual. For instance, in a sports surveillance environment we might use biometrics to determine that an individual is a tall and strong skinhead covered with tattoos and so on and (rightly or wrongly) classify him as a hooligan; alternatively, we might simply have used an RFID tag to determine that this is John Smith who is, according to police information (which, however, could also be mistaken), a hooligan. A decision on the action to be taken could then be made, given that a hooligan has been detected somewhere.

In an effort to expand the current example, additional biometric analysis could be performed resulting in the determination that this individual is acting in an aggressive manner (e.g., from gait analysis, see Chapter 5) or is drunk or is asleep or even, for example, is in constant and close peaceful interaction with another individual, whom we eventually classify as his girlfriend (being female, etc), thus surmising that the individuals observed are non-violent. The more complex a system becomes, the more prejudices it may end up incorporating (e.g., "if you are in the company of a woman, you are less likely to act violently") but it is clearly possible to avoid excess sensitivity to major prejudices (e.g., "skinheads are hooligans") and to improve the objectivity of the reasoning performed (e.g., by detecting violent *behaviour*).

---

[95] Chapter 2 above 'Defining profiling: a new type of knowledge?'.

The capability suggested above is also highly desirable in applications that can support partial profiling. Here, as much (non-biometric) information as possible is collected about each individual. The system is able to base its decision-making, classification or *interpretation* on the potentially incomplete data available. Biometric sensors can then be used to offer additional information to the system. Since incomplete data can be handled, the more new data the biometric component can offer, the better the expected performance will be. We should note the importance of the fact that the biometric data being collected can be of a dynamic nature (e.g., physical biometrics, such as body temperature, retinal state or behavioural biometrics, such as gait).

Biometrics, serving as links to an individual's profile, offer the opportunity to create a *trace* of an individual's actions, daily activities and transactions. This might be justified, for instance, for tracking an individual who is considered to be a suspect or a potential criminal. Thus, if/when this person engages in an illegal action, a *backtracking process* would provide important information that may reveal previously committed but not detected illegal acts.

Security reinforcement through the integration of biometrics into security systems is another important application of biometrics. The main aim is to take advantage of their identification and verification capabilities in an effort to "protect the present" by using information from the past. Thus, for example (non-biometric) "watch lists" are composed including wanted persons or based on other conventional criteria (e.g., police records of people acquainted with known criminals). This approach, however, cannot really offer any answers when it comes to the virgin illegal act of a person, suicide terrorists and generally people for whom no enrolled data exist. Biometric profiling in this case promises to fill in the gap. The cooperation of psychologists and technologists is hoped, amongst others, to provide reliable and robust criminal profiling (Nykodym et al. 2005; Rogers, 2003; Woodworth and Porter, 2000), so that the detection of *potential* criminals will also be possible. Technology performance will determine possible real applications. For instance, if *false positives* (the system raising an alert for an innocent subject) are not totally eliminated, the system cannot be fully automated. However, *guiding human decision making*[96] can be extremely valuable. *False negatives* (the system not detecting real criminals) determine the reliability of the system.

Another application of context sensitive profiles lies in daily commerce with advertising purposes. A person enters, say, a supermarket; the system extracts a general profile of this person, e.g., age, gender, temperament or performs identification and uses an existing profile of this person; it then uses this information to propose a new product by sending an sms to the person's mobile phone, or otherwise notifying him/her. Different biometric technologies, e.g., monitoring keyboard and mouse interaction to assess an emotional state, could be applied to purely electronic e-commerce interactions. Again, system performance will make the difference between a useful service and spamming.

---

[96] http://en.wikipedia.org/w/index.php?title=Decision_support_system.

Our last example closes the application loop by returning to user verification in a roundabout but interesting manner. In some conventional applications, e.g., credit card fraud monitoring, perfect security cannot be guaranteed but user behaviour is profiled; if, for instance, a card has not been used in several months and a large sum is suddenly charged on it, an additional check is typically performed. Similarly, biometric security cannot be flawless and may in some cases be compromised. However, if an extensive biometric *profile* accompanies each identity, then an individual fraudulently using somebody else's identity would still appear incongruent to the associated profile. An additional security check could then be performed.

7.3 Risks

Deployment of a biometric system in an important real-world application gives rise to three distinct and serious types of risk: (a) the system might be attacked and compromised by an adversary, (b) the system itself may suffer from (serious) imperfections and have an adverse affect on individuals it influences and (c) the intentional, correctly implemented capabilities of the system may encroach on the user's rights.

7.3.1 System Attack

The first type of risk is the one most often analysed. Much research takes place focusing on identifying and analysing the possible points of attack to a biometric system (Uludag and Jain, 2004; CCBEMWG, 2002). Indeed, especially in security applications, the presentation of any method is incomplete without an analysis of possible attacks against it. Therefore, we will not discuss this in detail but there exists one important problem that is not always dealt with and should be stressed. An attack against a biometric system can exploit a weakness of either the design or the implementation of the system. Researchers and commercial developers alike tend to present their systems in terms of their design and analyse how these systems are designed to withstand attack. Everybody knows that a bug in the *implementation of a system* creates an additional vulnerability but this is very hard to analyse systematically and is rarely emphasised specifically enough.

Furthermore, a real system has physical substance to its implementation, which can also be attacked. A trivial but potentially overlooked example is that no matter how intelligent the software used to process the video captured by a camera is, if someone simply destroys the camera, the software will fail. As a more involved example, consider that user profiles in a large-scale application are likely to be stored at a central site of the service provider, or even at a trusted third party's site for privacy reasons. An attacker intending to commit identity fraud could enhance an identity theft attack by immediately afterwards launching a denial of service attack against the central database. A final example of a very serious risk that must be assessed is that of an insider attack: an employee of the service provider could maliciously corrupt a profile database. Of course, it might be countered, a bank employee might similarly corrupt account databases. The real difference between these two cases, however, is that, in large-scale applications, the intentional corruption of a *database containing the biometric profiling information* that is gradually performed can be far harder to detect, due to its lower immediate impact as a secondary authentication mechanism to the system, although subversive attacks of this sort could have very serious consequences in the long term.

We next consider the latter two kinds of risk, where flawed biometric profiling may have an adverse affect on individuals it influences. We illustrate these issues with some representative examples. Note that these risks are generally hard to distinguish a priori, as both arise from flawed system functionality – regardless of whether this is caused by a flawed implementation or a flawed overall conception. One problem that clearly mixes these risk types is that real-world applications may be based on immature technology for reasons of marketing, politics, etc., or even simply unjustified optimism.

7.3.2   System Performance

The underlying risks stemming from the current performance limitations (Snelick et al. 2005; Gibbons et al. 2005) of biometric techniques and biometric systems (see Chapter 5) comprise a bottleneck for the adaptation of biometric applications by either enterprises or governments (Ashbourn, 2004). Even when designed and implemented, focusing on a highly-constrained application posing restricted requirements, current biometric systems cannot perform flawlessly. Biometric identification and verification still produce *false negatives* (not recognise a person with enrolled biometric data) and *false positives* (recognise a person as someone else with enrolled biometric data) as well as proceed to inaccurate or false classification of actions or behaviours.

Depending on the application-based requirements of the system, these performance imperfections may or may not allow the final use of the system. A typical example lies in law enforcement. Although much research effort is focused on criminal profiling, the automation of this process and its integration with biometric profiling are still rather immature. The performance metrics of biometric systems, such as false negatives rate or false positives rate, still indicate failure at rather *unacceptable rates* for applications of such a high importance. The consequence of less pervasiveness in people's lives could then be innocent citizens being unjustifiably monitored, with their right to *anonymity* and *privacy* being set aside.

7.3.3   System Capabilities

Smart surveillance systems installed either in public or private areas (e.g., at the office) for security purposes combine human tracking with activity recognition and offer advanced surveillance. The development of such technologies combined with the rapid proliferation of camera deployment in public and private facilities, however, gives rise to fears that an *electronic trace* of every person's actions and movements will be stored, posing serious threats to the person's right to anonymity and civil liberties. Eventually, such systems could be able to produce a profile of each monitored person, including the person's habits, daily activities, interests and people this person is involved with in business and personal relationships.

Using biometrics as personal data or profile linkers, a more precise and full description of each person will be composed gathering information from different sectors, such as business, education, health and criminal records. Taking into account that some biometrics (e.g., fingerprints, iris and DNA) include medical information, the profile of the person may be updated with information on his/her prognostics concerning the development of certain diseases. For example, genetic disorders may be detected by the further processing of raw data related to malformed fingers (Prabhakar et al. 2003). Thus, the person may have to face racism and discrimination based on his/her past actions, religion, ethnicity, medical record or potential future health vulnerabilities. The possibility of this data linking being the result of *unauthorised* and *sometimes unnecessary collection* and *use of data* (Cavoukian, 1999) is rather high and the user will be deprived of the right to control their personal data (Johnson, 2004) or remain anonymous (Arndt, 2005). Such personal data disclosure could then lead to access to specific areas being denied to him/her, provision of services being *prioritised* according to *extracted privileged groups* of people, the rehabilitation of previously convicted people who will be recognised in public areas becoming even harder, enterprises filtering out candidates for a job based on their medical or criminal records and so on.

As a person gradually becomes aware of being monitored and that his/her actions, expressed wishes, emotions and preferences, interests and habits are being used to construct a profile, he/she may become a victim of his/her desire to live the profile that he/she would like to have constructed for him/herself and thus even change his/her way of life and finally lose his/her identity. See chapter 15 for a much more thorough discussion of such issues.

There is a clear need for *legislative control* of biometric profiling applications in order for such risks to be minimised. A counterbalancing force that could be profitable for many large markets but could also maintain these risks at a high level is, simply, excessive public sympathy for biometric profiling applications. These applications have the potential to offer users the services that they most highly appreciate. The users themselves may thus feel the related legal protection to be an impediment to further exploitation of these applications - and laws that are universally scorned by users will fail to be effective if their application depends on user cooperation. For example, many users today feel that their GSM phones should reveal location information so that they can enjoy location based services without paying for GPS. Similarly, in some cases certain people might protect themselves by simply refusing to use such applications. However, this refusal itself could lead to discrimination when others automatically assume that it implies they have something to hide.

7.4   Conclusions

In this chapter, we have presented an overview of the growing opportunities as well as the concomitant risks stemming from biometric profiling - a rather revolutionary use of biometrics, which diverges from the core capabilities of biometrics, i.e., identification and verification. Biometrics, either as a source of valuable profiling information or universal linkers of existing profiles, promises to open up new prospects in profiling by enriching an individual's profile with information that is the closest to who this person is and what that person does. Both the rapid improvement of biometric techniques and the refinement of underlying technologies allow for these presented new possible applications to be regarded as quite realistic. Hence, there is an intensified need to detect and specify the resulting crucial risks and the key concerns, which derive both from the capabilities as well as the vulnerabilities of biometric profiling.

7.5   Need for Legal Analysis of Biometric Profiling

Els Kindt*

Biometric profiling has so far received little attention by legal authors. One of the reasons is that the technology is still under development and the processes are sometimes difficult to understand without an appropriate introduction to the biometric techniques used. Nevertheless, it is clear that biometric profiling will be further explored and used by various interested parties, in the public and private sector, in the near future. Biometrics raise specific concerns in relation to profiling because biometrics contain the potential to identify, authenticate or to distinguish the individuals involved. In addition, biometrics will soon be used in large-scale applications, e.g., for biometric passports. One should recognise that biometric profiling touches different fields of law, depending on the technologies and the purposes for which it will be used. The use of biometric profiling for intrusion detection purposes raises different legal issues compared to the use of the technique for recruitment or assessment in a human resources environment. A recurring issue will be the application of the personal data protection legislation and the right to privacy but other fundamental rights may also be involved, such as the right to non-discrimination, as will be explored in more depth in part III. This reply will briefly point to some of the legal issues that are specific to biometric profiling.

7.5.1   Introduction

In the aforementioned chapter, the authors discuss uses of possible future biometric profiling applications. Some of the examples that they describe provide a notion of what biometric profiling could mean or how it could be used. The example of the

---

*Katholieke Universiteit Leuven ICRI

individual, who is categorised as a hooligan based on some biometric traits and profiling but with additional biometric analysis, is classified as not dangerous based on his behaviour of slow interaction with another individual, shows how surveillance systems may use biometric profiling in the future. The other example of the use of biometric characteristics for enriching online profiling data gathered for e-commerce purposes, such as the measurement of the keyboard and mouse interaction for assessing the emotional state of an individual, will certainly be considered useful by companies once the techniques are fully developed.

7.5.2 Definition

For a proper understanding and analysis of biometric profiling, it is necessary to try to further define the concept of biometric profiling. The present efforts in the field of international biometric standardisation and in particular the efforts relating to the development of definitions and vocabulary, do not include a definition on biometric profiling as such.[97] The ongoing work of the International Organisation for Standardisation (ISO) in the field of biometrics, however, does refer to 'biometric profiles', in particular to the profiles of employees and seafarers.[98] The purpose of this work is to see whether there is a need for standardisation and to develop an approach to the development of standards for these profiles. The present work is mainly intended to standardise the interchange of the (biometric) data of these profiles. Little is known about the content of this standardisation effort. No documents of this study group have been published as of yet. On a commercial website, biometric profiling is described as a "scientific measurement of unique physical or behavioural characteristics of individuals and teams (...)" and "comparing the (...) pattern of behaviours to a (...) 'template' by which an extremely accurate 'profile' can be produced (...)".[99] The authors of the previous chapter have rightfully pointed out that not only traits that are uniquely linked to an individual could be used for biometric profiling purposes but also human characteristics with a low inter-person

---

[97] See text of Standing Document 2, version 5 – Harmonized Biometric Vocabulary, of subcommittee SC 37, *biometrics*, of the Joint Technical Committee ISO/IEC JTC 1, *Information Technology*, dated 31 January 2006, a working document, available at http://isotc.iso.org/livelink/livelink/fetch/2000/ 2122/327993/2262372/2263033/2299739/JTC001-SC37-N-1480.pdf?nodeid =4954581&vernum=0 (hereinafter 'Harmonized Biometric Vocabulary document').

[98] See Study Group on Profiles for Biometric Applications (Group 4) of ISO/IEC JTC 1, SC 37, *biometrics* and the standards ISO/IEC FCD 24713-1, ISO/IEC CD 24713-2 and ISO/IEC NP 24713-3 under development, see also at http://www.iso.org/iso/en/CatalogueListPage. CatalogueList?COMMID =5537&scopelist=PROGRAMME.

[99] See the description of biometric profiling given by the Thornhill Consultancy (based in the U.K) at www.allaboutmedicalsales.com/profiles/ thornhillconsultancy/; for another description of the use of biometric profiling, see e.g., http://www.flintbox.com/technology. asp?page=600&showall=on.

variability (e.g., gender but probably also weight, ...) ('soft biometric characteristics'). Therefore we could endeavour to describe biometric profiling in general as 'the use, by automatic means, of biometric characteristics, whether biological or behavioural characteristics, whether unique for a given individual or not, for extracting and applying (group) profiles to individuals'.[100] Few biometric profiling applications presently exist. One of the applications in which biometric profiling might have been used to some extent, is the Computer Assisted Passenger Pre-screening System, known as CAPPS II, deployed by the Transportation Security Administration (TSA) in the United States. Due to heavy criticism the system in all likelihood is no longer in use but has probably been replaced by the TSA with a new screening system.[101] Another application in which biometric profiling might be planned to be used, is for the exchange of information on terrorist profiles by EU Member States.[102]

7.5.3 *Legal Aspects*

Few legal authors have discussed biometric profiling. The use of biometric data in profiling data processing activities, however, raises questions. The Working Party on the protection of individuals with regard to the processing of personal data (Article 29 Working Party) has already expressed, in its 'working document' of August 1, 2003, concerns about the use of biometric data in general. The Article 29 Working Party states that the processing of biometric data will in most cases be considered as the processing of personal data. The Working Party discusses inter alia the risks of central storage of the biometric data, the danger that biometric data may include sensitive data and the collection of the data without knowledge of the individual. It may be relevant to question whether the issues discussed in this opinion remain the same for the use of biometric data for profiling purposes.

---

[100] At the time of writing this reply, there is not yet a page (in English) on biometric profiling in www.wikipedia.org.

[101] TSA finally dropped the CAPPS II programme in mid-2004, after it was obliged to disclose drafts of privacy assessment documents in which it deleted information and which did not indicate that compliance with the Privacy Act was guaranteed. The Electronic Privacy Information Center (EPIC) stated on its website, however, that TSA announced in September 2004 plans to replace the programme with a new programme, so-called 'Secure Flight', which includes, according to EPIC, many elements of the CAPPS II programme.

[102] See the draft council recommendation on the development of terrorist profiles, prepared by the Working Party on Terrorism, Council of the European Union, 14 October 2002, 11858/02 ENFOPOL 117, also available at http://72.14.205.104/search?q=cache:ttyKlOHz4vAJ: europapoort.eerstekamer.nl /9345000/1/j9vvgy6i0ydh7th/vgbwr4k8ocw2/f%3D/vgb9flbmvdzx. doc+11858/1/02&hl=nl&gl=be&ct=clnk&cd=2, mentioned and discussed by G. HOSEIN, 'Threatening the Open Society: Comparing Anti-terror Policies and Strategies in the U.S. and Europe', Privacy International, December 13, 2005.

7.5.4   Distinction Between 'Soft' and 'Hard' Biometric Characteristics

The authors have referred to the use of biometric characteristics as a link to other profiling information as one of the main applications of biometric profiling. In case the biometric data, which is part of the centrally stored profile, is capable of linking the profiling information with a specific person (because the biometric characteristics contain sufficient identification or verification capabilities, e.g., a facial image), the aforementioned risks of central storage of biometric data discussed in the opinion document of the Article 29 Working Party remain applicable. The question remains, however, if the central storage of soft biometric characteristics used in profiling applications, which do not include biometric information about an individual that permits identification of that person, contains similar risks (e.g., central storage of information about an individual's length or weight). At first sight, some may argue that the concerns of the Article 29 Working Party are not applicable to the central storage of soft biometric characteristics. The article 29 Working Party has focused on biometric applications that allow the identification or verification of the identity of persons.[103] However, the central storage of soft biometric information enriching the profile of the individual may in combination with profiling applications result in sensitive information (e.g., about the health of the person, i.e., overweight as a result of a comparison between height and weight). Soft biometric characteristics and profiling may also have the capability to qualify individuals in groups based on human characteristics (tall, short, angry people, etc.). This qualification of individuals according to human characteristics by profiling applications may need to be better protected than the qualification of individuals based on consumer behaviour (e.g., by a bank or insurance company). One of the reasons is that a general consumer profile may change over time or can be manipulated, while most of the physical characteristics 'stick' to the person and cannot be easily changed. Therefore, a profile constructed using information about the physical or behavioural characteristics of an individual and the use of profiling based on these characteristics, even if these characteristics cannot identify the individual but are stored centrally, may need more protection than a general profile (e.g., a general profile based on click stream information). Although the risks of central storage of soft biometric characteristics are not the same as those of the central storage of biometric data, which permit identification or verification of identity, appropriate regulation of the use and storage of soft biometric characteristics may be required. The distinction between soft biometric characteristics and other biometric characteristics, which permit individualisation and identification, is therefore also relevant for legal analysis purposes.[104]

---

[103] See Article 29-Data Protection Working Party, *Working document on biometrics*, 1 August 2003, p. 3, available at http://ec.europa.eu/justice_home/fsj/privacy/docs/wpdocs/2003/wp80_en.pdf.

[104] Another example that shows that this distinction is relevant is the discussion about the use of unique identifiers of biometric characteristics. 'Soft biometric characteristics', for example, should not be retained in the discussion about risks of unique identifiers, as 'soft biometric characteristics' are not unique to the given person and do not permit one to identify a given person.

7.5.5   *Informational Privacy*

Another concern which needs to be further analysed is the increased risk of loss of control by the data subjects over their personal data, in the case of profiling practices that include biometric characteristics. Some biometric data (soft and hard biometric characteristics) can easily be captured without the knowledge of the individuals involved (e.g., the facial image by surveillance cameras). This is different from most other personal data, which is either directly provided by the data subjects themselves, or which is indirectly provided by the data subject who knows, should know or explicitly or implicitly consents to the processing of personal data upon the use of a (digital) product or service, e.g., the use of a payment or shopping card, the use of Internet access etc. Biometric characteristics can be collected and processed in situations in which a data subject is not aware of and has no reason to believe that his personal data is being processed (e.g., voice recognition (over the phone), face recognition in public places, etc.). In case biometric information, which is unique for a person, is processed in order to link it with his profile information, the profile information may 'follow' the data subject wherever he goes. The capture of the biometric characteristics of a given person in a certain place may be sufficient to have access to other profiling information. The Article 29 Working Party has recommended that biometric data should not be collected without the knowledge of data subjects.[105] The concern of the Article 29 Working Party in this context is the risk of unknown identification or verification of an individual as such. The technologies, however, are evolving in a way that the capture of biometric data without the knowledge of the individuals involved, or at least with a minimum of trouble or awareness by the individual, becomes possible. The development of RFID is an example thereof. It is certain that these technologies will be used by public authorities and also by private parties. The hidden or easy identification or verification of individuals will no longer be an entitlement to the public authorities, regulated by law but will also become available to the private (commercial) sector. The entities obtaining such information about the identity of persons are able to use this information (as a unique identifier or not) in relation with other information contained in public or private databases, owned by public or private parties. The linking of the biometric information with information in profiling databases is one of the applications. At present, people are often not informed of or, if they are informed, do not understand, the way their personal information is used in profiling applications. In some situations, in particular when the data have not been handed over by the data subject to the controller, the obligation imposed on the data controller to inform the data subject is diluted or even not applicable anymore.[106] Linking biometric information with profiles may therefore seriously affect the informational privacy of the individuals, not only in the case of automated decisions but also in a general way. Additionally, biometric systems include the possibility of false matches and false refusals. Further

---

[105] Article 29-Data Protection Working Party, *Working document on biometrics*, 1 August 2003, p. 8, available at http://ec.europa.eu/justice_home/fsj/privacy/ docs/wpdocs/2003/wp80_en.pdf.

[106] See Article 11 1 and 2 of Directive 95/46/EC.

research is required with regard to the extent the data protection regulation and the fundamental right to respect privacy need to take the functionalities of the evolving technologies of biometric profiling into account. The contribution of the authors in the aforementioned chapter is very valuable, in the sense that it brings future applications of biometric profiling already to the attention of a wider audience.

7.5.6 Discrimination

The authors of the aforementioned chapter have also rightfully briefly pointed to some other negative effects that biometric profiling may have on individuals. We want to refer to the effect that the collection and use of biometric information in profiling may have with regard to discrimination. The collection and use of sensitive information, such as information relating to race or ethnic origin, are in principle forbidden. The collection of facial images, in the form of pictures, will reveal in many cases such sensitive information. Even though the profiling application will in principle carefully avoid explicitly processing data of a sensitive nature, in order not to breach the discrimination legislation, the use of biometric data could increase the risks that the profiling practices take race or ethnic origin into account. This will depend, in the first place, on whether or not the application uses the captured biometric sample ('raw data') or template.[107] In captured biometric samples, the information about the race or ethnic origin is easy to discover. In the case where only templates are used, the calculation of the features of the captured biometric samples and the extent to which this calculation can be done without taking any characteristics on race or ethnic origin into account, will be important. If such a template is sufficient, 'discrimination proof' seems to be something for specialists and will have to be certified in one way or another, as laymen will not be able to discern this. The legislation in general does not contain any provisions in this regard.

7.6 Bibliography

'Anthropology. The study of ethnicity, minority groups, and identity', Encyclopaedia Britannica, 2007.
Arndt, C., 'The loss of privacy and identity', *Biometric Technology Today*, Vol. 13, No. 8, Elsevier Science, 2005, pp. 6-7.
Article 29 Data Protection Working Party, *Working document on biometrics*, 1 August 2003. Available at: http://ec.europa.eu/justice_home/fsj/privacy/docs/wpdocs/2003/wp80_en.pdf.
Ashbourn, J., 'Where we really are with biometrics', *Biometric Technology Today*, Vol. 12, No. 4, Elsevier Science, 2004, pp. 7-9.
Cavoukian, A., 'Consumer Biometric Applications: A Discussion Paper', 1999. Available at: http://www.ipc.on.ca.

---

[107] See definition of 'biometric template' (3.2.2.2.8.2) and 'biometric sample' (3.2.2.2.9) in Harmonised Biometric Vocabulary document, cited in footnote 97, p. 140.

Cheng, Y., O'Toole, A., Abdi, H., 'Classifying adults' and children's faces by sex: Computational investigations of subcategorical feature encoding', *Cognitive Science*, Vol. 25, pp. 819–838, 2001.

Common Criteria Biometric Evaluation Methodology Working Group (CCBEMWG), *Common Criteria – Common Methodology for Information Technology Security Evaluation – Biometric Evaluation Methodology Supplement*, Version 1.0, August 2002.

Farkas, L., *Anthropometry of the Head and Face*, Raven Press, 2nd ed., 1994.

Foresti, G., 'Active Video-Based Surveillance System', *IEEE Signal Processing Magazine*, Vol. 22, No. 2, *IEEE Signal Processing Society*, Piscataway, NJ, 2005, pp. 25-37.

Gibbons, M., Yoon, S., Cha, S.-H., Tappert C., 'Evaluation of Biometric Identification in Open Systems', *Lecture Notes in Computer Science*, 3546, Poster I, Springer-Verlag Berlin Heidelberg, 2005, pp. 823-831.

Hildebrandt, M., Backhouse J. (eds.), *Descriptive analysis and inventory of profiling practices*, *FIDIS Deliverable 7.2*, European Union IST FIDIS Project, Brussels, 2005, pp. 1-116. Available at: www.fidis.net.

Hampapur, A. et al., 'Smart Video Surveillance: exploring the concept of multiscale spatiotemporal tracking', *IEEE Signal Processing Magazine*, Vol. 22, No. 2, 2005, pp. 38-50.

Hosein, G., 'Threatening the Open Society: Comparing Anti-terror Policies and Strategies in the U.S. and Europe', *Privacy International*, December 13, 2005.

Jain, A. K., Dass S. C., Nandakumar, K., 'Can soft biometric traits assist user recognition?', *Proceedings of SPIE Biometric Technology for Human Identification*, Vol. 5404, Orlando, FL April 2004a, pp. 561-72.

Jain, A. K., Ross A., Prabhakar, S., 'An introduction to Biometric Identification', *IEEE Transactions on Circuits and Systems for Video Technology, Special Issue on Image- and Video-Based Biometrics*, Vol. 14, No. 1, IEEE Circuits and Systems Society, January 2004b.

Jain, A.K., Lu, X., 'Ethnicity Identification from Face Images', Proceedings of SPIE International Symposium on Defense and Security: Biometric Technology for Human Identification, 2004.

Johnson, M., 'Biometrics and the threat to civil liberties', *Computer*, Vol. 37, No. 4, IEEE Computer Society Press, 2004, pp. 90-91.

Joint Technical Committee ISO/IEC JTC 1, 'Text of Standing Document 2, version 5 – Harmonized Biometric Vocabulary, of Subcommittee SC 37, *biometrics, Information Technology*, dated 31 January 2006, a working document. Available at: http://isotc.iso.org/livelink/livelink/fetch/2000/2122/327993/2262372/2263033/2299739/JTC001-SC37-N-1480.pdf?nodeid=495 4581&vernum=0.

Khan M. K., Zhang, J., 'Improving the security of a flexible biometrics remote user authentication scheme', *Computer Standards & Interfaces*, Volume 29, Issue 1, January Elsevier, 2007, pp. 82-85.

Kryszczuk K., Drygajlo, A., 'Addressing the Vulnerabilities of Likelihood-Ratio-Based Face Verification', *Lecture Notes in Computer Science*, 3546, Springer-Verlag Berlin Heidelberg, 2005, pp. 426-435.

Nykodym, N., Taylor R., and Vilela, J., 'Criminal profiling and insider cyber crime', *Digital Investigation*, Vol. 2, No. 4, Elsevier, December 2005, pp. 261-267.

Prabhakar, S., Pankanti, S., Jain, A. K., 'Biometric Recognition: Security and Privacy Concerns', *IEEE Security and Privacy*, Vol. 1, No. 2, IEEE Computer Society, 2003, pp. 33-42.

Rogers, M., 'The role of criminal profiling in the computer forensics process', *Computers & Security*, Vol. 22, No. 4, Elsevier, May 2003, pp. 292-298.

Smith, An., *The Ethnic Origins of Nations*, Oxford: Basil Blackwell, 1987.

Snelick, R., Uludag, U., Mink, A., Indovina, M., Jain, A., 'Large-Scale Evaluation of Multimodal Biometric Authentication Using State-of-the-Art Systems', *IEEE Transactions on Pattern Analysis and Machine Intelligence*, Vol. 27, No 3, IEEE Computer Society, 2005, pp. 450-455.

Uludag, U., Jain A. K., 'Attacks on biometric systems: a case study in fingerprints', *Proceedings of SPIE-EI 2004*, San Jose, CA, 2004, pp. 622-633.

Woodworth, M.,Porter, St., 'Historical Foundations and Current Applications of Criminal Profiling in Violent Crime Investigations', *Expert Evidence*, Vol. 7, Springer Netherlands, 2000, pp. 241-264.

Chapter 8
Profiling and Location-Based Services (LBS)

Lothar Fritsch

Location-based services (LBS) are services that position a person's mobile phone to provide some context-based service. Some of these services – called 'location tracking' or 'push LBS' applications - need frequent updates of the current position to decide whether a service should be initiated at the current moment – or to deduct from a location profile a future point in time for service provision. Thus, such distributed and ubiquitous systems will continuously collect and process locations in relationship to a personal context of an identified customer, combining personal information with other data streams (e.g., weather data or financial information). This chapter will introduce the concept of location as part of a person's identity. The role of location profiles in information systems is developed and related to identity management, privacy and geographical information systems (GIS). Furthermore, this contribution will outline how the knowledge about a person's private life and identity can be enhanced with data mining technologies on location profiles and movement patterns.

Finally, some preventive measures such as temporal and spatial cloaking, MIX-zoning and location dummies for protecting location information from unwanted profiling are explained.

8.1 Introduction: Location, Privacy and 'Mobile' Identity

Location data may at first seem trivial. Location is a pair of coordinates on a two-dimensional or three-dimensional grid, defining a position unambiguously, e.g., in the WGS-84 standard, which defines the coordinate grid used on planet Earth (EUROCONTROL, 1998). Location data may have a time stamp. Location data from a particular source can be aggregated over time and it can be linked to a person. Thus, I will first explore the relationship of location and identity before introducing geographic information systems, data mining and profiling.

8.1.1 Location and Identity

Some assumptions about location and identity seem trivial. At nighttime, a person's location is usually where his or her home is. During workdays, the location is

Goethe University Frankfurt (JWG)

M. Hildebrandt and S. Gutwirth (eds.), *Profiling the European Citizen:*
Cross-Disciplinary Perspectives.
© Springer Science + Business Media B.V. 2008

probably the workplace. But there is more. Location determines belonging to social groups, from which social status can be derived. Sociologist Gary Marx defines location as a part of human beings' identity (Marx, 1999), which has been applied to LBS and privacy (Fritsch, 2005), where the question of volatility and stability of profile information is raised. Clearly, location constitutes a context that can be used to deploy a context-based service. Gary Marx clearly defines locatability as one of his seven dimensions of identity: *"(...) identification can refer to a person's address. This involves location and "reachability", whether in actual or cyberspace (a telephone number, a mail or e-mail address, an account number). This need not involve knowing the actual identity or even a pseudonym. But it does involve the ability to locate and take various forms of action such as blocking, granting access, delivering or picking up, charging, penalising, rewarding or apprehending. It answers a "where" rather than a "who" question. This can be complicated by more than one person using the same address."* (Marx, 1999). This section presents a concept of mobility and location as being temporary identifiers: identifiers such as location are only of value if the reachability of the subject they belong to is provided.

Consideration of Pfitzmann and Hansen (2003) reveals the identity paradigm of the Privacy Enhancing Technology community: *"Identifiability is the possibility of being individualised within a set of subjects, the identifiability set. (...) An identity is any subset of attributes of an individual, which uniquely characterises this individual within any set of individuals. So usually, there is no such thing as "the identity" but several of them."* According to this definition, location is just a mere attribute of an identity. But location changes quickly. Obviously, some attributes are less volatile than others. How will identity management deal with this volatility? Does the concept of mobility put new requirements on the model of identity? What is a "mobile identity"? The above attribute model obviously needs a freshness concept to be able to distinguish fresh from expired attributes. I do not intend to express that old location attributes are worthless in profiles but if the fact they are old is not known to the application, confusion may be created for its users, as noted in Section 4.2 on dataveillance in Hildebrandt and Backhouse (2005). Freshness introduces time into the set of attributes. Thus, a "mobile identity" could be a form of identity that is unique even though location and time attributes can change at will. The challenge of mobile identity management in LBS is thus to find a way to provide a certain amount of identity control to the subjects but at the same time provide reach ability and re-identifiability for the user-to-application provider connection. Clearly, most of the privacy threats identified above result from a combination of a location and time attribute with other attributes, or within the context of the whereabouts (e.g., "This location is within the red light district").

A solution for privacy-friendly LBS with identity management has to hide as many attributes from observers as possible, as the location information has to be available to the application provider for the provision of the service. At the same time, the reachability of the user generally enables business transactions. Thus, the combination of attribute-hiding identity management with untraceable reachability are a solution for privacy-friendly LBS. If these two properties are to be implemented in a way to support the business models of location tracking, the location-based services can be equipped with privacy-respecting technologies. This assures users they have control over personal data release and identification, as required in the survey research, e.g., for the most privacy-aware group in Sheehan's typology (Sheehan, 2002). This group could possibly be convinced to use mobile on-line services, providing industry a base of usually older, more mature and financially attractive customers who care about privacy. Sholtz (2003) assumed that there is little long-term value in profile information from an economic point of view. A risk centred point of view might be different, though. Formally, Gruteser and Grunwald outlined some threats (Gruteser and Grunwald, 2003), where they postulate that from tracking a person's frequent nighttime location, they can guess his/her identity by looking it up in public phone directories. This will be discussed further below.

8.1.2   Geographical Information Systems (GIS)

Combined with geographical information systems (GIS), many contexts of a place can be identified – ranging from data about the neighbourhood via criminal statistics to local risk levels of natural disasters. Michael Curry states his concern about this and calls for ethical standards in Curry (1996). Recent product deployments like 'Google Earth' put these tools into the hands of the general public (Google, 2005). Ethically problematic is not only the privacy-invading character but also the possibilities to manipulate and misinform with maps, as described by Monmonnier (1996). Privacy, GIS and positioning technology in combination can be even more invasive, as highlighted by Monmonnier (2004). Technologies involved in such privacy threats can be categorised as follows:

- Position tracking technologies
- Data warehouse technologies
- Geographical databases & information systems (GIS)
- Meta databases with geo-coded data

In addition to these factors, some a-priori knowledge about contexts of everyday life, holidays, social conventions and suchlike can be an input in the above information systems.

8.1.3   Data Mining and its Applications

Data mining has been defined by many authors. Two definitions are presented here for clarity:

Knowledge discovery is the nontrivial extraction of implicit, previously unknown and potentially useful information from data. (Frawley, Piatetsky-Shapiro, Matheus, 1992).

Data mining is the search for relationships and global patterns that exist in large databases but are 'hidden' among the vast amounts of data, such as a relationship between patient data and their medical diagnosis. These relationships represent valuable knowledge about the database and objects in the database and, if the database is a faithful mirror, of the real world registered by the database (Holsheimer, Siebes, 1991).

Data mining evolved with relational databases. Most of the original data mining work centred on processing relations and attributes in such databases. Classic applications are fraud detection in financial or insurance matters or warehouse optimisation based on customers' preferred buying patterns. Threats to privacy from data mining on customer databases have been well-discussed. An overview of privacy threats and ethical questions in customer data collection and profiling can be found in Foxman and Kilcoyne (1993).

Data mining technologies are now available for different kinds of geographic information. Classification of land surfaces based on satellite intelligence and the mining of meta data layers of GIS are two examples. Meta data layers such as crime rate and wealth, classified by area, have been in use for years to obtain customer scoring and to fight mail-order fraud. Land surveying with satellite data might reveal how a farmer cares for his land – or whether he uses the right amount of fertiliser. The concept is called "precision farming". An overview of basic data mining technologies can be found in Chapter 4 above. More applications of GIS data mining can be found in Monmonnier's book (2004).

8.1.4   Profiling

Profiling a person is more than just data matching. Roger Clarke defines profiling as follows: "Profiling is a data surveillance technique that is little-understood and ill-documented but increasingly used. It is a means of generating suspects or prospects from within a large population and involves inferring a set of characteristics of a particular class of person from past experience, then searching data-holdings for individuals with a close fit to that set of characteristics." (Clarke, 1993). Thus, profiling targets at the selection of candidates out of the mass that have particular characteristics, or finding patterns over people's data that can be applied to find similar people. In Hildebrandt and Backhouse (2005), a semiotic model of knowledge discovery in databases describes in six consecutive steps how new knowledge is extracted from data. This will be applied below in Section 8.2.2 to describe location data mining.

As an example, for the application of the geo-coded profiling techniques, we examine the location track of a hypothetical person's day on Santorini Island. A compressed track is shown in Fig. 8.2. For simplicity, the location recordings of the person while staying at the same place are noted as a time interval. Only selected positions are shown in Fig. 8.1. For the start, the position data is time stamped (hence the time marks to the right) and then combined with GIS data containing road information and points of interest to create a map.

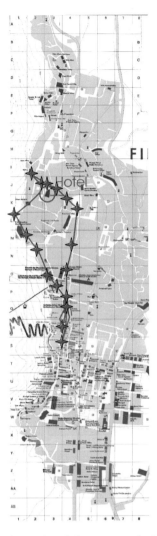

Fig. 8.1 Map of Fira with location track and time stamps of a hypothetical person. Excerpt of map "Santorin" (World Mapping Project), published by Verlag Reise Know-How, Bielefeld (www.reise-know-how.de)

From the road information, we can deduce with high probability the preferred roads or paths of the person, as you can see in Fig. 8.2. Additionally, by noticing that the person was using the area marked as "hotel" several times a day, one can guess that this must be the person's home. Looking at the time stamps adds more information. When you look at Fig. 8.1, the information in timestamps 1 and 19 clearly indicate that the person sleeps at the hotel location. Also, by observing timestamps 3 and 9, the person spends most of the daytime at the hotel as well. One can guess that the person is either an employee of the hotel or is participating in an ongoing event. Meal times reveal that for lunch and dinner, the person left the hotel

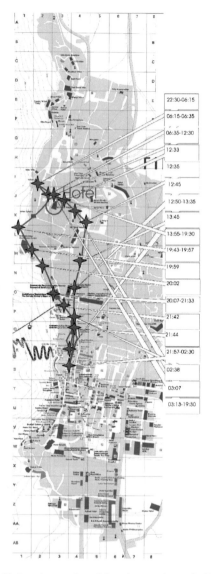

	22:30-06:15
	06:15-06:35
	06:35-12:30
	12:33
	12:35
	12:45
	12:50-13:35
	13:45
	13:55-19:30
	19:43-19:57
	19:59
	20:02
	20:07-21:33
	21:42
	21:44
	21:57-02:30
	02:38
	03:07
	03:13-19:30

Fig. 8.2 Map of Fira with location track and location marks as in Fig. 8.1. Excerpt of map "Santorin" (World Mapping Project), published by Verlag Reise Know-How, Bielefeld (www. reise-know-how.de)

to spend time at two locations in the old town. Using the points-of-interest (POI) database on the GIS, we find the candidate restaurants. What does this tell us about the nutritional habits, religion, health and budget of the person? Can we buy the credit card transaction data for these restaurants from Amex to learn more? Also, notice the dinnertime path was on the edge of the cliff, unlike the lunchtime path. The cliff points west into the sunset. Was the person therefore alone for the romantic view? Timestamp 16 reveals a long stay at – thanks to GIS – an old town dancing club. Dancing obviously went on for a long time. So, most likely there was no company on the cliff path or bad table manners or both. Timestamps 17 and 18 indicate slow progress back to the hotel, compared to the lunchtime progress. Is this due to intoxicating beverages or due to company? Here, timestamp 19 does not help. Unfortunately, the full day at the hotel can be credited to work, hangover or company alike. Only the minibar billing on the credit card will most likely tell.

In this example, we used a time stamped location track, a GIS with some POI data and some common sense to create a behavioural profile of a person. We were able to guess some context and find interfaces to other databases that elaborated our knowledge.

8.2   Contextual Profiling

8.2.1   Spatial and Temporal Dimensions of Location Tracking

Location data can be analysed at singular points in space or time as well as in intervals of either of them or both. The extent of analysis happens along the time axis or within geographic boundaries, which I call dimensions. The respective gain of information for profilers or related risk for the person being observed differs greatly based on the spatial and temporal dimensions. Generally, location tracking applications seem to be perceived to be more threatening than the one-time positioning of a person, as Barkhuus notes in Barkhuus and Dey (2003). A matrix of temporal and spatial dimensions is constructed from Barkuus & Dey's insight in table 1, where the matrix illustrates the kind of information that can be deducted about a person from the respective dimension category.

8.2.2   Context Acquisition from Temporal and Spatial Data

Personal information can be gained starting from knowledge about a person's identifier (which is not the identity but a set of identifying information, e.g., a name, a pseudonym, an address, etc.) and his/her location track by applying temporal and spatial context. Temporal context is, for example, a person's time zone, along with time-dependent social habits, e.g., lunch breaks, Spanish siesta or night shift working. Spatial context can be derived from geographic information systems, which contain many layers of information, much more specialised than mapping or navigation data. As described by Curry (1996) and Monmonnier (2004), existing GIS data layers include information about crime rates, property values, wealth, health,

Table 8.1 Personal information deducible from temporal and spatial dimensions

		Spatial dimension	
		At one point	*Within an area*
Temporal dimension	*At one moment*	**Singular:** Know about the status quo of time and space at one moment.	**Spatial snapshot:** For individuals: makes no sense as one can only be in one place at one moment in time. For groups: can reveal relationships, cliques, collaboration.
	Within a time window	**Time-linear:** Can reveal workplace, home, social context and information about personal preferences (e.g., restaurant type).	**Two-dimensional:** Reveals shopping habits, dating habits, driving speeds and other information.

education, employment, race, pollution, noise, natural hazards and much more. Context acquisition follows an algorithmic scheme that I have constructed below:[108]

1. Collect time-coded location data for some time (preferably days or weeks to operate in the two-dimensional category in Table 8.1).
2. Construct some temporal context of interest (e.g., private time vs. job time).
3. Check for a geographical pattern of interest in the location data track (e.g., places frequently visited or unusual places rarely visited, etc.)
4. Extract geographic coordinates along with their spatial and temporal information.
5. Query geographic information systems about locations and extract meta data (e.g., "…is an office building").
6. Conclude from temporal context, spatial context and geographic meta data, e.g., the workplace, the home place, sports and other personal data.

Notably, this algorithm works without knowing the person. It is enough to be able to re-identify him/her in the dataset. It can be used for example within a WiFi hot spot or mobile phone tracks that leave unique technical parameters as identifiable information. Using the algorithm above, we learn much about a - yet unknown - person's preferences and frequent behaviour.

Next, the old-fashioned databases enter the stage.

---

[108] The algorithm is inspired by Usama Fayyad's and Evangelos Simoudis' knowledge discovery algorithm presented in their 1995 tutorial "Knowledge Discovery and Data Mining" at the Fourteenth International Joint Conference on Artificial Intelligence (IJCAI-95). Documentation can be found online at www-aig.jpl.nasa.gov/public/kdd95/tutorials/IJCAI95-tutorial.html.

8.2.3 Data Mining, Combination and Profiling

As defined above, data mining follows relations in relational databases to find "knowledge". Various methods from disciplines such as artificial intelligence, statistics, computational linguistics and stochastic methods are deployed on collections of data. The correlation between shopping habits and location, communication habits and location, movement and health data, social contexts and other items can be mined from the databases.

The application of profiling techniques on geographic and database information could lead to new kinds of marketing, insurance or anti-terrorism systems. People's movement patterns combined with other features could be used to segment customers, generate health insurance conditions or arrest suspects. Numerous business models of LBS-enhanced applications have been published. A taxonomy of the applications can be found in Fritsch's and Muntermann's survey of application hindrances.[109] It can be expected to see them enter the market soon.

8.3 Countermeasures & Self-Protection

The protection against geo-coded data mining and profiling has three components: identity protection, camouflage and a legal and social framework for technology regulation. Each of these items will be discussed below. Following the distinction in Section 2.2 of Gutwirth and De Hert (2005) and the further discussion in Chapter 14 of this book, protective measures are divided into opacity and transparency tools. Opacity tools serve the purpose of hiding personal information to enable unobservable, individual actions that enable individual freedom. Transparency tools are used to create open, understandable and fair practices when dealing with personal information.

8.3.1 Identity Protection

A person's identifying data should be protected while using location-based services. If the location track is not personalised, it cannot be combined with any other personal data. Furthermore, the amount of data that can be accumulated about a person should be limited, to avoid identity guessing from movement patterns. Identity management systems with frequent pseudonym changes and anonymous access to services provide the means to reach these goals. The simplest form of identity management occurs in Fig. 8.3, where the mobile operator offers pseudonym translation services to the user before the application data traffic is forwarded into MIX cascades.

---

[109] [=350 - Fritsch 2005 Aktuelle Hinderungsg…=].

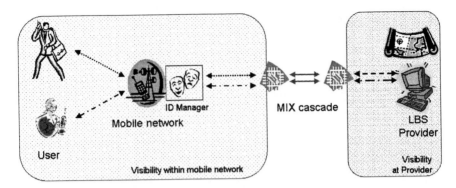

Fig. 8.3 Minimalist Mobile Network Identity Management approach

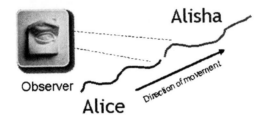

Fig. 8.4 Naive pseudonym change reveals pseudonym connection

More advanced identity management approaches introduce policy management. Here, a user can set a policy about location forwarding with her mobile operator and at the same time, issue anonymous credentials that identify the policy. The credential is then given to the LBS provider as a voucher. Please note though that naïve use of pseudonym change mechanisms can reveal all your pseudonyms used with a service, as illustrated in Fig. 8.4. To prevent this from happening, MIX-Zoning will be discussed later in this text (see Fig. 8.7). Identity Management can be either an opacity or a transparency tool, depending on its particular deployment in a context. It is an opacity tool in the context of identity camouflaging (e.g., by pseudonym translation). It can be a transparency tool towards users or businesses that clarifies rules, practices and visibility of data.

8.3.2 Camouflage

The generation of false information about identity, identifiable movement patterns and time disturbances will provide protection against unauthorised geographic profiling. Early concepts have been suggested by Gruteser and Grunwald (2003). Concepts include:

Temporal cloaking: the time intervals for location queries are regulated to avoid micro-measurement of a user's position. This concept is illustrated in Fig. 8.5.

Spatial cloaking: precision of location information is reduced to a level tolerable by the application but will not be delivered too precisely. This intentional degradation of position precision prevents the collection of too precise information on a person's movements on a high-resolution level. Spatial cloaking is illustrated in Fig. 8.6.

MIX-zoning: to allow for unobservable change of pseudonyms (and solve the problem described in Fig. 8.4), a zone of unobservability is created where users can go to perform their pseudonym change. As soon as many users do this simultaneously, an anonymity set is created. The concept is inspired by Chaum's MIX (Chaum, 1981). An example of MIX zoning for the purpose of pseudonym change protection is shown in Fig. 8.7.

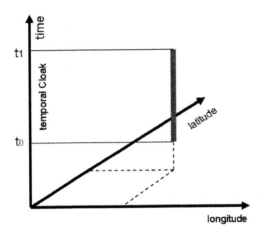

Fig. 8.5 Temporal cloaking

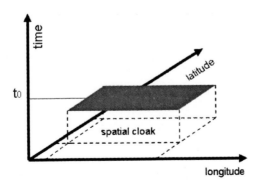

Fig. 8.6 Spatial cloaking

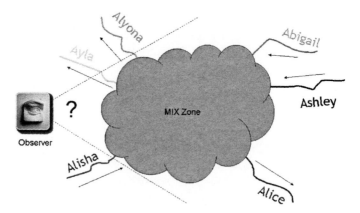

Fig. 8.7 A MIX zone

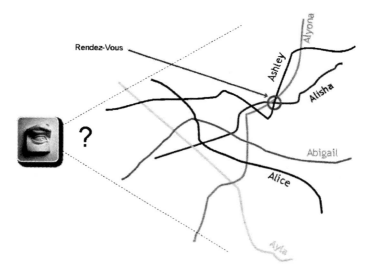

Fig. 8.8 Location dummy traffic, Rendezvous point

Temporal cloaking adds uncertainty to the point in time the position of a person was measured. The relying service, using the data, does receive a position datum but only knows this is not the person's current position but from some time in the past. The usefulness of this approach is limited in terms of privacy protection. Temporal cloaking only seems applicable in contexts where a service tracks a person frequently (e.g., a pollen warning scenario, as used in Koelsch et al. (2005) but with low-resolution requirements on position and timing Spatial cloaking is effective in circumstances where a tracking service does not require high-resolution position information (e.g., for pollen warnings). Here, the information is intentionally degraded to a degree where no daily routine is contained.

Location dummy traffic: MIX zones are effective to protect and obfuscate pseudonym changing events. Unfortunately, MIX zones might not always have enough people in them at the moment when they are used. To improve on this problem, the concept of dummy traffic in MIX communication can be adapted. Location track dummy traffic is performed with dummy users, which are artificially generated location tracks with a certain non-compromising behaviour. The dummy pseudonyms are registered with the LBS application and will be used for pseudonym changes.

When a user wishes to change to a different pseudonym, the dummy system ensures that some of his alternative or dummy pseudonyms will cross the user's path at a rendezvous point, where the change will happen. The now unused pseudonym takes up a dummy life of its own, in a temporary or permanent continuation of the previous path. This mechanism can take up a used pseudonym and carry it around the town virtually. The challenge here is the generation of realistic movement patterns that do not compromise the pseudonym owner by, e.g., entering the town's red light district. The application of this protection measure is restricted to LBS infrastructures that allow for the injection of artificially created position data (e.g., the GPS device scenario or some special instance of the intermediary scenario described in Fritsch (2005)).

All camouflage technologies are opacity technologies.

8.4 Legal and Social Framework

Finally, a legal and social framework is required on top of the technical infrastructures. To make sense of innovations like the LBS applications with privacy protection, possibly based on trusted platforms that can enforce system constraints, a legal and social environment for the technologies must be created. Regulation is a controversial topic but for many fields that are problematic in other parts of society, there is evidence that regulation does not only complicate markets but also provides the creation of new markets. For an outlook on how economic theory can favour regulation of pollution problems and possibly the privacy problem, Paul Sholtz presented some interesting examples in Sholtz (2001) and Sholtz (2003). To enable market participants to distinguish the quality of systems and parties, a public quality certification scheme can prove useful, as found in Backhouse et al. (2005).

Much of today's regulation in Europe deals with consent to and knowledge about personal data processing by the data subject (e.g., the EC Directive on privacy and electronic communications).[110] Socio-legal frameworks are thus clearly transparency tools, as binding rules of system deployment create transparency about the conditions and consequences of service deployment or users' participation in information processing with personal data.

Further discussion of this topic can be found in Part III of this book.

---

[110] D 2002/58/EC.

8.5   Conclusion

Summarising the challenges posed by combined data mining and geographic data mining, applied to location tracks, infrastructures for location-based applications have to offer reliable functionality to prevent misuse of personal information. As seen in Section 8.3, the development of technical countermeasures is in a very early phase of maturity. Similar to research in privacy-enhancing technology, it will take time for technology to mature, develop end-user usability and make its way into the application systems. With the possible countermeasures, users will have to rely on other people's IT systems correctly functioning. Thus, with the development of geographic data mining technologies and LBS, there is a strong need to research and specify ways to develop privacy-respecting infrastructures (PRI).[111] PRI – unlike the self-protecting focus of privacy-enhancing technologies (PET) – should be integrated within a regulatory, economic and technological framework. Some ideas of possible frameworks have been explored in Koelsch et al. (2005) by the deployment of PET on all nodes of a distributed LBS scenario, under consideration of the existing legal framework and end-user centric research. Generally, data protection policy of the future should take trusted platform technology under consideration. This form of restrictive computing base could ensure correct, fair function of LBS systems and geographic databases and generate assurance with a certification system.

8.6   Reply: Mind My Step?

Ronald Leenes*

Lothar Fritsch's contribution addresses the powerful inferences that can be made by combining the location of mobile phones with data from GIS systems and data mining techniques. Indeed, the combination of such data offers a rich picture of mobile phone users and their behaviour. Why and when should we worry and how does it relate to location-based services (LBS)? In this reply, a distinction is made between profile data triggered by location data on the one hand and by profiles constructed on the basis of location data, what is called location-based profiling, on the other. Location-based profiling by mobile operators is not likely to happen because of the computational complexity and limited added value in comparison to normal LBS. The state is a more likely user of detailed rich profiles because it claims to need more and more data on its subjects in order to fight terrorism and crime.

---

*Tilburg Universiteit, Tilburg Insituut for Law, Technology and Society (TILT)

---

[111] See also Fritsch et al. (2006) for an approach to specification of privacy-respecting location-based services.

8.6.1   Introduction

Until recently, profiling in the digital world was mainly based on aggregating and processing data generated by Internet applications such as web browsers, email, online forums and mining enterprise databases. The rapid proliferation of mobile devices, particularly mobile phones and the convergence of mobile technology and 'traditional' Internet applications have significantly increased the potential to construct personalised profiles of the users of online and mobile services. As Fritsch shows, powerful inferences can be made by combining location data generated by locatable devices, data from GIS systems and data derived from data mining techniques. In this reply I will look a little deeper into the possibilities and problems related to combining profiling and locatable devices.

8.6.2   Location Profiling Decomposed

Making a distinction in types of profiling enabled by locatable devices and data sources, there is, first, the classic profiling based on techniques such as data mining in databases. This results in personalised or group profiles that in the mobile context are triggered by location data provided by a locatable device, such as a mobile phone. Many location-based services, if they make use of profiles, belong to this category. An example is the use of the inference, based on mining a supermarket's purchase records, that an individual likes Mexican food to subsequently send him text messages around dinnertime containing addresses of nearby Mexican restaurants whenever he is in a city other than his home town. The essential characteristic of this type of service is that there is a pre-existing profile (or alternatively, a set of user preferences), which is triggered into action by location data. The profile determines the salient features (food preference, favourite pastime, et cetera.) that can be linked to locations through applications, such as the Yellow pages and GIS applications.

The second category of profiling starts with locations. Here, two kinds can be distinguished: profiling on the basis of only the location data and profiling on the basis of location data enriched with explanations for the patterns in these data. The first kind of profiling provides less information than the latter, because it only shows what (ir)regularities in movement occur and when they occur. However, even these patterns can tell us something about the mobile phone user's behaviour. For instance, during a particular month, say July, the phone is far away from its usual locations. This particular pattern could be due to the fact that the user is away on holiday in a foreign country.

The second kind of profiling combines location data and other data as discussed by Lothar Fritsch. This activity could be called *location-based* profiling or, if considered from the perspective of producing knowledge about an individual, *location-based inferencing*. Location-based inferencing involves tracking, or sampling, the location of a mobile device, typically a mobile phone (e.g., GSM, UMTS), at regular intervals. The samples in conjunction with other data sources, such as GIS systems, can subsequently be used to derive information about the location and, potentially, about the individual at this location. The data from GIS applications and other sources are used to detect and explain patterns in the location data produced by the user's locatable device.

The location-based inferences can be used to provide services to the user, such as giving personalised advice. For instance, common denominators that explain why the profiled individual was in particular places could be derived from frequently visited (kinds of) locations. To do so, the service would need to associate location data to relevant objects, events, or people at those places. GIS systems, Yellow pages, et cetera, can play a role here. For instance, the locations where a person resides during dinnertime could be used to query a Yellow pages-like system to see if there are commonalities in behaviour.[112] Regularly being in the vicinity of Chinese restaurants during lunchtime could be one. This could signify that this individual not only goes near Chinese restaurants but also frequents them and may even have a liking for Chinese food. This information in turn could be used to offer the individual location-based services: pointing out nearby Chinese restaurants in unfamiliar cities around lunchtime.

Of course, it is easy to imagine more exciting examples. It is also easy to see the problems associated with this kind of 'intelligent advice'. Section 8.7.4 will examine these problems.

Location based profiling can also be used for other purposes other than providing individualised services to the profiled individual.[113] It can also be used for inclusion and exclusion, stereotyping and stigmatisation and surveillance and monitoring.[114] An example that wears thin is that sexual preferences sometimes can just as easily be inferred as food preferences. Depending on who has access to the profile, this may have consequences for the individual, irrespective of whether these preferences relate to legal or illegal conduct. Even information about harmless hobbies, such as keeping Cobra snakes and visiting Gothic parties, may affect people's judgments and hence, have an effect on the person being judged, even if the information is completely irrelevant for the context of judgment.[115]

8.6.3   Getting close to the user

Lothar Fritsch's contribution raises questions that warrant further elaboration. Location data extends the possibilities of profiling, because it allows location data to be connected to objects and people. Combining location data of different devices

---

[112] Given the accuracy of location determination on the basis of GSM equipment, only an area of a certain size, depending on the number of base stations in a particular grid, can be determined, not the exact location (see, for instance, T D'Roza and G Bilchev, 2003; W. Millar, 2003).

[113] I will confine myself here to personalised profiles and leave group profiles out of the discussion. See chapter 2 of this volume for an extensive discussion on these two forms of profiling.

[114] See Custers, 2004; Clarke, 1994 for a detailed account of these types of profiling effects.

[115] Physically challenged people, black people, women, the elderly and so forth, all have experience with the effects of stereotyping and discrimination.

makes it possible to determine who else was, or was not, near a particular location. But apart from this, is it any different from other kinds of profiling?

Location-based profiling shares many of the general features of profiling: certain aspects of an individual's behaviour are monitored and attributes or characteristics are derived by means of mathematical or statistical operations on the data.[116] What sets location-based profiling apart from other forms of profiling is the omnipresence of the data collection. Mobile devices produce data that can be collected from the moment they are switched on; there is no way to prevent data collection while it is on. Although web-profiling (see chapter 9) is equally non-transparent as location-based profiling – web users often do not know whether data is being collected – web users at least have some control over the data being collected. Websurfing generally requires (conscious) actions of the users: they visit particular websites, click on buttons, fill out forms, enter search queries, type in particular words or sentences and so forth. The data used for the profiling, therefore, stems from discrete events. This allows web surfers to avoid falling victim to certain types of profiling. If they do not want to run the risk of being stigmatised as computer nerds, they could abstain from visiting sites such as Slashdot.org[117] or use technical means, such as anonymisers, to obfuscate their identity (their IP in this case).

Location data, on the other hand, is generated much more continuously and unobtrusively. Mobile phones generate location data whenever they are on. Many people are completely unaware of this. Apart from the techniques described in Fritsch's chapter, the only way to prevent data from being generated is by switching the device off.[118] The monitoring and subsequent profiling of location data therefore is even more intrusive than monitoring Internet-related behaviour. It happens all the time and everywhere.

Because of the continuous data generation, the use of location data has to be considered very carefully. Some locations are hard to avoid and being there may easily induce false hypotheses[119] that are particularly hard to refute.

In the case of location-based services, the location data will generally be used in conjunction with user preferences or user profiles created and used with the subject's

---

[116] See chapters 3 and 4 of this volume for an extensive overview of tools, techniques and methods for profiling.

[117] This is not the preferred way of avoiding being profiled because it forces a wrong choice on the user. The choice should be to allow or disallow profiling, instead of having to choose between exhibiting or refraining from certain behaviour. Visiting Slashdot is, after all, neither a crime nor morally wrong. See also chapter 14 of this volume.

[118] Which obviously severely limits the use of the device: you can place calls but cannot be called.

[119] For instance, on foot the shortest way from the University of Amsterdam's law faculty, where I sometimes go for meetings, to Amsterdam Central Station is through the red-light district. The location data generated when I stopped to answer a tourist's questions about the area on my way from the law faculty to the station could make me appear as looking for some 'sexual relief', just because I was pausing in the red light district? Would I later remember that I stopped to answer the tourist's questions?

consent. The danger here lies in the fact that an LBS provider potentially can make the match between the user preferences/profile and their location. The combination reveals user preferences or behaviour that people may want to keep private. For this reason, the EU FP6 PRIME project[120] explores solutions to maintain a strict separation between the three parties involved in providing the location-based service: the LBS provider (who provides the service), the location intermediary (who provides the location data) and the mobile operator (who provides the communication, localisation and bills the user). This separation limits the possibilities of personalised profiling because each of the three parties involved lacks the necessary data for really purposeful profiles.

The dangers of using location data for location-based profiling are far greater. Combining location data and data sources so as to facilitate explanations for being at those locations potentially provides an abundant and complete picture of mobile phone users and their activities, which could render them fairly transparent.

8.6.4 The Users of Location-Based Profiling

Further issues that can be elaborated in more detail concern the feasibility of location-based profiling and why people would bother at all to develop and use location-based profiling.

It is conceivable that despite efforts such as those exhibited in the PRIME project and implementing the counter measures described by Lothar Fritsch, mobile phone operators will engage in location-based profiling. They may, for instance, want to enhance their location-based services in the way described in the Chinese food example. However, I am not convinced that they will. Inferring that I probably live close to a primary school based on the fact that this is the only point of interest close to where I spend most nights is one thing. Providing useful services on the basis of profiling large amounts of location data and combining these with other data sources is another. Managing and analysing these huge data sets may prove to be fairly difficult.

To understand why, we need to take a closer look into the mechanics of enriched location based profiling. The location of a cell phone is determined by the Base Transceiver Stations (BTS) used for relaying the mobile phone's data to the terrestrial network. The simplest way to obtain a location fix is determining which BTS is closest to the mobile device. The cell phone is within a certain radius of the given BTS. This radius depends on the distribution of base stations and, according to D'Roza and Bilchev, this radius was around 500 metres in urban regions and up to 15 km in rural zones in 2003 (D'Roza and Bilchev, 2003, p. 22). Since then, the accuracy has improved due to an increase in Base Transceiver Stations. The accuracy can be further

---

[120] See the projects public portal at <http://www.prime-project.eu>, especially deliverable D4.2.a: evaluation of the initial prototypes.

improved by determining which of the antennas of the BTS picks up the strongest signal. This facilitates determining a pie segment of say, 120% degrees (given a BTS with three antennas) with a given radius. Triangulation and time difference calculations can further improve the accuracy of the location fix. However, even then, the accuracy of the location fix is at best in the tens of metres range.[121] This means that most location fixes possibly trigger a large set of objects, such as restaurants, schools, banks, offices and shops that could be considered as potential explanations for the mobile phone's location. This makes it difficult to draw conclusions concerning these data. Furthermore, there may even be multiple reasonable candidates for any kind of behaviour. Suppose it is known that a particular location fix is related to someone having dinner, then often not only Chinese but also Indian, Italian and even McDonald restaurants will be nearby as well. Statistical techniques may derive interesting patterns and be useful to sort out preferences across datasets but the computational efforts to derive useful data from the match between location and GIS data will be considerable, if not prohibitive. Especially because, depending on the sample frequency of the location fixes, the amount of data can be considerable.

The chances of deriving spurious results are also considerable. Making useful inferences may therefore be even more non-trivial than in the case of 'traditional' profiling. The chances of providing suggestions to the profiled users on the basis of the location-based profiles that are just off and therefore completely useless, seem considerable in my view. Of course, the profiled individual could be asked to acknowledge the conclusions inferred from the statistical processes: "I observe that you often seem to visit Chinese restaurants, do you really fancy these?" but I wonder whether this is a good idea.

This brings us to the fundamental question with respect to location-based services based on location-based profiling. The amount of location data that needs to be stored and processed easily outweighs the added value of trying to derive patterns and explanations from the data, not to mention the computational complexity of matching the location data with GIS data and other data. So, what is the advantage of using location-based inferencing over just *asking* the mobile phone user about their preferences? In other words, why not leave the initiative to specify under which conditions, or when, a service is to be provided to the user?

Mobile operators and others are eager to provide location-based services but this does not require location-based profiling. LBS service providers do need location data for their services. The kind of service to be provided determines the role of the location data in the process. Pull services require the user to state when a location fix needs to be obtained. The location fix is subsequently used to fulfil the user's request, such as where is the nearest pharmacy. The user decides when and for what reason the location data is used. Push services depend on the user to determine under what conditions a location should trigger some (informative) action.

---

[121] Tests carried out in the US by VoiceStream in the light of E-911 emergency calls found E-OTD accuracy to be 75 metres for 67% of calls and 259 metres for 95% of calls, according to <http://www.seitti.com/story.php?story_id=2362>.

Alternatively, another entity, such as a government agency, could specify the conditions for triggering actions. In a location-based emergency warning system, the government, for instance can decide to send all mobile phones in a particular area a text message informing them what to do.

A more likely user of rich profiles may be the state. In the post 9/11 era, the state claims to need more and more data on its subjects in order to fight serious crime and terrorism. Location data will probably play an increasing role in this respect, precisely because it allows correlating individual behaviour to objects, places and other individuals.

Location data is already being used in criminal investigations. For example, in what is known in the Netherlands as the Deventer Murder Case[122], the fact that the suspect made a phone call near a BTS located in Deventer around the estimated time of the death of the murder victim was considered as evidence to support the claim that he had killed her. Interestingly enough, the defence lawyer contested that the phone call was made near the BTS. Expert witnesses supported the defense's claim by stating that atmospheric circumstances could cause mobile phone signals to 'drift' to base stations further away than usual and that the defense's statement that the suspect was some x kilometres away from the crime scene at the time of the crime was indeed plausible.[123]

Another case of the use of location data is provided in a report on the usefulness of retaining traffic data, produced by Mevis (2005). This report describes a case where a series of car thefts involving expensive cars was solved by tracking the users of mobile phones that had been close to the BTS nearest to the location of the stolen cars at the estimated time of the car thefts.

Both cases concern single location fixes and do not involve profiling. The continuous tracking of mobile devices can easily be done and could indeed be useful to monitor suspects. A step further is also quite conceivable: using watch lists of locations and objects that trigger alerts when a mobile device (of a suspect) comes near. But also advanced location-based profiling techniques could be on the radars of law enforcement and anti-terror agencies. The same kind of inferencing described for deriving food preferences could be used to detect suspicious behaviour. An admittedly far fetched and stereotypical example is that the correlation of a particular mobile device being in Pakistan, Iran, Dodewaard (the location of one of the Dutch nuclear power plants), various locations close to mosques, as well as heavy-duty van dealerships, could lead to suspicion of preparations for an attack on the nuclear power plant.

The drawbacks and risks of such an approach are the same as for 'ordinary' location-based profiling but the consequences for those profiled could be much more grave.

---

[122] The complete file of the case can be found at *http://www.rechtspraak.nl/Actualiteiten/Dossiers/Deventer+moordzaak/Deventer+moordzaak.htm.*

[123] This case also shows that location determination by means of mobile phones is not without problems.

8.6.5   Conclusion

Location data offers additional possibilities for the use of profiles, both in the guise of location-based services that make use of data derived from profiles, as well as by providing the input for new types of profiles. The first usage does not differ very much from location-based services, which are used for customer set preferences. The latter is significantly different because it adds a very detailed spatial and temporal dimension to profiling that goes beyond those already present in traditional profiling techniques. The possibility of the continuous collection of location data and correlating these to objects, locations, time and other people potentially creates valuable information concerning the behaviour of mobile phone users. The use of this information in profiles may have a great impact on the profiled subjects and thus calls for utmost care by the profilers.

8.7   Bibliography

Backhouse, J., et al., 'A question of trust: An economic perspective on quality standards in the certification services market', *Communications of the ACM*, Vol. 48, No. 9, ACM Press, Wash. DC, 2005, pp. 87-91.

Barkhuus, L. and Dey, A. 'Location Based Services for Mobile Telephony: a study of users' privacy concerns', *Interact*, Zurich, 2003

Chaum, D. 'Untraceable electronic mail, return addresses, and digital pseudonyms', *Communications of the ACM*, Vol. 4, No. 2, Wash. DC, 1981.

Clarke, R., 'Profiling: A Hidden Challenge to the Regulation of Data Surveillance', *Journal of Law and Information Science*, Vol. 4, No. 2, 1993.

Clarke R., 'The Digital Persona and its application to Data Surveillance', *The Information Society*, Vol. 10, No. 2, Taylor and Francis, 1994, pp.77 -92.

Custers, Bart, *The Power of Knowledge. Ethical, Legal, and Technological Aspects of Data Mining and Group Profiling in Epidemiology*, Wolf Legal Publishers, Nijmegen, 2004.

Curry, M. R. 'In plain and open view: Geographic information systems and the problem of privacy', *Proceedings of the Conference on Law and Information Policy for Spatial Databases*, Department of Geography, University of California, Santa Barbara, California, 1996.

D'Roza, T and G. Bilchev, 'An overview of location-based services', *BT Technology Journal*, Vol. 21, No. 1, Springer Netherlands, January 2003, pp. 20-27.

EUROCONTROL, WGS-84 Implementation Manual, Brussels, Belgium, 1998.

Foxman, E. R. and Kilcoyne, P., 'Information Technology, Marketing Practice and Consumer Privacy: Ethical issues', *Journal of Public Policy & Marketing*, Vol. 12, No. 1, AMA Publications, USA,1993, pp. 106-119.

Frawley, W., Piatetsky-Shapiro, G. and Matheus, C., 'Knowledge discovery in databases: An Overview', *AI Magazine*, Vol. 13, No. 3, AAAI Press, California USA, 1992, pp. 57-70.

Fritsch, L. 'Economic Location-Based Services, Privacy and the Relationship to Identity', *1st FIDIS Doctoral Consortium, European Union IST FIDIS Network of Excellence*, January 25, 2005, Riezlern, Austria.

Fritsch, L., Scherner, T. and Rannenberg, K., 'Von Anforderungen zur verteilten, Privatsphären-respektierenden Infrastruktur', *Praxis in der Informationsverarbeitung und Kommunikation (PIK)*, Vol. 29, No. 1, 2006, pp. 37-42.

Google 'Google Earth Webservice and Geographic Information System', http://earth.google.com

Gruteser, M. and Grunwald, D., 'Anonymous usage of location-based services through spatial and temporal cloaking', *First International Conference on Mobile Systems, Applications, and Services (MobiSys'03)*, 2003, pp. 31–42.

Holsheimer, M. and Siebes, A., *Data Mining: The search for knowledge in databases*, Amsterdam, 1991.

Hildebrandt, M., Backhouse, J. (eds), *Descriptive analysis and inventory of profiling practices, FIDIS Deliverable 7.2*, European Union IST FIDIS Project, Brussels 2005. Available at www.fidis.net

Gutwirth, S., De Hert, P., 'The democratic constitutional state and the invention of two complementary legal tools of power control: opacity of the individual and transparency of power', Hildebrandt, M. et al. (eds), *Implications of profiling practices on democracy and rule of law, FIDIS Deliverable 7.4*, European Union IST FIDIS Project, Brussels, 2005. Available at www.fidis.net

Koelsch, T., et al. 'Privacy for Profitable Location Based Services', *Proceedings of the Security in Pervasive Computing Workshop (SPC) 2005*, Boppard, Springer, pp. 164-179.

Marx, G., 'What's in a name? Some reflections on the Sociology of Anonymity', *The Information Society*, Vol., 15, No. 2, Taylor & Francis, 1999, pp 99-112.

Mevis, P. et al., 'Wie wat bewaart heeft wat' (He who saves has savings), Faculteit Rechtsgeleerdheid, EUR, 2005.

Millar, W., 'Location information from the cellular network – an overview', *BT Technology Journal*, Vol. 21, No. 1, Springer Netherlands, January 2003, pp. 98-104.

Monmonnier, M., *How to lie with maps*, University of Chicago Press, Chicago, 1996.

Monmonnier, M., *Spying with Maps: Surveillance Technologies and the Future of Privacy*, University of Chicago Publishers, Chicago, 2004.

Pfitzmann, A. and Hansen, M. 'Anonymity, Unobservability, and Pseudonymity – A Proposal for Terminology', v0.21, 2003.

Sheehan, K., 'Toward a Typology of Internet Users and Online Privacy Concerns', *The Information Society*, Vol. 18, No. 1, Taylor and Francis, 2002, pp. 21-32.

Sholtz, P., 'Transaction Costs and the Social Costs of Online Privacy', *First Monday*, Vol. 5, No. 6, A Great Cities Initiative of the University of Illinois at Chicago Library, 2001.

Chapter 9
Collecting Data for the Profiling of Web Users

Emmanuel Benoist[124]

Internet technology allows web site administrators to monitor users visiting their sites. In the beginning the basic protocol used for the web (http) did not consider the concept of a *session*. It was impossible to recognise whether two requests came from the same user. Developers then found ways to follow visitors and implemented logins and shopping carts. These solutions included cookie session IDs encoded in the URL, or more recently the creation of a virtual host for each visitor. These mechanisms have also been used for statistical purposes, to study the behaviour of groups of users (group profiling) and to predict the behaviour of a specific user (user profiling).

Usually, collecting information is not in itself reprehensible; however, the use of the data is more critical. One can never be sure if it will be used for statistics (on anonymised data), for one-to-one marketing, or be sold to a third party. The W3 Consortium has published a standard called P3P, giving web site administrators the possibility to declare their policy regarding privacy in a machine readable format. Unfortunately, most people are not yet aware of the sensitivity of collected data; there is therefore no wide resistance to the creation of huge interoperable databases.

9.1 Anonymous Feeling of Web Surfers

For most Internet users, the World Wide Web gives the feeling of anonymity. Surfing the web only requires a computer from which anyone can access billions of web pages without giving any username or password. Visiting web pages does not require explicit identification and is therefore considered anonymous. At the same time, web site administrators want to discover who their customers are. They developed tools for tracking users in order to establish profiles and to better target their clients.

Administrators are assisted in gathering information about their customers by the unawareness from the customers themselves. Since many people believe that nobody cares about what they do on the Internet they do not protect themselves. It is therefore easy to gather a lot of information concerning the acts of people surfing on the Internet. The webmaster can not only see the set of goods purchased but also

Virtual Identity and Privacy Research Centre (VIP)

[124] English review by Tony Ambrose (IEFO - University of Bern, Switzerland).

M. Hildebrandt and S. Gutwirth (eds.), *Profiling the European Citizen:*
Cross-Disciplinary Perspectives.
© Springer Science + Business Media B.V. 2008

the list of all goods that were only viewed. It is possible to track every movement of each client, from where he or she came, to the last visited page and the user is unaware of being monitored. The user thinks, "Since I did not login, nobody knows who I am." This feeling is erroneous. It is possible to track any user on any site. It is also very easy for an ISP or an employer to register any movement someone makes on the Internet.

Profiling a web user requires two fields of expertise: data collection and data analysis. The ability to collect data relies on the web architecture itself. A system administrator can only report what has been sent to him. This means that he will have to use all the features of the underlying protocols of the web, such as TCP/IP and HTTP, to gain information about the visitor. Additionally, the information stored about each user is huge and sparse. It has to be analysed to be used for profiling.

In the next section, we will address the technical specificities of the Internet protocols used by web site administrators (and hackers) to track web surfers. We will then focus on the legitimate uses of such profiling and finish with a description of privacy threatening activities that can be found on the Internet.

9.2 Specificities of the Web Architecture

The World Wide Web is mainly based on two standards: TCP/IP and HTTP. We will see how they can be used to collect information about the user visiting a site.

The TCP/IP protocol is the basis of any exchange on the Internet. It allows the connection of two computers, one of them is called the server, the other is the client.[125] This structure is known as a client-server architecture. This is used for web but also for mail, file transfer and any networked application. To establish a connection, the client will ask the domain name server (DNS) to translate the server name that has been given by the user - for instance, www.fidis.net - into an Internet protocol (IP) number used as an address for communication between the computers - for instance, 80.237.131.150. The two computers can then build a connection, for which the client (i.e., the user's machine) must communicate its own IP address.

Once a TCP/IP connection has been built, the communication starts between the two computers. On the web, the *language* for exchanging information is called HTTP (Hyper-Text Transfer Protocol). This protocol is used to transfer files of any type, however, they are often html, gif, or jpeg.

In order to monitor the comportment of a user, server administrators will use the features of both TCP/IP and HTTP.[126] Since a connection has been built between

---

[125] *"A client is a computer system that accesses a (remote) service on another computer by some kind of network"*: http://en.wikipedia.org/wiki/Client_%28computing%29.

[126] See *Web Security, Privacy & Commerce*, where Garfinkel and Spafford (2002) give more details about security and privacy.

the client and the server, the server knows the IP address of the client. Using a *reverse DNS* called nslookup, it can also access the name of the computer (e.g., pinguin.bfh.ch), the country in which it is located and which ISP has been used.

The next level to be monitored is the exchange of information taking place in the HTTP connection. The browser has to send a description of itself to the server. It sends its operating system (e.g., Windows XP, Windows 2000 or MacOS X), its name and version (e.g, Microsoft Internet Explorer 6). It also sends the preferred language of the person using this computer. These features can be used by the server to send the right information to the visitor. The page, for example, could appear directly in the users native language.

Another type of monitoring is done using a *session*. A session corresponds to one visit from a user to a web site. HTTP does not offer direct support for a session. It is therefore said to be *session-less*. This means that once the client has received the requested page the connection is broken. Therefore, unlike FTP (File Transfer Protocol), it is not possible to know whether two requests have been sent by the same person. This can be problematic since such information is needed to login to a restricted area, hold goods in a shopping cart and for virtually any type of web application. The protocol gives the server the possibility to send a small piece of information to the client that the client will always send back. This information is called a cookie. A cookie is sent once by the server and the client includes the information in the cookie in any request it sends to the server as long as the cookie is still valid. Cookies were designed to store preferences of users in their browsers. They are nevertheless not used for this purpose anymore but rather to store the session IDs that identify each session. For the duration of the session, the client includes its identifier in each request. "I am client number 12345678754321". The server can then store in a database all the properties of this user (e.g., his access privileges, his username, the contents of his shopping cart etc.).[127]

Cookies are not only storable for a session but can also be stored for long-term usage. Some cookies have a validity of 30 years. They are used for monitoring the visits of a user over a long period of time. The user just has to be identified once and the server can build a complete profile of this user even if the user is not aware of having given any personal information months ago.

For security reasons, it is not possible for a web site to set cookies for another web site. So user IDs are web site specific. It is nevertheless sometimes useful to merge information coming from various web sites. This information is used for banner advertising or for profiling users on a larger scale. Web site administrators had to find a trick to be able to do this. To accomplish this task they inserted the same image provided by a third *(spy)-server* on each of the monitored web sites. This image can contain enough information to link all the users in the different sites. The sort of profile that could be created from this link is: "50% of Amazon clients are also Google users." But it can also be much more precise in user profiling.

---

[127] Cp. *PHP and MySQL Web Development* by Welling and Thomson for an implementation of these principles in PHP.

For example: "Mr Hans Muster living in Biel Switzerland (information gathered from the bookshop where he ordered a dictionary) is gay (since he regularly visits a gay web site) and travels to Bern each week (known from his account at the railway company e-shop)." We can see that one system designed with a harmless goal can also be misused.

HTTP is transferred as clear text over the Internet. This means that any information can be monitored by anybody listening to the connection. This includes the employer, the ISP (Internet Service Provider), or any hacker. They could listen to any communication concerning one particular machine. They can track all the information this machine sends to any web site (including cookies) and extract a very large amount of information from these data. The secure protocol used for encrypted transfer is known as HTTPS (for secure HTTP). It is used for the exchange of sensitive data (such as a password). It prevents any unwanted third party (hacker) from listening to the data being transferred between the PC of the user and the server he visits. But this protocol requires much more bandwidth than normal HTTP and is therefore not extensively used.

9.3   Legitimate Uses of Profiling

The first use of web profiling is purely statistical, for example, to discover the way visitors arrived at the monitored site. This can be done using a field sent in any http request called *URL-Referrer*. This gives an administrator a list of URLs referring to pages on his site and also (more valuable), the list of the keywords used in search engines to access the site.

The next thing to be studied is the way people navigate a site. Site administrators track the way visitors surf from one page to another when just browsing and the way they act before buying. Such results can be used to improve the usability of a web site, change the layout and function of menus and adapt the content of the pages. Administrators can also see the effect of work done, for instance, if certain pages are visited, or if people quickly find the desired information. This information can be used to model one or more *user profiles* and find their properties (regarding navigation on the site or amount of money spent, for instance). Such profiling deals with a lot of data that needs to be represented. The underlying graph is high dimensional and sparse; its study relies on powerful statistical and algorithmic profiling (Hyung, 2005; Brij Mesand, Spiliopoulou, 2000; Guandong et al., 2005).

Most marketing specialists want to implement one-to-one marketing. This means targeting information and special offers towards each specific client. They want to provide agents, geared to the interests and preferences of users, by monitoring clients' behaviour (Godoy, Amandi, 2005; Hyung, 2005). In both of the previous cases, it was possible to work on anonymous data. For one-to-one marketing, however, nominative data is needed to be able to send one person a personalised offer. This can be done using cookies (as seen previously) but since some browsers block the cookies, another solution exists. The session ID is directly encoded in the URL of the resource or as a hidden field in the forms that are used within the session. On such web sites, users usually have accounts and log into the system. This is used to merge information concerning different visits. While visiting the site, the client could receive an advertisment for a given product or be informed that all clients having bought this book have also bought another. One can, for instance, try to model co-occurrences of patterns (users who bought book XY, also bought CD XZ), or categorise users (rich, poor, educated, etc.) using clustering.

It is often useful to have the possibility to cross information coming from different web sites. For instance, people paying for a banner on a web site want to know the exact number of clients who clicked on this banner. They want to determine if these users were customers or only visitors. They want to know which advertisement is the best and compare the *quality* of customers coming from one site or from another. The amount of information required for such statistics is huge and could be used for purposes that users might not accept; if they only knew.

9.4 Privacy Threats and Counter Measures

The possible misuse of the information collected on web sites is multiform. It begins with reselling e-mail lists to *marketing specialists* (a.k.a. spammers) and ends by reselling all this information to a central database used for more potentially detrimental purposes, such as scoring people applying for insurance or credit. Collecting data, however, is often legitimate or even legally required (for e-commerce, for instance) but the misuse of information is an existing risk that should not be underestimated.

In Europe, reselling personal data without the consent of the provider is often forbidden[128] but it may be legal in other parts of the world. If a firm has collected a large set of information, we can expect this information to be sold to a company aggregating data. If the data was not released then shareholders would complain, since this would be a misuse of the resources of the enterprise. It can only be the role of a state (or of the European Union) to protect the customers from such attacks, since firms themselves do not have any direct interest in protecting privacy.

The aspiration to privacy is fundamental in a democracy.[129] There already exists many possibilities for users to protect the secrets of their lives. The first method used to prevent the profiling of users was to prohibit the use of any cookies. Some browsers can be configured such that they never send any cookies. This works well but is not that efficient, since sessions can be emulated by other means. Some servers can insert the session identifier (session ID) at the end of the address of all the

---

[128] Cp. The European Data Protection Directive D 95/46/EC, extensively discussed in part III.

[129] Cp. the discussions in part III of this volume.

links of all the pages they send. This number is not a cookie but since it is part of the address, it is sent to the server each time the user wants a new page.[130]

IP addresses can easily be changed. The only IP known by the server is the one of the machine sending the final request. But the HTTP protocol authorises the use of *proxies*, which are machines serving as buffers and/or filters for a lot of computers. Such machines can also be used remotely. This means that a user in France can pretend to be in Germany but the ISP or employer can still monitor the traffic of the person, since it often supplies the proxy service. It is possible to use a string of proxies, starting on the local machine with a small encrypting proxy and ending anywhere. This is called a MIX. This gives the possibility for the user to send any request and to obtain any response encrypted. Since many people can use the same MIX, it is not possible to use this IP address to monitor a specific user. Some web sites prefer to deny access to people coming from known MIXes, in order to prevent anonymous access.

The W3 Consortium[131] defined a set of standards for web site administrators to describe their site policy concerning data protection. This is known as the Platform for Privacy Preferences (P3P). A web site can describe its privacy policy in a way that a browser can understand. It is a great improvement. Before P3P, each user had to browse the site in order to find a human readable policy but most users never did this. The W3C provides a solution for a machine to automatically compare the privacy preferences of the user and the ones of the server. If there is an incompatibility, the user either receives a warning or is not allowed to access the site. Such a solution relies on the goodwill of the web site administrators. There is no way in the P3P to verify that the site does what it pretends to do. For instance, if a site holds information for delivering a good, there is no way to prevent someone (or even the firm itself) from selling the collected data to another company.

9.5   Conclusion

Profiling web users is vital for most web sites. Administrators use profiling to improve the quality of sites, verify the efficiency of advertisements and to offer better services to identified users. But the amount of information collected without the consent (and even the knowledge) of the users is very large. The possibilities for misuse are extreme. Privacy enhancing technologies exist but they are nevertheless not used because the understanding of the power of tracking technologies is very low among the general population. This knowledge gap is a risk for the entire information society. This society is mainly based on exchanges (of goods, money or information) but the basis for any exchange is trust. What would happen

---

[130] The session ID is sent in the URL for GET requests (links and small forms) and as a hidden field for POST requests (used mainly in large forms).

[131] The W3 Consortium (www.w3.org) is responsible for defining the standards of the World Wide Web. For instance, HTML, XML, CSS and XHTML have been standardised by it.

if a major player in the e-commerce industry was involved in a privacy fraud scandal?

States (or groups of states such as the European Union) have to provide rules and guidelines such that privacy can remain protected. The industry itself also has to find regulations to prevent harmful activities and to allow the sites respecting customers to be recognised.

9.6 Reply: Web Usage Mining for Web Personalisation in Customer Relation Management

Els Soenens*[132]

Web personalisation based on web (usage) mining for Customer Relation Management is gaining in popularity. However, appraisals of these profiling practices are often contradictory. Some welcome personalisation while others oppose to it. At the end, both privacy and autonomy of consumers should be respected in order to strengthen the relationship between consumers and companies. How can this be done? Do Privacy Enhancing Technologies and P3P offer enough protection? In this reply it is argued that we have to move one step further and look at the possibility of opening up the databases and disclosing the profiles they contain; in this way, consumers will be able to co-construct their own 'digital consumer identities', which are currently in the hands of the owners of database technologies. This way out is perceived to be suitable next to those of the PET and P3P solutions and comes close to the fruitful 'principle of minimum data asymmetry' of X. Jiang.

9.6.1   Introduction

In the first part of this chapter, Benoist concluded with the question 'what would happen if a major player in the e-commerce industry was involved in a privacy fraud scandal?'. Whether or not customers trust companies, such scandals are indeed not unthinkable in the domain of personalisation. Web personalisation, which is based on web usage mining, implies that a lot of data is being collected which may be misused without the customers' consent. However, personalisation based on web usage mining has become a profitable tool in Customer Relationship Management and it has been welcomed by many consumers.[133] This reply does not want to discard the

---

* Law Science and Technology Studies (LSTS), Vrije Universiteit Brussel (VUB)

---

[132] English review by Dionisis Demetis (London School of Economics).

[133] A lot of consumers like personalisation because of the fact that they are *automatically* offered services and products suitable to their needs. In fact, the research of Treiblmaier et al. (2004) found that in the group of people who were classified as 'data sensitive users' 21% of them still valued personalisation. For the group of people classified as 'rather data insensitive users', this percentage increased to 72.

advantages of personalisation for companies and customers alike but it will aim to find ways for safeguarding a citizen's dignity, autonomy and privacy.

This reply is organised as follows. Firstly, personalisation and web usage mining are shortly presented. Secondly, Privacy Enhancing Technologies (PET's) and the Platform for Privacy Preferences (P3P) are discussed as suitable safeguards in consumer protection. Thirdly, inspired by the principle of minimum information asymmetry, we look for solutions that can work alongside those provided by Privacy Enhancing Technologies and P3P.

9.6.2   Web Personalisation and Web Usage Mining

'In a metaphorical sense, the consumer's soul is being captured in a matrix of data while his/her body and mind are being pampered by technologies of seemingly obsequious personalisation.' (Dholakia and Zwick, 2001: 2)

Web Personalisation

'Web personalisation can be described as any action that makes the web experience of a user personalised to the user's taste' (Mobasher et al., 2000: 141). The profile of a user's taste is not only based on personal data.[134] One can distinguish several types of information that can be used to construct a profile of a user's taste.[135] As indicated by van der Hof and Prins in this volume, Crossley, Kings and Scott (2004: 100) distinguish 'declared information, inferred information and behavioural information'. We can relate the distinction to the difference Treiblmaier et al. (2004) make between personalisation and customisation. According to Treiblmaier et al. (2004: 2), 'customisation requires users to explicitly control the adaptation process' whereas personalisation based on web usage mining is driven by the secondary (mis-)use of traces that people leave behind while surfing on the Internet. Seen from the clients' perspective, customisation is a far more active process than personalisation because at least part of the information has been 'actively declared'. Personalisation, on the other hand, can occur without the consent or even the awareness

---

[134] Personal data is understood in its legal meaning as defined by the Directive 95/46/EC concerning the protection of individuals regarding the processing of personal data and free movement, art. 2 sub a: 'personal data' shall mean any information relating to an identified or identifiable natural person ('data subject'); an identifiable person is one who can be identified, directly or indirectly, in particular by reference to an identification number or to one or more factors specific to his physical, physiological, mental, economic, cultural or social identity.

[135] A relational description of data, information and knowledge (in relation to profiling) is given by Hildebrandt (2006, 548 - 552): 'one could say that a profile is knowledge to the extent that it turns data into information, allowing one to discriminate between relevant and irrelevant data (in a specific context).'

of citizens. Personalisation based on web usage mining is primarily derived from 'behavioural information'.[136] Authors such as Won (2002: 31) argue that the term 'impersonal personalisation' would suit the practice even better.[137]

Web usage mining

The automatic and real-time adjustment of web services and products is done by a recommender engine, presenting the online part of personalisation based on web usage mining (Mobasher et al., 2000). Normally, web usage mining also contains an offline process in which the essential data preparation and mining stages are performed.

Web usage mining is a special case of web mining in that it uses 'data that describes the pattern of usage of web pages, such as IP addresses, page references and the data and time of accesses' as input for the mining stage (Srivastava et al., 2000: 13). For an elaborated technical description of personalisation based on web usage mining we refer to Mobasher et al. (2000), since a technical understanding of web usage mining is not the objective of this reply. Recently, Privacy Preserving Data Mining (PPDM) techniques have been developed.[138] PPDM algorithms focus on the protection of sensitive data and/or sensitive knowledge while still allowing the mining of useful patterns from databases.[139] However, even when using PPDM, web usage mining makes it easy to personalise websites and services without the awareness of people. That is where the shoe pinches.

In this reply we do not reject personalisation per se. However, we do propose ways to enhance the privacy and autonomy of citizens that are subject to personalisation.[140] In the next section, we take a deeper look into the instruments that concentrate on the protection of (informational) privacy.

---

[136] 'Behavioural information is information passively recorded through user logins, cookies and / or server logs': Crossly, Kings and Scott (2004: 100). See Chapter 6 of this volume, section 6.2 'Setting the Stage: Personalisation and Profiling'.

[137] Actually, personalisation uses all types of information to construct consumer profiles. Won (2002:31) speaks of impersonal personalisation because (web) personalisation (also) relies on 'inferred information'. According to Crossly, Kings and Scott (2004, 100) inferred information is 'information indirectly associated with users, such as by identifying similar interests'. In the light of group profiling, it could be argued that personalisation is not really personal.

[138] For an overview of PPDM algorithms, see: Bertino, Nai, Parasiliti (2005: 121-154) and Oliveira, Zaiane, (2004: 7 – 17). See also Meints, M., section 4.8 in this volume.

[139] Sensitive data includes for example, personal data, identifiers, names, addresses, medical and census records. Sensitive knowledge, in the area of PPDM, is knowledge about sensitive activities or characteristics of categories of people. See also the difference Oliveira and Zaiane (2004: 9) make between 'individual and collective privacy preservation'. However, it can not always be known in advance whether or not the KDD process will produce sensitive or non-sensitive knowledge.

[140] We follow the definition Agre and Rotenberg (2001:7) who state that privacy is 'the freedom from unreasonable constraints on the construction of one's own identity'.

9.6.3   (Informational) Privacy Safeguards: PETs, P3P and Anonymizer.com

Consumers play an important role in safeguarding informational privacy when they surf the web. For example, both privacy enhancing technologies (PET's) and the Platform for Privacy Preferences (P3P) place the burden on the citizens' side. As explained by Benoist (this chapter), PET's and P3P are already available to protect one's privacy while surfing the Internet. However, authors such as Coyle (1999) and Clarke (2001) criticise P3P because they believe that this privacy protocol does little to really protect privacy.[141] Roger Clarke (2001) even calls it a 'Pseudo-PET'. The Electronic Privacy Information Centre (EPIC, 2000) arrives at conclusions similar to those of Coyle and Clarke in their report 'Pretty Poor Privacy: An Assessment of P3P and Internet Privacy'.

Vis-à-vis the technical safeguards, anonymisers can be useful to protect one's privacy, because anonymity hinders the disclosure of personal identifiable information. However, this does not mean that anonymous data cannot be 'triangulated'[142], creating the possibility of identification (Berendt et al., 2002). Furthermore, while using a trusted third party such as anonymizer.com, we have to take into account the abilities of the party that wants to perform personalising. In particular, the situation depends on the capacity to analyse traffic via anonymiser.com at the point of entry and exit respectively. When a person interested in performing personalisation has this power, the source and destination of the communication could be linked. However, in the (typical) case that only the user side of the traffic can be verified, the request coming from anonymizer.com is the only action seen.

The anonymiser administrator is trusted not to reveal the links between the source and destination of the communications but in the event that the web site administrator has (exceptional) powerful capacities to analyse the input and output traffic of the anonymiser, there is no reason to trust the web site administrator. Furthermore, if more people are using anonymizer.com and no differentiation can be made regarding the identity of different users, then the web site administrator will perceive only one 'personality'. As a result, the constructed profile of the 'aggregated' user will be applied to all these 'undifferentiated' users. In this case,

---

[141] P3P was thought to accomplish users' privacy preferences while surfing the World Wide Web. However, P3P especially seems to push the exchange of personal data and little to no garantuees vis-à-vis minimum obligations of web providers to accomplish that the users' privacy preferences are built in. Fundamentally, privacy has rather gained the status of a exchange product between consumers and web producers rather than a human right. See for instance: 'P3P is nothing more than a 'privacy policy declaration' standard. That's a mere fraction of what it was meant to be and of what the situation demands.': Clarke (2001). See Clarke (2001), Coyle (1999) and EPIC (2000) for more arguments against P3P.

[142] 'Triangulation is the combination of aggregated information and anonymised information to identify and reveal particular characteristics of an individual': Berendt, Mobasher and Spiliopoulou (2002).

the constructed profile does not enable correct personalisation, which can be disadvantageous for both the profilers and the customers.[143]

Legal safeguards to privacy are discussed elsewhere in detail (see chapters 13, 14 and 15 of this volume). It is nevertheless interesting to stress that the European Data Protection Directive puts consumers in an ironic situation. Technically speaking, anonymity provides a safeguard to the privacy of citizens. However, legally speaking anonymisation of data thwarts the applicability of the European Data Protection Directive (95/46/EC) (see chapter 13). Thus, it does not seem odd to look at the advantages of being identifiable. Authors such as Schreuders et al. (2005) argue that from the moment a group profile – a profile which need not be derived from anonymised personal data - is applied to an identifiable person, we can speak of the processing of personal data. This argumentation implies that the protection of the directive is applicable when group profiles are applied to identified or identifiable persons. In addition every person, whether or not identifiable, can appeal to article 15 (1) of the Directive to object to the application of group profiles if these profiles are exclusively based on automated decision making.[144] The danger in the case of web personalisation based on web usage mining is that as a matter of course people simply do not know if certain profiles are being applied to them.

The safeguards proposed so far mainly concentrate on informational privacy. Consumers can enhance the protection of their personal data on the Internet; however web personalisation establishes some serious consequences that go well beyond the level of (informational) privacy. This reply argues that personalisation, based on web usage mining, has the potential to affect not only the privacy but also the autonomy and identity building of people.[145] Akin, Cuijpers et al. (this volume) state that the 'core privacy challenge of personalisation lies in (…) the implications for the way our lives are typified and our identities constructed'.[146]

---

[143] Muchas gracias a Claudia Diaz (KULeuven – COSIC, FIDIS) por la explicación. Note that the interpretation is on my account. If you are interested in the topic, it is suggested to read Claudia Diaz' PhD Thesis 'Anonymity and Privacy in Electronic Services.' (KULeuven 2005). The thesis is available at: http://homes.esat.kuleuven.be/~cdiaz/papers/Thesis-cdiaz-final.pdf.

[144] Art 15 (1) of the Data Protection Directive (D 95/46/EC) states that 'member states shall grant the right to every person not to be subject to a decision which produces legal effects concerning him or significantly affects him and which is based solely on automated processing of data intended to evaluate certain personal aspects relating to him, such as his performance at work, creditworthiness, reliability, conduct, etc.'.

[145] The relation between privacy, autonomy and identity building is visible in the definition of privacy by Agre and Rotenberg (2001). See Hildebrandt for an elaborate discussion of this relation in chapter 15.2.4 of this volume.

[146] The potential threats of personalisation to the identity of persons have been clearly described in chapter 6 of this volume. The authors also discuss other potential consequences of personalisation as 'price discrimination' and threats 'to the freedoms (of speech, of consuming, of conscience, sic.) and societal interests' (as cultural and political diversity, sic.).

9.6.4   In Defence of Autonomous Identity Building for Consumers: The Principle of Minimal Data Asymmetry

The use of database technologies and profiling enables marketers to take control over the construction of citizens' consumer selves (Zwick and Dholakia, 2004; Poster, 1995; Plant, 1997).[147] Consequently, web usage based personalisation challenges not only the privacy but also the identity building of citizens. This becomes even clearer if we realise that personalisation is about categorising consumers. Categorising people based on digitally constructed consumer selves that are 'formulated, stored and exchanged well outside the sovereignty of the physical consumer' (Dholakia, Zwick, 2005:8), can easily limit the freedom of choice and the autonomy of citizens.[148] Essentially PET's and P3P are not able to sort out these limitations of choice and autonomy for citizens because PET's and P3P hardly change the level of control over *database technologies* (Zwick and Dholakia, 2004).[149] Therefore the question remains – how can citizens influence their digitally constructed selves according to the view they have of themselves (especially regarding the pattern with which they consume)?

A possible way could be found in the principle of minimum information asymmetry formulated by Jiang (2002). Jiang (2002:10) proposes 'to minimise the information asymmetry between data owners[150] and the data controllers'. His statement suggests actions in two directions: it urges to decrease 'the flow of information from data owners to data collectors and users' while simultaneously 'increasing the flow of information from data collectors and users back to data owners' (Jiang, 2002: 4). Whereas the first action could be done by PET's and anonymisers, the second action can be realised by allowing consumers to '*access and alter the code and content of the database*', as Zwick and Dholakia (2004) suggest. In other words, the idea of opening up the databases directly to the citizens combined with the use of PETs and P3P, could bring about the fulfilment of the principle of minimum information asymmetry.

So far, several companies have made efforts to provide the opportunity to look into the applied profiles and to alter the information according to which customers were categorised. One of these companies is Amazon.com, which uses not less than '23 independent applications of personalisation' on their website (Cranor, 2003).[151] Amazon's 'browsing history' function remembers the searches of people even if they are not

---

[147] Zwick and Dholakia (2004), Poster (1995) and Plant (1997) clearly explain this by using post-structuralist insights.

[148] See van der Hof en Prins (chapter 6 of this volume) where they state 'personalisation, however, provides a new dimension in that it may force individuals into restraining one–dimensional models, based on criteria set by technology and of those who own and apply the technology'.

[149] Note that, 'even the most trivial recorded details have great value': Berry and Linoff (2000).

[150] In theory, the consumers are the data owners of their (personal) data. However, database technologies extract a lot of (personal) data from consumers – often in invisible (and subtle) ways. With the help of personalisation applications, the marketeers and database owners obtain more control over the construction of the consumer selves.

[151] Cranor refers to Riedl (2001: 29-31).

signed in and this browsing history function is not necessary limited to one surfing session. However, it is possible to block the browsing history function or to delete certain items from 'your browsing history'. Since Amazon.com has decided to open up the databases (at least partly) and to enable (registered) customers to change the profiles applied on them, a 'strong link' is created between the consumers and Amazon's profiling applications (Zwick and Dholakia, 2004).[152] As such, consumers may experience increased control and power over their representations in the database.[153]

Personalisation can work well but as stated in chapter 6 of this volume, transparency and quality are essential aspects of good personalised services. Transparency in personalisation services could be perceived as annoying by some companies. However, when performed fairly, the practice of opening up database profiles to customers seems to provide a real win-win situation for both consumers and online firms (Zwick and Dholakia, 2004).

9.6.5   Conclusion

In this reply we have elaborated the distinction between customisation and personalisation as a consequence of web usage mining. Customisation refers to personalised services based on profiles explicitly controlled by web users, while personalisation refers to personalised services based on data mining without the consent or even awareness of the web user. Utilitarian thinkers may value web personalisation because of its economical merits. Indeed, personalisation does have advantages for e–commerce companies and customers.[154] However, if one takes a deontological point of view, the *act* of secondary use of web log data in order to personalise without explicit consent, can never be perceived as ethically justified (Treiblmaier et al., 2004: 8).[155] Moving away from this black-and-white picture, this

---

[152] A 'strong link' relates for example to the question 'Why was I recommended this?' and the option customers have to indicate 'Not interested'. In contrast to a 'weak link' which is a mere 'sign-in process' that allows multiple consumer identities per person but *does not* enable changing the profiles applied on the surfer: Zwick and Dholakia (2004: 26).

[153] We are not blind to the criticisms of Amazon.com. Amazon.com has been criticised for not being straightforward when it comes to their privacy policy. It has been stated that Amazon.com uses its subsidiary company Alexa to collect personal information on customers: see EPIC Digest (2001). Also, Amazon.com does not make it possible to look into and change *all* gathered information. There is a difference in providing the opportunity to change 'your' profile and providing access to all gathered (personal and non personal) information!

[154] See also van der Hof and Prins, section 6.3.3 of this volume: 'Inclusion and exclusion, however, do not necessarily have to be perceived as bad. Inclusion or exclusion may be considered economically useful, because it will do a better job of getting the right information and services to the right persons'.

[155] According to the deontological point of view, customisation (as understood by Treiblmaier et al.) could be performed without ethical concerns, because it needs the explicit control of users in the adaptation process: Treiblmaier et al., 2004.

reply concentrates on ways *how to* enhance the protection of citizens' privacy and thus of their consumer autonomy and identity in cases of web personalisation through web usage mining. We argue that those who own database technologies now have (massive) control over citizens' consumer behaviour and identity building. As a result, consumer safeguards should not be limited to the protection of informational privacy. Actually, this reply stipulates that privacy must be understood in its relation to identity building.

Following Jiang's principle of minimum information asymmetry, we have looked for ways to establish more symmetry in the relation between customers and database owners. We believe that the combined efforts of consumers and companies are needed. On the one hand, consumers must make use of the existing solutions, offered by the Platform of Privacy Preferences and Privacy Enhancing Technologies, to protect their personal data. On the other hand, consumers should be given possibilities in order to not to be treated as passive subjects of web personalisation.[156] To turn consumers into more active and controlling partners, companies should firstly stress if and which personalisation applications are being performed upon (potential) customers. Secondly, once the personalisation applications are known, the consumers should be entitled, not only with a right to avoid being the target of automatic group profiling, but - presuming personalisation is not necessary bad - consumers should also be given a right to change the profiles that are (and could be) applied to them.

We believe that the actions proposed can enhance the autonomy and control of citizens over their digital consumer selves. In a sense, 'controlled personalisation' comes close to what Treiblmaier et al. (2004) understand as 'customisation'. Still, our suggestions will not create a *deus ex machina* to all risks of personalisation.

9.7   Bibliography

Agre, P. E., Rotenberg, M, *Technology and Privacy: The New Landscape*, MIT, Cambridge, Massachusetts, 2001.

Berendt B., Mobasher, B. and Spiliopoulou, M., 'Web Usage Mining for E-Business Applications', *ECML/PKDD-2002 Tutorial 'Text Mining and Internet Content Filtering'*, Helsinki, 19 August 2002.

Berry, M.J.A. and Linoff, G., *Mastering data mining: the art and science of customer relationship management*, Wiley, New York, 2000.

Bertino, E., Nai F., I., Parasiliti P. L., 'A framework for evaluating privacy preserving data mining algorithms', *Data Mining and Knowledge Discovery*, Vol. 2, No. 11, Springer publ., New York, 2005, pp. 121-154.

---

[156] In chapter 15 of this volume, the authors, Gutwirth and De Hert, refer to the Foucaultian concept 'resistance'. They explain that 'resistance' is essential for balances of power *and* for personal freedom. We believe 'restistance' is therefore also important in web personalisation based on web usage mining.

Clarke, R., 'P3P Re-visited', 2001. Available at: http://www.anu.edu.au/people/Roger.Clarke/DV/P3PRev.html

Cranor, L.F., ' 'I Didn't Buy it for Myself'. Privacy and E-commerce Personalization', *Proceedings of the 2003 ACM Workshop on Privacy in the Electronic Society*, ACM Press, Washington DC, 2003, pp. 111- 117.

Coyle, K., 'P3P, Pretty Poor Privacy? A social analysis of the platform for privacy preferences P3P'. Available at: www.kcoyle.net/p3p.html

Dholakia, N., Zwick, D., 'Privacy and consumer agency in the information age: between prying profilers and preening webcams', *Journal of Research for Consumers*, Vol. 1, No.1, online journal sponsored by UWA business school and the graduate school of Management. Available at: http://web.biz.uwa.edu.au/research/jrconsumers/academic/academic_article.asp?IssueID=9&ArticleID=3

EPIC, 'Pretty Poor Privacy: An Assessment of P3P and Internet Privacy', June 2000. Available at http://www.epic.org/reports/prettypoorprivacy.html

EPIC Digest 06/05/2001. Available at http://www.privacy.org/digest/epic-digest06.05.01.html

Jiang, X., 'Safeguard Privacy in Ubiquitous Computing with Decentralized Information Spaces: Bridging the Technical and the Social', paper presented at '*Privacy in Ubicomp*', *Workshop on socially informed design of privacy-enhancing solutions in ubiquitous computing*, Sweden, September 29, 2002. Available at: http://guir.berkeley.edu/pubs/ubicomp2002/privacyworkshop/papers/jiang-privacyworkshop.pdf

Garfinkel, S. and Spafford, G., *Web Security, Privacy & Commerce*. O'Reilly, second edition, 2002.

Godoy, D., Amandi, A., 'User profiling for web page filtering', *IEEE Internet Computing*, Vol. 9, No. 4, IEEE Computer Society, Wash. DC, 2005, pp 56-64.

Hyung, Joon Kook, 'Profiling multiple domains of user interests and using them for personalized web support', *Lecture notes in computer science*, Vol. 3645, Advances in Intelligent Computing, International Conference on Intelligent Computing, ICIC Hefei, China, August 23-26, 2005, Proceedings, Part II, Springer, Berlin - Heidelberg, 2005, pp. 512-520.

Hildebrandt, M., 'Profiling: From Data to Knowledge, The challenges of a crucial technology', *DuD, Datenschutz und Datensicherheit*, Vol. 30, No. 9, Vieweg-Verlag, Wiesbaden, 2006, pp. 548-552.

Masand, B., Spiliopoulou, M. (eds), 'Web usage analysis and user profiling', *international WEBKDD'99 workshop*, San Diego, CA, USA, August 15, 1999; revised papers, Lecture Notes of Computer Science, LNAI, Vol. 1836, Springer, Berlin-Heidelberg, 2000.

Mobasher, B., Cooley, R., Srivastava, J., 'Automatic Personalization Based on Web Usage Mining', *Communications of the ACM*, Vol. 43, No. 8, ACM Press, New York, 2000, pp. 141-151.

Oliveira, S.R.M. and Zaiane, O.R., 'Toward standardization in privacy preserving data mining', *Proceedings of the ACM SIGKDD 3rd Workshop on Data Mining Standards*, 2004, pp. 7–17. Available at: http://www.cs.ualberta.ca/ zaiane/postscript/dm-ssp04.pdf

Plant, S., *Zeros + Ones: Digital Women + The New Technoculture*, Doubleday, New York, first edition, 1997.

Poster, M., *The Second Media Age*. Cambridge Polity Press, Cambridge, 1995.

Riedl, 'Personalization and Privacy', *IEEE Internet Computing*, Vol. 5, No. 6, IEEE Computer Society, Washington D.C., 2001, pp. 29-31.

Schreuders, E., *Data mining, de toetsing van beslisregels en privacy (Data mining examining decision rules and privacy)*, ITeR, No. 48, Sdu Pu, Den Haag, 2005.

Srivastava, J., Cooley, R., Deshpande, M., Tan, P-N., 'Web Usage Mining: Discovery and Applications of Usage Patterns from Web Data', ACM *SIGKDD Explorations*, Vol. 1, No. 2, ACM Press, New York, 2000, pp. 12-23.

Treiblmaier, H., Madlberger, M, Knotzer, N., Pollach, I., 'Evaluating Personalization and Customization from an Ethical point of View: an empirical study', *Proceedings of the 37th Hawaii International Conference on System Science*, Big Island, HI, USA. IEEE Computer Society, 2004.

Vriens, M., Grigsby, M. 'Building Online Customer-Brand Relationships', *Marketing Management*, Vol. 10, No. 4, American Marketing Association publications, Chicago, 2001, pp. 34-39.

Welling, L., Thomson, L., *PHP and MySQL Web Development*. Sams, Indianapolis, Indiana, March 2001.

Won, K., 'Personalization: Definition, Status and challenges ahead', *Journal of Object Technology*, Vol. 1, No. 1, Chair of software engineering at EHZ Zurich, 2002, pp. 29 – 40. Available at www.jot.fm/issues/issue_2002_05/column3

Xu, G., et al., 'Towards user profiling for web recommendation', *Australian Conference on Artificial Intelligence*, Proceedings. Lecture Notes in Computer Science, Vol. 3809, Springer, Berlin - Heidelberg, 2005, pp. 415-424.

Zwick, D., Dholakia, N., 'Whose Identity is it anyway. Consumer representation in the age of database marketing', *Journal of Macromarketing*, Vol. 24, No. 1, Sage Publications, New York, London, Delhi, 2004, pp. 31– 43.

Chapter 10
User Profiling for Attention Support at School and Work

Thierry Nabeth

Advances in technologies, with the design of personalised systems, have opened the possibility to use profiling not only as a tool of surveillance but also as a way to better support people in their learning and working activities. This chapter proposes to illustrate this perspective of profiling for providing user attentional support within the domains of education and work.

10.1 Introduction

Attention appears to represent one of the key factors for learning or working performance. The most effective learners and knowledge workers are not necessarily the most intelligent or the brightest ones but are the most effective at filtering and selecting the most relevant information and at allocating their cognitive resources. This ability to manage attention efficiently is even more critical in the context of new methods of learning and working within the Information Society. In this context, learners and knowledge workers have access to a huge amount of information and are more on their own (or autonomous) in defining and organising their work or their learning. As a consequence, they are more exposed to an information flood and to solicitation, they are subject to cognitive overload (having to perform too many things at the same time) and they are more at risk of procrastination or to engage into activities that are very ineffective.

One of the solutions that can be proposed to address this "attention" challenge resides in the design of ICT systems that are aware of the attentional dimension and are able to support the individuals or the groups with filtering and selecting the most relevant information and helping them allocate, in the short or in the long term, their cognitive resources. However, the realisation of such "attention informed systems" relies to a large extent on the ability to profile the users, for instance determining the user's current level of attention or how these users have allocated their past efforts. We will see in this chapter that profiling for supporting attention

Institut Européen D'Administration Des Affaires (INSEAD), CALT

M. Hildebrandt and S. Gutwirth (eds.), *Profiling the European Citizen: Cross-Disciplinary Perspectives.*
© Springer Science + Business Media B.V. 2008

consists both in the behavioural biometric profiling of the user's activities (see chapter 5 for an in-depth presentation of this concept) and the profiling consisting in the exploitation of the digital traces that people leave in the log files of information systems when they are interacting with these systems.

The objective of this chapter is to help understand the profiling issues by examining the contexts of the support of attention in schools and in virtual communities.

The first part of this chapter presents the concept of attention for learning and for work and indicates which different approaches and mechanisms can be used to support and manage attention. In the second part of this paper, we analyse how profiling intervenes in the design of systems that are able to provide some attention support to the users. We also briefly examine the issues (such as the limitations and risks) relating to the profiling of users. In the next part of this chapter, we present AtGentive, a research project aimed at designing systems to support attention in the domains of education and work. We finally conclude by summarising our findings and indicate new directions of work and expected future use of personal profiling to enable the design of advanced (personalised) applications in order to better support the human and group cognitive processes.

10.2   Attention in the Context of Learning and Work

"We live in an age of information overload, where attention has become the most valuable business currency" (Davenport, T.H. and Beck J.C., 2001)

10.2.1   What is Attention?

Attention is a concept that has been extensively explored in the discipline of psychology and relates to the state of allocation of cognitive resources on a subject. Attention is connected to several cognitive concepts such as perception, arousal, memory and action. In order to be attentive, a person has to be in a state (that can be conscious or unconscious) of sensing the environment, of processing or of memorising signals and reacting upon them if necessary.

Attention can be associated with a set of processes that enable and guide the selection of incoming perceptual information in order to limit the external stimuli processed by our bounded cognitive system and to avoid overloading it (Chun and Wolfe 2001). Attention can either be conscious and controlled voluntarily by the subject or be unconscious and driven by stimuli. In the first case, attention can be associated with the allocation of the "conscious" brain and corresponds generally to an intellectual activity in which the person is currently engaged (such as having a conversation, writing a report or executing a task requiring some concentration by the subject). In the latter case, attention is related to a set of "pre-attentive" processes, receptive to different stimuli and reacting automatically (e.g., in sudden luminance changes, some stimuli are impossible to ignore). These two categories of attention are however not totally independent but interact constantly. For instance "conscious" attention may be able to control the pre-attention when forcing the focus on searching a particular item.

The concept of attention has also been studied in disciplines other than psychology such as Communication (Media study) and Management. In these disciplines, attention is usually considered at a higher level of abstraction, analysing the longer-term effects of cognitive resource allocation and on people's interaction. For instance, advertisers and TV producers are known to have acquired a real mastery of capturing and maintaining people's attention (Gladwell, 2000). In particular, one of the central elements in Communication is to ensure that people are 'listening' and remembering the messages that are broadcasted to them. In Management Sciences, Davenport and Beck (2001) define attention as a "focused mental engagement on a particular item of information" and can be considered both at the individual and at the organisational level (an organisation can also be attentive). Other areas of Management include the effective allocation of peoples time (and the infamous mythical person-month problems depicted in Brooks (1995)) but also the different strategies used to manage interruptions, the different human resource management tools used to align people's attention and the organisational attention (via incentives and appraisal systems) and the way to motivate people (an important means to have people allocate their attention).

10.2.2   Attention in the Knowledge Economy

The ability to efficiently manage attention has become one of the most critical elements for learning and working performances within the Information Society.

Indeed, in an online setting, learning approaches often rely on active, experimental, distributed and social learning models that are less linear than the traditional class-room-based learning ones. In this context, the learners are more on their own; they have less guidance and cannot situate themselves with others and adjust their behaviour accordingly. Even in the presence of strong commitment, optimal time allocation and the effectiveness of learning or collaborative processes are harder to evaluate. The learners also have fewer points of reference to situate themselves, do not receive any direct pressure from a tutor or from their peers and can more easily procrastinate, or engage in learning activities that are very ineffective.

In the case of work in the "knowledge economy", the situation is not different. Knowledge workers are engaged in a multitude of projects involving a variety of actors from different horizons (from different functions, cultural background) with whom they have to collaborate. They also have to process more information and solicitation than in the past, originating from a variety of sources and available in different forms (news, email, instant messaging, etc.). Finally, they are more autonomous and more responsible for their lines of actions. As a consequence, knowledge workers are more at risk to be overwhelmed by too much information and too many interruptions and also to manage inefficiently the execution of the many tasks they have to accomplish for their work (Davenport and Beck, 2001). At the organisational level, increased competition and pressure from the shareholders has augmented the effort expected from the employees: people are asked to do more with fewer resources and in less time.

At the same time, humans' cognitive capabilities have not radically changed. For instance, human beings still have the same memory retention of a short-term memory with a maximum capacity to manipulate 7 (+- 2) chunks of information at any given time (Miller, 1956). They also have the same very limited ability to effectively conduct several tasks at the same time and in particular, as Rubinstein, Meyer and Evans (2001) have demonstrated, they are very bad at switching from one task to another.

Technologically, if new tools have appeared to better support learning and work activities, they have so far been unable to fully counterbalance the new needs resulting from modern work and business environments. In some cases, technologies, by being at the origin of additional sources of distraction and interruption, have even aggravated the situation.

These new conditions have typically resulted in a situation of information and cognitive overload for the learners and for the knowledge workers and consequently in the need for new tools and new approaches to address this problem.

10.3   Supporting Attention in the Knowledge Economy

One of the solutions that can be proposed to address this "attention" challenge resides in the design of ICT systems to help users manage their attention more effectively. These systems can intervene by enhancing people's cognitive capabilities (such as the filtering processes we have described previously) but also by increasing the relevance of the interaction (via some personalisation) and by automating some of the learning and working tasks.

Practically, the support of attention in these systems can intervene at three levels:

(1) The discernment / perception level.
(2) The metacognitive (reasoning) level.
(3) The operational level.

10.3.1   Enhancing User's Perception (Watching Like a Hawk)

The first means to support the users' attention consists in enhancing their perception capabilities. Increasing perception means being able to augment the ability to spot relevant information and to discard irrelevant pieces from a huge mass of information.

Different approaches and mechanisms can be proposed to enhance users' perception and in particular to discriminate the "good information" from the noise. The first approach is related to the design and the presentation of information in a way that facilitates the comprehension of this information and therefore helps to reduce the cognitive overload. A variety of mechanisms can be proposed to facilitate the comprehensibility of the information. For instance, following the pioneering work of Anne Treisman on pre-attentive processing, attributes displayed by an information item, such as the form, colour, texture, size, location, order and motion (see (Healey, 2006) for a partial list of pre-attentive visual features), can contribute to increased conspicuity, i.e., the quasi-instantaneous understanding of the nature of an object by a simple glance. Artefacts, metaphors or visual tags (e.g., the symbol of a book or the picture of a person) have also been used for a long time to facilitate user's perception, by allowing them to manipulate higher level concepts. Indicators summarising the information (for instance a number reflecting the popularity of a document) can be used to provide a synthesis view of the information and help to reduce the perceived complexity of the world. This approach was formalised a long time ago by Bier, et al. (1993) via the concept of the MagicLens. This last approach has more recently been adapted to a social context with the term "social translucence" for ensuring the activity of a group is more visible (Erikson et al., 2002). Finally, personalisation can also be used to increase people's perception by presenting only the information that is the most relevant to a particular user (indeed, information that may be considered as good for one person may be considered as noise for another one and vice versa).

10.3.1.1 Profiling and Perception Support

Obviously, the provision of mechanisms enhancing the user's perception is very dependent on knowing this user and therefore on the profiling of this user and to some extent to the groups to which this user belongs. In particular, knowing the characteristics of this user such as interest, context of work, role within the organisation (or grade for the student) as well as his current working or learning states (is the user engaged in an activity that requires all his/her attention and thus should not be interrupted?). This information can be exploited in order to decide the relevance of an item to a user (the same information may be important to one user and meaningless to another). The user profile may also inform the system as to the best way to intervene, typically maximising the impact and reducing the distraction.

10.3.2 Providing Attention Metacognitive Support

The second way of supporting user's and group's attention consists in helping them to **better understand the way they are managing their attention** and in particular helping them to acquire a metacognitive understanding of how they are proceeding in managing their attention. Practically, the support for this level can consist in the provision of mechanisms that can help them to assess their current attention-related practices. Other mechanisms can consist in diagnostics tools helping the user to analyse their behaviour (is it attention effective?) and situate them (compare with others). Finally, metacognitive support can consist in guidance, helping them to improve their practice in a way that is more attention effective. More concretely, the mechanisms that can be proposed may include the display of the information related to the activities in which people are engaged (for instance how much time they have spent on these activities); some comparison of the activities with others and some guidance on how to improve their current attention-management practices.

10.3.2.1 Profiling and Metacognitive Support

As in the previous case, profiling, i.e., the observation of the users' actions, is critical for providing attention meta-cognitive support. This information about users' activities can be displayed as statistics visualising how they are allocating their attention. These data can also be exploited in order to elaborate a diagnostic related to the effectiveness of the users' attention allocation. For instance, this analysis may help to identify the less attention effective activities (low value activities consuming a lot of time), or provide an analysis of the way the users are interrupted when accomplishing their tasks. This analysis can also consist in providing the users some comparisons to help them situate their practices. Finally, this information, as well as users' information such as role and preferences, can be used to propose attentional guidance (for instance with suggestions of practices that could be attention effective for this user).

10.3.3 Providing Attention Operational Support

As indicated previously, people are very ineffective at working on too many things at the same time because of the limited human multitasking capabilities (people can think of only one thing at a time and as indicated by Rubinstein, Meyer and Evans (2001), switching from one task to another is costly).

The last category of support of attention consists therefore in providing operational support of the learning or working processes in a way that is effectively related to the allocation of attention with regard to many tasks to accomplish or of many interruptions to deal with. Examples of components and mechanisms providing operational attention support includes systems that help to organise the time or that help to manage interruption, such as an agenda. Other mechanisms providing operational support are related to the support of the management of interruptions. People (knowledge workers and students) are indeed frequently interrupted in their activities with the consequence that their concentration is broken, or requires them to switch their attention to other tasks (with the associated cost). Examples of mechanisms for managing interruption consist in better managing the flux of the interruption and in particular in filtering the irrelevant interruption, or in lessening the negative consequences of interruption by minimising distraction.

10.3.3.1 Profiling and Operational Support

Even in the case of the support of the working process, obtaining access to users' information appears to be important. For instance, an agenda may have to be aware of the interest or the availability of a person in order to determine whether to send a notification. Mechanisms for managing the interruption may also need to be aware of the state of the attention of the user in order to decide the most appropriate time to interrupt the user, as well as the more effective method to use (the most adequate mode of interruption may indeed vary, depending on the person). Profiling may also be useful to determine the context of the activity in which the user is engaged and his/her current role, so as to propose more relevant support to this user.

10.3.4 Profiling Issues

As we have seen in the previous sections, profiling the activities of the user appears to be one of the key elements for the design of Information Systems supporting user attention in the three dimensions (perception, metacognition and operation).

This profiling, nonetheless, raises a series of issues such as:

- The real possibility of capturing the user's data.
- The limitation related to the processing of these data and inferring something useful out of them.
- Privacy issues.

10.3.4.1 Biometric Profiling Issues

The capture of biometric behavioural data (see chapter 5 for a description of behavioural biometric) represents one of the most important challenges in the design of systems supporting user's attention. For instance, the access to psycho-physiological data that can be used to profile the attentional state may appear difficult to deploy and be too intrusive for the end-user. For example, the activity of the brain can be measured with several techniques. Probably the most feasible online measurement technique is electroencephalography (EEG). In EEG, brain activity is measured with electrodes placed on the scalp. EEG involves relatively small equipment and the electrodes can be applied on the subject with little restriction to the position and movements of the person (compared to, e.g., functional magnetic resonance imaging).

However, it is needless to say that such a measure can currently only be performed in a laboratory setting. Moreover, most psychophysiological measures can reflect a multitude of psychophysiological phenomena, including emotional arousal and cognitive activity (Coan and Allen, 2004), making the result not absolutely reliable. In a similar way, technologies used for tracking eye movements are even more cumbersome and costly and difficult to apply in a real situation. Finally, such data are very sensitive because they deal with physiological information that can be exploited in very different contexts, such as health (such information can reveal an illness), performance measure (for instance measuring intelligence) or privacy (similar instruments are used to detect liars). Definitely, the learner or the knowledge worker will think twice before adopting such systems. To summarise, even if the extraction of attentional information from psychophysiological signals appears promising, it still represents challenging tasks that are difficult to fulfil today. Firstly, the conditions it requires (intrusive hardware), secondly, the risks linked to the interpretation of these data and thirdly, it can raise several privacy issues for which we have little experience.

10.3.4.2 Digital Traces Issues

The digital traces that originate from the person's activities in digital environments represent another source of data that can be very relevant for profiling related to user's attention. It is also the source of data that can be the most likely exploited for the design of advanced ICT based systems. The capture of activity information (versus biometric information) does not appear to be as difficult to achieve, since this information is readily available, in particular, if one considers that these data are often already collected in different log files. Besides, with a general trend towards the adoption of concepts originating from the web 2.0 phenomenon, digital environments are increasingly exposing their data via the exportation of RSS feeds, or via the availability of APIs (Application Programming Interfaces) allowing external applications to connect to these platforms. For instance, it is easy to procure access to the feeds of the latest postings in a personal blog, the changes happening in a Wiki, the list of the latest items bookmarked by an individual using a social bookmarking service such as del.icio.us[157],the presence of an individual in an instant messaging service, the new events in a calendar service or to activities of a person in a social networking service such as Facebook.[158] In some cases, web 2.0 has even generated services such as 'Twitter'[159] which aims to allow people to record their activities with ease (using SMS, instant messaging, email, etc.) and to expose them to a group of other people (typically friends). The interpretation of

---

[157] Del.icio.us http://del.icio.us/

[158] Facebook http://www.facebook.com/

[159] Twitter http://twitter.com/

these digital traces also appears to be simpler than in the case of biometric data, even though it may also be subject to errors, since the systems are often aware of the context of the activity in which the user is engaged. Activity information can tell us a lot about the level of attention and commitment of a particular user. For instance, the observation of the number of connections to a system can help us to identify users that are less committed. The observation of the number of actions from the users that have connected can help us to determine if a user is actively engaged in an action or is inattentive. The determination of the level of contribution from a user (for instance how many postings or documents the user has posted) is an element that can represent a good indicator of commitment and therefore of attention. However, the effective analysis of these data may be difficult to achieve and may depend, in part, on the cognitive profile of the user. For instance, a person performing a lot of activities may indicate a person who is very dedicated to her work. It may also indicate an inexperienced person who is not very effective at learning or working. To summarise, the exploitation of a person's activities (peoples logging information) appears to be easier than the observation of the psychological information but may also face the barrier of human complexity. Besides, the observation of a person's information may also raise similar privacy issues, in particular if they are used not only to support the attentional process but also for the evaluation of the learner by educational institutions or for the appraisal of the knowledge worker by organisations. Finally, the multiplication of the sources of data originating from a variety of digital environments may raise the question of the difficulty for a user to keep track and to control the use of these data. These different traces may also be used for purposes that are totally different than the one that was originally intended, such as the screening of an individual applying for a position in an organisation. For instance, it is now common in the United States for recruiting companies to use the Internet as a means to conduct a background research on prospective employees.[160] Yet, we have observed in response to this situation the appearance of a certain number of answers such as the arrival of services proposing to individuals to identify and erase their digital traces.[161] More interestingly, it is useful to mention that these digital trace issues are not unknown and are explicitly being addressed by an initiative aimed at better controlling them. More specifically, AttentionTrust[162] is an initiative aimed at better controlling the digital traces (also referred to as attention meta-data) and in particular to guarantee that these data are only disclosed to legitimate services.

---

[160] For instance an article from the New York Times reported how the social networking sites have been used to disclose 'embarrassing' information leading to the rejection of job applications. Finder Alan (2006); For Some, Online Persona Undermines a Résumé; The New York Times US, June 11th, 2006. http://www.nytimes.com/2006/06/11/us/11recruit.html

[161] An example of a service for erasing the digital traces is Reputation defender. http://www.reputationdefender.com/

[162] AttentionTrust. http://www.attentiontrust.org/

10.4   Attention Support in the AtGentive Project

10.4.1   AtGentive, an Overview

The concepts presented in this chapter derive from research conducted in AtGentive, a research project partially funded by the European Commission, aimed at investigating the use of **agent-based ICT systems for supporting the management of the attention of young learners or adult knowledge workers**, in the context of learning environments and collaborative environments. AtGentive relies on a model of support of attention (Roda, 2006) that has been elaborated in the course of the project, which is based on a survey of existing theories on the subject of attention (Roda and Thomas, 2006). This model has been operationalised with the design of ICT systems providing a variety of mechanisms for supporting the attention of the users in simple or sophisticated manners. In the first case, these mechanisms include tools which help to extract and to visualise the activities of the users so as to provide an assessment about the actions to which they have dedicated their attention. For instance, some of these tools include the feeds from all the different actions that the users have performed during a session (when they have connected, what areas they have visited, what documents they have read or have created, who they have enquired about, etc.) as well as their graphical visualisation in order to help identify the relevant information (the most or least active people, the resources that are most accessed by the whole group, etc.). In the second case, intelligent agents are used to analyse user's activities and hence, can proactively intervene to assist and guide the users in managing their attention in a more effective way. For instance, an agent intervention can consist in the popping-up of an artificial character aiming at stimulating a pupil that has not interacted with the system for a long period of time, or the notification to a user of an item of particular importance (such as an abnormal burst of activity in the virtual community platform).

Two applications domains are used to validate the concepts generated in this project: (1) AtGentSchool: an e-learning application aiming at supporting the attention of a group of pupils in a school. In this case, profiling consists in the observation of the students by the different means available in order to determine their attentional states and profiles. It is expected that knowing about the attentional state of individuals (e.g., distraction) and of their attentional profiles will help to design better learning systems; (2) AtGentNet: an attention aware virtual community platform aiming at supporting the knowledge exchange of a group of managers that are engaged in an offline training programme and that use the platform to interact between these sessions. In this second case, profiling people's activities and determining the level and the nature of the contributions of the different participants, can be used to set up mechanisms stimulating the participation of this community and therefore the value it offers to its members.

10.4.2   Profiling in AtGentive

Needless to say, profiling represents a critical element for the functioning of the different mechanisms used to support the attention in the AtGentive system. Firstly, it is at the origin of the core data that are used as input to the visualisation mechanisms aiming at supporting the attention of the user. Secondly, these data also represent the principal source of information used by the agent mechanisms to conduct the reasoning and later on, to proactively intervene with the user with relevant actions. As a consequence, the quality of the AtGentive systems is directly correlated with the quality of the profiling. From this perspective, profiling is considered as an element to be optimised at all costs, since any improvement will have a direct impact on the efficiency of the system by providing better visualisations and more relevant interventions.

However, should this desire for profiling prevail at all costs and should trying to control the attention of the user always be desirable, especially as this seems to pose some problems related, for instance, to privacy? The answer to this question is obviously no and the project has already identified a certain number of issues that could prove critical for the beneficial adoption of the AtGentive systems and their effectiveness. For instance, it may be considered very inadequate to profile the real time level of the attention of an adult leaner and then to generate an agent intervention requesting this learner to "go back to his/her lesson", even if this can probably be done with young learners (note: we will not enter here into the debate of the most adequate control and the level of authority in the case of supervising children who are in learning). Adults are supposed to be responsible persons who are more autonomous in their learning processes and they should, more generally, be motivated in a less directive way than young children (Knowles et al., 1998). In a similar way, tracking adult activities in a platform can have a detrimental effect, in particular if the participants perceive this as a tool of surveillance, introducing an unacceptable pressure. In a learning community, the participation in a knowledge exchange is performed on a voluntary basis and is motivated by the perception of the users that they are obtaining some value out of it.

In this project, we have tried to avoid the pitfalls mentioned previously by delimitating the contexts of use and actions in such a way that these profiling issues do not represent a problem: in the case of the classroom of pupils, the profiling is mainly executed to stimulate the activity and to guide the students and not used as a tool for evaluating them; in the case of the community of managers, profiling is also performed to bring more transparency to the exchange process with the objective of stimulation and not as a tool of control. It is clear however that in some other contexts, the usage of AtGentive systems could raise some more serious issues. For instance, in the case that the profiling would become a tool of surveillance and for grading via the observation of their activities or in the case of managers, we would reject the use of an AtGentive system to track people's commitment to their work.

10.5   Conclusion and Future Work

We believe that the next generation of e-working and e-learning systems will not serve their users more but will serve them better. These new systems will be able to achieve this objective by providing better support to the human processes and in particular by better adapting to the user's needs and at a higher level. In particular, this next generation of e-working and e-learning systems will be systems that will adapt to their users and not the other way around, as is the case today. These systems will also be able to take the human dimension more into account, which they will do by supporting the cognitive process of the users more closely.

In this context, profiling is one of the most critical elements to fulfil this vision, since it represents the key mechanisms that will be used by these systems to know about their users. Indeed, for e-work and e-learning, the purpose of profiling is not the identification of the users but understanding them. As a consequence, the ability to provide better services will directly depend on the capacity of these systems to determine the characteristics of their users in order to provide services in a way that is more relevant.

In this chapter we have tried to provide a glimpse of this category of systems. We have first tried to identify the different sources of information that can be used as an input for profiling the user so as to design more advanced ICT systems. Our conclusion is that, even if biometric data have not reached a level of maturity to make it usable today, the large availability of the digital traces that the web 2.0 phenomenon has reinforced, makes these digital traces a good candidate for effectively building advanced ICT systems relying on profiling. Then, we have presented some ongoing work that we are conducting in a research project, AtGentive, aimed at designing a system relying on the profiling of the user. The objective of this project is to investigate how to support user's attention in the context of learning and work, both at the individual and at the group level. In this chapter, we have more particularly looked at profiling as a critical component for providing attentional support, indicated what kinds of personal information (including both digital traces of user's activities present in log files, as well as the biometrical data) could be extracted and used and what the different associated issues (such as difficulty or privacy) are.

To be frank, it will still take some time before this next generation of systems can provide deep (cognitive) and personalised support for the work and the learning processes to be ready for the "real world", even if the deployment of a preliminary version of our system appears to be promising. However, this chapter has helped to understand more concretely how to provide this advanced support. It also underlines the importance of profiling in the design of these systems, as well as the different issues associated with this profiling (such as the capture of user data, the processing of these data and privacy issues). After reflection, systems taking the benefits of profiling, which is a condition for their emergence, are not necessarily that far away. They are actually starting to happen in some manner if we think of the new systems such as FaceBook, del.icio.us and the likes that have emerged as part of web 2.0 and for which the management of the users and group activities represents a central component. Finally, this chapter has also presented a more positive vision about the use of profiling, which should not be perceived only as a tool of authentication or control of the individual but also as a way to better support people's activities.

10.6   Acknowledgement

The work described in this paper was partially sponsored by the EC under the FP6 framework project AtGentive IST-4-027529-STP and the Network of Excellence FIDIS European Union IST-2002-507512. We would like to acknowledge the contributions of all project partners.

10.7   Reply: Profiling Individual and Group E-learning – Some Critical Remarks

Ruth Halperin*

Profiling is seen to hold promise in the context of e-learning, offering tools with which to diagnose learners and hence provide instructional interventions that better accommodate their needs. Rather than assuming a 'one size fits all' approach, common in traditional classroom teaching, profiling mechanisms embedded within e-learning environments take account of the diversity apparent among individual learners. These include a wide range of personal variables such as cognitive style, self-regulation and previous knowledge. Similarly, as Nabeth argues in this chapter, profiling users' activities in the context of collaborative learning appears to be beneficial in stimulating member's participation and interaction.

Having underlined the apparent advantages of learner profiling, this reply moves on to consider some of the difficulties associated with the application of profiling capabilities within learning environments. First, we explore the extent to which such tools can provide an accurate diagnosis of the learner's state. Underlying assumptions of the assessment process and its application are addressed. Following this, the implications of the 'back end' monitoring inherent to the profiling activity are analysed with particular attention given to the context of online discussion forums. Potential problems of resistance are brought to the fore, resulting from learners feeling watched-over and sensing the environment as controlling.

10.7.1   Profiling and Learner-Centred Environments

Profiling is seen to hold promise in the context of e-learning, offering tools with which to diagnose learners and hence provide instructional interventions to better accommodate their needs. Rather than assuming a 'one size fits all' approach, common in traditional classroom teaching, profiling mechanisms, when embedded within e-learning environments can take account of the diversity apparent among individual learners. Individual differences that are seen to influence learning processes and their outcomes include a wide range of variables such as cognitive style, previous knowledge and self-regulation skills (Zimmerman and Schunk, 1989). Indeed, the design of *learner-centred* environments is regarded as key, particularly in the context of prevailing constructivist approaches to learning (Duffy and

---

*London School of Economics (LSE)

Cunningham, 2001). Within the constructivist framework, learning is seen as an active process in which learners construct new ideas or concepts from the basis of their current and past knowledge. As knowledge and experience vary considerably among learners, for a learning environment to be effective, individual diversity must be accommodated.

10.7.2 Profiling Individual Learning

The use of profiling as discussed in this chapter coincides with the constructivist approach to learning as the information derived from the use of profiling tools is aimed at *supporting* the learners in their individual (and thus unique) learning path. In particular, the use of profiling as a means of providing metacognitive support is a case in point. Metacognitive processes and associated skills assume the leading role of the learner, rather than that of the teacher. In discussing the three types of support (perception, metacognitive and operational) Nabeth seems to suggest that the recipients of the resulting 'profile' are the users (learners) themselves. In this context of profiling, privacy issues would appear less problematic; however, different problems become apparent. First, the basis upon which diagnosis is derived remains questionable and doubts may be raised as to the accuracy and reliability of the resulting profile and thus, its usefulness to the learner. As Nabeth points out, the use of psycho-physiological techniques are deemed unfeasible (and problematic at any rate) so that the profiling of the user is reliant on some interpretation of activity data. Yet, the inference process of learners 'state of attention' remains unclear. For example, what data may be used in order to define an activity a learner has performed as 'low' (or high) value? Keeping the notion of learner diversity in mind, it can be argued that an activity of low value for one may well be of high value to another. Thus, an automated assessment in terms of standard quantitative values would seem inappropriate. Furthermore, it is suggested that the user's activities can be displayed as statistics visualising how they are allocating their attention. Offering information to the user in this way appears useful but what are the underlying categories of the activities and can they be taken to represent an accurate description of students' attention allocation? Since cognitive processes are not readily available for observation, determining one's state of attention is not a simple task.

Further complexity arises from the extent to which learners are able to make constructive use of the profiling information provided. As compellingly discussed, information overload, multitasking and the need to deal with ever growing amounts of information in a-linear environments challenge one's ability to manage attention efficiently. We should therefore ask if providing further information relating to 'self-profile' or notifications (as suggested in the discussion on operational support) will indeed support the learner or rather, add to the existing load. Perhaps profiling information should be provided with caution and focus mainly on metacognitive skills, since effective allocation of attention is significantly a manifestation of these sets of skills.

10.7.3 Profiling Group Learning

When considering the application of profiling tools in the context of e-learning, it is important to distinguish between individual learning as discussed above and group learning (or collaborative learning) explored in the following. As Nabeth argues, profiling user activity in the context of online group interaction should prove beneficial in stimulating member participation and interaction. However, some drawbacks become evident and might lead to problems of user resistance. Unlike profiling information in the context of individual learning, profiling user activity in group learning is typically used by teachers or moderators rather than by the learners themselves. In a recent study conducted with postgraduate learners (Halperin, 2005), students were profiled inasmuch as their online participation and contribution to discussion forums was concerned. Relying on the user tracking facility provided by the e-learning application, moderators were able to obtain an accurate picture of the involvement level of each student whilst refraining from playing an active role in the interaction itself. Whereas increased participation was documented as a result of this intervention, negative attitudes and resentment also emerged as a consequence. More specifically, the 'back end' monitoring inherent to this profiling activity was met with resistance as learners felt watched-over and sensed the environment as controlling. This is particularly alarming as the delegation of control from teachers to learners is considered pedagogically crucial (Nachmias, 2002) and online discussion forums are seen as a prominent vehicle for facilitating this transition (Harasim, 2000).

10.7.4 Conclusion

Profiling in the context of e-learning appears to be highly beneficial, especially in light of the efforts to design learner-centred environments. Yet, the application of profiling techniques as discussed in this chapter raises a number of challenges that call for further exploration. In the context of individual learning, difficulties associated with diagnosing attention states are highlighted as well as the question of whether learners may be able to make effective use of such 'self-profiles'. In the case of group learning, the problem of resistance was brought to the fore, pointing to issues of control as they become associated with profiling activities.

10.8 Bibliography

Bier, E. A., Stone, M. C., Pier, K., Buxton, W., DeRose, T. D., 'Toolglass and magic lenses: The see-through interface', Proceedings 20th annual conference on Computer graphics and interactive techniques, 1993, pp. 73-80.

Brooks, F. P. Jr., *The Mythical Man-Month: Essays on Software Engineering (20th Anniversary Edition)*, Addison-Wesley, 1995.

Chun, M. M. and J. Wolfe, 'Visual Attention', in Goldstein E.B., *Blackwell's Handbook of Perception*, Oxford, UK, Blackwell, 2001, pp. 272-310.

Coan, J. A. and Allen, J. J. B., 'Frontal EEG asymmetry as a moderator and mediator of emotion', *Biological Psychology*, 67, Elsevier B.V. Netherlands, 2004, pp. 7-49.

Davenport, T. and Beck J., *The Attention Economy*, Harvard Business School Press, 2001.

Duffy, T. M., Cunningham, D. J., 'Constructivism: Implications for the Design and Delivery of Instruction', in Jonassen, D. H. (Ed.), *Handbook of Research for Educational Communications and Technology*, AECT, 2001.

Erickson, T., et al., 'Social Translucence: Designing Social Infrastructures that Make Collective Activity Visible', *Communications of the ACM* (Special issue on Community, ed. J. Preece), Vol. 45, No. 4, ACM Press, USA, 2002, pp. 40-44.

Gladwell, M., *The tipping point: How little things can make a big difference*. Boston et al.: Little, Brown, 2000.

Halperin, R., *Learning Technology in Higher Education: A Structurational Perspective on Technology-Mediated Learning Practices. Doctoral Thesis.* London School of Economics and Political Science, University of London, 2005.

Harasim, L., 'Shift Happens: Online Education as a New Paradigm in Learning', *Internet and Higher Education*, Vol. 3, No. 1-2, Elsevier Science, Netherlands, 2000, pp. 41-61.

Healey C. G., 'Perception in Visualization', 2006. Available at: http://www.csc.ncsu.edu/faculty/healey/PP/

Miller, G.A., 'The Magical Number Seven, Plus or Minus Two', *The Psychological Review*, Vol. 63, APA Journals, Washington DC, 1956, pp. 81-97.

Nachmias, R., 'A Research Framework for the Study of a Campus-Wide Web-based Academic Instruction Project', *Internet and Higher Education*, Vol. 5, No. 3, Elsevier Science, Netherlands, 2002, pp. 213-229.

Roda, C., *Conceptual Framework and Application Scenarios; Project AtGentive, Deliverable 1.3*, 2006. Available at: http://www.atgentive.com/

Roda, C. and Thomas J. (Eds), 'Special Issue: Attention Aware Systems', *Computers in Human Behaviour*, Vol. 22, No. 4 Elsevier, Netherlands, 2006.

Rubinstein, J. S., Meyer, D. E., & Evans, J. E., "Executive Control of Cognitive Processes in Task Switching", *Journal of Experimental Psychology: Human Perception and Performance*, Vol. 27, No. 4, APA Journals, Washington DC, 2001, pp. 763-797.

Zimmerman, B. J., & Schunk, D. H. (Eds.), *Self Regulated Learning and Academic Achievements: Theory, Research and Practice*. Springer-Verlag, New York, 1989.

Chapter 11
Profiling of Customers and Consumers - Customer Loyalty Programmes and Scoring Practices

Meike Kamp, Barbara Körffer, and Martin Meints

Profiling is increasingly being applied to customers and consumers. The main purposes are risk assessment and fraud prevention, for example in the financial sector and the housing industry (also called scoring) and advertising and market research, for example via customer loyalty programmes. Within this article both areas of application of profiling practice are described and analysed concerning the technical and legal aspects, especially with respect to the European Data Protection Directive 95/46/EC (hereafter, the abbreviation D 95/46 EC is used).

In the first section of this chapter general types of customer loyalty programmes (two party and three party contracts) are described. The legal aspects, elaborated in detail in the study "Kundenbindungssysteme und Datenschutz", commissioned by the "Verbraucherzentrale Bundesverband e.V. (vzbv)" and carried out by the Independent Centre for Privacy Protection (ICPP) are mapped to the corresponding articles of the D 95/46 EC and summarised. This section concludes with a good practice example, the LN-Card, a customer loyalty programme that can be used by the readers of a local German newspaper, the "Lübecker Nachrichten" (LN). This programme was awarded with a regional privacy seal in 2004.

In the second section of this chapter a definition of scoring and a general description of credit scoring practices is given, which highlights the difference between credit scoring applied by a credit institute and credit scoring operated by a credit information agency (third party service). In this context the most common criteria employed in the scoring process will be described. This is followed by a technical classification of the scoring practices and a legal analysis focused on three aspects. These aspects include criteria that have to be met to achieve a scoring practice that complies with Article 7 of D 95/46 EC, conditions under which scoring becomes an "automated individual decision" in the context of Article 15 of the D 95/46 EC and the need for transparency from the perspective of the customer.

11.1 Introduction

Profiling is increasingly being used for marketing purposes, risk management and other applications in the financial sector, where the focus of the profiling endeavour is typically the consumer. In this chapter, customer loyalty programmes as a contractual instrument to gather and process customer data for marketing and credit

Unabhängiges Landeszentrum für Datenschutz Schleswig-Holstein, Germany (ICPP)

M. Hildebrandt and S. Gutwirth (eds.), *Profiling the European Citizen:*
Cross-Disciplinary Perspectives.
© Springer Science + Business Media B.V. 2008

scoring purposes (e.g., for risk management in the financial sector) are described and analysed with respect to European data protection legislation.

11.2   Customer Loyalty Programmes in Germany

Customer loyalty programmes have become increasingly popular during the last five years in Germany. The main premise is to gain customer loyalty by granting a certain amount of discount. We observe two types of customer loyalty programmes on the German market:

- *Two party relationship programmes, where we have a direct contract between customer and vendor*
- *Three party relationship programmes, with relationships between each of the parties: customer, vendor and the system operator granting the discount.*

Figure 11.1 illustrates the three party relationship:

Within the three party relationship, the customer's personal data are processed by the system operator and in most cases additionally by the vendor (at least for the vendor's own customers).

If the processing of data is necessary for the performance of a contract to which the data subject is party then the data processing should be based on a regulation following Article 7 lit. b of D 95/46/EC of the European Parliament and the Council of 24 October 1995 on the protection of individuals with regards to the processing of personal data and on the free movement of such data. If used for the purpose of the contract, which is the granting of discount, these requirements are typically fulfilled by the processing of the name, address, one further piece of contact information (e.g., a telephone number if communication with the data subject is required in

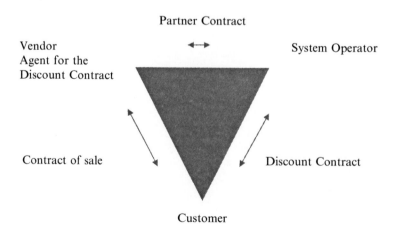

Fig. 11.1 Illustration of the three party relationship in a customer loyalty programme

the context of the contract), the time and place of card deployment and the price of purchased goods.

Besides the data required for discount purposes, in most cases additional personal data is collected, for example date of birth, several contact addresses (telephone numbers, e-mail, etc.), information about purchased goods and information on personal circumstances of life (e.g., family status, number of children, income, etc.)

These data are mainly used for market research and advertising purposes using profiling techniques. As a general rule they can only be processed on the basis of informed consent that fulfils the requirements stated in Article 2 lit. h of D 95/46 EC on the processing of personal data. This implies that the consent is freely given and based on sufficient information about the intended processing of the customer's data.

In a study[163] ordered by the "Verbraucherzentrale Bundesverband e.V." (vzbv) and carried out by the Independent Centre for Privacy Protection (ICPP) in December 2003, sixteen customer loyalty programmes were investigated. When compared against the benchmark of the German Federal Data Protection Act (BDSG), numerous major and minor shortcomings and violations were found. A central weakness of all programmes investigated was that because of trade secrecy, the place and time of the storage of the data and the way and purpose of the processing was not described sufficiently. On the grounds of insufficient information, a declaration of consent - which has to be based on free will - is legally ineffective.

11.2.1 *European Legal Grounds*

Based on European legislation[164] the German Federal Data Protection Act (BDSG) has several sections relating to customer loyalty programmes. Those directly based on D 95/46 EC are summarised in this chapter together with the findings of the study.[165]

Usually, customer loyalty programmes employ customer account cards. From a data protection perspective, the contract between the customer and either the discount-granting company or an operator of the account card system can be interpreted in two distinct parts: (1) discount related part: rewarding customers' loyalty by granting discounts and (2) collection of additional data: collecting and processing additional personal data for different purposes, such as advertising, direct marketing and market research.

---

[163] The Study Kundenbindungssysteme und Datenschutz. Gutachten im Auftrag des Verbraucherzentrale Bundesverband e.V. is available via: http://www.datenschutzzentrum.de/wirtschaft/kundbisy.htm.

[164] Directive 95/46/EC, 24th October 1995, on the protection of individuals with regard to the processing of personal data and on the free movement of such data.

[165] The Study Kundenbindungssysteme und Datenschutz Gutachten im Auftrag des Verbraucherzentrale Bundesverband e.V.

For the first part of the contract, Article 7 lit. b of D 95/46 EC on the protection of individuals with regard to the processing of personal data and on the free movement of such data is relevant. This Article limits the use of personal data with regard to the discount related part of a contract. In detail, this means that the contract partner of the customer is allowed to store and process only the following data: name, address, **year** of birth, **one** further piece of address information (phone, email, etc.), time and place of card deployment, price of purchased goods / services and discount amount and data related to the purchased goods only if they are necessary for computation of the discount amount.

For further data, the free and informed consent of the customer is required. Requirements for the consent are regulated in Article 2 lit. h of the European Directive on the processing of personal data. In addition, for data processing in general, Article 10; Article 11 (information of the data subject) and Article 12 (right of access) apply.

Consequences, particularly from Article 2 lit. h of the European Directive on the processing of personal data, are that the customer agreeing to the further use of his/her personal data has to know the details and consequences of the collection and processing of the data. In addition, the decision is not considered to be freely entered into if the participation in the loyalty programme depends on an agreement for the collection and processing of additional personal data. To gain a legally effective declaration of consent, the customer has to be informed about the following facts (a) who is responsible for the data and the data processing, (b) which categories of data will be processed, (c) for what purpose they are processed, (d) how the processing is done (phases and data flows), (e) to whom data are transferred, (f) that decision of consent is voluntarily and what the consequences of a refusal of consent are and (g) that the given consent may be revoked at any time.

From a technical perspective, in this context, the data are used for personalised and group profiling, in most cases of a non-distributive type. Typically, the following data mining techniques are applied: association rules (personalised profiling), classification (group profiling) and clustering (group profiling) (Schweizer 1999, also c.f. chapters 2.3.2 and 3.2).

11.2.1.1 Findings of the Study

In the aforementioned study, sixteen federal and several regional customer loyalty programmes were investigated for their compliance with the BDSG. All programmes investigated showed defects, some minor and some major. A typical example of failure to comply was that of collecting more data than necessary for correct implementation of the discount without the consent of the customer. In other cases the participation in the discount programme depended on consent to further usage of personal data, thus no freedom of choice was given. Occasionally the exclusion of personal data from the declaration of consent was not implemented in a privacy-compliant way. In some cases, the possibility to opt-in or opt-out was not implemented in the contract, thus the customer had to cancel the part of the contract he did not agree with (c.f. also chapter 13.2.1.2). In rare cases conditions of entry and privacy policies were sent to the customer only after acquiring his/her consent – this essentially means that there was no consent at all because the customers could not know the conditions in advance. In some cases the information that consent was voluntary was missing and the consequences of refusing the declaration of consent were not pointed out. In many cases the planned processing of personal data was not sufficiently described – therefore the declaration of consent was not completely based on a free decision.

In some cases such defects were subsequently remedied by the operators of the loyalty programmes.

11.2.1.2 Case Study: The LN-Card

For the LN-Card, a customer loyalty programme for the readers of a local German newspaper, the "Lübecker Nachrichten" (LN), the privacy seal of the "Independent Centre for Privacy Protection Schleswig-Holstein" (ICPP) was granted.[166]

The LN-Card is an example of a three party relationship, so the loyalty programme can be used with other participating regional vendors. The contract with the users of the card is limited to the granting of an account, additional purposes to process personal data are not defined. Consequently only a minimum of personal data, essentially required for the purpose of the contract, is collected and processed. The user is informed in an exemplary way and contracts with vendors and external service providers define rights and obligations with respect to the processing of personal data very proficiently.[167]

Credit Scoring

11.2.2 Definition and Purpose of Credit Scoring

Credit scoring is used within the credit decision process for the purpose of estimating the risk of credit failure. Credit scoring aims to quantify the likelihood that the prospective borrower will not meet his/her credit obligations, i.e., that he or she will fail to repay a loan.[168] For the estimation process a statistical model is created. This is done by analysing relevant attributes from a relevant set of people to assess which personal criteria have a statistical effect on the creditworthiness of a person and to measure the degree of this effect. These parameters and their relative importance are compiled in a statistical model, which is often developed as a so-called "scorecard".

---

[166] See http://www.datenschutzzentrum.de/guetesiegel/register.htm.

[167] See http://www.datenschutzzentrum.de/guetesiegel/kurzgutachten/g041006/

[168] See www.wikipedia.org for "credit score".

In many scorecards not only the criteria and their relative importance are considered but also the combinations of certain parameters. The individual credit score is then calculated by setting the scorecard with specific information from the prospective borrower. The credit score is commonly quoted as a number that is allocated to a certain percentage of the statistical likelihood of credit failure.

From a technical perspective credit scoring in most cases is group profiling of a non-distributive type (c.f. chapter 2.3.2). Typically, scoring uses data mining techniques for classification; this approach can also be understood as directed group profiling (c.f. chapter 3.2). In some documented cases logistic regression algorithms are used.[169]

11.2.3   Credit Scoring Practices

Credit scoring is operated by specialised enterprises or credit reporting agencies selling the credit scores across the credit service sector. The credit reporting agencies develop credit scores based on their credit history databases and deliver the score, in many cases together with the credit report, to a credit institute. Credit scoring is also operated by credit institutes or by the banks themselves. In these internal scoring systems the bank's own experiences e.g., experiences with the balancing and debiting of bank or credit accounts can be considered. Commonly, banks or credit institutes incorporate an external credit score as a parameter in their internal scoring.

The credit score can influence the credit decisions in different ways. It is used to estimate the qualification for a loan, to assign a credit limit, to assign an interest rate or to assign the term of a loan/duration of a credit.

In many scoring systems certain criteria are identified as "K.O.-criteria". Meeting such criteria is essential and failure to meet them means that the scoring is not conducted and a credit score is not generated. For example, the age of an applicant is commonly selected as a K.O.-criterion such that under-aged applicants are excluded from the credit decision process. In other cases, criteria such as unemployment or a negative credit history can rule out the credit scoring process, with the consequence that the applicant is expelled from obtaining credit or a loan. The credit or loan can also be denied in cases where the credit score falls below the so-called "Cut-Off-Score".

The following chapters refer to the use of credit scoring within the decision process, from the application for credit until the credit decision. The process of generating or defining profiles and optimisation of the profiling algorithms e.g., by using anonymised data of credit applicants is not investigated in this section.

---

[169] For example in Germany the Schufa, see Der Hessischen Landtag, *Drucksache 16/1680 in der 16. Wahlperiode vom 11.12.2003*, S. 21, Wiesbaden 2003. Available at: http://www.denic.de/media/pdf/dokumente/datenschutzbericht_2003.pdf.

11.2.4   Commonly Used Criteria in Credit Scoring Systems

Parameters that are employed in credit scoring can be divided into contractual parameters, financial criteria and demographic characteristics.

Commonly used contractual parameters are the number of accounts, the number of credit cards, the number of loans or credits, securities, duration of contractual relationships between the credit service and the prospective borrower, management of the contracts, balances of the accounts, account turnovers, overdrafts etc. As for financial criteria, credit scorings can incorporate securities, real estate, capital, income, costs, insolvencies, number of personal credit report requests, number of credit applications etc.

Demographic characteristics that are commonly employed in the scoring are address, number of tenancy changeovers, age, sex, number of children, neighbourhood, family status, education, profession, name of the employer, nationality, religion, car ownership etc. Parameters such as address or neighbourhood are used because scoring suppliers and credit services believe that a poor neighbourhood is an indication of low income and low payment behaviour. It is typically assumed that people of a kind gather together. The number of tenancy changeovers is used as an indicator of absconding debtors.

11.2.5   Data Protection Aspects of Credit Scoring

Credit scoring is used to predict the creditworthiness of a person and hence quantify one aspect of the data subject's personality. In the process of scoring, different kinds of personal data are compiled into a personal profile. Thus the practice of credit scoring deserves a closer look in the context of the D 95/46 EC. According to the object of the Directive, member states shall protect the right to privacy of natural persons with respect to the processing of personal data. Therefore the Directive is applicable only in cases where personal data is processed. Art. 2 (a) of the Directive defines personal data as "any information relating to an identified or identifiable natural person". The credit score is "personal data" in the sense of Article 2 (a) of D 95/46 EC. Article 2 (a) is applicable because the credit score is based on or developed by an analysis of all kinds of "personal data" from the prospective borrower. The bank allocates the calculated credit score to the applicant and refers to this value for the prediction of the likelihood of credit failure. For the scoring credit institute or credit reporting agency, the credit score is therefore information relating to the identified person / the applicant.

11.2.5.1   Compliance with Article 7 of the Data Protection Directive

Since the Data Protection Directive is applicable, the legitimacy of credit scoring depends on whether the requirements of Article 7 of D 95/46 EC are met. In Article

7 of D 95/46 EC conditions are specified under which personal data may be processed. Credit scoring complies with Article 7 if the applicant (data subject) has given his or her consent (Article 7 (a)) or if the credit scoring is necessary for the performance of a contract to which the data subject is party or in order to take steps at the request of the data subject prior to entering into a contract (Article 7 (b)).

11.2.5.2 The Data Subject's Consent

Under Article 2 (h) of D 95/46 EC the data subject's consent shall mean any freely given specific and informed indication of his wishes by which the data subject signifies his agreement to personal data relating to him being processed. In the case of credit scoring, an informed indication as required by the Directive can be assumed only if all relevant factors of the scoring process are known by the credit applicant. First of all, the scoring banks or credit institutes have to identify themselves as the data controller. Secondly, the applicant has to be informed about the purposes of the credit scoring. Therefore the credit institute has to explain the credit scoring as a method of minimising the risk of credit failure by predicting the likelihood of repaying the loan. If the credit institute incorporates an external credit score in the internal scoring process, the applicant has to be informed about the identity of the companies that deliver the credit score. The credit institute has to disclose what kind of personal data is processed when operating the scoring system. The credit institute shall explicitly notify the applicant if personal data are processed that derive from a different contractual relationship or was collected in other ways than from the credit application. If special categories of data (Article 8) are processed, the prospective borrower has to give his or her explicit consent to the processing of those data (Article 8 2. (a)).

11.2.5.3 Processing Necessary for the Performance of a Contract or in Order to Take Steps at the Request, Prior to Entering into a Contract

If the credit service has not obtained the data subject's consent, then the scoring is legitimate only if it is necessary for the performance of a contract or in order to take steps at the request, prior to entering into a contract. Since the credit scoring takes place before the credit agreement is concluded and after the prospective borrower has applied for the credit, the credit scoring has to be necessary in order to take steps at the application prior to entering into the contract. The wording "at the request" shall guarantee that the processing of the personal data is carried out on the initiative of the data subject.[170] The credit scoring takes place after the prospective borrower has applied for credit and is therefore carried out on his or her initiative. As a risk management tool, it can also be a necessary step for the decision of whether to grant credit or not and can therefore be necessary in order to take steps prior to entering into the contract. Of course it is not an indispensable step in order to accomplish the primary contractual purpose. But Article 7 (b) of D 95/46

---

[170] Dammann/Simitis, EG-Datenschutzrichtlinie Kommentar, 1. Auflage Baden-Baden 1997, Art 7 Punkt 3.

EC limits the legitimate data processing not to indispensable steps in order to accomplish the primary contractual purpose.[171]

In fact, the credit institute has to have a tool to minimise the risk of credit failure in order to conduct credit services for various people. It depends on the concrete methods and operations of the scoring to determine whether credit scoring is risk management in compliance with D 95/46 EC or not. Credit scoring is only necessary in the sense of the Directive if it has a crucial significance for the quantifying of creditworthiness and risk of credit failure. The incorporated parameters and criteria are very important factors in measuring the significance of the credit scoring. To comply with the requirements of the Directive, the mathematical or statistical significance of the parameters is not the only relevant criterion. In addition, the parameters have to meet a certain standard of plausibility and coherence in the context of creditworthiness.[172] Therefore parameters that permit only implausible assumptions about the solvency and willingness to pay of the scored applicant as well as parameters that are not individually controllable, shall be excluded. Demographic characteristics in particular have a great potential to be indirect and lead to implausible conclusions. Hence, parameters such as the number of tenancy changeovers, the address or the neighbourhood have great potential for leading to incorrect purely statistical conclusions, when the individual circumstances are not considered. Examples of this are frequent work-related tenancy changeovers (e.g., for soldiers, top managers) or living in a "bad" neighbourhood, e.g., living close to the train station in order to be more flexible for frequent work-related travelling.[173]

The use of parameters such as age, sex, race, sexuality, disability and religion may cause unjustified discrimination, considering the principle of equal treatment. The European Directives 2000/43/EC and 2004/113/EC prohibit direct or indirect discrimination based on sex or race when providing goods and services available to the public, irrespective of the person concerned. If those parameters are used in credit-scoring then the very fact that they are used leads to the conclusion that they have an effect – positive or negative – on the score. If a person is consequently treated less favourably in the credit decision process, then the Directives are applicable.[174]

The processing of financial data can also be illegitimate, for example parameters such as the number of personal credit report requests have to be excluded from the credit scoring. The right to access under Article 12 of D 95/46 EC is one of the basic privacy rights. Therefore, the number of requests for a personal credit report cannot be held against the borrower. From a consumer protection perspective it is also questionable if the number of credit applications should be incorporated in the scoring. The consumers must have the right to compare prices when applying for

---

[171] Dammann/Simitis, EG-Datenschutzrichtlinie Kommentar, 1. Auflage Baden-Baden 1997, Art 7 Punkt 3.

[172] Unabhängiges Landeszentrum für Datenschutz Schleswig-Holstein, 'Scoringsysteme zur Beurteilung der Kreditwürdigkeit – Chancen und Risiken für Verbraucher', Forschungsprojekt im Auftrag des BMVEL, S. 72ff.

[173] Unabhängiges Landeszentrum für Datenschutz Schleswig-Holstein, 'Scoringsysteme zur Beurteilung der Kreditwürdigkeit – Chancen und Risiken für Verbraucher', Forschungsprojekt im Auftrag des BMVEL, S. 72ff.

[174] See Directives 2000/43/EC, 2000/78/EC, 2002/73/EC and 2004/113/EC.

credit. Hence, the number of credit applications should not have an adverse effect on the credit score.

11.2.5.4 Automated Individual Decision (Article 15 of the Data Protection Directive)

Depending on the operation of the scoring and the way it is embedded in the credit decision process, credit scoring can generate an automated individual decision. If the credit decision is solely based on the credit score of the applicant, credit scoring is an automated processing of data intended to evaluate the creditworthiness of the data subject under Article 15 (1.) of the Data Protection Directive. Article 15 (1.) of D 95/46 EC addresses the credit services or banks that make the credit decision. Whether this decision is based on an internally developed or externally delivered credit score is irrelevant. The determining factor for the application of Article 15 is that credit scoring is an evaluation of the personal aspects relating to the prospective borrower that is accomplished by a machine rather than a human.

In this context the "Cut-off Score" is the most apparent example of an automated decision. In addition, the credit score can have such a great impact on the credit decision that the whole decision process has to be characterised as an automated process. If the credit officer routinely adopts the estimation indicated by the credit score without reconsidering and verifying the decision with the individual circumstances, Article 15 (1.) is applicable.

If the credit scoring has a tendency to generate an automated individual decision, the credit service has to establish suitable measures to safeguard the legitimate interests of the prospective borrower, such as arrangements that allow him to state his point of view (Article 15 (2.) (a)). For that purpose, the credit service shall notify the prospective borrower about his or her corresponding right.

11.2.5.5 Transparency Aspects

In cases where the credit service does not obtain consent for the credit scoring, the service nevertheless has to inform the applicant about all relevant factors (methods, parameters and right of the data subject to express his own point of view) of the scoring. More importantly, he has to make sure that the credit scoring is an integral part of the contract. The credit service shall take care through organisational arrangements that the credit decision is not based solely on the credit score and to inform the applicant accordingly.

The credit service has to communicate the actual credit score as well as the parameters and the logic of the processing at least in the case of the automated decision referred to in Article 15 of the Data Protection Directive if the applicant so requests. If the credit score has been developed by an external firm, this firm has to give the applicant access to this kind of information.

From the perspective of the Data Protection Directive, the credit agency or credit institute needs to inform or grant access to data for the data subject only. This does not include a general description of the scoring practice for the general public.

11.3   Conclusion

In this chapter, customer loyalty programmes and scoring in the financial sector were introduced and analysed based on the results of two studies.

In the context of customer loyalty programmes sixteen programmes in Germany were investigated. The contracts with the customer usually have two parts: (1) a discount related part and (2) a part for the collection of additional data. Legal grounds with respect to the European legal framework for both parts were analysed and compared with the findings from the survey. All programmes showed defects, many of them related to (a) the legal grounds for the processing of personal data and (b) the way the declaration of consent was implemented. In some cases the defects were remedied by the operators of the loyalty programmes and in one case the privacy seal of the "Independent Centre for Privacy Protection Schleswig-Holstein" (ICPP) was granted.

Credit scoring is used within the credit decision process for the purpose of estimating the risk of credit failure. It can influence the credit decisions in different ways. It is used to estimate the qualification for loans, to assign a credit limit, to assign an interest rate or to assign the term of a loan/duration of the credit. From a privacy perspective credit scoring can be legitimate if the prospective borrower has given his or her informed consent or if the credit scoring has become an integral part of the contract according to Art. 7 (a) and (b) of D 95/46 EC. To comply with the Directive the incorporated criteria must have a statistical significance, have to be plausible and coherent in the context of creditworthiness and shall not interfere with any discrimination prohibitions or other interdictions of use. To safeguard the privacy rights of the applicant, he or she must be informed about the relevant factors of the credit scoring. In accordance with Article 15 of D 95/46 EC, the credit services have to make sure that the credit decision does not become an individual automated decision based solely on the credit score.

11.4   Reply: Profiles in Context: Analysis of the Development of a Customer Loyalty Programme and of a Risk Scoring Practice

Ana Canhoto*

Profiling can be seen as an act of communication between three levels which are very different in nature: 1) the technical level that captures and manipulates the data, 2) the formal level of rules and policies and 3) the informal level of human interactions. While the main article analyses the first two levels, this reply focuses on the third one.

The technical aspects of profiling are embedded in the formal ones and these are interpreted through the prevalent informal characteristics of the context in which the profiles are

---

* Henley Management College

developed and used. As a result, two groups operating in different informal contexts may react differently to the same formal or technical initiative. The reply examines how the same formal initiative – the Directive 95/46/EC – translates into different technical solutions in the two applications considered in chapter 11, because of the different nature of strategic objectives informing the development of such profiles.

Customer loyalty programmes, one of the applications considered, aim to encourage or reward actions that are considered positive by the organisation. By opposition, the other application considered, risk scoring programmes, aim to discourage particular types of behaviour. The analysis of how the informal context cues application of the formal legal requirements and translates it into specific technical solutions will assist the reader in abstracting from the two applications considered to different industry, legal or technical circumstances.

11.4.1 Introduction

The article by Kamp et al. analyses two instances of profiling – customer loyalty and credit scoring – and reflects on the extent to which the two practices described comply with European data protection legislation, in particular article 7 of the Directive 95/46/EC. The authors consider that in light of the Directive, the two applications analysed collected far more data than is deemed necessary. Additionally, in both cases, provision of service by the organisation depends on the data subjects granting further access by the organisation to personal data. There are interesting differences, however, regarding the nature of the superfluous data collected, the information given to the data subjects and the data mining techniques employed (Table 11.1). In this article, we examine the differences and suggest that they are not the result of random factors. Rather, we argue, they reflect the nature of the context in which the applications emerged or are used.

Social science researchers are encouraged to look beyond functionalist explanations for why things are as they are. This paper addresses this challenge by looking at the context in which the profiling applications emerge and are used. Understanding how the context cues the application of legal requirements and translates them into specific technical solutions assists the reader in abstracting from the two applications considered to different industry, legal or technical circumstances.

Table 11.1 Differences identified

Difference\ Application	Customer loyalty	Credit scoring
Data collected	Extensive collection of personal data	Extensive collection of product related, as well as personal data
Information given	Systematic failures identified	It is clear that personal data will be collected and examined
Data mining techniques	Association, classification and clustering	Mostly classification. In some cases, also regression

11.4.2   Customer Loyalty Programmes and Credit-scoring Programmes

A customer loyalty programme, as described by Humby et al. (2003):

> *'opens a two-way exchange of value, a sort of commercial conversation. The outcome of that conversation (...) depends on the quality of the benefits being offered to both parties. For the customer, quality is about how relevant it is to them and how valuable and tempting the 'thank you' is. For the retailers, it is about how clearly they can hear what the customers are saying to them through their actions. (...) The message (...) can be heard through the mechanism of the loyalty programme.' (page 26)*

A credit scoring programme, on the other hand, represents an assessment of someone's credit risk and reflects the person's ability to repay debts. The score helps the potential lender to decide whether or not to provide a loan and at what rate. It enables users to evaluate and manage risk exposure. Furthermore, credit scoring models are usually developed using a large sample and considering many different variables.[175]

In summary, customer loyalty applications are exploratory and focused on the individual, whereas credit scoring ones are confirmatory and focused on classes. As a result, one may expect customer loyalty applications to be rather more intrusive than credit scoring ones but the later may be more discriminatory than the former, in the sense that credit scoring may result in the denial of service to potential customers as a result of them falling into certain general categories. We now examine the differences identified in Kamp et al.'s study.[176]

11.4.2.1   Data Collected Over and Above Application Requirements

The customer loyalty application collects far more personal data than would be strictly necessary for the purposes of rewarding loyalty to a particular retail outlet. Indeed, a simple log of the frequency and value of purchases should be all that is needed to reward buyers' loyalty. Collecting, storing and processing the supplementary data described is costly and it is doubtful that organisations would do it unless there is some economic benefit in doing so. The extension of supplementary personal data collected, therefore, suggests that the loyalty rewarding feature may be a means, rather than an end, to the profiling exercise.

The credit scoring application also collects extensive personal data. Additionally, organisations using this application also tend to collect extensive product related

---

[175] For a decription of credit scoring and its impact on customers the reader is referred to Leyshon, A. and N. Thrift (1999, 434-466).

[176] This analysis is based on the Informal-Formal-Technical Framework described in Canhoto, A. I. and J. Backhouse (2007, 408-419).

data over and above the logical requirements of a credit scoring application. Rather, Kamp et al. suggest, information such as the number of personal credit reports requested or of credit applications made tell the lending organisation more about the data subjects' market awareness than their ability to repay a loan. Such information might help the lending organisation decide, for instance, whether or not to provide a particularly competitive interest rate to a potential client.

11.4.2.2   Information Given to the Data Subjects

In the case of the customer loyalty application, there seems to be systematic failures regarding the information given to the data subjects concerning both their rights and the extent to which personal data is collected and processed. Such an attitude by the organisations reveals that they are pursuing a very aggressive strategy of data collection.

In the case of the credit scoring application, it is very clear to the data subjects that their personal data will be collected and examined as part of the interaction with the organisation. Moreover, to a certain extent, such collection is done as a result of the data subjects' request, when they apply for a loan. The organisations' actions mirror the relative power that such organisations have, as they are trading a product that is highly desired or needed, by the data subjects.

11.4.2.3   Data Mining Techniques Used

Even though the Directive does not address issues of particular data processing techniques, it is still interesting to reflect on the differences observed by Kamp *et al.* This is because, as noted in chapter 3, the choice of algorithm is partly influenced by the function to be performed by the model.

The customer loyalty applications described by Kamp et al. use a mixture of models, most notably association, classification and clustering models. The wide range of models used reflects the varied nature of the questions asked from the data. Association models, for instance, describe significant relations between the data, whereas clustering models look for natural groupings among the data items. That is, these models are exploratory and actively look for meanings in the data set. They are particularly suitable for a descriptive exercise.

Credit scoring profiles, on the other hand, rely mostly on classification models. Such models consist in examining the features of a newly presented object and assigning it to one of a predefined set of classes. Regressions are similar to classification models but refer to the future. The choice of models for the credit scoring profiling is appropriate for a matching exercise, where analysts have clear expectations about patterns of behaviour and intend to pigeonhole data subjects in clear, previously established categories.

For an overview of the various data mining techniques, the reader is referred to section 3.2.

11.4.3 Conclusion

The audit of compliance developed by Kamp et al. highlights how the same formal initiative – the Directive 95/46/EC – is translated into two very different technical solutions. By broadening the analysis of the differences to include contextual elements such as the nature of strategic objectives informing the development of the profiles, we identify the origin of such differences. Applications that aim to learn about or describe patterns of behaviour are more likely to be intrusive and focused on the individual. Applications based on long established profiles and used to pigeonhole observations rather than explain them, are more likely to raise issues of discrimination than the later, as it may result in the denial of a service by the organisation.

11.5 Bibliography

Dammann, U., Simitis, S., EG-Datenschutzrichtlinie Kommentar, 1. Auflage Baden-Baden 1997, Art 7 Punkt 3.

Der Hessischen Landtag, *Drucksache 16/1680 in der 16. Wahlperiode vom 11.12.2003*, S. 21, Wiesbaden 2003. Available at: http://www.denic.de/media/pdf/dokumente/datenschutzbericht_2003.pdf

Canhoto, A. I., 'Ontology-based interpretation and validation of mined knowledge: Normative and cognitive factors in data mining', Nigro, H. O., Cisaro, S. E. G. and Xodo, D. H., *Data mining with ontologies: implementations, findings, and frameworks*, Hershey, NY, Information Science Reference, 2007, pp. 84-105.

Canhoto, A. I. and Backhouse, J., 'Profiling under conditions of ambiguity—An application in the financial services industry', *Journal of Retailing and Consumer Services*, Vol. 14, No. 6, 2007, pp. 408-419.

Humby, C., Hunt, T. et al., *Scoring points: how Tesco is winning customer loyalty*, London, Kogan Page, 2003.

Leyshon, A. and Thrift, N., 'Lists come alive: electronic systems of knowledge and the rise of credit-scoring in retail banking', *Economy & Society*, Vol. 28, No. 3, 1999, pp. 434-466.

Liebenau, J. and Backhouse, J., *Understanding Information: An Introduction*, Macmillan, London, 1990.

Schweizer, A., *Data Mining Data Warehousing – Datenschutzrechtliche Orientierungshilfe für Privatunternehmen*, Orell Füssli Verlage, Zürich 1999.

Unabhängiges Landeszentrum für Datenschutz Schleswig-Holstein, 'Scoringsysteme zur Beurteilung der Kreditwürdigkeit – Chancen und Risiken für Verbraucher', Forschungsprojekt im Auftrag des BMVEL, S. 72ff.

Verbraucherzentrale Bundesverbandes e.V. – ULD, 'Kundenbindungssysteme und Datenschutz. Gutachten des Unabhängigen Landeszentrums für Datenschutz Schleswig-Holstein (ULD) im Auftrag des Verbraucherzentrale Bundesverbandes e.V.', 2003. Available at: http://www.datenschutzzentrum.de/wirtschaft/Kundenbindungssysteme.pdf

Chapter 12
Profiling in Employment Situations (Fraud)

Nils Leopold and Martin Meints

Profiling in employment related situations has found increasing application during the last ten years as an instrument for electronic (and in some cases highly automated) employee monitoring. In the first part of this article the European legal grounds for workers' data protection are described; the Data Protection Directive 95/46/EC is only one but an important part of the existing European legal framework. General principles for data protection at the workplace derived from this European legal framework are outlined.

In the second part, examples of profiling practice in employment situations will be described and analysed concerning legal and technological aspects based on case studies that are raised in, among others, Privacy Commissions in Germany. Core elements of a legally compliant implementation will be outlined. The case studies include: e-mail analysis and profiling applied by intrusion detection / intrusion prevention systems, skill management tools and fraud prevention, for example, in the retail sector through embezzlement by cashiers

12.1 Introduction

Within organisations such as private enterprises or public authorities, profiling has gained increasing importance as an instrument to ensure security in a general sense. Areas of potential application of profiling are prevention of fraud committed by employees, performance monitoring and management and establishing internal and external information security (see, for example, Lasprogata, King, Pillay 2004). Typical examples for the application of profiling are fraud prevention (for example, in the retail sector through embezzlement by cashiers), direct and indirect supervision by tracking of employees (for example, in postal services, logistics or call centres, where skill management tools and access control systems can be used to monitor hours of work) and profiling on log-files for example in firewall systems and intrusion detection / prevention systems.

Like many other new technologies, in this context profiling potentially causes a shift in the informational balance and as a consequence the balance of power in favour of the employer. Data protection achieved great attention as a

Unabhängiges Landeszentrum für Datenschutz Schleswig-Holstein, Germany (ICPP)

M. Hildebrandt and S. Gutwirth (eds.), *Profiling the European Citizen:*
Cross-Disciplinary Perspectives.
© Springer Science + Business Media B.V. 2008

modern legal instrument **with the aim of re-balancing the power relationship between employers and employees**. It seems to be one of the important challenges of the information society, to manage the complex processes of the integration of IT-technology into the everyday work life of European citizens – especially in terms of privacy rights.

An employment relationship implies, as a general rule, a subordinate (legal) relationship. It is a contract whereby the employee agrees to perform the work for certain wages, under the authority of the employer. This means that the employer is contractually allowed to exercise authority over the employee. Additionally, the employee in most cases uses the infrastructure owned by the employer/company in order to carry out his assigned tasks. However, the individual is only subject to the authority of the employer insofar as this is embodied in the specific employment relationship, in other words, as is relevant for the employment contract. Furthermore, the existence of an employment contract does not lead to the suspension of basic fundamental rights of the employee at his workplace. The right to privacy and the basic principles of data protection have to be taken into account and have to be respected by the employer from the very beginning and all the way through to the end of a contractual relationship.

In this chapter, legal grounds for data protection in an employment situation will be summarised. In addition, three example applications of profiling in employment situations will be presented and analysed with respect to data protection.

12.2   Legal Grounds with Respect to Data Protection in the Working Context

Data protection regulation in the workplace aims to re-establish an informational balance between employer and employee. Thus, it provides for general principles concerning the processing of personal data in the work context and guarantees the rights of the workers to know about their data being processed as well as the right to be informed about, right to object to and the right to correct false data. Data protection at the workplace protects the workers dignity and freedom. Their individual rights to privacy are supposed to be acknowledged and strengthened in the working context. The applicable data protection rules have to be interpreted in the light of the fundamental rights granted in the ECHR and in the EU Constitution (still a draft). In addition, in a number of contexts, the privacy rights of workers have to be weighed against the equally protected constitutional rights of employers, for instance property rights.

Relevant regulations with respect to data protection are:

- Council of Europe's 1981 Convention (108) for the Protection of Individuals with regard to Automatic Processing of Personal Data
- OECD's 1980 Guidelines on the Protection of Privacy and Transborder Flows of Personal Data
- Council of Europe's Recommendation (86) 1 on the Protection of personal data used for social security purposes

- Recommendation No. R(89)2 of the Council of Europe on the protection of personal data used for employment purposes
- 1990 UN Guidelines Concerning Computerised Personal Data Files (UN Economic and Social Council E/CN.4/1990/72 from 20 February 1990 – not binding
- **1995 European Commissions' Directive on the protection of individuals with regard to the processing of personal data (95/46/EC)**
- 1997 Protection of Workers' personal data (ILO Code) – not binding
- Council of Europe's Recommendation (97) 5 on the Protection of Medical Data
- 2002 European Union Directive concerning the processing of personal data and the protection of privacy in the electronic communications sector (Directive on privacy and electronic communication, 02/58/EC)
- European Convention for the Protection of Human Rights and Fundamental Freedoms from 1950 and corresponding jurisdiction of the ECHR
- European Treaty establishing a constitution for Europe signed by the Heads of States and Government 29 October 2004 – not binding

Article II-68 Treaty establishing a constitution for Europe: Protection of personal data

1. Everyone has the right to the protection of personal data concerning themselves.
2. Such data must be processed fairly, for specified purposes and on the basis of the consent of the person concerned or some other legitimate basis laid down by law. Everyone has the right of access to data that have been collected concerning him or her and the right to have it rectified.
3. Compliance with these rules shall be subject to control by an independent authority.

Additionally, one should mention that numerous member states have already passed specific data protection legislation covering single aspects of the workplace, such as for the "dawning" practice of genetic testing in some member states (e.g., prohibition in Austria by law). Also, there is a trend for sector-specific legislation to be observed covering issues of data protection at the workplace as a whole (Finland was the first country to implement this).

12.2.1 Data Protection at the Workplace – Most Relevant Legislation in the Profiling Context

To provide a platform for the analysis of the following three cases of data protection at the workplace, the most relevant data protection legislation is summarised. In chapter 13, a more detailed description of relevant data protection aspects in the profiling context is given.

12.2.1.1   EU Directives

From all of the aforementioned pieces of legislation, which constitute the basic international legal background on data protection at the workplace, the EU-Directive from 1995 as well as the 2002 Directive on privacy in the electronic communications sector are the most important because of their binding character and their detailed regulation.

Data protection laws in the EU confer individual rights to any person concerned by the processing of personal data (e.g., right of access, right to rectify). *As a general rule, these rights apply fully to the employer-employee relationship and the only possible exceptions are those allowed by Directive 95/46/EC (Article 29 working party opinion on the processing of personal data in the employment context, WP 48, 8/2001).*

The same applies to the Directive 2002/58/EC – Directive on privacy and electronic communication – as far as the use of telecommunications, e-mail and Internet by employees is concerned. The main precondition for its applicability is but one aspect: according to recital 10 of the Directive 2002, in the electronic communications sector Directive 95/46/EC applies in particular to all matters concerning the protection of fundamental rights and freedoms, which are not specifically covered by the provisions of the 2002 Directive, including the obligations on the controller and the rights of individuals.

Directive 95/46/EC applies to the processing of personal data wholly or partly by automatic means and to their processing by other means once they form part of a relevant filing system (criteria of quick retrievability) or are intended to do so. Personal data means any information relating to an identified or identifiable natural person. Processing in the meaning of the Directive can be understood as any collection, use or storage of information about workers by electronic means. Also the processing of sound and images is explicitly included in the Directive as possibly being electronic personal data, thus bringing, e.g., video surveillance within the scope of the Directive. The Directive applies to all data controllers and thus does not differentiate between public and private employers.

12.2.2   Relations Between National Labour Law and Directives

There are complementary and sometimes supplemental relationships between the two fields of law. Especially in those European countries that provide for collective agreements between employers and workers, this often also results in agreements on the possible extent of surveillance or performance monitoring aspects (e.g., in Norway or in Germany with the workers councils). These agreements function as a supplement to the already existing European legislation on data protection but also provide for more effective ways of implementing data protection rules at the workplace.

12.2.2.1   General Principles

Broadly speaking, the general interests of employers to routinely monitor the performance of his employees up to a certain extent have to be acknowledged.

The same applies to surveillance measures on a more or less random basis. Employers should always be aware of the fact that almost all surveillance measures taken will fall within the scope of the data protection laws and thus will also have to meet the requirements of the given provisions of the EC Directives. This means that the data processed should be collected for specified, explicit and legitimate purposes. The results should not be misused for other purposes. The collection should also be adequate, relevant and not excessive in relation to the purpose for which they are collected. The storage of these data should not be longer than is necessary for the purpose and a legal ground for collecting according to Article 7 and 8 of the Directive 95/46/EC is needed. In most cases the employees must be informed in advance about the processing of personal data by the data controller, according to Articles 10 and 11 of the Directive 95/46/EC.

12.2.2.2 Problems with Consent in the Working Context

The **consent** of the data subject is probably the most problematic criterion of Article 7 Directive 95/46/EC when being applied to the workplace context. According to Article 2 paragraph (h) of the Directive, consent is defined as a freely given and informed indication of the wishes by which the data subject signifies his agreement to personal data relating to him being processed. However, there are significant doubts whether the consent of the individual should be qualified as freely given in the workplace context. Freedom implies the possibility of choice. The choice not to give consent to the processing of one's own data thus should in no case lead to negative consequences taken by the employer, including the risk of losing the job. The fear of facing negative consequences, for instance losing a job, always has to be taken into account when evaluating the quality of consent in data protection legal context. A high unemployment rate in all European countries is proof of one of the most challenging structural problems of the EU internal market. With almost all parts of society nowadays facing this risk and thus possibly ending up in a degrading line towards poverty, there are clear signs of individuals more or less consciously abandoning their right to privacy in the face of this risk.

As a consequence, the Article 29 Working Party has explicitly put a general question mark behind consent as a possible legitimation in the workplace context: "The Article 29 Working Party takes the view that where, as a necessary and unavoidable consequence of the employment relationship, an employer has to process personal data it is misleading if it seeks to legitimise this processing through consent. Reliance on consent should be confined to cases where the worker has a genuine free choice and is subsequently able to withdraw the consent without detriment" (Working Party Paper No. 48: 23).

The first complete sector-specific national regulation on data protection (Finnish Law on Data Protection in the workplace from 2001) draws the same conclusion under Section 3, where it is stated: necessity principle: "The employer is only allowed to process personal data that is directly necessary for the employment relationship and concerns management of the rights and obligations of the parties to the relationship or benefits provided by the employer for the employee, or arises from the special nature from the work concerned. **No exceptions can be made to this provision, even with the employee's consent**" (unofficial translation by the Finnish Ministry).

Local workers' representatives, for instance works councils within companies in numerous EU member states, can be powerful substitutes in contributing to the workers' rights - especially in terms of protecting their data protection rights.

12.3   Example 1: Surveillance of E-mail Communication and Internet Access in the Private Sector

One of the more complex problems of workers' data protection is the use of the Internet and e-mail by employees. There are a number of tools and applications on the market allowing for the automated analysis of e-mails of employees[177] allowing for hidden mail forwarding, mail analysis and reporting. From a technical perspective this is personalised profiling, using data mining techniques for association (i.e., if there is specific content, then it is a private mail with a likeliness of X%, c.f. sections 4.3.4).

In the context of IT security, intrusion detection and intrusion response systems are implemented. Based on configurable surveillance policies, the network traffic of hosts or network segments is monitored and potential security incidents are reported. Intrusion response systems in addition allow for blocking of specific, predefined network traffic. Though intrusion detection is typically aimed at threats from external networks e.g., the Internet, their use to prevent information theft from within an organisation, for example by employees, has gained importance as well.[178]

Some intrusion detection systems use heuristics to analyse network traffic data[179], though obviously with limited quality. This approach is also referred to as anomaly detection. From a technical perspective this is non-distributive group profiling using data mining techniques for classification (classes are typically normal and abnormal network traffic).

Every organisation has to first define an overall Internet and e-mail policy in order to give transparent advice to their employees and set limits on its possible use. The data protection issue at stake is to what extent employers should be allowed to monitor these communication infrastructures.

In cases where an employer permits the private use of e-mail services, this has to be qualified as "offering public telecommunication" and thus makes Directive 2002/58/EC applicable instead of Directive 95/46/EC. This leads to the application

---

[177] For example http://www1.seattlelab.com/Products/SLMailPro/email_monitor.asp, http://www.email-monitoring.net/ and http://www.siterecon.com/Email-Monitoring-Service.aspx.

[178] See for example http://www.networkcommand.com/IDS/ids.html, http://www.securityfocus.com/infocus/1514 and http://www.gfi.com/news/en/lansim3launch.htm.

[179] See http://www.securityfocus.com/infocus/1728.

of two different protection regimes setting different standards concerning the possibilities of employers to intercept and monitor employee activities, depending on whether private e-mail communication is allowed or not.

In the case of permission, Articles 5 and 6 of the Directive 2002/58/EC in particular have to be respected. Both the privacy of traffic data of the e-mail and the content are to be respected by the employer. As a consequence, surveillance measures concerning e-mail accounts of workers that may be used for private purposes must meet the strict confidentiality requirements. Monitoring of these accounts for the purpose of checking individual working performances is prohibited. Two of the few exceptions from the strict prohibition of storage, disclosure or notice of contents are following concrete suspicions of criminal offences and the collection of evidence in preparation of criminal prosecution procedures.

Practical solutions in order to avoid the two different applicable legal regimes may include the complete restriction of the private use of e-mail for the whole staff. Employees can instead be offered the use of web-mailing services on the Internet. Another practical solution for employers is to offer two different e-mail addresses. The official mailing account will then be open to full monitoring as long as this is communicated to the employees sufficiently. The other account might still be official in a sense but is left for occasional private use. In any case, there have to be guidelines defining under which circumstances which persons shall be able to take notice of traffic data or even the content of the data. Evidence of severe misconduct, for instance reasonable suspicion of passing on business secrets, might be one of the reasons for infringing on an employee's e-mail privacy.

12.4 Example 2: Human Resource and Skill Management

Some modern Human Resource Management tools aim at pooling, profiling and ranking/scoring the potential and the capacities of all employees with regard to their age, qualifications, working performance and salary, etc. in order to optimise deployment within the company.[180] From a technical perspective, in this context distributive group profiling is used. Typically, data mining techniques for clustering or classification are applied.

Since there can be advanced and complex programming involved, the employees effected must be informed about the logic of the programme. They also have the right to be regularly updated about the results of their data being processed. Since the legitimation of the processing according to Article 7 lit b might fail due to a lack of an inner connection with the purpose of the single working contract, consent given by all employees could be an option. Still, this might prove to be impossible, thus raising the question of other means of legitimation.

---

[180] For example, SAP HR as an integrated solution: http://www.sappress.de/katalog/buecher/titel/gp/titelID-717 or training tracking and skill management as a specialised solution for example: http://www.cebos.com/training-system.html.

As a possible solution, the employer could rely on Article 7 lit. f. of the Directive as a legal ground. Nevertheless, it would be necessary to additionally create safeguards for the employers, in order to prevent the legitimate interest of the employer from being overridden by the interests for fundamental rights and freedoms of the data subject (see Art. 7). Thus, specific technical and organisational measures taken by the employer are required, e.g., the system has to guarantee that identification of data subjects is kept no longer than necessary within the system (system of pseudonymity), Article 6 lit. e of the Directive and that it is protected against unauthorised disclosure (Article 17, para 1). A practical way to take account of the fundamental rights of the data subjects would be to restrict the use of the system. For example, it can only be operated if two persons are present simultaneously, one of them associated with the employer, the other associated with the employee. Finally, the results of the scoring process must not be applied to the workers automatically but should be presented with the option for each employee to object and to challenge the results being processed (Article 15 para 2).

12.5   Example 3: Fraud Prevention in Retail

Supermarkets use profiling to detect unusual cash flows, which are often caused by cashier embezzlement.[181] Cash refund transactions are especially scrutinised.

There are some well-known techniques for fraudulently taking money out of a cash register. One example is the use of fake certificates for bottle deposits for usually small amounts of money. In the profiles, cashiers using this method can be determined by a higher rate of refund transactions than average. Further investigation is necessary but can be carried out in a targeted fashion. In addition, data mining is used to generate insight into fraudulent techniques as yet unknown.[182]

Based on this information we can deduce that from a technical perspective personalised as well as non-distributive group profiling (cf. chapter 2.3.2) is being used. Thus it is expected that data mining techniques for association, clustering and classification are used in this context.

A retail chain based in Switzerland claims to have caught fifty of their cashiers fraudulently taking money from the cash till within two months. By using such profiling techniques, they claim to have saved €200.000.[183]

A supermarket chain in Germany wanted to introduce, in co-ordination with the workers council, a fraud prevention system. To this end, they approached the ULD to check the legality of its use with regard to data protection.[184]

---

[181] For example http://www.fujitsu.com/de/services/retail/lossprevention/, http://www.torexretail. de/german/loesungen/einzelhandel/loss-prevention/loss_prevention.php?navid=55 and http:// www.evolution.com/news/GRMediaKit.pdf.

[182] See http://www.quarks.de/dyn/18298.phtml.

[183] See http://www.3sat.de/3sat.php?http://www.3sat.de/nano/cstuecke/71247/index.html.

[184] Result of the study see http://www.datenschutzzentrum.de/material/themen/wirtscha/lossprev. htm.

German data protection regulation in principle allows for the agreement of the social partners within the company to serve as the legal basis for the processing of personal data. The employment contract of the workers affected could not be identified, since the use of the software opened up the possibility for, at least in theory, total surveillance of all workplaces and all cashiers. Even coffee-breaks or the performance speed of single employees could permanently be monitored. This goes beyond the necessity for the execution of the employment contracts, cp. Article 7 (b) of the European Directive 95/46/EC. There is also an overriding interest of the data subjects not to become the object of a complete workplace surveillance structure which would have to be acknowledged in a general weighing of interests, cp. Article 7 (f) of the Directive. The weighing of interests would have to give sufficient consideration to the fact that the use of the software system will unavoidably also touch the fundamental rights of those employees who cannot be alleged of any criminal negligence. These innocent workers would have to take the risk of being accused as a result of the analyses being carried out.

The social partners' agreement on the use of the system had to take into account that by its very nature it is producing suspects at a time where there are no concrete clues or no evidence of a criminal act having been committed. It also has to be taken into account that all workers' rights are being infringed on and that it allows for a complete profiling of performance in the usage of the cash registers. In order to conform with the fundamental rights of the employees and the provisions and principles of data protection law, the ULD demanded that the agreement provided the following regulation:

the purpose-binding principle forces a limit on data being processed in the future. An analysis of older data inventories is prohibited. The employees have to be informed in advance that the system will be activated and basic information on its purposes has to be given.

The interests of the employees make it mandatory not to directly connect disciplinary action with the evaluation of the results, Article 15 of the European Data Protection Directive. Misinterpretations of the results could lead to unfair practices and discrimination, thus it has to be stated in the agreement that the results will not be used for personalised performance monitoring purposes, etc. Analyses of single supermarket performances are possible.

The monitoring of cash register use is reduced to intentional manipulation only. The whole system should only be run by the use of pseudonyms which means that the cashiers could only be identified by their cash register number. Identification may only be carried out if there is concrete evidence for a person to be under suspicion.

All data providing evidence of justifiable suspicion have to be stored also on behalf of the suspect such that they can use them to prove innocence.

The concept governing authorisation and access to the system should limit the number of users to the responsible auditing staff. Further technical and organisational measures have to be taken in order to legitimise and secure the transmission of the data from the separate legal entities to the central auditing unit.

12.6   Summary and Conclusions

European legislation relevant in the context of data protection in the workplace is quite complex, as the overview in section 12.2 shows. In this chapter three case studies illustrating relevant application scenarios for profiling in the workplace were introduced and analysed.

In the first case the use of private e-mail at the workplace was elaborated concerning two relevant European Directives and the existing instruments for e-mail monitoring and analysis. If the employer offers the employee an account for private as well as business e-mails, monitoring e-mail communication is for the most part legally prohibited. As a result, employers should strictly discriminate between e-mail accounts that are used for private e-mail at or from the workplace and those that are used for e-mail on behalf of the employer only. Different approaches to implement these different types of accounts have been suggested.

The second case study analyses the use of human resource and skill management. Relevant questions in this context proved to be appropriate legal grounds to run such a system, transparency of the system's operations and purpose binding for the use of the results.

In the third case study the use of profiling for fraud prevention in retail was explored. In addition to the elaboration of reliable legal grounds for the introduction and application of fraud prevention systems, limitations on data to be collected and analysis were suggested and discussed. Especially in this case, the collection and use of data beyond the scope of the system needs to be prevented by technical and organisational means. This should include co-operation with, e.g., works counsels.

12.7   Reply: The Use of Labour Law to Regulate Employer Profiling: Making Data Protection Relevant Again

Paul De Hert*

The strength of data protection as a legal framework for the balanced application of profiling techniques in employment situations should be assessed with prudence. As a set of rules and guarantees focusing on the individual person, it does not fit well in an area of society where power differences between the parties concerned are considerable. The only legal vocabulary that is accepted and recognised is the one used in collective labour law, where union and employee-representatives discuss most issues, including the ones that concern individual rights. The success of data protection will depend on its ability to find its way into this collectivised vocabulary. But how strong is the vocabulary of labour law?

* Vrije Universiteit Brussel (VUB) and Tilburg Universiteit, Tilburg Instituut for Law, Technology and Society (TILT)

12.7.1 The General Framework: An Empty Shell[185]

The work relationship between employer and employee is characterised by an unequal balance of power. Negotiation and consultation procedures between employers and employees aim to ease the consequences of this unequal relationship. The employer cannot assert his authority with regard to all aspects of the employee's personality and activities. The context of the working conditions presents specific characteristics that have been described by the European Court of Human Rights. Thus, in the case Niemitz v. Germany: *"Respect for private life must also comprise to a certain degree the right to establish and develop relationships with other human beings. There appears, furthermore, to be no reason of principle why this understanding of the notion of "private life" should be taken to exclude activities of a professional or business nature since it is, after all, in the course of their working lives that the majority of people have a significant, if not the greatest, opportunity of developing relationships with the outside world. This view is supported by the fact that, as was rightly pointed out by the Commission, it is not always possible to distinguish clearly which of an individual's activities form part of his professional or business life and which do not."*[186]

Employers should therefore accommodate workers' privacy. Not accommodating privacy in the workplace can result in a lack of employee trust, creativity and health (Business for Social Responsibility Education Fund, 2001). In many cases, workplace monitoring can seriously compromise the privacy and dignity of employees. Surveillance techniques can be used to harass, discriminate and create unhealthy dynamics in the workplace (PHR, 2004). Usually the answer given to these challenges is based on the principles of data protection. Employers are recommended to accommodate data protection rights for their employees. This includes notice, employee participation in drafting a monitoring policy and employee access to information collected under the policy. This is also the core of Leopold's and Meints' analysis, be it that their analysis is clearly European. In practice, this means that recommendations are presented as a result of an analysis of legal texts. They are more than just recommendations, *they are law.* Employers in Europe do not have a moral but a legal duty to accommodate data protection rights, it is more than just good will or enlightened management.

What strikes the reader is the complexity of the analysis. We learn that in European countries the collection and processing of personal information is protected by the EU Data Protection and the Telecommunication Privacy Directives.

---

[185] Most of the articles quoted by the author can be viewed on http://www.vub.ac.be/LSTS/.

[186] 23 November 1992, Series A nr. 251/B, par. 29. See also the case Halford v. United Kingdom, 27 May 1997, *ECR* 1997-III, par. 44: *"In the Court's view, it is clear from its case-law that telephone calls made from business premises as well as from the home may be covered by the notions of "private life" and "correspondence" within the meaning of Article 8 para. 1 (art. 8-1) (see the above-mentioned Klass and Others judgment, loc. cit.; the Malone v. the United Kingdom judgment of 2 August 1984, Series A no. 82, p. 30, para. 64; the above-mentioned Huvig judgment, loc. cit."*

The latter provides for confidentiality of communications for "public" systems and therefore does not cover privately owned systems in the workplace. In these cases the former applies. The result is unsatisfactory. There are two different protection regimes depending on technicalities and we are advised to consider a distinction between private and professional use of e-mail services. Leopold and Meints conclude their analysis under 'Example 1' with the suggestion that the complete restriction of the private use of e-mail for the entire staff might be one of the practical solutions. This recommendation - promoting medieval privacy protection - is illuminating but contradicts the spirit of the Court's findings in *Niemitz*, viz., that in modern life it is not always possible to clearly distinguish which of an individual's activities form part of his professional or business life and which do not.

The principles of data protection rights laid down in the two European Directives are general in scope and linked to many subtleties. Every principle seems to have its exception and every exception gives birth to new exceptions, this time with the emphasis on the scope of the exception. Their application to workplace privacy issues is not always clear. Close your eyes and try to recall what Leopold and Meints have to say on their three examples (surveillance of e-mail-communication and Internet access; human resource and skill management; fraud prevention in retail). The taste in our mouth is technical and procedural. Substantive solutions or answers did not make it into our legal memory. Does data protection have anything to say on substantive issues regarding profiling?

Through the years I have lost a part of my passion for the European data protection regulations and the analysis carried out in terms of data protection. The threats are usually aptly identified and there is a good amount of lip-reading done of the privacy and data protection rights but how about the outcome of the exercise? In 2001 the *Registratiekamer*, the Dutch Data Protection Registrar, published a lengthy list of guidelines for employers planning to implement online employee monitoring systems in the workplace, based on the (then) new Personal Data Protection Act, signed on July 6 2000. These included requirements that a company must discuss the entire system and its usage with the relevant unions and work councils, as well as publishing details of the discussions and the system to the staff. Interestingly, the Dutch Data Protection registrar skated around the contentious issue of personal e-mail at work, saying that, if possible, personal and professional e-mail should be kept separate but, if this cannot be carried out, then monitors should attempt to ignore obviously personal e-mail (Gold, 2001; De Hert, 2001). This kind of legal output has a chilling effect on the reader, at least on this reader. The mountain brings forth a mouse. Employers have nothing to fear with regard to data protection, they can push through as far as they want. Employers, who are open and willing to respect data protection 'rights' must feel like they are sacrificing competitiveness and business advantages. This is even more so when they start reading in newspapers about their colleagues in other countries. With the American Management Association finding that nearly 3/4 of major businesses monitor their employees[187] and with the 2000 U.K RIP Act allowing for most employers to monitor without consent (Crichard, 2001), it must be difficult to explain to employers on the European continent that they cannot monitor their employees at will, as do their American and British colleagues. One of the challenges of European data protection will be to overcome a "race to the bottom" - development in the area of human rights as a consequence of internationalisation. Whereas good communication to parties involved about differences in the legal systems with countries outside the EU will probably lead to more acceptance of the EU legislation, less is true about differences in legal systems within the EU. It is striking to note that the preamble of the 1995 Directive discusses internal market problems due to privacy restrictions in certain EU countries, but does not consider the race to the bottom problems due to the lack of privacy guarantees in certain EU countries. At one time the Commission envisaged a new Directive to harmonise differences in data protection regulation regarding workers (De Vries, 2002) but apparently and sadly this initiative lost momentum.

12.7.2   The Data Protection Move Towards Labour Law Instruments: Transcending Technicalities

There are several models for data protection regulation: comprehensive or sectoral laws; self-regulation and regulation through technology (PHR, 2004). The European approach to regulation is well known: general laws on the European and national level that govern the collection, use and dissemination of personal information by both public and private sectors with an overseeing body that ensures compliance. Traditionally, this approach is contrasted with the United States preference for sectoral laws, governing, for example, video rental records and financial privacy, enforced through a range of mechanisms. Although many European and American authors express strong attachment to the European approach[188] there are alternative viewpoints (Blok, 2001 and 2002: Bergkamp, 2002). Equally, there are reports showing that successful strategies against excessive camera surveillance are driven by the citizens using administrative enforcement mechanisms, rather than by the data protection authorities using data protection mechanisms (Bennett & Bayley, 2005). In recent writings we have therefore applauded the development at the EU level, and at the level of the member states to draft sectoral laws used to complement

---

[187] For a helpful overview of workplace privacy issues, mainly in the United States, see the Electronic Privacy Information Centre (EPIC)'s *Workplace Privacy Page* http://www.epic.org/privacy/workplace/; and Solove & Rotenberg, 2003.

[188] "A major drawback with this approach is that it requires that new legislation be introduced with each new technology, so protections frequently lag behind. The lack of legal protection for individual's privacy on the Internet in the United States is a striking example of its limitations. There is also the problem of a lack of an oversight agency" (PHR, 2004). For more detail about the different approaches, see De Hert, 2002b.

comprehensive legislation by providing more detailed protections for certain categories of information, such as telecommunications, police files or consumer credit records.

The turn in data protection writings and practices towards labour law, not quite theorised but nontheless present in Leopold's and Meints' analysis, is to be understood along the same lines. Through it, there is an attempt to benefit from the advantages of both sectoral laws *and* self-regulation, in addition to enjoying the advantages of a general framework.

At first sight this turn is not evident: the European data protection framework is of a general nature and it provides for general concepts and proper enforcement machinery. However, more is needed to penetrate social sub-spheres such as labour law and labour practices. The demonstration of Leopold and Meints convincingly shows that data protection has at least something to say about profiling at the workplace but not much insight is given about the enforceability of the solutions and recommendations they arrive at. Based on my knowledge of the European, Belgian and Dutch case law - showing unfamiliarity with data protection concerns or preferential treatment of employer interests, there is no reason to be cheerful (De Hert, 2002a; de Vries, 2002; De Hert & Loncke, 2005; De Hert & Gutwirth, 2006).[189] Hence, the use of labour law and its self-regulatory characteristics: absence of time-consuming formal procedures needed for 'real' or formal legislation, ability for easy adaptation to changing circumstances, creation of rules, build on values that the relevant parties are already familiar with, more awareness due to self-legislation and more willingness to comply (Koops, et al., 2006).

---

[189] In a recent Dutch case, the applicant requested a court order for a bank ('Dexia') to supply relevant personal data. He demanded to be provided with a complete overview of all processed personal data, including information about the purposes of the processing, the recipients of the data and the sources of the data. Further, the applicant demanded copies of: the lease contract, the risk profile, certificates of the shares referred to in the contract, certificates of dividend payments, the credit-worthiness survey ('credit-score'), written reports about telephone calls and every other document that concerned him. The court was of the opinion that the applicant had no right to obtain a copy of the contract. However, Dexia had to give information about the contract data, to the extent that they could be defined as personal data. The same was true for the requested copies of the dividend payments. The court stressed that Dexia had to submit information about all personal data, irrespective of the existence of a legal obligation to process these data. There was for example, no obligation for Dexia to set up a risk profile. But if data are processed to construct such a profile, they have to be included in the overview provided to the data subject. However, the court decided that Dexia could make use of one of the exemptions provided by the Act, namely that a controller is not obliged to provide an overview of the personal data if this implies a disproportionate administrative burden for him. Dexia demonstrated to the court that their duty to respond to a similar request had seriously upset its organisation and had already cost more than a hundred thousand euros. For this reason the court rejected the applicant's request and decided that in this instance Dexia would not have to provide the overview of the personal data. *Dexia v applicant*, 12 July 2005. The decision (in Dutch) is published on www.rechtspraak.nl under number LJN AS2127. See Jos Webbink and Gerrit-Jan Zwenne, 'The scope of Access Rights under the Dutch Data Protection Act', via http://www.twobirds.com/english/publications/articles/Access_Rights_under_the_Dutch_Data_Protection_Act.cfm. We learn from the Dexia case that profiling in an employment situation aiming to prevent further or establish fraud committed by employees is regarded as individual profiling covered by the Directive when it aims to identify the fraud. On the contrary, data mining techniques to generate insight on fraudulent behaviour and methods will be justified by group profiling when the information is not convertible to any particular person. The real purposes regarding the application of the data processing are decisive.

12.7.3   The Turn of Data Protection to Labour Law Instruments: Transcending Individuality and Individual Consent

There are however more than 'language' factors accounting for this striking turn from data protection law to labour law. In particular we draw attention to the collective dimension of privacy. The distinction between first, second and third generation human rights has never been very solid. First generation rights also serve collective interests. Freedom of assembly, for instance, laid down in article 11 of the European Convention on Human Rights contains a straightforward illustration of this proposition: "Everyone has the right to freedom of peaceful assembly and to freedom of association with others, including the right to form and to join trade unions for the protection of his interests". In a similar vein, does the protection afforded by the privacy right benefit groups? The right to have a certain name given to a child offers protection to persons belonging to certain minority groups (Gilbert, 1992). We saw above the recognition of the right to privacy in *Niemitz* as a right to develop relationships with the outside world. The legal and material environment needed for such a development cannot be the creation of one individual. It is a collective good that should in principle be open to everyone. To claim rights with such a strong collective basis, associations of all kinds are far better placed than individual ones (De Hert & De Schutter, 1998). If privacy has a future, the legislation behind privacy will, so we believe, have to allow associations defending privacy by opening privacy procedures for associations. This will contribute to an objectivation of privacy and data protection conflicts and provide solutions when individuals are not willing to take up their rights (with a heavy collective dimension). We note that this call for recognition of the collective dimension of privacy is not new in international human rights law. Rights are defined in a certain context and this context changes or may change. New refugee patterns have brought legal scholars to recognise that today's society is in need of a set of refugee rights that are not only accorded to the individual refugee but in certain cases also to refugee groups in need of protection (Jackson, 1991; Hathaway & Neve, 1997; Parrish, 2000; Fitzpatrick, 1996).

Partly, data protection regulation recognises this collective dimension of privacy through its administrative features: special watchdogs are created and delicate processing activities are subjected to notification and checking procedures.[190] Contemporary data protection, viz. data protection after the 1995 Directive, has shifted away from this by replacing a system of regulation based

---

[190] These procedures for notifying the supervisory authority are designed to ensure disclosure of the purposes and main features of any processing operation for the purpose of verification that the operation is in accordance with the data protection principles. In order to avoid unsuitable administrative formalities, exemptions from the obligation to notify and simplifications are allowed, except in cases where certain processing operations are likely to pose specific risks to the rights and freedoms of data subjects by virtue of their nature, scope or purposes, such as that of excluding individuals from a right, benefit or a contract, or by virtue of the specific use of new technologies. In addition a system of prior checking is made possible for risky processing operations and in the course of the preparation of new legislation regarding the protection of personal data.

on the idea that processing activities need to be legitimate by a system based on the idea that processing activities need *consent*. It would not be feasible to analyse this in great depth but the 1995 Directive, inspired by Dutch pragmatism and its ability to conceive everything as a potential candidate for trade, has amended some of the basis intuitions of the Council of Europe Convention of 28 January 1981 for the Protection of Individuals with regard to Automatic Processing of Personal Data by making consent a valuable option in almost all cases. In practice, this implied a complete redrafting of some national data protection bills of older date that did not recognise consent as a legal ground for the legitimate processing of data (Leonard & Poullet, 1999). We are, for that reason no great admirers of the 1995 EU Directive boasting in its preamble that "the principles of the protection of the rights and freedoms of individuals, notably the right to privacy, which are contained in this Directive, give substance to and amplify those contained in the Council of Europe Convention of 28 January 1981" (comp. with Gutwirth, 2002).

Leopold and Meints rightly consider consent of the data subject as one of the most problematic criteria of Art. 7 of the 1995 Directive when being applied to the workplace context. According to Article 2 para (h) of the Directive, consent has to be defined as a freely given and informed indication of the wishes by which the data subject signifies his agreement to personal data relating to him being processed. Many companies traditionally use consent as the legal basis to process workers' personal data to a third country. Workers are then asked to sign a so-called 'consent form' agreeing to the processing. Such forms often concern a whole list of personal data and rarely give explanations as to the consequences of not agreeing to the processing by the worker. In fact, these forms are habitually seen by the employers as a formality: "let the workers sign and then it is OK" (Blas, 2002). The foolishness of the European legislator when introducing consent as a legal ground in the sphere of human rights has provoked some reaction from the member states. The Dutch Data Protection Law defines consent as any freely given, specific and informed indication of wishes by which the data subject signifies his agreement to personal data relating to him being processed (Article 1, letter i of the WBP). Again, this is not much help for the regulation of the working sphere. The Working Party rightly takes the view that where consent is required from a worker and where there is a real or potential prejudice that arises from not consenting, the consent is not valid in terms of satisfying either article 7 or 8 of the Directive, as it is not freely given. If it is not possible for the worker to refuse, it cannot be considered as consent, as this must at all times be freely given. A worker must therefore be able to withdraw consent without prejudice. The Working Party underlines the fact that where, as an unavoidable consequence of the employment relationship an employer has to process personal data, it is misleading if it seeks to legitimise this processing through consent. Reliance on consent should be confined to cases where the worker has a genuine free choice and is subsequently able to withdraw consent without detriment (Working Party, Opinion 8/2001).

Blas has brilliantly identified the elements that should be taken into consideration for the correct interpretation of the requirements regarding consent

(Blas, 2002).[191] Consent for profiling operations should be freely given and has to be specific. This means in particular that it should specifically be given for each individual profiling operation, not for profiling in general. The requirement for information implies that the data subject should be aware or made aware of the particular risks of the profiling operation. The consent will only be valid if the data subject has been sufficiently informed. If the relevant information is not provided this exception will not apply. It is not sufficient if the data subject has been informed about the intended profiling operation and has not objected to it (opt-out construction). This is not a clear indication of the wishes of the data subject. Because the consent must be unambiguous, any doubt about the fact that the consent has been given would also render the exception inapplicable.

One could question the wisdom of the European legislator in inserting consent as a general legal ground, knowing that Europe is a continent of workers rather than autonomous Greek Gods. Overseeing these requirements regarding consent makes one realise that consent is difficult to apply when the profiling envisaged would cover the data of numerous data subjects (Blas, 2002). In such a case, the information has to be given in a complete and appropriate way to all the data subjects and consent has to be obtained from all of them in order to enable profiling. In addition to the fact that this whole operation can be time consuming and might involve considerable expense (for instance if the data subjects are in different locations), the use of consent for this kind of case shows some other practical inconveniences. For instance: what does the controller do if some of the data subjects give their consent and others do not?[192] Also, what does the controller do if some of the data subjects decide to withdraw their consent at a later stage?[193] Strategically, the turn to labour law can be understood as a way to overcome the burdens of consent for the employer willing to profile more than one employee. Freedom implies the possibility of choice, as Leopold and Meints rightly note, but what is left for the individual worker to choose when worker representatives have decided upon their rights?

12.7.4 Assessing the Role of Labour Law

The foregoing casts some shadow on the role of labour law in the area of privacy and data protection.[194] One could respond to this that this new role for representative

---

[191] In the following we stay close to the analysis of Blas (regarding transfers of workers' data to third countries) but we transpose her analysis to our subject matter.

[192] "If workers are free to say 'yes' or 'no' to the envisaged transfer there might be a considerable amount of workers opposing the profiling operation": Blas, 2002.

[193] "It should be borne in mind that data subjects (or where applicable their legal representatives) are free to withdraw their consent at any time. The decision to withdraw consent does not have a retroactive effect but the processing of the data of that data subject will have to be terminated from that moment on": Blas, 2002.

[194] Our finding that privacy is a collective good that needs to be upheld by collective means certainly does not imply that workers should give their rights away to representative workers bodies.

labour organisations could prove to be beneficial for human rights protection, since especially small firms do not always have the resources or talents to organise social dialogue with their workers in a proper manner and tend to decide without dialogue on the implementation of privacy-threatening technology such as cameras and profiles. Workers' associations would then be a better option. The adoption in Belgium of two privacy related 'Collective Labour Agreements', one on cameras and another on monitoring e-mail and the Internet, brought with it the appearance of new monitoring methods. On the grounds of a violation of a privacy related collective agreement, the unions can go to court, or demand the intervention of labour inspectors working for the Ministry of Employment and possessing police powers (De Hert & Loncke, 2005). These agreements have contributed to the acceptance of data protection rights by making them sound much more concrete. Hence, 'unique' new rights have entered the legal horizon in Belgium. Collective Labour Agreement 68 (16 June 1998) dealing with the protection of the private life with respect to camera monitoring at the workplace, explicitly prohibits secret surveillance, unless performed by law enforcement agencies[195] and prohibits permanent camera monitoring of employees. Temporary camera-surveillance is the only type of control that enables the control of the workers. This kind of surveillance is allowed in two circumstances: for the control of the performances of the employees and for the control of the production process. Of course, these categories are very broad but the main issue is that permanent monitoring is not allowed.

In a similar vein Collective Labour Agreement 81 (26 April 2002) on the protection of the private lives of employees with respect to controls on electronic on-line communications data, distinguishes between general and individual monitoring of employees. Resembling the example of Leopold and Meints regarding the fraud prevention system in the German supermarket chain, the Agreement pushes the employer to first turn to general monitoring. In principle, the agreement seems to suggest, the employer will first perform a general control without being able to determine what wrong-doing can be attributed to which employee. Only in the second instance can the employee responsible be sought. 'Individualisation' of electronic on-line communications data, as referred to in the agreement, means an action whose purpose is to process electronic on-line communications data collected during controls by the employer, in order to attribute them to an identified or identifiable person. Agreement 81 is based on the assumption that group profiling (without individualisation or personalisation) is less harmful for privacy-rights, although undoubtedly the impact of such a technique can be far reaching, even if no personalisation takes place.

A close reading of Collective Labour Agreement 81 (26 April 2002) recalls our 'data protection experience' of the mountain and the mouse: in most cases

---

[195] Secret monitoring can be introduced provided that the provisions of the law of criminal procedure are met. This means that only the Public Prosecutor can organise such a camera surveillance. Within the context of a labour agreement it is strictly forbidden.

'individualisation' is possible without mediation. Recourse to general monitoring is only made obligatory in situations of minor importance. Elsewhere we have identified the events of September 11 as a driver behind the privacy unfriendly provisions in Collective Labour Agreement 81. The workers' representatives at the negotiation table obviously did not do a good job. This was partly due to a lack of case law in favour of employee's interests. Only after the conclusion of the Agreement, the news spread that the French Court of Cassation had rendered an important judgment in favour of workers' privacy with regard to the use of the Internet and e-mail.[196] This Judgement immediately provoked more privacy friendly judgements in Belgium but did not have an impact on the drafting of Collective Labour Agreement no. 81. It is therefore often heard that this agreement is a product of the period after 9/11 and *before* the judgement of the French Court of Cassation.

With this observation, we return to our description of models of regulating data protection. Labour law in some way allows for forms of self-regulation, in which companies and industry bodies establish codes of practice and engage in self-policing. In theory, there is nothing wrong with this, especially not in the light of our finding that the general provisions of the EU Directive regarding consent do not fit into the reality of the working sphere. However, in many countries, especially the United States, efforts to achieve more balanced outcomes for data protection through self-regulation have been disappointing, with little evidence that the aims of the codes are regularly fulfilled. Adequacy and enforcement are the major problems with these approaches. Industry codes in many countries have tended to provide only weak protections and lack enforcement (PHR, 2004). We wrote that judges are often unfamiliar with data protection and the work of the data protection authority. Most significant in this respect is the important judgment of the Belgian Court of Cassation (27 February 2001), omitting all reference to international and national data protection *and* the Collective Labour Agreement no. 68 of 16 June 1998. Both areas of law with their specific but complementary legal instruments were ignored and evidence gathered through secret monitoring by the employer was legally accepted in court. Is data protection really better off with labour law in its stable? Of course but in a legal system that refuses to distinguish between secret profiling and legitimate or transparent profiling, labour law will not do what data protection law is unable to do. Elsewhere in this volume, Gutwirth and I have defended the view that stronger allies (such as criminal law prohibitions) are needed to realise transparency and other key values of data protection. The fact that human rights are at stake does not make self-regulation or regulation through labour law actors illegitimate – public interest can be very well served by these models of regulation - but it does force the central legislator to be more alert and to intervene if necessary (Koops, et al., 2006).

---

[196] Cass., 2 October 2001, *Dalloz*, Jurisprudence, 2001, no. 39, 3148-3153, annotated by P.-Y. Gautier, via www.droit-technologie.org.

12.8 Bibliography

Art. 29 Data Protection Working Party, *WP No. 48 Opinion 8/2001 on the processing of personal data in the employment context*, adopted on 13 September 2001. Available at: http://ec.europa.eu/justice_home/fsj/privacy/docs/wpdocs/2001/wp48en.pdf.

Art. 29 Data Protection Working Party, *WP No. 55 Working document on the surveillance of electronic communications in the workplace*, adopted on 29 May 2002. Available at: http://ec.europa.eu/justice_home/fsj/privacy/docs/wpdocs/2002/wp55_en.pdf.

Bennett, C., J., Bayley, R.M., 'Video Surveillance and Privacy Protection Law in Canada', in Nouwt, S., de Vries, B.R., Prins, C. (eds.), *Reasonable Expectations of Privacy? Eleven Country Reports on Camera Surveillance and Workplace Privacy*, T.M.C. Asser Press, the Netherlands, 2005, pp. 61-90.

Bergkamp, L., 'EU Data Protection Policy. The Privacy Fallacy: Adverse Effects Of Europe's Data Protection Policy in An Information-Driven Economy', *Computer Law & Security Report*, Vol. 18, No. 1, Elsevier, Netherlands, 2002, pp. 31-45.

Blas, D.A., 'Transfers of personal data to third countries in the employment context: the use of international databases for workers' data', *Privacy & Informatie*, Jaargang 4, No.1 Kluwer Juridische Uitgevers, Belgium, 2002, pp. 24-28.

Business for Social Responsibility Education Fund, *Striking a Balance: e-Privacy in the Workplace*, 2001.

Blok, P., *Het recht op privacy. Een onderzoek naar de betekenis van het begrip 'privacy' in het Nederlands en Amerikaans recht*, Den Haag: Boom Juridische uitgevers, 2002.

Blok, P., 'Protection des données aux Etats-Unis' Chapter 1, Title IV in De Hert, P., (ed.), *Manuel sur la vie privée et la protection des données*, Ed. Politéia, Brussels, update No. 7 (2001), pp. 3-40.

Crichard, M., 'E-Mail Monitoring- Eavesdropping At Work — Is It Legal?', *Computer Law & Security Report*, Vol. 17, No. 2, Elsevier, Neth., 2001, pp. 120-121.

De Hert, P. & De Schutter, O., 'Straatsburg, videosurveillance en het vorderingsrecht van verenigingen' [Video-Surveillance and Organisations before the European Court], *Algemeen Juridisch Tijdschrift (A.J.T.)*, No. 16, Mys en Breesch, Gent, 1998, pp. 504-511.

De Hert, P., 'Internetrechten in het bedrijf. Controle op e-mail en Internetgebruik in Belgisch en Europees perspectief', [Employer control of e-mail and Internet in Belgium and Europe], *Auteur&Media*, No. 1, 2001, pp. 110-116.

De Hert, P., 'Kenbaarheid van bedrijfscontrole op e-mail en internetgebruik. Factoren die spelen bij de chaos rond dit leerstuk [Foreseaability of Surveillance by Employers of E-mail and Internet. Factors that Contribute to the Vagueness of Privacy Protection], *Privacy & Informatie*, Jaargang 4, No. 1, Kluwer Juridische Uitgevers, Belgium 2002a, pp. 26-30.

De Hert, P., 'European Data Protection and E-Commerce: Trust Enhancing?' in Prins, J.E.J., Ribbers, P.M.A. Van Tilborg, H.C.A. Veth, A.F.L & Van Der Wees, J.G.L. (eds), *Trust in Electronic Commerce*, The Hague, Kluwer Law International, 2002b, pp. 171-230.

De Hert, P., Loncke, M., 'Camera Surveillance and Workplace Privacy in Belgium', in Nouwt, S., de Vries, B.R., Prins, C. (eds.), *Reasonable Expectations of Privacy? Eleven Country Reports on Camera Surveillance and Workplace Privacy*, T.M.C. Asser Press, the Netherlands, 2005, pp. 167-209.

De Hert, P. & Gutwirth, S., 'Privacy, data protection and law enforcement. Opacity of the individual and transparency of power' in Claes, E., Duff, A. & Gutwirth, S. (eds.), *Privacy and the criminal law*, Antwerp/Oxford, Intersentia, 2006, pp. 61-104.

de Vries, H., 'Rechtspraak over 'mailen en 'surfen', *Privacy & Informatie*, Jaargang 4, No.1, Kluwer Juridische Uitgevers, Belgium, 2002, pp. 4-9.

European Commission, *Second stage consultation with the community social partners on the protection of personal data in the employment context from 30/10/2002*. Available at: http://europa.eu.int/comm/employment_social/news/2002/oct/data_prot_en.html.

Fitzpatrick, J., 'Revitalizing the 1951 Refugee Convention', *Harvard Human Rights Journal*, Vol. 9, Harvard Law School and Harvard Human Rights Program, Harvard, 1996, pp. 229-253.

Gold, S., Dutch Employers Can Monitor Employees' Online Activities", *Newsbytes* (01/10/01) Available at: http://www.newsbytes.com/news/01/160295.html.

Gilbert, G., 'The Legal Protection Accorded to Minority Groups in Europe', *N.Y.I.L.*, Vol. 23, Cambridge University Press, Cambridge, 1992, pp. 67-104.

Gutwirth, S. *Privacy and the Information Age*, Lanham, Rowman & Littlefield Publ., 2002.

Hathaway, J., Neve, R.A. 'Making International Refugee Law Relevant Again. A Proposition for Collectivized and Solution Oriented Protection', *Harvard Human Rights Journal*, Vol. 10, Harvard Law School and Harvard Human Rights Program, Harvard, 1997, pp. 112-137.

Hendrickx, F., *Protection of workers' personal data in the European Union: Part I – general issues and sensitive data; Part II – surveillance and monitoring at work*; Tilburg 2002. Available at: http://europa.eu.int/comm/employment_social/labour_law/docs/dataprotection_hendrickx_ combinedstudies_en.pdf.

Jackson, I.C., 'The 1951 Convention relating to the Status of Refugees: A Universal Basis for Protection', *International Journal of Refugee Law*, Vol. 3, No. 3, Oxford University Press, Oxford, 1991, pp. 403-413.

Koops, B.-J., et al., 'Should self-regulation be the starting point?', in Koops, B.-J. et al. (Eds)., *Starting Points for ICT Regulation*, The Hague, TMC Asser Press, 2006, pp. 109-150.

Lasprogata, G., King, N. J., Pillay, S., 'Regulation of Electronic Employee Monitoring: Identifying Fundamental Principles of Employee Privacy through a Comparative Study of Data Privacy Legislation in the European Union, United States and Canada', *Stan. Tech. L. Rev.* 4, Stanford 2004. Available at: http://stlr.stanford.edu/STLR/Articles/04_STLR_4/index.htm.

Leonard, Th. & Poullet, Y., 'La protection des données à caractère personnel en pleine (é)volution. La loi du 11 décembre 1998 transposant la directive 95/46/C.E. du 24 octobre 1995', *Journal des Tribunaux*, Larcier, Belgium, 22 May 1999, 378 ff.

Parrish, M., 'Redefining the Refugee: The Universal Declaration of Human Rights as a Basis for Refugee Protection', *Cardozo Law Review*, Vol. 22, No. 1, 2000, pp. 223-267. Available at: http://www.cardozo.yu.edu/cardlrev/pdf/221Parrish.pdf.

PHR, *Privacy and Human Rights 2004*. Available at: http://www.privacyinternational.org/article. shtml?cmd[347]=x-347-82589&als[theme]=Privacy%20and%20Human%20Rights&headline =PHR2004, consulted 13 November 2004.

Solove, D.J., Rotenberg, M., *Information Privacy Law*, Elective Series, Aspen, 2003.

Working Party, Opinion 8/2001 on the processing of personal data in the employment context, adopted on 13 September 2001, 5062/01/EN/Final, WP 48.

Part III
Profiling, Democracy and Rule of Law

In this part we will look into the relevant legal framework and assess the adequacy of the existing framework in terms of democracy and rule of law.

Chapter 13
Cogitas, Ergo Sum. The Role of Data Protection Law and Non-discrimination Law in Group Profiling in the Private Sector

Wim Schreurs, Mireille Hildebrandt, Els Kindt, and Michaël Vanfleteren

This chapter focuses on the legal uncertainty regarding the applicability of data protection law in the case of profiling. This legal uncertainty stems amongst others from the definitions of personal data, data processing and data controller in EU regulations as well as from the possible exclusion of anonymous data from the applicability of data protection law. We will show that it is perfectly possible to construct and apply profiles without identifying the person concerned in the sense of data protection law.

We will build our legal analysis gradually upon the three different steps that exist in the construction and application of profiles: the collection of personal data and other information to construct the profile; the construction of the profile upon personal and anonymous data and the application of a group profile to a group or an individual. For each level, we will analyse whether and how data protection law applies. We will use case law and legal doctrine in our analysis.

As a result of the legal uncertainty that we find in data protection law, we will then try to find answers in privacy and anti-discrimination law, with a special focus on legislation and jurisprudence in the case of racial and ethnic profiling.

13.1 Introduction

Profiling is the process of 'discovering' correlations between data in databases that can be used to identify and represent a subject and/or the application of profiles (sets of correlated data) to individuate and represent a subject or to identify a subject as a member of a group or category. In the case of group profiling the subject is a group (which can be a category or a community of persons).[197] Any particular individual

---

Wim Schreurs, Mireille Hildebrandt Vrije Universiteit Brussels (VUB), Els Kindt, Michaël Vanfleteren (KULeuven-ICRI)

---

[197] Chapter 1, section 1.2. In a legal context, a data subject is mostly understood as a person. However, to understand group profiling it is of crucial importance to face the fact that the subject of a group profile is a group (a category or a community) and not an individual person. In the case of non-distributive profiles, the application of the group profile to an individual member of the group can lead to a wrongful attribution of risks or preferences. See section 1.3.2 of chapter 1. 'The group profile represents thus an abstract person, rather than one particular individual': Hildebrandt, M., Backhouse, J. (Eds.), 2005:10.

M. Hildebrandt and S. Gutwirth (eds.), *Profiling the European Citizen:*
Cross-Disciplinary Perspectives.
© Springer Science + Business Media B.V. 2008

that is considered as a *member* of that group may be subject to an application of the group profile.[198] The more sophisticated a group profile becomes, due to the availability of ever more (relevant) data, the more it inclines towards a personalised profile and the more subtly it will discriminate between members and non-members.[199] As described in many of the chapters of this volume, the application of group profiles can affect us in a number of ways, especially in the case of the increasing automation of decision taking, social interaction and doing business.

To try to assess this impact from a legal perspective, we discuss two legal fields that both aim at the protection of individuals: data protection law with regard to the processing of personal data and anti-discrimination law with regard to the treatment of individuals on the basis of group profiles. We will limit ourselves to an analysis of profiling in the private sector (a civil setting).[200]

13.2   Group Profiling and Data Protection Law[201]

13.2.1   *General Introduction to the Data Protection Directive 95/46 EC*

Data protection law applies when personal data are collected or processed. However, Data Protection Directive 95/46 does not apply to the processing of personal data (i) concerning *legal persons*, (ii) carried out by a natural person in the exercise of activities that are *purely personal or domestic*, such as correspondence and the holding of records of addresses and (iii) carried out for the purposes of *public security, defence, national security* or in the course of State activities in areas of criminal law and other activities that do not come within the scope of Community law.[202] Since we will focus on the private sector, we assume that these exceptions do not apply. It should be obvious that these exceptions seriously limit the applicability of the protection offered by the Directive. Personal data means 'any information relating to an identified or identifiable natural person (data subject)'. An identifiable

---

[198] 'Instead of discriminating a person from all other persons, group profiling seems to focus on identifying a person with a certain group of persons': Hildebrandt, M., Backhouse, J. (Eds.), 2005:16. See chapter 1 about the consequences of applying non-distributive profiles, or non-universal generalisations.

[199] Cp. chapter 6 of this volume.

[200] Privacy law, consumer protection law, e-commerce law etc. are not further discussed in this chapter.

[201] We limit ourselves in this text to the two important European Directives on data protection: Directive 95/46/EC of the European Parliament and of the Council of 24 October 1995 on the protection of individuals with regard to the processing of personal data on the free movement of such data, *Official Journal* L 281, 23 November 1995, pp. 31-50 (Data Protection Directive 95/46) and Directive 2002/58/EC of 12 July 2002 concerning the processing of personal data and the protection of privacy in the electronic communications sector, *Official Journal* L 201, 31 July 2002, pp. 37-47 (Directive on Privacy and Electronic Communications).

[202] Article 3 § 2 of the Data Protection Directive.

person is 'one who can be identified directly or indirectly, in particular by reference to an identification number or to one or more factors specific to his physical, physiological, mental, economic, cultural or social identity'.[203] Data protection does not apply when no reasonable possibility exists to link the data with an identifiable person[204]: this is the case when personal data are rendered anonymous in such a way that the data subject is no longer identifiable.[205]

It may be important that data protection should apply to group profiling.[206] Data protection law creates rights and obligations that apply from the moment personal data are processed *and* most of these rights and obligations cannot be found in other fields of law. In order to underline the importance of its application, we first discuss these general rights and obligations. We then indicate why the application of data protection law is important, in particular at the moment of the *construction* of the profile. We will finally treat the difficult question of whether and when data protection law applies in the case of group profiling.

The general rights and obligations of data protection law, often called 'data protection principles'[207] can be found in Data Protection Directive 95/46. If data protection law applies, personal data must be (i) processed fairly and lawfully, (ii) collected for specified, explicit and legitimate purposes and not further processed in a way incompatible with those purposes, (iii) adequate, relevant and not excessive in relation to the purposes for which they are collected and/or further processed and (iv) accurate and where necessary, kept up to date and in a form that permits identification of the data subject for no longer than is necessary.[208]

Personal data can only be collected and processed (v) if the data subject has unambiguously given his consent or in other situations, which however all have in common that in

---

[203] Article 2(a) of the Data Protection Directive 95/46/EC. For the purpose of this article, we will not make a distinction between sensitive and non-sensitive data. We will consider all data as non-sensitive for the purpose of this text. Sensitive data differ from non-sensitive data in the sense that processing of sensitive data is principally prohibited and requires extra protection. In this sense, the safeguards we describe can be seen as minimal safeguards that apply or should apply to sensitive data. See also chapter 14 of this volume.

[204] Recital 26 of Data Protection Directive 95/46/EC: 'whereas, to determine whether a person is identifiable, account should be taken of all the means likely reasonably to be used either by the controller or by any other person to identify the said person'. After the text for this chapter was finalised, Opinion 7/2007 on the concept of personal data was published on 20th June 2007 by the Art. 29 Working Party (01248/07/EN, WP136).

[205] Recital 26. See infra.

[206] Contra Koops, B-J., in Hildebrandt, M. & Gutwirth, S., (Eds.), 2005: 69: 'A more important issue is why we should really be concerned with data protection. (...), it is outdated and doomed to fail in the current information society. Data storage devices and data networks are here to stay. They create such huge opportunities for collecting and processing data (...) that trying to prevent data collection and trying to restrict data processing is banging one's head against a brick wall. (...). Instead of focusing on the early, enabling stages of data processing, it should concentrate on the later, usage stage of data processing.'

[207] The data protection principles have been articulated in the OECD Guidelines Governing the Protection of Privacy and Transborder Data Flows of Personal Data, 23 September 1980.

[208] Article 6.1. of Data Protection Directive 95/46/EC.

these situations the processing of data must be 'necessary'.[209] The data controller must (vi) inform a data subject of his representative's identity, of the purposes of the processing for which the data are intended and of the recipients or the categories of recipients of the data.[210] The data controller is (vii) responsible for the confidentiality and the security of the personal data and must notify the processing to a national supervisory authority.[211] Furthermore, the Data Protection Directive indicates the national law applicable when data are processed in different member states[212] and prohibits the transfer of personal data to third countries that do not ensure an adequate level of protection.[213] Finally, the data subject has a right of individual participation, which means that he has the right to obtain from the controller, amongst others, confirmation as to whether and for which purposes data relating to him are being processed, as well as 'knowledge of the logic involved in any automatic processing of data concerning him, at least in the case of automated decisions'.[214]

We claim that it is important that data protection principles apply *especially* to the collection of personal data used to construct the profile.[215] We have four reasons for this assumption.

First, the mere collection of personal data does not necessarily fall within the scope of privacy, anti-discrimination, computer crime or other laws. Processing is often necessary in communications or transactions, in which case data protection law at least guarantees the aforementioned rights and obligations.[216] Privacy and anti-discrimination law may, e.g., only offer protection if a profile is applied after the data have been processed.

---

[209] See Article 7 of Data Protection Directive 95/46/EC. For example, processing must be necessary for the performance of a contract, for compliance with a legal obligation, for the protection of a vital interest of the data subject etc... See infra.

[210] Article 10. However, two provisions can be regretted, regarding the obligation to provide the data subject with the 'categories of recipients' of the data. First, not the names of the recipients but only the categories of recipients must be indicated. This explains why it suffices that websites only mention that data are shared with 'partners' or 'affiliated companies' without indicating the names of the recipients, requiring a special request from the data subject who wants to be further informed. Second, the communication of the categories of recipients to the data subject is only required in as far as such further information is necessary, having regard to the specific circumstances in which the data are collected, to guarantee fair processing. The vagueness of these requirements seems to paralyse effective implementation.

[211] Articles 16, 17 and 18 of Data Protection Directive 95/46/EC. Upon notification to the national data protection supervisor - which must be done in many cases but not always - the controller must inform the national supervisory authority of the categories of personal data processed and of the purposes of processing, hereby indicating the measures taken to protect the confidentiality and security of the data.

[212] Article 4, which aims to create more legal certainty.

[213] Articles 25 and 26.

[214] Article 12.

[215] Contra Koops, Reply in Hildebrandt, M. & Gutwirth, S., (Eds.), 2005: 69.

[216] If data protection would not apply at the level of collection, we would not have the guarantee that 'our' personal data are secured and kept confidential; that they are are kept in a form that permits identification of the data subject for no longer than is necessary; that we are informed that companies are using our personal data to make profiles; that our personal data cannot be transferred to countries that do not offer adequate protection, etc.

Second, data protection law may offer us the *last resort* to hinder the construction of group profiles. By objecting to the collection or - at the moment of collection - the further processing of personal data for profiling purposes, data protection may provide means to effectively prevent automated profiling as such. If profiling is a problem in that it creates an excessive amount of 'dossiers' (files) about individual persons, even if we are treated equally and without infringement of our privacy, because it facilitates undesired discrimination and privacy infringements, the collection level may offer the most adequate means to prevent the excessive construction of profiles in our society. In principle, it allows us to prevent the collection of data from which profiles can be inferred or which can be used to profile us as members of a relevant group. After collection, personal data may be made anonymous, in which case data protection no longer applies. Hindering the construction of profiles through data protection law may be an interesting track, since a new concern could be that a vast collection of personal data allows something that non-automated profiling practices cannot provide to the same extent: the inclusion of a detailed personal history in the construction of a profile.[217] If, e.g., we have been poor for the last twenty years and we suddenly win the lottery, the profile will not forget our former poverty.[218] If we have been a thief at the age of 18, we may be confronted with this for the rest of our lives if our past remains included in our present interactions.

Third, data protection at the moment of collection will concern data of individuals other than just those to which the group profile will be applied; the construction of a group profile does not necessarily include the processing of data of those to whom it will be applied. A supermarket may for example use your and my personal data to construct a profile and apply the profile to another person (by sending personalised advertising, because the profile seems to apply to him). Thus data protection at this level provides protection both for those whose data are used and for those to whom profiles inferred from them may be applied.

Fourth, data protection reflects a rather objective tool to protect individuals. It gives more legal certainty than privacy or anti-discrimination law because it simply applies when personal data are processed. The questions of when privacy is at stake or when someone has been treated unfairly are more difficult to answer than the question of whether personal data have been processed.[219]

---

[217] This counts in particular for personalised profiling.

[218] Contra A. Kundig (2002:24): 'We have to face quite *paradoxical effects* of unlimited electronic storage and instant communication: while the individual can be confronted at any time with a complete record of all his / her actions in the past, *history* is becoming an endangered species since (1) many more decisions are made on a day-to-day basis, without traces of strategic thinking and (2) virtually all electronic media are subject to fast (as measured on historic scales) decay both physically and logically (through sheer lack of access software).'

[219] '*[Data Protection] simply applies when personal data are processed. Hence the complex and subjective question 'is this a privacy issue?' is substituted by a more neutral and objective question 'are personal data processed?'*': Hildebrandt, M. & Gutwirth, S. (Eds.), 2005: 25.

To discuss whether data protection law applies to profiling, we distinguish three steps in profiling: i) the collection of personal data and information to construct the group profile, ii) the construction of the group profile upon anonymous data and iii) the application of the group profile. We will now shift from the focus on the general rules of data protection to their application in the context of data collection, construction and application of profiles. We will provide some examples to assess the possible importance and implications in practice.

13.2.1.1 The First Step: Collection of Personal Data and Other Information to Construct Profiles

Any information can be used to construct profiles and personal data are an important part of that information. Before personal data are rendered anonymous they need to be collected. At this point, some questions arise.

The first question arises when data are collected from persons whereas these data cannot *reasonably* be linked to the person to whom the data relate. This can be the case when, e.g., only the length or weight of all visitors is measured, or when movements of people in a supermarket are registered. The latter example can be rather interesting: suppose a shopping trolley with a display of advertisements and discounts is presented to the customer according to the following knowledge incorporated in a profile: if the trolley moves fast and the intervals between movements are short, advertisements and discounts for expensive and basic products are displayed (since this correlates to the profile of a customer in a hurry). If the trolley moves slowly and the intervals between movements are long, advertisements and discounts for cheap but special products are displayed (since this correlates to a customer having time to shop). Suppose the trolley does not identify the customer but only registers its movements throughout the store, hereby pushing information according to the profile of the movements. By moving the trolley around, the individual moves himself into the application of a profile and at the same time, he may provide new data to adjust and thus reconstruct the profile. With some imagination, this example represents a broad range of possible applications. Is the shopping behaviour, namely the moving of a shopping trolley by an anonymous customer considered as personal data? Personal data means any information *relating to* an identified or *identifiable* natural person.[220] An *identifiable* person however is one that can be 'identified directly or indirectly, in particular by reference to (…) one or more factors specific to his physical, physiological, mental, economic, cultural or social identity'.[221] To determine whether a person is identifiable or not, 'account should be taken of all the means likely reasonably to be used either by the controller or by any other person to identify the said person'.[222] In other words, the Directive

---

[220] Article 2 (a) of Data Protection Directive 95/46/EC.

[221] Article 2 (a) of Data Protection Directive 95/46/EC.

[222] Recital 26 of Data Protection Directive 95/46/EC.

does not apply when *no reasonable possibility exists of linking* the personal data to an identifiable person. This means that the collection of information relating to the trolley is not necessarily subject to data protection law. The Explanatory Memorandum of the Dutch Data Protection Act explicitly states that (translated) 'not every coincidental or technical relation between data and a person is sufficient to make the data personal data'.[223] A Dutch Report on RFID concludes the same (translated): 'The same counts of course for data relating to tangibles such as purchases or clothes. The fact that these things can be connected with a certain person, e.g., because one can see that a person carries the products, does not make the information about the products personal data, even if the product information is collected with RFID'.[224] On the other hand, if the trolley movements can be linked to a particular individual, e.g., through fingerprints or through a link with the list of purchases, data protection law is clearly applicable.

If data protection applies to the collection of personal data (when the data collected are not anonymous) and the personal data are processed for the purpose of constructing profiles, a second question arises: do data subjects have the right to be informed that data relating to them will be made anonymous in order to construct profiles? This is important because most profiles are constructed upon the collection of personal data, e.g., through customer loyalty programmes or cookies. We will argue that the data subject must be informed of the fact that personal data relating to him can be made anonymous for the purpose of constructing profiles. Today, most websites with decent privacy disclaimers already inform the customer of this purpose, e.g., when cookies are used. Looking at the Data Protection Directive brings us to the same conclusion: on the one hand, article 6.1.b. states that personal data must be collected 'for *specified, explicit* and legitimate purposes and may not [be] further processed in a way incompatible with those purposes'. On the other hand, Art. 10 and 11 dictate that the data controller is responsible to provide the data subject with 'the purposes of the processing for which the data are intended'. Exceptions such as the ones in Art. 10 and 11 do not extend to the purpose specification and are thus not valid.[225] A counter argument - that data subjects must not be informed of the purpose of rendering anonymous data to construct group profiles – may be found in article 6.1.b. This article continues that '*further* processing of data for historical, *statistical* or scientific purposes shall not be considered as incompatible provided that member states provide appropriate safeguards'. However, recital 29 of the Directive states clearly that 'these safeguards must in particular rule out the use of the data in support of measures or decisions regarding any particular individual'.

---

[223] *Kamerstukken II* 1997-1998, 25 892, nr. 3, p., 47 of the Dutch Data Protection Act (Wet Bescherming Persoonsgegevens).

[224] Zwenne G-J & Schermer, B., 2005: 43.

[225] Cfr. Supra: Articles 10 and 11 state that only *further* information such as the (categories of) recipients of the data and the existence of the right of access and the right to rectify data, must *not* be provided if not necessary 'having regard to the specific circumstances in which the data are collected, to guarantee fair processing in respect of the data subject'. This does not relate to the purpose specification principle.

The word 'any particular individual' is very relevant at this point, since it does not merely relate to the data subject but to any particular individual, subject to measures or decisions based on the use of statistical techniques. Thus, although the question remains of whether one can speak about *any particular individual* in the case of group profiling, one can argue that this is the case, because at some point group profiles may be applied to particular individuals. This would mean that when my data are used to build group profiles and the group profile is applied to another individual, one could speak of a measure or decision regarding any particular individual and the Directive applies. Finally, an exception from the purpose specification principle at the moment of collecting data for constructing group profiles, can *not* be found in the fact that 'the principles of protection shall not apply to data rendered anonymous in such a way that the data subject is no longer identifiable'[226] if it concerns personal data that are made anonymous only *after* being collected.

We can conclude that the purpose of constructing group profiles does not have to be specified when no personal data are collected. If personal data are collected though and used for profiling purposes, this purpose has to be specified in as far as it aims for more than just statistics: as soon as it may support measures and decisions towards at least one particular individual, the purpose of profiling should be specified, even if the data will be rendered anonymous after the collection.[227]

The right to be informed about the purpose of data collection would not be that important (even if useful) if the data subject would not have the right to *object* to this particular type of processing, namely anonymisation of personal data for the purpose of constructing profiles. As indicated above, data protection law could have a real impact on profiling if the data subject could object to the anonymisation of his personal data, thus hindering the construction of profiles. This raises the question of whether data subjects can object to personal data being rendered anonymous in order to construct group profiles.

13.2.1.2 A Step In Between: Anonymisation of Personal Data

The first question to be answered is why one would object to anonymisation. Most privacy advocates spend a lot of time advocating anonymisation, as it seems the safest key to protect personal data. This is, however, not the case when we consider profiles. As explained in the first part of this volume, automated profiles may constitute rich and intimate knowledge on people. This is true of personalised profiles and of group profiles. Both can be based on anonymous data. In the case of a

---

[226] Considerans 26.

[227] We would like to point out that, even if the purpose of profiling has to be specified, the purposes are often too broadly or not understandably described in the general terms and conditions of the service provider. Also, an effective control on the principle of finality, e.g., by supervisory authorities, does not really exist. Another problem is that most of the time the data subject does not know what data is being processed, whether legally or illegally. In this case one cannot expect the data subject to claim that his data have been collected and processed for purposes that are incompatible with the Directive.

personalised profile this may seem highly unlikely but, e.g., the profiling of web serving in combination with biometric behavioural profiling can produce a very specific individuated profile without linking it to an identifiable person. It may, for instance, be linked to specific keystroke behaviour (without access to the IP address). In this case the entire profile may be inferred from data that belong to one individuated person but it can also be mixed with similar personalised profiles to create a group profile. The fact that group profiles can be based on anonymised data should not be a surprise. The point is that such highly specialised profiles, based on anonymised data, may not fall within the scope of the Directive because they do not contain personal data. In this case, both the persons whose data were used to construct the profile and the persons to whom the profile is applied, have no access to 'their' profiles, while these profiles may impact their lives to a much greater extent than the use of their personal data per se could do.[228] For this reason it may be important to resist anonymisation, as this will result either in the applicability of the Directive, or – if the data controller does not use the data – in preventing the use of one's personal data for the construction of profiles.

It would be a simplification and incorrect to say that rendering data anonymous as such is an act that does not fall within the scope of data protection law. Rendering data anonymous does fit the definition of personal data *processing*: ''processing' shall mean any operation or set of operations, which is performed upon personal data, whether or not by automatic means, such as collection, recording, organisation, storage, *adaptation or alteration*, retrieval, consultation, use, disclosure by transmission, dissemination or otherwise making available, alignment or combination, blocking, *erasure or destruction'*.[229]

Since rendering data anonymous is an act of data processing, one could argue that data subjects indeed have the right to object to their personal data being used to construct profiles, even if this is done after their data is anonymised. The consent principle of data protection law plays a major role here. Article 7 of the Data Protection Directive states that to be legitimate, the processing of personal data may only take place if the data subject has (a) *unambiguously given his consent* or if the processing is *necessary* for (b) the performance of a contract to which the data subject is party, or for taking steps at the request of the data subject prior to entering into a contract, or (c) compliance with a legal obligation to which the controller is subject, or (d) protecting the vital interests of the data subject, or (e) the performance of a task carried out in the public interest or in the exercise of official authority vested in the controller or in a third party to whom the data are disclosed, or (f) the purposes of the legitimate interests pursued by the controller or by the third party or parties to whom the data are disclosed, except where such interests are overridden by the interests or fundamental rights and freedoms of the data subject. In most of these cases, the collection for the purpose of profiling seems not necessary, in which case unambiguous consent must be given. Consent means 'any freely given specific and informed

---

[228] In the case of automated decisions based on profiling, art. 15 of the Directive may be applicable, see section 13.2.1.4 below.

[229] Article 2 (b) of the Data Protection Directive.

indication of his wishes by which the data subject signifies his agreement to personal data relating to him being processed'.[230] However, the effect of the requirement of consent is relative. Data subjects are frequently forced by the controller to give consent for the processing of data for several purposes. In the end, 'consent is often turned into a pure formality without offering any guarantee'.[231]

A Munich Regional Court ruled that consent within consumer loyalty programmes[232] could not be obtained by a 'pre-selected check box' stating that consent is given.[233] 'The pre-selection of the checkbox establishing consent for the utilisation of data for other than contractual purposes requires the data subject to opt out. According to the court, this violates the principles of the Federal Data Protection Act (Bundesdatenschutzgesetz). Furthermore, there is a risk of deception, since the data subject is made to believe that by not consenting he would violate the rule.'[234]

The Article 29 Data Protection Working Party concluded that the definition of consent 'explicitly rules out consent being given as part of accepting the general terms and conditions for the electronic communications service offered.'[235]

In June 2004, the Court of First Instance of Nanterre (France) judged that the online subscriber contract of AOL France, a famous French portal, contained abusive clauses regarding the subscribers' collected data (including their pseudonyms and shopping behaviour). These personal data could be transferred to the U.S. and to affiliated partners and be used 'to offer products and services that may be of interest to the subscriber'. The claimant - a French consumer protection organisation - claimed that these general terms and conditions 'allowed analysis of consumer behaviour' and that 'only express consent by the subscribers can allow AOL to transfer the data to other companies'. AOL France countered that the terms and conditions provide the right to opt-out of this processing.[236] The Court concluded that the terms in this standard contract allowed data transfer 'to persons that the subscriber did not choose, for unknown operations that may involve selling and

---

[230] Article 2(h) of the Data Protection Directive. When sensitive data are processed, this consent must be *explicit* (Article 8).

[231] Gutwirth, S., 2002: 99-101.

[232] Cp. section 11.2 above.

[233] Landgerichts München, 9 March 2006, Az.: 12 O 12679/05 (nicht rechtskräftig), http://www. justiz.bayern.de/lgmuenchen1/presse/presse1.html.

[234] Premium Global E-Law Alert, Newsletter from Baker & McKenzie, 3 April 2006.

[235] Art.29 Data Protection Working Party, *Opinion on the use of location data with a view to providing value-added services, 25 November 2005 (WP 115)*, available through http://europa.eu.int/ comm/justice_home/fsj/privacy/workinggroup/wpdocs/2006_en.htm; See also Art. 29 Data Protection Working Party, *Opinion 5/2004 on unsolicited communications for marketing purposes under Article 13 of Directive 2002/58/EC*, 27 February 2004 (WP 90).

[236] Tribunal de grande instance de Nanterre,2 June 2004 (UFC Que Choisir vs. AOL Bertelsmann Online France), available at http://www.legalis.net/jurisprudence-decision.php3?id_article=1211. For an English analysis, see David Naylor & Cyril Ritter, 'B2C in Europe and Avoiding Contractual Liability: Why Businesses with European Operations Should Review their Customer Contracts Now', http://www.droit-technologie.org,, 15 September 2004.

direct marketing' so the subscriber 'would see his behaviour customised, analysed and becoming a target for e-commerce companies'. 'The subscriber', the Court continues, 'does not receive something in return for this transfer of his own personal data to third parties or affiliated companies, which brings along a disequilibrium where AOL neither provides information on the economic reasons of these transfers, nor on the advantages it takes from it'. The final conclusion of the Court was that 'the principle of express consent that the subscriber must give for each transfer of his personal data allows to attract his attention to this operation and to obtain a carefully considered consent. [Therefore], the principle of opt-out (...) does not have a sufficient protection level for the subscriber and this follows clearly from the lecture of the contract, since the clause that permits the objection to the transfer represents a single line in a contract of 11 pages in 2000 and 13 pages in 2003 and demands a manipulation that the subscriber does not control at the moment of subscription or throughout the execution of the contract'.

If an argument can be found for anonymisation of personal data *without* the unambiguous consent of the data subject, it must be in the 'balance criterion' of article 7(f): 'The processing is necessary for the purpose of legitimate interests pursued by the controller or by a third party or parties to whom the data are disclosed, except where such interests are overridden by the interests or the fundamental rights and freedoms of the data subject'. But even in this case, the Directive grants the data subject a right to object in two situations.

First, 'at any time on *compelling legitimate grounds* relating to his particular situation, to the processing of data relating to him, *save where otherwise provided by national legislation*. If there is a justified objection, the processing instigated by the controller may no longer involve those data'; this means that the right to object is not an unconditional right but one that can only be exercised in particular situations. The question is what are compelling legitimate grounds to object a certain processing? This is not clear, especially regarding the anonymisation of personal data by a data subject who may at the end *not* be subject to the application of the inferred group profile. An interesting approach could be to make a difference between an objection to the collection of data per se (e.g., by requiring anonymity) and a partial objection that relates to particular data, to particular processing operations or even to particular transfers of the data.[237] In the case of an objection against a particular processing operation, the individual 'may agree to be included in a telephone directory but not in an inverted directory, just as he might accept having his data included in the Intranet of a government department but not on the Internet'.[238] Compelling legitimate grounds may exist when privacy may substantially be affected, e.g., when the names of candidates in recruitment procedures are disclosed on the Internet.[239] Member states may limit the right to object when the exercise of this right itself can have undesired effects. An example of a detrimental effect could be 'an objection to

---

[237] Mallet-Poujol, N., 2001:79.

[238] Mallet-Poujol, N., 2001:80.

[239] See EDPS - European Data Protection Supervisor, 2005:58.

the introduction of certain health data in a network intended to facilitate the communication of patient records between health-care professionals hindering the main purpose of the activity, i.e., optimum circulation of information among professionals. If the information is to circulate properly and be used, it must be reliable.'[240] The right to object must thus be assessed on a case-by-case basis and the outcome will mainly depend on the provisions in the national legislation of member states.[241]

Second, the data subject shall be granted a right to object 'on request and free of charge, to [object to] the processing of personal data relating to him which the controller anticipates being processed for the purposes of direct marketing or to be informed before personal data are disclosed for the first time to third parties or used on their behalf for the purposes of direct marketing and to be expressly offered the right to object free of charge to such disclosures or uses.'[242] The right to object to these specific purposes of processing seems more relevant and unconditional, which is confirmed by the French Cour de Cassation: 'the refusal of telephone subscribers to be subjected to commercial direct marketing constitutes, in that it relates to the protection of their private life, a legitimate reason for objecting to the use of their registered data for purposes of digital processing with a view to setting up direct marketing files'.[243] Moreover, this right has been further strengthened by the opt-in principle for unsolicited communications for the purpose of direct marketing in the Privacy and Electronic Communications Directive 2002/58.[244]

On the basis of this analysis, we advocate a paragraph in the Directive that includes a right to be informed of the anonymisation of personal data, a requirement of unambiguous consent to the anonymisation and, if consent would not be required, a right to object to anonymisation that must be clearly assessed when it is exercised on compelling legitimate grounds relating to particular situations of data subjects and that must be unconditional in the case of processing for direct marketing purposes.[245]

13.2.1.3   The Second Step: The Construction of the Profile from Anonymous Data

We have dealt with the rights and obligations that apply *before* personal data are rendered anonymous and with an alleged right to be notified of, provide consent for

---

[240] Cullen International, 'Chapter II: General rules on the legality of personal data processing'.

[241] The Commission concluded in its report on the implementation of the Data Protection Directive that the implementation of Article 7 differs quite substantially between member states: European Commission (2003: 10-11).

[242] Article 14 of the Data Protection Directive.

[243] Cass. 29 June 1999, D. 1999.IR. 244, cited by Mallet -Poujol, 2001: 81.

[244] Article 13. See infra.

[245] The consent and objection approach may sound quite impossible to realise, since these requirements would as a result apply to every form of data processing, including the deletion of personal data. We may, however, find an argument that no consent is required for the deletion of data in article 7 (ii) that states that no consent is required if the processing is necessary for compliance with a legal obligation to which the controller is subject.

and object to the anonymisation of personal data. The next level, the construction of profiles, generally deals with data after they have been rendered anonymous. Data subjects, especially those to whom a group profile is applied, may have an interest in having access to the knowledge and potential secrets implied in the profile and the reasoning why certain actions or decisions may be taken towards them on the basis of the profile. We want to have access to such information when we match the criteria of a profile in a private setting, to be able to anticipate the actions and decisions that may impact our life.

Another matter of concern is the fact that group profiles may incorporate falsified presumptions, such as statistics that wrongly presume that mobile phones will cause cancer or information that people from a certain area have for instance been exposed to radioactive radiation. Knowledge of the logic involved could support an objection to the use of such profiles, even if no personal data of an identifiable person are collected to construct the profile.

Article 12 of the Data Protection Directive gives the right to the data subject to obtain from the controller 'knowledge of the logic involved in any automatic processing of data *concerning him* at least in the case of the automated decisions referred to in article 15.1'. The problem is that this right cannot be invoked if there are no personal data and thus no data subjects involved. However, this does not mean that the right of access to the logic involved remains virtual. We could look at the two other levels in which personal data are indeed processed and in which data subjects are indeed involved. Granting a right to know the logic involved at the level of *collection*, before the data are collected, would be interesting but difficult to defend in practice. The automatic processing occurs after the collection and may vary: a typical characteristic of automated profiles is that they are adjusted in real time and that new knowledge will constantly be added after the moment of collection. Also, data collection does not necessarily imply automated decisions concerning the data subject whose data are collected to construct the profile. However, data subjects may have a recognised interest in knowing the logic involved from the moment that the profile is applied to them: in this case, the data subject is situated at the application level. This level will now be discussed.

13.2.1.4   The Third Step. The Application of the Group Profile[246]

Besides privacy, anti-discrimination and other laws, data protection may play an important role when group profiles are applied to persons. However, applicability of the Data Protection Directive at application level generally depends on the identifiability of the person targeted - if the application of a profile gives rise to some activity that falls within the scope of 'processing' as defined in article 2 (b) of the Directive.

---

[246] '*Human behaviour* and our *system of values* are influenced by the tools we use and the importance we attribute to them or, as Neil Postman said in [45]: "...embedded in every tool is an ideological bias ...': A. Kündig, 2002: 24; Postman, N., 1993.

The application of group profiles implies that the group profile has to be activated in one way or another. To know whether data protection law applies at the level of application of the profile, we have distinguished two situations. Either personal data of identifiable persons are processed to activate the profile (e.g., the shopping trolley is dedicated to an identified customer), or only data relating to non-identifiable persons or other information are processed to activate the profile (e.g., the shopping trolley moves fast). If a group profile applies to an identifiable person, data protection law (discussed above) applies. If the group profile is not applied to an identifiable person, such as in the example of the (anonymous) user of the shopping trolley, one could argue that data protection law does not apply.

Of particular importance when an identifiable person matches the criteria of the profile, is article 15 of the Data Protection Directive, which concerns 'automated individual decisions' and which is strongly related to profiling. Article 15(1) states: *'every person has the right not to be subject to a decision which produces legal effects concerning him or significantly affects him and which is based* solely *on automated processing of data intended to evaluate certain personal aspects relating to him, such as his performance at work, creditworthiness, reliability, conduct, etc.'* However, article 15 (2) continuous with an exception: *'a person may nevertheless be subjected to an automated individual decision if that decision is taken [a] in the course of the entering into or performance of a contract, provided the request for the entering into or the performance of the contract, lodged by the data subject, has been satisfied or that there are suitable measures to safeguard his legitimate interests, such as arrangements allowing him to put his point of view, or [b] is authorised by a law which also lays down measures to safeguard the data subject's legitimate interests'.*

Although 'profiling' is not expressly mentioned in this article, the original proposal for this article included the word 'profile', stating that data subjects have the right "not to be subject to an administrative or private decision involving an assessment of his conduct which has as its sole basis the automatic processing of personal data defining his profile or personality".[247]

Article 15(1) offers protection to *every person* who is subject to decisions that are based solely on automated processing of *data*, not specifying that this must be an automated processing of *his or her* personal data. The use of extensive data profiles of individuals by powerful public and private institutions indeed deprives the individual of the capacity to influence decision-making processes within those institutions, should decisions be taken on the sole basis of his *data shadow*.

Bygrave has analysed the possible impact of article 15 on automated profiling.[248] According to Bygrave, article 15(1) does not directly *prohibit* a particular type of decision-making or profile application. Rather, it confers on persons a right to prevent them from being subjected to such decision making, if their personal data are

---

[247] See Article 14 of the Proposal for a Council Directive concerning the protection of individuals in relation to the processing of personal data (COM(90) 314 final - SYN 287, 27.07.1990), *Official Journal* C 277 of 5 November 1990, 8.

[248] Bygrave, Lee A., 2001:17–24; Bygrave, Lee A., 2000:67–76.

processed. This would 'leave the actual exercise of the right to the discretion of each person and allow, in effect, the targeted decision making to occur in the absence of the right being exercised'. In other words, Bygrave suggests that the data subject involved must actively exercise his right not to be subjected to automated decision making. Furthermore, Bygrave analyses the difficulties that exist in interpreting the provisions of article 15. It is not easy to anticipate what should fall within the cumulative conditions of the article: do personalised advertising banners, that automatically adjust their content according to the visitor's profile, involve an automated decision that significantly affects data subjects; when do decisions produce legal effects; when do decisions 'significantly affect' data subjects; in which case can a decision be said to be based solely on automated data processing?

A completely different approach to the application of group profiles to individuals may be found in Directive 2002/58 on privacy and electronic communications, namely in its article 13 regarding unsolicited communications for direct marketing purposes. This article states that the use of electronic communication, such as e-mail and SMS, for the purposes of direct marketing may only be allowed in respect of subscribers who have given their *prior consent* (*opt-in*), except where the electronic contacts were obtained directly from the customer in the context of a sale of a product or service for similar products and services, provided that the customer has a clear and easy opportunity to object to such use at the moment of collection and on the occasion of each message (*opt-out*). Electronic communications are defined as 'any information exchanged or conveyed between a finite number of parties by means of a publicly available electronic communications service. This does not include any information conveyed as part of a broadcasting service to the public over an electronic communications network except to the extent that the information can be related to the identifiable subscriber or user receiving the information'.[249] Direct marketing has not been defined in the Directive. It is clear, however, that the communications need to have a commercial content in order to fall under the opt-in regulation of Directive 2002/58.[250, 251]

Let us now go back to the example of the shopping trolley, in which an anonymous person receives automated messages on the display of his trolley, based upon his movements through the supermarket. The question is whether the application of

---

[249] Article 2 (d) of Directive 2002/58/EC.

[250] Recital 40 states: 'Safeguards should be provided for subscribers against intrusion of their privacy by unsolicited communications for direct marketing purposes in particular by means of automated calling machines, telefaxes and e-mails, including SMS messages. These forms of unsolicited *commercial* communications...'.

[251] EU Directive 2000/31/EC on Electronic Commerce defines "commercial communication" as "any form of communication designed to promote, directly or indirectly, the goods, services or image of a company, organisation or person pursuing a commercial, industrial or craft activity or exercising a regulated profession". The following do not in themselves constitute commercial communications: information allowing direct access to the activity of the company, organisation or person, in particular a domain name or an electronic-mail address; communications relating to the goods, services or image of the company, organisation or person compiled in an independent manner, particularly when this is without financial consideration.

the profile should be considered as an electronic communication for which the opt-in (and at least the opt-out regime) is applicable. In this case, the data subject must always give prior consent to receive those communications; at least he would always have the right to opt-out of receiving these communications. The definition of electronic communications does not hinder the application of this article to unsolicited communications: these relate to *any information* exchanged or conveyed between a *finite number of parties* (the number of recipients is indeed determined by the group profile and therefore limited). The last part of the definition seems to be written especially for the application of profiles, since broadcasting services can rely on profiles, e.g., in case of broadcasts to everybody in a street that matches a group profile. These broadcasting services cannot be excluded from the opt-in/opt-out principle to the extent that the information can be related to the identifiable subscriber or user receiving the information.

To apply these provisions, a broad interpretation of electronic communications is at least necessary but this is not unthinkable when taking into account the technology-neutrality of the Directive. Considering any unwanted electronic communication of personalised or targeted information such as spam, regardless of the content and regardless of the technological means, would offer an interesting approach.

13.2.2 Conclusion. How to Enforce Data Protection Rights?

We have advocated in this text that the application of data protection is important for several reasons, especially where other laws do not foresee guarantees or do not offer the same guarantees that data protection law does. Individuals (should) have the right to object to profiling in certain situations. Whenever the construction or the application of profiles takes place, they should have the right to know who, when and why the data relating to them are processed.

The most common criticism of data protection is that it encompasses merely procedural rules - without really protecting individuals. Apart from that, individuals seem scarcely concerned and do not read information relating to the processing of data relating to themselves. The right to object to certain forms of processing is very seldom exercised while we are increasingly, almost constantly, exposed to personal data processing. In addition, infringements of data protection law are not often prosecuted[252], if they are ever noticed.

However, we do not agree that these facts prove that data protection law could not be tenable in our future information society. They prove that the incentives for both

---

[252] In Belgium, where the implementation of Directive 2002/58/EC provisions on unsolicited communication for the purpose of direct marketing took place already in 2003 (Wet van 11 maart 2003 betreffende bepaalde juridische aspecten van de diensten van de informatiemaatschappij, *B.S.* 17 maart 2003; Koninklijk Besluit 4 april 2003 tot reglementering van het verzenden van reclame per elektronische post, *B.S.* 28 mei 2003), no single person has yet been prosecuted for sending spam. See T-zine (Tijdnet), 'No spam law cases in Belgium', 14 April 2006.

data controllers and data subjects to comply or make use of data protection are not in place. As will be indicated in chapter 15, we may need to (re)design the technological infrastructure to enforce compliance by data controllers and to provide the tools to access both data and profiles for data subjects. In this sense, one could think of rules, imposed by legislation and coded in technology. Mandatory data protection rules and the applicable margins of negotiation would be embodied - in a user-friendly format - into a technological device such as a personal digital assistant. Such a technologically embodied – or ambient - law could provide an adequate mix of flexibility and rigidity within an ambient intelligent environment, being at once generic (concerning legal protection that cannot be overruled) and contextualised (by allowing contractual freedom within the margins of such legal protection).

13.3 Group Profiling and Anti-discrimination Legislation

13.3.1 *Introduction*

In this section, we examine what role anti-discrimination laws play regarding the construction and the use of group profiles.[253] Typically, group profiles will be used to select individuals as members of a group, while other individuals who do not fit the profile are excluded. For the purpose of this legal analysis, we focus primarily on the use of group profiles by private suppliers in a commercial or civil setting, such as the use of profiles for the selection of customers for granting access to a given place (access control) or for (not) providing a service (e.g., an insurance contract or in an Ami environment, any service for which the individual matches the criteria set forth by the group profile of the provider). The use of a group profile in these situations results in the classification of individuals and may lead to unfair treatment. However, the question is whether this treatment could be seen as "discrimination" under current anti-discrimination law.

Our analysis aims to provide the basis for further discussion of the legal consequences of the use of group profiles in the private sector, rather than providing final statements or answers for these relatively new practices which are steered by rapid technological developments. The greater use of group profiles seems to be inevitable and will increase with the availability of enormous amounts of data, brought together from different sources in data warehouses where the (often anonymous) data is aggregated and then analysed in an automated manner (data mining).[254] During the process of data mining and profiling, a set of previously unknown patterns or correlations between the data of a particular group of people is deduced from the

---

[253] See also Koops, B - J, in Hildebrandt, M., Gutwirth, S., (Eds), 2005: 68.

[254] See part I of this volume. The described process is sometimes also described as 'knowledge discovery in databases'. For an overview of the process, see also Borking, A., and Van Amelo, 1998.

databases, which results in a group profile. This group profile can then be applied to a specific group of persons who are likely to engage in a predicted behaviour or act. Group profiling is a practice that interests the private and the public sector.[255] We will not deal with potential issues of the use of group profiles by public authorities for criminal law or law enforcement purposes.

13.3.2 Anti-discrimination Legislation

To understand whether anti-discrimination law can provide recourse should it be found that data protection legislation does not apply to the construction and/or application of a group profile to individuals or would offer too limited protection, we will take a closer look at Article 14 of the European Convention on Human Rights (the 'Convention')[256] and Article 1 of Protocol No. 12 to the Convention ('Protocol No. 12').[257,258] These articles contain a negative obligation for the parties to the Convention (that is, signatory states) not to discriminate against individuals. This would mean, that if profiling practices conducted by public bodies representing

---

[255] See also Hosein, I., 2005: 17.

[256] Convention for the Protection of Human Rights and Fundamental Freedoms, *European Treaty Series, N° 5*, also available at http://conventions.coe.int/Treaty/en/Treaties/Word/005.doc (last visited on 12 April 2006).

[257] Protocol No.12 to the Convention for the Protection of Human Rights and Fundamental Freedoms, *European Treaty Series, N° 177*, also available at http://conventions.coe.int/Treaty/en/Treaties/html/177.htm. The Protocol No. 12 has been opened for signature since 4 November 2000 and came into force on 1 April 2005 after ten ratifications (there are as of 12 April 2006 22 signatory states (without ratification) and 13 ratifications (list available at http://conventions.coe. int/Treaty/Commun/ ChercheSig.asp?NT=177&CM=8&DF=4/12/2006&CL=ENG). Protocol No.12 differs from Article 14 in that it contains a general prohibition on discrimination. It is intended to remedy the limited scope of Article 14, which contains a prohibition on discrimination only in relation to the rights and freedoms stated in the Convention. Article 14 reads as follows: " The enjoyment of the rights and freedoms set forth in this Convention shall be secured without discrimination on any ground such as sex, race, colour, language, religion, political or other opinion, national or social origin, association with a national minority, property, birth or other status". Article 1, paragraph 1, of Protocol No. 12 is as follows: "The enjoyment of any right set forth by law shall be secured without discrimination on any ground such as sex, race, colour, language, religion, political or other opinion, national or social origin, association with a national minority, property, birth or other status".

[258] Several other international treaties also contain a prohibition on discrimination, including, without limitation the Universal Declaration of Human Rights and the International Convention on the Elimination of All Forms of Racial Discrimination of 1965. The EC Treaty and the EU Constitution also contain in several articles an express prohibition of discrimination (see, e.g., Article 13 of the EC Treaty introduced by the Amsterdam treaty). Accordingly, the Council has adopted, for example, Council Directive 2000/43/EC of 29 June, 2000 implementing the principle of equal treatment between persons irrespective of racial or ethnic origin (*O.J.*, L180/22). The principle of equal treatment is, as confirmed by the Court of Justice, one of the fundamental principles of community law. Based on this international legislation, national states have adopted various national non-discrimination laws (which will not be discussed in detail in this section).

the state (i.e., the (local) government) were proven to be discriminatory, these provisions could be invoked by an individual who could require the government to cease the discriminatory profiling practice in any particular case ('vertical effect').

Whether one could require the legislator to take measures to eliminate discrimination that might be created by, for example, private parties, is less certain. This is relevant, however, to the extent that profiling practices are or will often be used by private (commercial) organisations. It is generally accepted that the aforementioned provisions impose, in principle, not a positive obligation upon the states to take action in the case of discriminatory practices by private parties.[259] However, there are indications in legal doctrine and case law that this principle is not that strong and that in the future, states could be required to take measures to eliminate discrimination, for example by enacting new legislation eliminating specific forms of discrimination.[260] It should be noted, however, that such positive obligations in the area of relations between private persons would probably concern, at the most, relations in the public sphere normally regulated by law, for which the states have a certain responsibility (including, for example, arbitrary denial of access to restaurants).[261] Therefore, if specific forms of group profiling by a specific sector would be proven to be discriminatory, it is conceivable that in the future one could require that legislative measures should be taken in order to limit the practices of group profiling that are discriminatory.[262] This is related to the theory that although the provisions are in principle directed to states, private parties can claim the application of the provisions of the Convention, to some extent, also in private relationships ('horizontal effect' or 'third-party applicability' or 'Drittwirkung'). Therefore, we could conclude by saying that there are arguments to defend where group profiling practices of a private supplier are discriminatory, directly or indirectly, individuals or a group of individuals could probably not only require from a state to enact specific legislation in order to apply the non-discrimination principle in private relations but could also demand that the non-discrimination principles be applied to the profiling practices of private parties and, for example, request to prohibit the practices.

The wording of Article 14 of the Convention and Protocol N° 12 is very broad: discrimination 'on any ground such as sex, race, colour, language, religion, political or other opinion, national or social origin, association with a national minority, property,

---

[259] See also the Explanatory Report to Protocol No. 12, recital 25.

[260] In this context, the Explanatory Report to Protocol No. 12 is also relevant: "On the other hand, it cannot be totally excluded that the duty to 'secure' under the first paragraph of Article 1 might entail positive obligations. For example, this question could arise if there is a clear lacuna in domestic law protection from discrimination. Regarding more specific relations between private persons, a failure to provide protection from discrimination in such relations might be so clear-cut and grave that it might engage clearly the responsibility of the state and then Article 1 of the Protocol could come into play (...)" (recital 26).

[261] Explanatory Report to Protocol No. 12, recital 28.

[262] Compare, for example, with legislative measures which have been taken by several states in order to eliminate discrimination between men and women.

birth *or other status'* is prohibited. It was not the intention to expressly enumerate all additional non-discrimination grounds (e.g., age). The reference to 'other status' leaves it quite open as to which other criteria used in the relation with profiling practices could be considered "discriminatory".[263] Therefore the question remains which 'other statuses' may be grounds upon which one shall not discriminate, e.g., the financial status of an individual, the history of purchases of an individual or the history of damages under an insurance contract? These criteria are often used in commercial profiling practices as the basis for distinguishing groups of customers for different direct marketing strategies or for applying diverging contract terms. With increased data processing in private and public services, for example in the banking and insurance institutions, using tools for analysing data and constructing and applying profiles of clients, becomes a new practice and the individual track of customers and their profiles becomes increasingly important. The practices of black lists, credit scoring or the sharing of other information, have received some attention during the last couple of years. The Article 29 Data Protection Working Party has adopted a working document on blacklists in which it warns about these practices, by describing several examples but without analysing in depth the consequences and the legitimacy of the processings.[264] In Belgium, judges have looked into information sharing and black listing practices within the insurance sector but have waived the complaints of the individuals concerned, by deciding that the interests of the companies outweighed the interests of the individuals.[265]

For the non-discrimination provisions to apply, it is sufficient that there is (1) a difference in treatment (2) between 'persons' or 'groups of persons' in 'analogous' or 'relevantly similar situations' (3) without 'objective and reasonable justification'.[266] There is an 'objective and reasonable justification' if one pursues a 'legitimate aim', the distinction is pertinent and there is a 'reasonable relationship of proportionality between the means employed and the aim sought to be realised'. The claimant will have to identify and prove the discrimination. From the case law of the European Court of Human Rights, it appears that claimants sometimes have difficulties in proving that they were treated differently because of a characteristic, for example, social origin.[267] The claimants have to prove, not that they *have* different characteristics but that they have been discriminated *because* of these characteristics. If these principles are applied

---

[263] See and compare for example, ECHR, Van der Mussele v. Belgium, 23 November 1983, also available at: http://cmiskp.echr.coe.int////tkp197/viewhbkm.asp?action=open&table=1132746FF1 FE2A468ACCBCD1763D4D8149&key=12131&sessionId=6645501&skin=hudoc-en &attachment=true (last consulted on 10 April 2006) where the 'professional status' was considered and discussed as a possible unlawful ground of discrimination (but no violation of Article 14 of the Convention was withheld).

[264] Article 29 Data Protection Working Party, Working document on Blacklists, 3 October 2002, available at http://europa.eu.int/comm/justice_home/fsj/privacy/docs/wpdocs/2002/wp65_en.pdf.

[265] See, for example, Court of first instance of Brussels, 19 December 2000, M. X v. Datassur, *Computerrecht*, 2002, 30.

[266] A discriminatory practice could also be the equal treatment without objective and reasonable justification of persons whose situations are significantly different.

[267] ECHR, Olsson v. Sweden, 24 March 1988, Publ. Court, A, vol. 130, par. 92-93.

to the technology of (group) profiling, it seems that the categories of data and the logic involved in the process, would contain the evidence that a group has been selected (or not) because of a specific characteristic. Nevertheless, as this logic is part of a complicated technological process, including the use of algorithms and other deciding mechanisms, sometimes part of the proprietary rights of the owner of the profiling system, the individual, who is victim of the profiling practice will not, without due procedures of access to that technology, be able to provide such proof in a proceeding.[268] In case there is different treatment based on one of the criteria explicitly mentioned in Article 14 or Protocol N°12 (sex, race, colour, language, religion, political or other opinion, national or social origin, association with a national minority, property, birth or other status), it will not be so difficult to prove the discrimination. The discrimination is in this case called 'direct discrimination'. The provisions are clear in that different treatment based on one of the aforementioned criteria is prohibited. Therefore, (data) processes that include one of these criteria as a deciding factor, are not common. Service providers, including suppliers of profiling systems, will often carefully exclude such criteria. National legislations also often provide that discrimination on that basis is sanctioned with criminal fines. However, it is also possible that apparently neutral criteria, e.g., place of domicile or credit scores, are used but these criteria have, as an effect that a group that fits the criteria is excluded ('indirect discrimination').[269] If there is no 'objective and reasonable justification', that is, if the treatment does not pursue a 'legitimate aim' or if there is not a 'reasonable relationship of proportionality between the means employed and the aim sought to be realised' the treatment is discriminatory.[270]

13.3.3 Group Profiling and the Dangers of Indirect Racial or Ethnic Discrimination

Since the attacks of 11 September, there has been a rapid growth in measures introduced to prevent similar attacks. For this purpose, all kinds of measures are taken, including the set up of 'watch lists' based on profiles. Governments are involved in this and use not only their own information and databases but also commercial databases of private parties. A large scale programme that was set up in May 2004 required commercial airlines offering flights to or through the United States to

---

[268] It should be noted that under Directive 95/46/EC the data subject has a right to obtain information about the logic involved in any automatic processing of data concerning him but that this right is restricted to cases where the person is subject to an automated individual decision (see Articles 12 and 15 of Directive 95/46/EC). An automated individual decision is described as a decision which is based *solely* on automated processing of data. It is possible that data controllers would try to avoid giving information by inserting a non-automated element in the decision making process, in which case the right to obtain information about the logic would no longer apply.

[269] Profiling techniques may use variables which are not discriminatory but which correlate with discriminatory characteristics, so called 'masking'. See Custers, B., 2004: 57.

[270] See also Fredman, S., 2002: 106 ff.

communicate detailed and specific information on passengers, contained in their commercial reservation and check-in databases, to U.S. authorities before take-off (transfer of the so-called Passenger Name Record (PNR) data). The individual data and profiles of the passengers were compared upon arrival with other data and databases.[271] The Article 29 Data Protection Working Party has expressed its concerns about this practice in several opinions, also because the communication of that information is vulnerable to data mining and profiling practices.[272] Information about the profiling practices that were applied was not made public.[273] However, the data transferred contained elements which, if profiled could result in direct discrimination (although it seemed that there was a willingness to delete certain PNR codes and terms which are sensitive according to the 95/46/EC Directive (which includes for example, data about race)). Moreover, the Article 29 Data Protection Working Party stressed that specific codes, for example for meal preferences, should also be deleted. Such criteria could be used for indirect discrimination.[274]

There are, however, other examples on how criteria used in group profiling, which at first sight do not entail racial or ethnic discrimination, might lead to a group of people being excluded due, indirectly, to their specific ethnic origin or race. There are some examples of such group profiling in the private sector. In 2000, the 'Hoge Raad' (Supreme Court) in the Netherlands had to deal with this issue in a case in which the owner of a discotheque had forbidden entrance, after irregularities, to a group of people who were staying at a particular address. The address was a centre where asylum applicants were awaiting their expulsion. It was generally known that the individuals staying at that address had characteristics, in particular physical, ethnical, geographical, cultural, historical or religious characteristics, which pointed to another race. The 'Hoge Raad' affirmed that indirect racial discrimination is 'to be understood as a measure that is at first sight

---

[271] Although this example relates to some extent to law enforcement, it is herein mentioned because use is made of private (and commercial) databases.

[272] See Article 29 Data Protection Working Party, Opinion 2/2004 on the Adequate Protection of Personal Data Contained in the PNR of Air Passengers to be Transferred to the United States Bureau of Customs and Border Protection (US CBP), 29 January 2004, available at http://ec. europa.eu/justice_home/fsj/privacy/docs/wpdocs/2004/wp87_en.pdf: 'This underlines the need for a cautious approach bearing in mind also the possibilities this opens up for data mining affecting, in particular, European residents and entailing the risk of generalised surveillance and controls by a third state' (last visited on 15 September 2006).

[273] It was difficult to analyse to what extent characteristics of the profile contained elements for direct or indirect discrimination.

[274] The Court of Justice has in the meantime annulled the decision approving the conclusion of an agreement between the European Community and the United States of America on the transfer of Passenger Name Record data invoking the wrong legal basis. See ECJ, C-317/04 and C-318/04, 30 May 2006, Official Journal, C 178, 29 July 2006, pp.1-2. However, on 6 October 2006, the EU completed negotiations on an interim agreement on the processing and transfer of passenger name record (PNR) data by air carriers to the U.S. administraion. The interim agreement will expire upon the date of application of any superseding agreement and in any event, no later than 31 July 2007, unless extended by mutual written agreement.

neutral but in fact affects, to a major extent, only individuals of a specific group, while the difference in treatment cannot be explained by objective reasons not relating to discrimination on a specific ground'.[275] The Hoge Raad concluded that such indirect discrimination is prohibited. Because the judge in the first instance had given a too restrictive interpretation of the term 'race discrimination', the 'Hoge Raad' annulled the judgement, which acquitted the owner of the dancing club. The Court of appeal that had reviewed the case, had stated that, while accepting that the practice of excluding individuals with a specific address could in the case at hand indeed qualify as indirect discrimination, the owner had used objective reasonable means to exclude that group. This was the case because, based on the facts of the case, he had no other means to limit the risk of fights. For this reason the Court of appeal acquitted the owner. One should note that a court will generally also take into consideration whether there are alternatives to reach the same goals and whether there are similar restrictions accepted in other countries (the 'consensus' principle). Similar practices of restricting access by dancing club owners were submitted to courts in Belgium.[276] Although the profiling executed by the dancing club owner in the case before the 'Hoge Raad' was, strictly speaking, not the result of the technological process of group profiling described above, the case is an illustration of profiling in the larger sense (but by using criteria which are used in group profiling) and contains some elements which are useful in order to study the impact of profiling techniques, the possible discriminatory effects and the way anti-discrimination laws are interpreted in some courts. In addition, the context of refusing access to a place such as a dancing hall is relevant in the sense that presently there are examples of dancing clubs where data relating to access and consumption (including biometric data) are processed in an extensive way.[277]

Another example of group profiling in the private sector that has received some attention is the practice of credit scoring. Credit scoring could be described as an 'automated processing of general and/or personal data, possibly combined with statistical and/or demographic data on a postal code basis in order to make a credit

---

[275] Hoge Raad, 13 June 2000, N° 00274/99, *Nederlandse Jurisprudentie*, 2000, 513, also available at the portal of Dutch court decisions, http://www.rechtspraak.nl/.

[276] See for example, Court of Appeal of Antwerp, 25 April 2000, also available at the portal of the Centre for Equal Opportunities and Opposition to Racism, at http://www.diversiteit.be/NR/rdonlyres/E7A60757-F6C5-40AD-BF00-75A8F6F4726F/0/r000425_antwerpen.pdf; Court of First Instance, Hasselt, 10 May 2000, also available at the portal of the Centre for Equal Opportunities and Opposition to Racism, at http://www.diversiteit.be/NR/rdonlyres/A35A813A-077B-44A1-9291-80EB9CB925FF/0/r000510a_c_hasselt.pdf. It should be noted that these were criminal cases and that these cases concerned 'direct discrimination'. While in the first mentioned case, the court decided that there was discrimination, the court in the second case acquitted the culprits.

[277] See Opinion of the Registratiekamer, Biometrisch toegangscontrolesysteem VIS 2000, 19 maart 2001, available at http://www.cbpweb.nl/downloads_uit/z2000-0080.pdf?refer=true&theme =purple (last visited on 15 September 2006).

profile by using a logical and transparent calculation model'.[278] The Dutch Data Protection Authority has warned about indirect discrimination in credit scoring practices.[279] Inhabitants of particular zones may obtain from credit score information brokers a lower credit score than others. Careful and transparent acceptance procedures for new clients should limit the risk that suppliers of services employ indirect discriminatory practices.[280] It should be mentioned that an important issue is on whom the burden of proof of the (non)-discriminatory practice is imposed. In principle, the (group of) individuals who claim that they have received discriminatory treatment, shall provide evidence of their claim. As already stated above, the burden of proof is difficult to meet.

The question remains whether states have a positive obligation to act in order to rule out direct or indirect discrimination in these settings. Based on the succinct analyses on the basis of selected (limited) case law, it seems that anti-discrimination laws nowadays will not always provide a clear answer in the case of (in)direct discrimination. It is certainly too early to make some general conclusions in this respect, based on this limited case law and legal doctrine but it remains useful to note that non-discrimination laws have their limits. Therefore, the right to privacy as a general human rights concept might be revisited in order to see whether it could be of (additional) use in this debate.

13.3.4   Concluding Remarks

From the brief analysis of the principles of non-discrimination legislation above, it is clear that group profiling techniques pose new challenges to the existing legal framework. Profiling techniques contain risks of direct and indirect discrimination and the anti-discrimination laws may not be sufficient in order to cope with the effects of this new technology.

13.4   Reply

Sarah Thatcher*

Building on the analysis performed in Chapter 13, this reply will consider the implications of these findings in a very specific data environment. As a result of recent national and EU

---

*London School of Economics (LSE)

---

[278] Article 1 of the Code of Conduct of the Dutch association of information brokers ('Nederlandse Vereniging voor Handelsinformatiebureaus'), available at http://www.nvhinfo.nl/htm/gedragscode.pdf.

[279] See, for example, Wishaw, R., 2000:37.

[280] For the practice of credit scoring and profiling, please see Chapter 11.3.

legislation, Internet service providers and telecommunications operators will be obliged to retain traffic data for a period of up to two years. The costs of storing these data are borne by the service provider. Once these databanks are established, the possibility arises that they will be extensively mined. First, the potential exists for government authorities to use AmI technologies to keep a 'watching brief' on data as it is collected, thereby building intricate profiles of the communication practices of citizens. Second, given that these data are being stored at the cost of the service provider, it is unreasonable to assume that service providers will not attempt to find ways of deriving commercial value from them.

The possible consequences of group profiling on this unprecedented scale will be considered in terms of both the data protection regime and the broad implications for democracy and the rule of law.

Schreurs, Hildebrandt et al. have considered both data protection and anti-discrimination law as defensive tools available to the citizen for fending off the unwanted advances of the private sector. In this contribution, they have acknowledged and set to one side the public sector impact on the privacy of citizens in connection with criminal law and law enforcement. The applicability of data protection law has been argued in a series of stages, from data collection through anonymisation to profile construction and application and then, finally, to enforceability. Further, anti-discrimination law has been considered in connection with the application of a group profile to determine the extent to which it may be effective to prevent both direct and indirect discrimination. The following analysis mirrors the framework used in Chapter 13.

13.4.1 Data Collection

It is clear that the data protection regime has relevance to the field of group profiling but it is subject to certain serious restrictions. The most far-reaching of these restrictions are those granted in favour of the public sector, highlighted by the public order exemptions[281] and data retention provisions[282] contained in the relevant EU legislation. Although the authors have explicitly excluded the public sector criminal law and law enforcement scenarios from their analysis, they are relevant to their arguments in the sense that they are a rationale for data retention on a grand scale. The 2006 Data Retention Directive[283] harmonises data retention provisions across the EU so that communications data, including traffic and location data but excluding content, are retained by service providers for between six months and two years. The purpose of such retention is "the investigation, detection and prosecution of serious crime"[284], a provision which is capable of very wide interpretation.

This is a serious derogation from the rights of the data subject, since he no longer has the right to object to the collection of personal communications data. Not only is

---

[281] D 1995/46/EC Art. 3(2); D 2002/58/EC Art. 15(1); D 2006/24/EC explicitly leaves intact the effect of these provisions.

[282] D 2006/24/EC Art. 3.

[283] D 2006/24/EC.

[284] D 2006/24/EC Art. 1(1).

data retained concerning the originator of the communication, who at least arguably has the right to decide whether or not to use a public network for that purpose, but data is also retained on the recipient, who has no choice in the matter. Although these data are supposedly for use only by competent national authorities, these and the procedures for access to retained data are defined by national law[285] and may in practice be very broad. This admits of the possibility that private organisations operating on behalf of the government may have access to this sensitive personal data and, of course, will be permitted to process the data. Group profiling on the basis of these data may well be a powerful tool for achieving the diverse ends of these organisations.

The Article 29 Data Protection Working Party (the "Working Party") has objected that the term "serious crime" in the Data Retention Directive does not constitute a sufficiently restrictive definition of the purposes of data retention; that such data should only be available to law enforcement authorities; that no mining of data should be permitted of individuals not suspected of an offence; and that judicial scrutiny should apply on a case by case basis.[286] It is clear that the UK regime, in particular, already goes beyond these recommendations, granting access to communications data not only to law enforcers and intelligence services but also to agencies as diverse as the Financial Services Authority, the Charity Commission, the Inland Revenue, Local Authorities and many Government Departments.[287] Already, the boundaries between the public and private sectors are being eroded as far as access to personal communications data is concerned and an artificial distinction between the two is increasingly difficult to draw. As a data subject, should I be any less concerned that my privacy is being invaded by a governmental agency rather than a commercial organisation?

More worrying still, perhaps, is the dichotomy at the heart of the Data Retention Directive. Although the data is retained for public order purposes, the holder of the data is, in most cases, a private, commercial organisation: the communications service provider. They hold such data at their own cost, although there may be a fee payable by the competent national authority on access. Given this financial and logistical burden, it is unreasonable to assume that service providers will not attempt to find ways of deriving commercial value from the data held. Implicitly acknowledging this possibility, the Working Party has recommended that communication service providers should be specifically excluded from processing retained data for purposes other than those falling within the Data Retention Directive, especially their own purposes.[288] To underpin this restriction, the Working Party further recommends that there be a logical separation between the storage systems for data retained for public order purposes and the storage systems used for business purposes. Nevertheless, there is nothing in the legislation to this effect and the suspicion

---

[285] D. 2006/24/EC Art. 4.

[286] Article 29 Data Protection Working Party Opinion 3/2006.

[287] Section 25(1) Regulation of Investigatory Powers Act 2000; Regulation of Investigatory Powers (Communications Data) Order 2003.

[288] Article 29 Data Protection Working Party Opinion 3/2006.

must be that service providers will attempt to find ways to derive commercial value from these data, the storage of which they are resourcing. Comprehensive communications data are surely extremely valuable for profiling purposes.

There are now, therefore, effectively two connected regimes of which data subjects must be aware: data retention and data protection. Under the data retention regime that applies to communications data, the data subject has no control over whether or not his personal data is collected. All personal data, apart from communications data, are still subject to the data protection regime, so that the data subject has some control over the collection of data. However, if the data cannot be linked back to an individual, it is not considered personal and there are no restrictions on data collection. For group profiling purposes, this is probably the most significant weakness of the data protection regime from the citizen's point of view.

13.4.2   Anonymisation

Once personal data are collected, either under the data retention or the data protection legislation, the normal data protection regime applies, so that the processing of that information is subject to the consent of the data subject. Consent may be 'given' to anonymisation of personal data for group profiling purposes but it might equally be given for the construction of the profile without anonymisation. This position is problematic if Gutwirth's view is accepted, that consent is often a formality without guarantee.[289] Not only must a data subject be concerned with all the personal data he has permitted to be collected but he must also be concerned with the communications data that has been collected as a matter of course under the data retention provisions. If the issue of consent is routinely fudged, the scope of the data now stored on an individual citizen may lead to a greatly increased level of processing activity so that greater numbers of group profiles are generated out of personal data, whether or not it has first been anonymised.

13.4.3   Construction of the Profile

Once the data has legitimately been anonymised, the data subject arguably has no further control over the use of those data, for example to construct a group profile. Likewise, if the data were not in the first place linkable to an individual and thus not subject to the data protection regime, profiles can be constructed with impunity. Where consent to use of personal data is not given, group profiles may in any case be constructed illegitimately and the data subject may never be any the wiser.

---

[289] Gutwirth, S., 2002: 99-101.

13.4.4   Application of the Profile

Schreurs, Hildebrandt et al. note that, where the application of a profile is activated by the processing of personal data, data protection law will apply, bringing with it the requirement of consent. In addition, it is argued that *any* person may prevent the automatic application of a group profile under Article 15(1) of the Data Protection Directive but the individual concerned may need to take positive action to do so. Even if this position is accepted, the problem, of course, is that the individual must know that a profile is being applied in order to prevent its application. In an era of increasingly pervasive computing, it is by no means obvious how an individual should be aware each time a profile is applied.

13.4.5   Enforcement of Data Protection Law

Enforcement of data protection law is a notoriously difficult area. As the authors point out, infringements are rarely noticed and prosecutions even more rarely brought. The technical solution proposed is not a convincing answer to what is essentially a socio-cultural problem. The personal digital assistant 'containing' the relevant rules within its technology would have to be the interface between the potential data subject and every transaction he makes. This hardly seems practicable, even in the medium term. In addition, technological solutions have historically been subject to socio-technical circumvention – the social engineering techniques of hackers being an obvious example – and there is no reason to believe that this will be any different in the future.

13.4.6   Anti-discrimination Law

Anti-discrimination law most often relates to very personal relationships as are found, for instance, in the employment context. Its application in a broader, commercial environment is less successful. The basic problem is that discrimination is fundamental to successful commerce. Subject to limited restrictions, freedom of contract is an elemental part of democratic society, so that a contracting party can generally choose his counterparty as he sees fit and contract on the terms he desires. Profiling is often apparent both in the choice of counterparty and in the terms of the contract. For example, an insurer of motor vehicles may choose to issue an insurance policy to a middle-aged woman with a clean driving licence who lives in a nice neighbourhood and yet may, with impunity, refuse to insure a teenage man with three accidents to his name who lives on a council estate, or at least insure him on adverse terms. Sex, age and, indirectly, socio-economic discrimination is apparent here, yet the commercial setting apparently negates its exploitative nature.

Anti-discrimination law may have a very limited utility in narrow circumstances but ultimately, economic imperatives will militate against its widespread use as a defence to the application of group profiles.

13.4.7 Conclusion

The authors of Chapter 13 have sought to show in positive terms how citizens might defend themselves against the construction of group profiles out of their personal data and the application of group profiles once constructed. This reply has concentrated on the negative and has sought to demonstrate how the individual may be exposed to group profiling. The data protection regime has many flaws but the greatest concern for citizens wishing to avoid the effects of group profiling is that it only applies to personal data. Where group profiles are constructed and/or applied as a result of data that cannot be traced to an individual, data protection law provides no assistance to the citizen. Anti-discrimination law, on the other hand, applies retrospectively but only in very limited circumstances of the most serious kind. It is unlikely to assist with the everyday, commercial interactions of citizens with organisations who are using profiles for commercial purposes.

The fact is that group profiling is nothing new: commerce has proceeded on this basis for millennia. It is merely the scale of the enterprise in the Information Society that has thrown up new concerns related to automation, ubiquity, opacity and lack of human discretion. It is impossible for a data subject to be aware of all the data about him and his life that subsist in databases across the planet and to manage the processing of this information effectively. The scale of the problem has eroded the power of the principle of consent. Data protection law does not, indeed cannot, go far enough. It is time to step away from the mechanism of data processing and look to purposes and impacts for the framework for a new protective regime.

13.5 Bibliography

Art.29 Data Protection Working Party, *Opinion on the use of location data with a view to providing value-added services, 25 November 2005 (WP 115)*. Available at http://europa.eu.int/comm/justice_home/fsj/privacy/workinggroup/wpdocs/2006_en.htm.

Art.29 Data Protection Working Party, *Opinion 5/2004 on unsolicited communications for marketing purposes under Article 13 of Directive 2002/58/EC*, 27 February 2004 (WP 90).

Borking, J., Artz, M., en Van Amelo, L., *Gouden Bergen van gegevens. Over Datawarehousing, data mining en privacy*, in Registratiekamer, *Achtergrondstudies en Verkenningen 10*, September 1998. Available at: http://www.cbpweb.nl/documenten/av_10_gouden_bergen_van_gegevens.stm?refer=true&theme=purple.

Bygrave, L. A., 'Minding the Machine: Article 15 of the EC Data Protection Directive and Automated Profiling', *Computer Law & Security Report*, Vol. 17, Elsevier, Neth., 2001, pp. 17 -24.

Bygrave, Lee A., *Privacy Law & Policy Reporter*, Vol. 7, HiTech Editing Pty Ltd., 2000, pp. 67–76.

Custers B., *The Power of Knowledge*, Wolf Legal Publishers, Nijmegen, 2004.

European Data Protection Supervisor (EDPS), 'Public access to documents and data protection', *Background Paper Series July 2005 n°1*, Brussels, European Communities, 2005. Available at: www.edps.eu.int/publications/policy_papers/Public_access_data_protection_EN.pdf.

European Commission, *First report on the implementation of the Data Protection Directive (95/46/EC)*, 15 May 2003, pp. 10-11. Available at: http://europa.eu.int/comm/justice_home/fsj/privacy/lawreport/index_en.htm.

Fredman, S., *Discrimination Law*, Oxford University Press, Oxford, 2002.

Gutwirth, S., *Privacy and the Information Age*, Rowman & Littlefield Publishers Inc, 2002.

Hildebrandt, M., Gutwirth, S., (Eds), *Implications of profiling practices on democracy and rule of law, FIDIS Deliverable 7.4*, European Union IST FIDIS Project, Brussels, 2005. Available at: www.fidis.net

Hildebrandt, M., Backhouse, J. (Eds), *Descriptive analysis and inventory of profiling practices, FIDIS Deliverable 7.2*, European Union IST FIDIS Project, Brussels, 2005. Available at: www.fidis.net.

Hosein, I., 'Researching the Ethics of Knowledge Management: The Case of Data Mining', in Department of Information Systems. London School of Economics and Political Science, *Working Paper Series* 135, 5 October 2005. Available at: http://is2.lse.ac.uk/wp/pdf/WP135.PDF.

Koops, B.J., 'Reply' in Hildebrandt, M., Gutwirth, S., (Eds.), *Implications of profiling practices on democracy and rule of law, FIDIS Deliverable 7.4*, European Union IST FIDIS Project, Brussels 2005. Available at: http://www.fidis.net/.

Kündig, A., *Basis for IT Assessment. An overview of the underlying technologies, their applications and the implications for individuals, society and business*, Swiss Centre for Technology Assessment, 2002. Available at: http://www.ta-swiss.ch/www-remain/reports_archive/publications/2002/TA43_2002.pdf.

Mallet-Poujol, N., 'Report: The place of the individual in a world of globalised information: rights and obligations' in *European Conference on Data Protection on Council of Europe Convention 108 for the protection of individuals with regard to automatic processing of personal data: present and future (Proceedings)*, Warsaw, Council of Europe, 2001. Available at: http://www.coe.int/t/e/legal_affairs/legal_co-operation/data_protection/events/conferences/DP(2001)Proceedings_Warsaw_EN.pdf

Naylor, D., Ritter, C., 'B2C in Europe and Avoiding Contractual Liability: Why Businesses with European Operations Should Review their Customer Contracts Now', 15 September 2004. Available at: http://www.droit-technologie.org/1_2.asp?actu_id=979&motcle=B2C&mode=motamot.

Postman, N., *Technopoly: The surrender of culture to technology*, Vintage Books, New York, 1993.

T-zine (Tijdnet), 'No spam law cases in Belgium', 14 April 2006.

Zwenne, G-J, Schermer, B., *Privacy en andere juridische aspecten van RFID: unieke identificatie op afstand van producten en personen [Privacy and other legal aspects of RFID: unique identification from a distance of products and people]*, Elsevier Juridisch, 's Gravenhage, 2005. Available at: http://www.nvvir.nl/doc/rfid-tekst.pdf.

Chapter 14
Regulating Profiling in a Democratic Constitutional State

Serge Gutwirth and Paul De Hert

In this contribution De Hert and Gutwirth rethink notions such as privacy and data protection against the background of the principles of the democratic constitutional state. They focus upon the necessity to differentiate between privacy and data protection in relation to the distinction they make between opacity and transparency tools. Proceeding by the prohibition of certain kinds of conduct, *opacity tools* tend to guarantee non-interference in individual matters by the state and private actors. Through these tools, the (constitutional) legislator takes the place of the individual as the prime arbiter of desirable or undesirable acts that infringe on liberty, autonomy and identity-building. Opacity tools are normative. *Transparency tools*, on the other hand, are meant to compel government and private actors to 'good practices' by focusing on the transparency of governmental or private decision-making and action, which is indeed the primary condition for a responsible form of governance. In other words, transparency tools tend to make the powerful transparent and accountable. For De Hert and Gutwirth *by default* privacy is an opacity tool and data protection a transparency tool.

De Hert and Gutwirth further argue that profiling is an activity which, in a principled way, should be organised by transparency tools, namely tools which ensure the visibility, controllability and accountability of the profilers and the participation of the concerned. Their principled stance is thus similar to the one held in data protection: *as a rule* the processing of personal data - collection, registration, processing sensu strictu - should not be prohibited but made conditional from the perspective of guaranteeing transparency. As such they do not defend *a principled* prohibitory approach aiming at the enforcement of the individuals' opacity against profilers.

14.1 Positions and Approaches with Regard to Profiling Practices

14.1.1 *Introduction*

At this stage of this book it has become redundant to stress the importance of (automated) profiling and the many applications, possibilities and opportunities it

Serge Gutwirth (VUB and EUR) and Paul De Hert (VUB and TILT)[290]

---

[290] Contact: serge.gutwirth@vub.ac.be & paul.de.hert@uvt.nl.

M. Hildebrandt and S. Gutwirth (eds.), *Profiling the European Citizen:*
Cross-Disciplinary Perspectives.
© Springer Science + Business Media B.V. 2008

includes for contemporary societies. As demonstrated in the preceding chapters, profiling takes place within all thinkable spheres, stages and contexts of the lives of individuals, citizens, groups and organisations. In this contribution we build further upon these descriptions and analyses in order to provide a different set of questions, addressing the issue of the legal regulation of profiling practices. Although our perspective takes into account the existing law, it is not descriptive, since it aims at identifying the different generic concepts and/or tools legislators and policy makers have at their disposal to comprehend the matter. We will try to show that two sorts of tools coexist, i.e., tools respectively enforcing the opacity of the individual and the transparency and accountability of the power. In our opinion these tools express a fundamentally different normative stance. Hence, the option for the one or the other must be considered to be significant from a policy point of view. In order to introduce this contribution we would like to shortly evoke two cases or positions by which we think we can intuitively enlighten the fundamental ideas upon which our approach is based.

14.1.2   The Google Case and Recent Dutch Legislation on Demanding Personal Data

The case against Google began January 18, 2006 when the Justice Department asked U.S. District Judge James Ware (San Jose, California) to order the company to comply with a subpoena issued August 2005. The subpoena called for a 'random sampling' of 1 million Internet addresses accessible through Google's search engine and of 1 million search queries submitted to Google in a one-week period. Essentially, it aimed at obtaining data from search engines to prove how easy it is to stumble over porn on the net. If it could have proven this, the result might have been onerous regulation for many websites. In court documents the U.S. government said it had tried to generate the same information using the Internet Archive website but did not obtain the results it wanted. Google was not the only set service firm that has received a request. The Justice Department conceded that it already had obtained data from other search firms such as Yahoo, AOL and MSN.

Google did however refuse to comply with the demand of the U.S. Department of Justice. The reasons behind this refusal are interesting. Google accepts requests tied to specific criminal investigations by law enforcement organisations but it opposes 'fishing expeditions' in which police forces or intelligence services request data and examine it for people that could have committed crimes or that match a certain profile. Google feared that the 'porn-request' would set a precedent and that there might follow requests to link people with searches for particular terms, such as bomb making materials. Google's worry is that governments would use the data to monitor and spy on civilians.[291] In more general terms one could say that Google has voiced some of the classic arguments against profiling practices and against the (subsequent) use

---

[291] Ward, M., 2006.

of 'soft information' (non verified information) by law enforcement agencies. These practices threaten the requirement that investigative actions should be based upon reasonable and material grounds of suspicion.[292]

Another position is taken by a Dutch law of July 2005[293] that amended the Dutch Code of Criminal Procedure giving law enforcement services and justice authorities more powers to demand personal information from public institutions and companies when this is required in relation to a criminal investigation. Previously, these institutions and companies were bound by the Dutch Personal Data Protection Act and therefore could in principle not provide those personal data. The new law, which entered into force in 2006, makes information and data, which is at the disposal of public institutions and industry, available to law enforcement agents, who from now on will have the power to demand 'identifying' information about an individual (e.g., someone's name, address, place of residence, date of birth or sex, client number, policy number or bank account number). However, the law is not limited to the aforementioned 'identifying information', it reaches further. The Public Prosecutor may also but under heavier conditions, request data on services provided, which indeed contribute to better assessing the pattern of behaviour of an individual. He or she may even demand 'sensitive data', which is personal data related to someone's religion, race, political affinity, health or sex life, be it under still more severe and narrowing conditions. The law translates the endeavour to limit the possibilities of these new powers of the Public Prosecutor with regard to the level of intrusion on a person's privacy they represent. While demanding 'identifying information' is accepted when investigating any crime, the request for information other than identifying data is only allowed for crimes carrying a four-year prison sentence. The power to demand sensitive information is further limited to investigations of serious crimes and subject to prior authorisation from the examining magistrate.

14.1.3 Comparing the Approaches

These two examples show different possible approaches to the issue of profiling. Firstly, the U.S. Justice Department defends the implicit position that it is legitimate to use (all) available and retraceable personal data for policy-making purposes. This entails that, in principle, all traces and data left by individuals are accessible and usable for governmental data mining operations. Which sites have you visited? Which places have you been with your mobile phone or your GPS-equipped car? Which services have you paid for? Which countries have you visited? This mass of data is plainly deemed to be available for mining and trawling and allegedly bear no

---

[292] The Google case ended with a settlement between the two parties and Google handing over 'some' not 'all' data; Anne Broache, 2006.

[293] Wet bevoegdheden vorderen van gegevens van 16 juli 2005, *Stb*, 2005, 390.

privacy-risk, at least if some rules are respected[294]: 'The Justice Department has forcefully dismissed all privacy concerns, saying that any search data obtained from Google would not be shared with anyone else, including federal law enforcement officers who could potentially find the information useful for investigations. The government has also said it is not interested in obtaining information that could be used to identify individuals but, rather, anonymous data about search patterns intended to help bolster its case [in favour of] anti-pornography filters'.[295]

Secondly, the position of the Dutch law is much more restrictive. It empowers the Dutch prosecuting authorities to demand personal data available in the public and the private sector in relation to a criminal investigation. However, the system is a gradual one: the more privacy-sensitive the data requested are, the more stringent the conditions for legitimacy of the request will be. The law enacted a regulation dependent on the type of data required and of the magnitude of the crimes at hand.

Thirdly, Google's resistance expresses the principled position that not all traces can be considered as a pool for data mining, serving other purposes than the original one. As a rule, personal data processed by private and public bodies during the performance of their tasks should not be available and correlatable for other purposes. On the contrary, there are stringent limits to the use that can be made of such data. Some of these limits are technically coined in terms of the 'purpose specification principle', which belongs to the hardcore of data protection law: personal data may only be processed for specified, explicit and legitimate purposes (see *infra*). When data are requested for other than the initially specified purposes, serious guarantees have to be built in. More concretely, in the case at hand: Google will only accept a clearly targeted mining action if there are reasonable indications or suspicions to believe that a person is involved in criminal activities.

It is not our purpose to demonstrate that there is such thing as a 'European' position that is superior to the position of the United States. On the contrary, the U.S. system, where judges have a final say in ordering or not to comply with subpoenas, guarantees judicial control that is absent in the Dutch system, built upon detailed legislation and the institution of the Public Prosecutor. Our purpose is to demonstrate that the positions we have just identified can be better understood from the perspective of the distinction of the two sorts of legal tools that are at the disposal of legislators and policy makers in a democratic constitutional state - opacity and transparency tools. Although these tools always co-exist and are articulated, we believe that it is quintessential to focus upon their different signification. After having described these tools (in part II) and linked them to the difference between privacy and data protection (in part III), we will discuss the issue of profiling and data mining (in part IV).

---

[294] The same 'principle of availability' is defended in the *Proposal for a council framework decision on the exchange of information under the principle of availability, COM (2005) 490 final* and in the 24 November 2005 *Communication from the commission to the council and the European Parliament on improved effectiveness, enhanced interoperability and synergies among European databases in the area of Justice and Home Affairs* COM (2005) 597 final, Brussels, 24 November 2005. See also: De Hert P. & Gutwirth, S., 2006a: 21-35.

[295] Taken from Anne Broache, 2006. The autor erroneously wrote 'against' but of course she means 'in favour of', we corrected this in the quotation.

14.2   The Democratic Constitutional State and the Invention of Two Complementary Legal Tools of Power Control: Opacity of the Individual and Transparency of Power[296]

14.2.1   The Democratic Constitutional State

As already extensively described in former publications[297], the early development of the democratic constitutional state during the 17th and 18th centuries gave birth to new ways to deal with power and power relations. The old omnipotent ruler gave way to a state organisation characterised by a series of embedded mechanisms of power limitation tending to the preservation of individual self-development and freedom. The 'new' system aims to guarantee both a high level of individual freedom and an order in which such freedom is made possible and assured. It has to establish a political institutional system within which, paradoxically, order/unity *and* diversity/liberty are possible. As a result of this double bind the democratic state is constantly under tension because the individual liberties must be tuned, reconciled or made compatible with a social order, which is, in its turn, precisely devised to be constitutive for the liberty of its individual participants. It must enforce an order while protecting individual liberty. A good balance between both aspects must be found and upheld, because on the one hand too much liberty leads to disintegration, chaos and ultimately to the destruction of individual liberty itself and on the other hand, too much order excessively limits individual liberty and leads to dictatorships or tyrannies, including Mill's proverbial tyranny of the majority.

We contend that the history and the practice of democratic constitutional states and the ways they combine fundamental and generic principles, such as the recognition of fundamental rights and liberties, the rule of law and democracy[298], always reveal the use and articulation of two distinct constitutional or legal tools. On the one hand there are tools that tend to guarantee non-interference in individual matters and *the opacity of the individual*. On the other hand we identified tools that tend to organise and guarantee the *transparency and accountability of the powerful*. These two instruments have the same ultimate objective, namely the limiting and controlling of power but they realise this ambition in a different way, from a different perspective. Hence, they provide the legislator with the possibility to translate different policy choices into two distinct sorts of legislation. From this perspective, both tools are a part of the means by which a democratic constitutional state can dynamically organise the relations between individual, social and state concerns and interests. In the sequel of this contribution we will connect the legal protection of privacy to the

---

[296] Chapters II and III of this contribution include parts of some of our formerly published work, namely De Hert P. & Gutwirth S., 2003: 111-162 and De Hert P. & Gutwirth S., 2006b: 61-104.

[297] Cf. footnote 296.

[298] For an extensive discussion of these three principles, see the publications of De Hert and Gutwirth, referred to in the footnote above.

first category of tools, the opacity tools and the regulation of the processing of personal data or 'data protection' to the second category, the transparency tools.

14.2.2   Opacity Tools: Opacity of the Individuals and Limits to the Reach of Power

Opacity tools protect individuals, their liberty and autonomy against state interference and also interference from other (private) actors. They are essentially linked to the recognition of human rights and the sphere of individual autonomy and self-determination. In sum, tools of opacity set limits to the interference of power in relation to the individuals' autonomy and thus their freedom to build identity and self. It can also be said that opacity tools imply the possibility and protection of the anonymity of individuals and their actions. The ideas behind such tools can be understood by recalling the function of the first generation of human rights. By recognising human rights, the revolutions of the 17th and 18th centuries in England, the U.S. and France laid the foundations for a sharper legal separation between the public and private spheres.[299]

Opacity tools, thus, are legal tools that enact a prohibition to interfere with the individual's autonomy and accordingly impose a hands-off or abstention policy from the state and private actors (as a result of the 'horizontal effect' of human rights, for example). In other words, it can be said that they enforce the anonymity of behaviour in our societies. Opacity tools set *limits* to the interference of the power with the individuals' autonomy and as such, they have a strong *normative nature*. The regime they install is that of a principled proscription: they foresee 'no, but …' law. Through these tools, the (constitutional) legislator takes the place of the individual as the prime arbiter of desirable or undesirable acts that infringe on liberty, autonomy and identity-building: some actions are considered unlawful even if the individual consents.[300]

14.2.3   Transparency Tools: Channelling Power and Making Power Transparent and Accountable

The second set of constitutional tools is connected to the principles of the democratic constitutional state that limit state powers by devising legal means of control of these powers by the citizens, by controlling bodies or organisations and by the

---

[299] See Ariès P. & Duby (eds.), 1987.

[300] It would be wrong to characterise opacity tools exclusively by their negative function of shielding and protecting the individual against interferences. They also have an important positive function. See below.

other state powers. Transparency tools are thus very different from opacity tools: they are mainly regulatory. Although their objective is (also) to control state (and other) powers, they do not proceed by drawing the boundaries of such power's reach. On the contrary, transparency tools tend to regulate accepted exercise of power. Transparency tools are not prohibitive but aim at channelling, regulating and controlling legitimate powers: they affect the way power can be exercised; they make the use of power legitimate. More concretely, transparency tools provide means of control of power by the citizens, controlling bodies or organisations and by other state powers.

Transparency tools intend to compel government and private actors to observe 'good practices' by focusing on the transparency of governmental or private decision-making, which is indeed the primary condition for an accountable and responsible form of governance. They define the principles by which the state and private actors must organise their conduct in relation to citizens. In other words, transparency tools tend to make the powerful transparent and accountable: they allow us 'to watch the watchdogs'. Transparency tools install a regime of conditional acceptance: they foresee 'yes, but ...' law. A good example is administrative law, which regulates the modalities of the executive power and ensures accountability by governmental actors.

14.2.4 Distinguishing Both: A Different Default Position

As we wrote, opacity and transparency tools belong to the same constitutional architecture. They were conceived simultaneously, at the historical moment of the conceptual birth of the democratic constitutional state, both with the aim of contributing to the control of power. Nonetheless, the tools of opacity are quite different in nature from the tools of transparency. Opacity tools embody normative choices about the limits of power, while transparency tools aim at the channelling of normatively accepted exercise of power. While the latter are directed towards the control and channelling of legitimate uses of power, the former are indicating where power should not come (protecting the citizens against illegitimate and excessive uses of power). Opacity tools are determining what is in principle out of bounds and hence, what is deemed so essentially individual that it must be shielded against interferences, while transparency tools regulate the exercise of power taking into account that the temptations of abuse of power are huge. The latter empower the citizens and special watchdogs to have an eye on the legitimate use of power: they put 'counter powers' or countermeasures into place. On the opacity side there is a prohibition rule, which is generally but not always (e.g., the prohibition of torture) subject to exceptions; on the transparency side there is a regulated acceptance.

In other words, opacity and transparency tools set a different default position: opacity tools install a 'No, but (possible exceptions)' rule, while transparency tools foresee a 'Yes, but (under conditions)' rule. If we were to apply the concepts to surveillance, the opacity approach would entail a prohibition of surveillance and imply a right not to be surveilled, while the transparency approach would regulate accepted surveillance and imply a right not to be under *unregulated* surveillance.[301]

14.2.5   The Example of Articles 7 and 8 EU-Charter of Human Rights

The differences between both sorts of tools appear clearly in Articles 7 and 8 of the Charter of Fundamental Rights of the European Union (incorporated in the Articles II-67 to II-68 of the Draft Constitution of the European Union).[302]

> Article 7: 'Everyone has the right to respect his or her private and family life, home and communications'.
>
> Article 8: 'Everyone has the right to the protection of personal data concerning him or her. Such data must be processed fairly for specified purposes and on the basis of the consent of the person concerned or some other legitimate basis laid down by law. Everyone has the right of access to data that has been collected concerning him or her and the right to have it rectified. Compliance with these rules shall be subject to control by an independent authority'.

Article 7 provides a good example of an opacity tool because it limits the possible interferences with the individuals' private and family life, home and communications. In a more generic way it can be said that this article protects the individuals' privacy. It is normative and prohibitive but, of course, the prohibition is not absolute. The rule is a 'no', *but* exceptions are thinkable under a number of conditions. In fact, art. 7 of the Charter is a reproduction of the first paragraph of art. 8 of the European Convention on Human Rights, which in its second paragraph does explicitly foresee the conditions under which the privacy-rights recognised by the first paragraph, can be limited by the state. A look at the existing legal exceptions to the protection of privacy and their acceptance by the case-law of the European Court of Human Rights very well shows that the opacity provided by privacy has in fact a rather limited scope. This does not affect the importance of the fact that the article recognises the principle of a prohibition of interference with an individual's private and family life, home and communications. In certain cases the Court ruled categorically against state intervention (for example in respect of homosexual relations).[303]

Article 8 of the Charter provides a good example of a transparency tool. It organises the channelling, control and restraint of the processing of personal data. Data protection legislation *regulates* the processing of personal data. It guarantees

---

[301] Tadros V., 2006b: 106-109.

[302] Our focus on privacy and data protection in the continuation of this text does not of course imply that privacy and data protection respectively, are to be considered as the only opacity and transparency tools.

[303] We provide the analysis of the case law of the Court in De Hert P. & Gutwirth S., 2006b: 82-93 and in De Hert P. & Gutwirth S., 2005: 141-175.

control, openness, accountability and transparency of the processing of personal data. In principle thus, data protection law is not prohibitive. As a rule, personal data may be processed provided that the data controller meets a number of conditions. The rule is a 'yes, but …' rule. Hence, data protection is pragmatic in nature: it assumes that private and public actors need to be able to use personal information and that this must be accepted for societal reasons, which predominate the concerned privacy interests.

The difference in logic between Articles 7 and 8 of the Charter of Fundamental Rights of the European Union is evident. The rationale for this different logic is less evident. What could be the reason to conceive privacy protection as an opacity tool and data protection as a transparency tool?[304]

14.3 Why Two Legal Default Positions with Regard to Regulation?

14.3.1 Privacy: Prohibitive Protection of Autonomy Against (Excessive) Steering

The legal protection of privacy is embedded in the contemporary democratic constitutional state, the values of individualism and the constitutional separation between state and church. Privacy legally translates the political endeavour to ensure non-interference (or opacity) in individual matters. Negatively stated, it protects individuals against interference in their autonomy by governments and by private actors.[305] It is a fundamental notion for a society that wants to limit power relationships. It is intimately linked with the idea that individuals are entitled to unshackle themselves from tradition, social conventions or religion and dissociate themselves, up to a point,

---

[304] In the next paragraphs we present a broad picture of privacy and data protection. When we speak of 'privacy', we mainly refer to article 8 ECHR and its interpretation by the Court of Strasbourg and the direct (and horizontal) effect of this article in the national legal systems and also to the national constitutional protection of privacy. When we speak of 'data protection' we refer to the vast body of international, supranational and national data protection legislations based upon the same principles (the EC-Data Protection Directive being our pre-eminent reference point). As a result, we do not enter into the debate about the values privacy *and* data protection are deemed to protect and enforce; we focus on the differences between privacy-rules and data protection rules. In a different perspective, in chapter 15.4 of this book, Hildebrandt analyses this underlying layer of values when she distinguishes between privacy (the value, defined by her as identity building) and privacy rights (the systems of legal regulation, such as art. 8 ECHR *and* data protection). According to her '[p]rivacy empowers the human person of flesh and bones to rebuild its identity, by protecting its indeterminacy; privacy rights, liberties and legal obligations empower the legal person with the legal tools to indeed seek such protection when it is violated'. From this point of view the concept of 'privacy' is attributed a much broader meaning than the one we give it in this contribution.

[305] Such a negative understanding of privacy can clearly be read in the formulation of Article 8 ECHR: no interference by public authorities is permitted unless necessary in a democratic society.

from their roots and upbringing. However, privacy also functions positively. Being the legal concept that embodies individual autonomy, it plays a quintessential role in a democratic constitutional state based upon the idea that its legitimacy can only result from a maximal respect of each person's individual liberty.[306]

The significant role of privacy, instrumental to the building of the citizen, should be understood in the light of Michel Foucault's argument that all power relationships presuppose a tension between the power and the individual resistance it appeals to. Power as a behavioural conduit - *une conduite des conduites* - always implies a moment of resistance, namely the moment when individuals consider behavioural alternatives. Foucault sees power as the relation between individuals, when one steers the behaviour of the other, even though the other has the freedom to act differently. Power, in this sense, is a strategic situation that leads individuals to behave in ways in which they would not spontaneously commit themselves.[307] Resistance, Foucault writes, is always at the heart of the balance of power. It is precisely at this elementary level that privacy comes in, since personal freedom embodies behavioural alternatives other than those induced by the power relation. In other words, privacy expresses the legal recognition of the resistance to or reticence towards behaviour steered or induced by power. From this point of view, privacy in a constitutional democratic state represents a legal weapon against the development of an absolute balance of powers, again proving privacy's essential role in such a state.[308]

The essential role of privacy in a democratic constitutional state explains why the legal provisions, such as art 8.1 of the ECHR are, by default, prohibitive and normative. They aim at setting limits to the reach of the intervention of states and others in individual matters. By default, they imply that beyond a certain point there is no more legitimate intervention. They legally draw the lower limit of interference in the different aspects of privacy, such as private life, the house, family life, communications and correspondence. Somewhere, even if this point has to be redetermined again and again, taking into account the context and the interests and rights

---

[306] About this concept of privacy see Gutwirth S., 2002.

[307] Cf. Foucault M., 1984: 313-314: 'L'exercice du pouvoir (...) est un ensemble d'actions sur des actions possibles: il opère sur le champ de possibilités où vient s'inscrire le comportement de sujets agissants: il incite, il induit, il facilite ou rend plus difficile, il élargit ou limite, il rend plus ou moins probable; à la limite il contraint ou empêche absolument; mais il est bien toujours une manière d'agir sur un ou sur des sujets agissants, et ce tant qu'ils agissent ou qu'ils sont susceptibles d'agir. Une action sur des actions'.

[308] So privacy imposes a balancing of power and resistance in all power relationships. This does - or at least should not - only apply to the interference of the state. The list also includes the business sector, companies, trade unions, police, doctors, etc. The legal system gives examples - some successful, some not - of attempts to safeguard the privacy of individuals by protecting it against powerful interests. Police services cannot invade the privacy of a home at will. Welfare workers also have to operate within limits. Homeowners do not have the unlimited right, despite the absolute right to property, to check on their tenants. Employers cannot check on their personnel and their telecommunication exchanges at will. Banks and insurance companies are, in principle, limited in their freedom to gather, process and pass on personal information.

at stake[309] somewhere there is a 'no go'. Somewhere there is a legal shield that bounces off intrusions.

14.3.2   Data Protection: The Regulation of the Processing of Personal Data

'Data protection' is a catchall term for a series of principles with regard to the processing of personal data. Through the application of these principles governments try to reconcile fundamental but conflicting values such as privacy, free flow of information, governmental need for surveillance and taxation, etc. The basic principles of data protection are spelled out in the international legal data protection texts produced by institutions such as the Organisation for Economic Cooperation and Development (OECD)[310], the Council of Europe[311] and the European Union.[312] Each of these organisations has produced what has become a classic basic data protection instrument, respectively the OECD Guidelines, Treaty 108 and the Data Protection Directive.[313] As stated, the EU has included the right to data protection in the European Charter of Fundamental Rights and the Draft Constitution (supra).

Generally speaking, data protection provides for a series of rights for individuals such as the right to receive certain information whenever data are collected, the right of access to the data and, if necessary, the right to have the data corrected and the right to object to certain types of data processing. Also, these laws generally demand good data management practices on the part of the data controllers and include a series of obligations: the obligation to use personal data for specified, explicit and legitimate purposes, to guarantee the security of the data against accidental or

---

[309] Notwithstanding privacy's core importance it is clear that it is a relatively weak fundamental right in the European constitutional tradition. Contrary to so called 'hard core' or absolute rights that must be respected even in times of emergency when derogations to other rights are justified (article 15 § 2 ECHR) and contrary to 'normal rights' (e.g., article 5 and 6 ECHR) which can be derogated from: in times of emergency (article 15 § 1), privacy, together with other rights enumerated in articles 8 to 11 of the ECHR, can be legitimately restricted in many cases. The conditions for permissible restrictions are listed in the second paragraphs of these Articles.

[310] Cf. OECD Guidelines Governing the Protection of Privacy and Transborder Data Flows of Personal Data, 23 September 1980 in *Guidelines Governing the Protection of Privacy and Transborder Data Flows of Personal Data*, Paris, OECD, 1980, 9-12; *International Legal Materials*, 1981, I, 317.

[311] Treaty 108: Convention for the protection of individuals with regard to automatic processing of personal data, Council of Europe, January 28, 1981, *European Treaty Series*, no. 108; *International Legal Materials*, 1981, I: 422.

[312] Data Protection Directive: Directive 95/46/EC of the European Parliament and of the Council of 24 October 1995 on the protection of individuals with regard to the processing of personal data on the free movement of such data, *Official Journal of the European Communities*, L 281, 23 November 1995: 31-50.

[313] This Directive has been supplemented by data protection provisions in a number of more specific Directives (cf. infra).

unauthorised access or manipulation and in some cases the obligation to notify a specific independent supervisory body before carrying out certain types of data processing operations. These laws normally provide specific safeguards or special procedures to be applied in case of transfers of data abroad.[314]

In principle, data protection is not prohibitive.[315] On the contrary, in the public sphere, it is almost a natural presumption that public authorities can process personal data, as this is necessary for the performance of their statutory duties, since, in principle, public authorities in democratic societies act on behalf of the citizens. The main aims of data protection consist in providing various specific procedural safeguards to protect individuals and promoting accountability by government and private record-holders. Data protection laws were not enacted for prohibitive purposes but to channel power, promote meaningful public accountability and to provide data subjects with an opportunity to contest inaccurate or abusive record holding practices. The rationale behind data protection in the public sector is the knowledge that authorities can easily infringe privacy and that in all administrative systems there is an urge to collect, store and use data, an urge which must be curtailed by legal regulation. A similar rationale explains the European option to regulate processing executed in the private sector.

Data protection regulations thus mainly belong to the category of transparency tools, as opposed to the protection of privacy that pertain to the tools of opacity. The wording of the data protection principles (the fairness, openness, accountability, and the individual participation principle, etc.) already suggest heavy reliance on notions of procedural rather than substantive justice. The data protection regulations created a legal framework based upon the assumption that the processing of personal data is in principle allowed and legal.

Nevertheless, a number of exceptions exist. For instance, a prohibitive rule applies to 'sensitive data' (data relating to racial or ethnic origin, political opinions, religious or philosophical beliefs, trade union membership or data concerning health or sexual preference). The underlying motive is that the processing of such sensitive data bears a supplementary risk of discrimination. The prohibition is nonetheless never absolute but derogations are (in principle) only possible in strictly defined

---

[314] For a more extensive description of data protection rules, see chapter 13 of this book.

[315] At first glance, however, the Data Protection Directive seems to create a system of general prohibition, requiring some conditions to be met for 'making data processing legitimate'. The impression is given that the basic logic behind it is of a prohibitive nature: 'no processing, unless...'. But this understanding is not correct for, firstly, the Directive was heavily inspired by and had to accommodate existing national data protection regulations, which were *not* based upon the prohibition principle. Secondly, the Data Protection Directive provides for a catchall ground for private data processing in its art 7f. According to this article, personal data can be processed without the consent of the data subject if the processing 'is necessary for the purposes of the legitimate interests pursued by private interests, except where such interests are overridden by the interests of fundamental rights and freedoms of the data subject.' For some authors this article even covers the processing of data for direct marketing purposes. Indeed, such an article obliges a serious analyst to doubt and even refute the idea that the processing of personal data is in principle prohibited or dependent on the consent of the data subject. Article 7f in fact spans the whole scale of possibilities and can obviously 'make data processing legitimate' for every conceivable business interest.

circumstances, for example, for reasons of national security. Another example can be found in Article 15 of the Data Protection Directive. This article gives individuals the right to object to decisions affecting them when these decisions are made solely on the basis of profiles.[316] In other words art. 15 proscribes the practice of making decisions about a person relying exclusively on automated data processing.[317]

---

[316] According to this article every person has the right 'not to be subject to a decision which produces legal effects concerning him or significantly affects him and which is based solely on automated processing of data'. Hence, in principle, decisions that significantly affect the data subject, such as the decision to grant a loan or issue insurance, cannot be taken on the sole basis of automated data processing. The data subject must also be able to know the logic on which these automated decisions are based. The article refers to automated processing of data 'intended to evaluate certain personal aspects relating to him, such as his performance at work, creditworthiness, reliability, conduct, etc.' The goal is to guarantee participation in important personal decisions. A dismissal based purely on the data from the company time clock is, as a result, unacceptable. It applies also to the rejection of a jobseeker based on the results of a computerised psychotechnical assessment test or to a computerised job application package. These decisions have to take professional experience or the result of a job interview into account. The automated test is insufficient and it applies to such sectors as banking and insurance. The EU member states have to enact provisions that allow for the legal challenge of computerised decisions and which guarantee an individual's input in the decision-making procedures. However, member states are allowed to grant exemptions on the ban on computerised individual decisions if such a decision '(a) is taken in the course of the entering into or performance of a contract, provided the request for the entering into or the performance of the contract, lodged by the data subject, has been satisfied or that there are suitable measures to safeguard his legitimate interests, such as arrangements allowing him to put his point of view; or (b) is authorised by a law which also lays down measures to safeguard the data subject's legitimate interests'. Art. 15, see Bygrave, L.A., 2001: 17-24.

[317] There is a ongoing debate about this article, because some authors (such as Bygrave cited in the former footnote) argue that the wording of the article ("Member States shall grant the right to every person not to be the subject to a decision ...") only creates a right to object, which would imply that as long as this right is not exercised, the automated decision making process is not illegal. An extensive analysis of this position is given in chapter 13 of this book. We think that this reasoning is wrong, because it would make the legitimacy of a purely automated decision dependent on the *implicit* consent of the concerned subject: if you do not object, you consent and you thus make the automated decision legitimate. This is not only an absurd position, because the main problem with automated decisions is precisely that the individual is *not* consulted but it is also sharply at odds with the Directive's understanding of 'consent' as a 'freely given specific and informed indication of his wishes'. We, from our side, are thus convinced that art. 15 of the Directive expresses a significant rebuttal of purely automated decisions about individuals. The Belgian legislator, for example, has evidently understood the Directive in the same way, since the Belgian law on data protection, implementing the Directive, uses unambiguously prohibitive wording: "A decision resulting into legal effects for a person or affecting him seriously, may not be taken purely on the basis of automatic data processing that is destined for the evaluation of certain aspects of his personality. The prohibition laid down in the first section is not applicable if the decision is taken in the context of an agreement or if it has its ground in a provision laid down by or by virtue of a law, decree or ordinance. In such an agreement or provision appropriate measures shall be taken for the protection of the legitimate interests of the data subject. At least he shall be allowed to bring up his standpoint in a useful way"; art. 12 bis of the consolidated text of the Belgian law of December 8, 1992 on Privacy Protection in relation to the Processing of Personal Data as modified by the law of December 11, 1998 implementing Directive 95/46/EC – *Unofficial English translation by K. Buyens, updated by Mieke Loncke*, see: http://www.law. kuleuven.ac.be/icri/documents/12privacylaw.php).

But again, both prohibitive features are accompanied by numerous exceptions that do not set strong and clear-cut limits to the targeted actions.

The foregoing shows that data protection regulations do promote transparency but (sometimes) also provide for opacity rules, e.g., when sensitive data are at hand. Inversely, the default position of privacy is opacity but it can also allow for transparency rules, e.g., when the Court of Strasbourg (or a national legislator) derogatively allows telephone tapping under strictly defined conditions (e.g., by legal regulation, for certain incriminations, limited in time, with control of the police, etc.).

14.3.3 Combining the Tools

It is up to the legislators and policymakers to consider both tools and to identify the kind of tools necessary for a given problem, especially with regard to technological developments. How much of which tool is necessary and when? Channelling power in the mist is doomed to fail; limits and points of departure are necessary. Transparency tools alone cannot, therefore, be enough. However, approaching new phenomena with heavy prohibitions may circumvent the legitimate interest of the state or block potentially interesting developments, for example, with regard to the use of a new technology. It may also lead to a situation in which the prohibitions are not respected. This would leave power relations uncontrolled, due to the lack of tools. Hence, an approach based only on opacity tools should also be considered with due care. The question then becomes how to combine the tools appropriately and how to calibrate the switch.

Of course, such an approach raises the question of the application of the distinct tools to (new) developments and techniques. When will opacity be called upon? When will transparency apply? How to choose between an opacity approach (proscriptive rules that limit or 'stop' power) and a data transparency approach (regulations that channel power and make it conditional and accountable)? In fact, raising the question as to what should be protected through opacity and what through transparency tools is raising other questions: what is, in a democratic constitutional society, so essential that it must be, as a rule, shielded from interference by others (public and private actors)? Which aspects of individual life in an open society must be protected against visibility? Which aspects of individual life should be withdrawn from scrutiny, surveillance and control? Where are hard norms needed? Where should ad hoc balancing of interests be replaced by a categorical balancing?

The answers to these questions must be formulated by reference to the basics of the democratic constitutional state as described above. Opacity and transparency tools each have their own roles to play and they are both indispensable. Neither will do without the other. They are not communicating vessels. Hence, for example, we do not think like Etzioni that public authorities cannot be denied technologies and means for crime fighting if their implementation is linked to enough transparency and accountability.[318] On the contrary, taking privacy seriously implies the making of normative choices: some intrusions are just too threatening for the fundamentals of the democratic constitutional state to be accepted even under a stringent regime of accountability. Other intrusions, however, can be felt to be acceptable and necessary in the light of other, sometimes predominating, interests. Only then, after such a normative weighing of privacy and other interests, privacy-invasive and liberty-threatening measures can, exceptionally and regrettably, be accepted and submitted to the legal conditions of transparency and accountability.

14.3.4   Is Data Protection a Good Starting Point for Regulating Profiles?

In practice, with new emerging technologies such as profiling, it will often work the other way around. Data protection, with its broad concepts such as 'personal data' and 'processing', is always triggered first. *Personal data* in the EU Data Protection Directive refer to 'any information relating to an identified or identifiable natural person.' There are no limits as to content or technology. Phone numbers and license plates, social security numbers, images, voices, genetic information, fingerprints are included in the definition of Article 2 of the Data Protection Directive. A person is identifiable as soon as identification is possible based on means that can reasonably be assumed to be used by the responsible data controller. The *processing* includes automated and manual processing. The Directive covers manual processing only if it constitutes a filing system and has a minimal structure. This condition does not, however, apply to automated processing because programmes have the capacity to merge and intertwine masses of loose data within seconds. The term 'processing' also needs to be given a comprehensive interpretation. The Directive imposes upon the member states a definition that says that it applies to any operation that is performed upon personal data. The rules cover each part of processing - 'collection, recording, organisation, storage, adaptation or alteration, retrieval, consultation, use, disclosure by transmission, dissemination or otherwise making available, alignment or combination, blocking, erasure or destruction.' It is worth highlighting that even the mere collection of personal data is covered by the Directive.

The conclusion is easy to make: data protection regulations apply in principle to the automated collection and processing of personal data. This implies that a number of rules are applicable from the default transparency perspective and that the processing of data must fulfil the foreseen conditions. However, as argued above, some data protection rules are proscriptive opacity rules: sensitive data may not be processed at all, unless exceptions apply. This could, for example, entail that video surveillance falls under this regime because images of a person (can) contain

---

[318] Etzioni A., 2002: 34: 'If accountability is deficient, the remedy is to adjust accountability, not to deny the measure altogether'.

racial, ethnic, health or religious information. Another opacity rule is that the secret collecting and processing of personal data is in principle forbidden: there must be openness to the processing.

Is this enough to regulate a technology such as profiling, however? We think it may be a good start but one should remain cautious. In the following paragraphs we will try to demonstrate that there might be a danger in entrusting regulation solely to the data protection mechanism in its current form.

14.4   Profiling and Data Protection: A Principled Position

14.4.1   Correlatable Humans

As the other chapters of this book demonstrate, over recent decades, individual and group profiling capacities have exponentially grown as a result of both the advances in technology and the increasing availability of readily processable data and traces. Today, an individual - consciously and unconsciously, voluntarily and involuntarily - leaves a vast amount of processable and thus correlatable electronic traces in his wake. The use of Internet, mobile telephones, electronic financial systems, biometric identification systems, radio frequency tags (RFIDs), smart cards, ubiquitous computing, ambient intelligence techniques, GPS and so forth all participate in the spontaneous and automatic generation of correlatable data. Add to this the use of still more pervasive and powerful data mining and tracking systems and the 'correlative potential' increases again. Such a 'correlative potential' can spawn an unlimited amount of profiles that in principle enable a permanent real-time analysis of the conduct of individuals and the affirmation of evaluations of and predictions about their behaviour, sensibilities, preferences, identity, choices, etc. *ad infinitum*. Such profiles can be used both by private (marketing, insurances, employment, private security) and public actors (crime and terrorism fighting, preparation of decisions, elaboration of tailor-made services, CAPPS II, etc.). We believe that these evolutions represent more than mere quantitative changes: they induce a significant qualitative shift that we have chosen to describe with the notions of 'correlatable human' and/or 'traceable or detectable human'.[319] This requires some explanation.

The scientific and statistical approaches of the 19th century were prestructured or stratified in the sense that human scientists and policy makers were searching for explicative etiological schemes: they chose to investigate the populations from the perspective of *certain* parameters that they believed to be relevant and pertinent. In other words, the correlations established were the result of oriented questioning; they were *measurements* meant to be meaningful and revealing. Research parameters

---

[319] The development of these concepts is the result of networked and interdisciplinary research carried out under the *Interuniversity attraction poles* programme (V/16) *The loyalties of knowledge. The positions and responsibilities of the sciences and of scientists in a democratic constitutional state* financed by the *Belgian Federal Science Policy* (see www.imbroglio.be).

were preliminarily stratified according to their presupposed pertinence. Lombroso researched the skulls of detainees and Quetelêt their social backgrounds, because they each believed that that parameter could provide etiology of criminal behaviour. In other words: the correlations established by 19th century scientists were the result of oriented questioning: the chosen parameters or variables were presupposed to explain the problem at hand. Today, however, such preceding questions (and the structuration/stratification of parameters they imply) are no longer needed to organise the search for correlations.[320] On the contrary, the emergence in itself of a correlation has become the pertinent or interesting information or knowledge, which in its turn will launch questions, suppositions and hypotheses. Things are going the other way around now: the upsurge of a correlation *is* the information, in scientific practice to begin with but of course also in a growing number of practices in economic, social and cultural life.

In this context Isabelle Stengers evoked the image of the bubble chamber[321]: a bubble chamber is a container full of saturated vapour such that if you have an energetic particle travelling through it, its many successive encounters with a gas molecule will produce a small local liquefaction: quantum mechanics tell us that we cannot define the path of a particle but, because of the bubble chamber, we can 'see' its 'profile'. According to this metaphor there are an unlimited number of detectors and detections surrounding us, as we act and live. Hence, we leave traces and 'profiles' that allow others to 'see' us. Compared to the 19th Century 'average human', this is the new point: the human is no longer identified and grasped in terms of meaningful, stratified categories only: (s)he is detectable and retraceable and thus 'correlatable'. The fundamental difference is that detections are much wider than measurements responding to addressed questions: independently, detections are *a-signifiantes*; they do not (yet) have a specific meaning but they can acquire a meaning as a result of the questions and concerns of the one who uses them. Detections *may* correspond to measures but first of all they are indeterminate.

In other words, the huge increase of processable traces (spawned by automatic detections), of linkability, convergence and interoperability and of available profiling/processing technologies have led to a qualitative shift whereby correlations and profiles can be generated before any preceding stratified interest. This is precisely why we say that humans have become detectable, (re)traceable and correlatable.

14.4.2   Origin and Scope of Data Protection in the Context of a Profiling Society

The origin of data protection lies, at least partially, in this qualitative shift in the practices of processing personal data. To us, the advent of data protection law is

---

[320] Cf. Chapter 3 and 4 of this book. In this paragraph we focus upon the growing possibilities and importance of 'inductive' profiling.

[321] See: www.imbroglio.be (restricted area, sorry)

related to an intuitive understanding by legislators of the shift described in the former paragraphs. Why otherwise would data protection provide for the protection of *all* data related to a person without any distinction as to e.g., their inherent level of 'privacy-sensitivity'?[322] In inventing and devising data protection, the legislator did *not*, in a principled way, *prohibit* the detection and the collection of traces. These activities were submitted to the transparency rules of data protection, which means that they were accepted in principle but submitted to rules guaranteeing control and accountability of the processors.

Data protection was conceptualised as a set of good practices aiming at minimising those risks: it provided a legal response to the questions raised by the pervasive collection and processing of the clouds of indeterminate data left by actors. This attests a redistribution of the legal approaches to these issues: although transparency is the default stance of the legal approach of the processing of personal data, prohibitive opacity rules within data protection still apply to determine which personal data answer stratifications or prestructured questioning. Think of data concerning race, religion and political affiliation. Indeed, these data additionally bear an immediate danger of discrimination. On the other hand, the transparency rules of data protection apply to the indeterminate detections that have not yet effectively been used and mobilised.

We contend that the invention of data protection is not only contemporaneous with the birth of the potential for the automated detection of individual traces but also that it formulates a legal response to the problems caused by these developments today. Data protection rules apply to profiling techniques (at least in principle).[323] The collection and processing of traces surrounding the individual must be considered as 'processing of personal data' in the sense of existing data protection legislation. Both individual and group profiling are indeed dependent on such collection and the processing of data generated by the activities of individuals. Without collecting and correlating such personal data, no profiling is thinkable. This is precisely why, in legal terms, no profiling is thinkable outside data protection.

There is an ongoing debate in contemporary legal literature about the applicability of data protection to processing practices with data that is considered anonymous, viz. data that does not allow the identification of a specific individual. This debate also has repercussions on the legal regime for profiling. Some contend that data protection rules do not prohibit processing practices that bring together data on certain individuals without trying to identify the said individuals (in terms of physical location or name). For instance, in the Google case discussed above, the U.S. government contended it was not interested in obtaining information that could be used to identify individuals, but rather anonymous data about search patterns, intended to help bolster its case against anti-pornography filters.[324]

---

[322] General data protection law is indifferent to this parameter: it merely applies to the processing of personal data, even if these data are (still) *a-signifiantes*. It is enough that the data relate to an identifiable person.

[323] We add "at least in principle" because we are well aware of the practical difficulties of effectively enforcing and implementing data protection, more particularly in the field of profiling.

[324] See Broache, 2006.

We have analysed this debate earlier[325] and the conclusion still stands: it is possible to interpret the European data protection rules in a broad manner covering profiling practices pertaining to humans. This is confirmed in chapter 13 of this book wherein, after a thorough legal analysis, W. Schreurs, M. Hildebrandt, E. Kindt and M. Vanfleteren advocate an inyerpretation of the data protection rules in which those rules generally apply to profiling practices at the moment of the building and application of the profiles. However, the courts have the last word on this and they have not yet spoken. The authors of chapter 13 however, indicate a number of problems that may be standing in the way of such an application, the most important being firstly, that group profiles are not personal data but abstract information extracted from anonymised data and secondly, that those group profiles can be applied to persons without identifying them which, of course, would imply the non-applicability of data protection rules. Another open issue mentioned is, indeed, that applicable data protection is not effectively enforced.

It is our belief that data protection *should* apply and that, if confusion remains, legal texts should be adapted so as to make this possible. Profiling practices lead to an accumulation of power in the hands of those that command them and to a loss of control by the concerned individuals. Therefore, they should be made transparent. Consequently, if the definition of 'personal data' ('any information relating to an identified or identifiable natural person') turns out to be a barrier to the application of data protection rules, this should not be taken as a reason to discard data protection but as a strong signal to start thinking and devising a new generation of data protection rules, wherein the 'identifiability' of the data subject is no longer a criterion. If technologies and socio-economic practices make it possible to control and steer individuals without the need to identify them, the time has probably come to explore the possibility of a shift from personal data protection to data protection *tout court*.

14.4.3   *Data Protection and Profiling: A Natural Pair*

Our finding that data protection applies or should apply to profiling practices is neither good nor bad news. Profiling in itself is neither good nor bad. We are neither technophobes nor techno-utopists and we discard both *boom* and *doom* scenarios for the future. All in all, profiling generates knowledge. This knowledge however, has the particular feature of being non-representational. Profiles do not so much aim to represent a current state of affairs but rather to predict future behaviours inferred from past actions. Profiles are patterns obtained from a probabilistic analysis of data; they do not describe reality. Taken to a more abstract level, profiling leads to the identification of patterns in the past, which can develop into a very useful and valuable probabilistic knowledge about non-humans, individuals and groups of humans in the present and in the future. Even

---

[325] De Hert, P., in Prins et al., 2002: 190-199.

if the past shows that a pattern occurs every time certain conditions are met, one cannot be 100% sure it will happen today and tomorrow as well. Based on its experience, an animal may associate a situation with danger as a result of the recognition of a certain pattern or profile and act consistently even if the situation, in reality, is not really a dangerous one (the human smell and the shuffling footsteps were not those of a hunter but those of an animal rights observer). Hence, profiling is as old as life, because it is a kind of knowledge that unconsciously or consciously supports the behaviour of living beings, humans not excluded. It might well be that the insight that humans often 'intuitively know' something before they 'understand' it can be explained by the role profiling spontaneously plays in our minds.

Therefore, there is no reason, by default, to prohibit automated profiling and data mining concerning individuals as such with opacity rules. Profiling activities should in principle be ruled by transparency tools, namely tools that ensure the visibility, controllability and accountability of the profilers and the information, control and participation of those concerned. Our principled stance is thus similar to the one held in data protection: as a rule the processing of personal data - collection, registration, processing sensu strictu - is not prohibited but subject to a number of conditions guaranteeing the visibility, controllability and accountability of the data controller and the participation of the data subjects. We are hence convinced that the principles of data protection are an appropriate starting point to cope with profiling in a democratic constitutional state as they impose 'good practices'.

Nevertheless, while the default position of data protection is transparency rules ('yes, but ...'), it does not exclude opacity rules ('no, unless'). In relation to profiling, two examples of such rules are very relevant. On the one hand, of course, there is the prohibition against the making and taking of decisions affecting individuals solely on the basis of profiling (Art. 15 of the Data Protection Directive). This seems obvious because in such a situation, probabilistic knowledge is applied to a real person. On the other hand, there is the (quintessential) purpose specification principle, which provides that the processing of personal data must meet specified, explicit and legitimate purposes. As a result, the competence to process is limited to well-defined goals, which implies that the processing of the same data for other incompatible aims is prohibited. Processing of personal data for different purposes should be kept separate. This, of course, substantially restricts the possibility to interconnect the different processing and databases for profiling or data mining objectives. The purpose specification principle is definitely at odds with the logic of interoperability and availability of personal data, which would imply that all comceivable databases concerning individuals can jointly be used for profiling purposes.[326] In other words, the fact that the applicable legal regime to profiling and data mining is data protection, it does not give a *carte blanche* to mine and compare personal data that were not meant to be connected.[327]

---

[326] Cf. De Hert, P., 2006 and De Hert P. & Gutwirth, S., 2006a: 21-35.

[327] Cf. European Data Protection Supervisor (EDPS), *Annual Report 2005*: 22-23. http://www.edps.eu.int/publications/annual_report_en.htm.

14.5 Conclusion

Humans have become detectable, (re)traceable and correlatable far beyond their control and the correlatable traces they produce start to live their own lives, becoming the resources of a very extensive, if not unlimited, network of possible profiling devices generating knowledge directly or indirectly concerning and/or affecting them. Such a shift demands careful monitoring from the perspective of the democratic constitutional state, because it likely entails a number of threats such as the influencing of individual behaviour (you act differently if you know that traces you leave will be processed), sharpening of power inequalities, loss of control, customisation and normalisation of conduct, consequent erosion of both negative and positive freedom and, last but not least, taking of unmotivated and unilateral decisions about individuals.

In this contribution we took at a closer look at the difference in nature between privacy and data protection, which received a separate formulation in the 2000 EU Charter on fundamental rights. This is rightly so: by default privacy is an opacity tool and data protection a transparency tool. This distinction is not absolute, however. Some opacity rules were incorporated in the European data protection framework, e.g., when sensitive data are at hand and when the original purpose of a data processing operation is neglected. In these cases the default position of data protection ('yes, but …'), is reversed ('no, unless …').

The rich set of principles of data protection are an appropriate *starting point* to cope with profiling as they submit it to 'good practices'.[328] Subsequently, profiling practices are always subjected to legal power management, even in the case of legitimate profiling. This, in our view, seems to be the major difference with the U.S. approach, where the data protection framework is conceived in less general terms[329] and where a solid legal framework for controlling ordinary or legitimate profiling is not present. The Google case teaches us that such a framework still has to be elaboratedPresently, this is done by judges and only in cases where firms such as Google refuse to cooperate.

On the other hand, there are two positive things that can be learned from the U.S. experience. Firstly, there is the American piecemeal approach towards privacy protection. Without striving for a general privacy and data protection framework, the U.S. legislator is willing to vote privacy and data protection regulations for specific, 'hot' issues. This ad hoc approach is not the result of coincidence but of culture. It exemplifies an essentially American way of looking at privacy and privacy threats in the sense that it relies on market principles, self-regulation of private

---

[328] We stress 'starting point', because we are well aware of some lacunae, problems and controversial issues related to the application of data protection to profiling practices. This is why we pointed at the option to consider devising a new set of transparency rules, a new generation of data protection rules, which would be similar to data protection but would apply regardless of the identifiability of the data subject.

[329] For a discussion: De Hert, P. in Prins, et al., 2002: 200-230.

parties and/or, on a strong civil society.[330] The government abstains from interfering. Koops and Leenes rightly contrast this with the European (continental) approach, favouring legal measures and legislation for the fair treatment of personal data.[331] They rightly identify Lawrence Lessig as a typical exponent of the U.S. approach. In his chapter on code and privacy in *Code and Other Laws of Cyberspace*, Lessig identifies two risks generated by profiling practices:[332] on the one hand the danger of normalisation of the population[333] and on the other hand violation of equality through discrimination, for instance between customers, based on profiles. Instead of calling only for legal measures, such as fair information practices, Lessig seeks the solution in privacy enhancing technologies and in the legal creation of property rights with regard to personal data.[334] The advantage of relying on property law over data protection law lies in the fact that property law facilitates ex ante control over personal data; only after consent may personal data be used. Obviously, the consent will only be given at the right price. In more general terms, Lessig defends the position that there are at least four modes to regulate behaviour, i.e., law, social norms, markets and 'code' or architecture, the point being to find the 'optimal mix' among these four modalities of regulation: policies 'trade off' among these four regulatory tools.[335] In the light of the many sceptical writings about the way European data protection works in practice (many say it does not offer adequate protection on the field), it becomes our task to follow closely alternative methods of regulation that are at hand and to amend current European policy options when the alternatives prove to be better.

Secondly, Europe can probably benefit from the U.S. ability to react with effective legal instruments whenever a need to react is recognised. If this image is true, one could say that there is a better predisposition to implement opacity tools in the U.S. constitutional tradition. Americans simply know better how to say 'no' in certain cases. In recent years, for instance, a number of American States have enacted legislation in order to prohibit 'racial profiling'. Not all states have enacted prohibitions and the definitions of (forbidden) racial profiling are not the same. Without going into technical details, we observe that a considerable amount of these regulations are far

---

[330] Hosein G., 2005.

[331] Koops, B.J., Leenes, R., 2005: 115-188.

[332] Lessig, L., 1999a: 154.

[333] This is done by presenting the person who fits a particular profile only the options the profiler wants him to see. Obviously, this scheme works best if the profiled subject is unaware of this selective feed of options. This kind of manipulation affects people's autonomy to make choices. Lessig writes: 'When the system seems to know what you want better and earlier than you do, how can you know where these desires really come from? (...) (P)rofiles will begin to normalise the population from which the norm is drawn. The observing will affect the observed. The system watches what you do; it fits you into a pattern; the pattern is then fed back to you in the form of options set by the pattern; the options reinforce the patterns; the cycle begins again;' Lessig L., 1999a: 154. On profiles and normalisation see also: Gutwirth S., 2002: 66-78 and Hildebrandt M., in chapter 15 of this book (sub 15.2.3).

[334] See also in Lessig, L., 1999b: 519-521.

[335] Lessig, L., 1999b: 506-514.

more precise and comprehensive[336] than the general prohibition on automated decision in Article 15 of the Data Protection Directive (discussed above).[337] Our comparison between the U.S. Google case and the 2005 Dutch Bill on demanding data furnishes a second illustration. The latter works without the intervention of a judge (the 2005 Dutch Bill allows the Public Prosecutor to demand 'sensitive data'), the former teaches us that profiling demands can be brought before a judge, which in the case of Google resulted in a concrete analysis of the necessity of the profiling practice in question.

Profiling should be addressed not only with a mix of modes of regulation (as Lessig argues) but this mix must also construct an appropriate articulation of opacity and transparency tools. Europe and the U.S. have something to learn from each other.

14.6   Reply: Addressing the Obscurity of Data Clouds

Ronald Leenes*

Gutwirth and De Hert proclaim data protection instrumental to privacy. Privacy incorporates notions such as individuality, autonomy, integrity and dignity. These values are affected by IT systems that use personal data. Data protection regulation aims to control the use of personal data to protect the fundamental values mentioned. Data protection regulation is therefore a transparency tool; it makes the powerful accountable. Modern profiling techniques potentially obscure the concepts and relations underlying the Data protection framework. Some types of profiles derived from data mining constitute digital persona on which decisions about individuals are taken. These profiles, by their very essence, may render incorrect representations of the individuals to which they are applied, possibly resulting in an unfair judgement. Transparency in the sense of explicating the profile or inference rules used to derive particular decisions about individuals seems to be a necessity to guarantee privacy protection. This will, however, not be welcomed by the users of the profiles. Opacity tools, such as Privacy Enhancing Technologies, may prove to be necessary complements.

14.6.1   Introduction

Gutwirth and De Hert in their illuminating contribution rightly make a distinction between privacy and data protection. Data protection is a means to help protect privacy. Privacy is a complex concept that incorporates and furthers equally complex

---

* Tilburg Universiteit, Tilburg Insitituut for Law, Technology and Society (TILT)

[336] See Gandy O.H. & Lemi B., 2005: 14-16.

[337] We recall that this article proscribes decision making affecting persons *solely* on the basis of automated profiles.

notions such as individuality, autonomy, integrity and dignity (e.g., Bygrave, 2002: 128-129). The use of IT systems affects these values. Decisions about individuals are taken by these systems by (autonomously) applying business rules and algorithms on the basis of data collected about these individuals. Because of the effects these decisions have on individuals and the values mentioned earlier, data protection regulation is important. The collection, processing and use of personal data has to be regulated to promote that decisions about individuals are based on data that are lawfully obtained, adequate, accurate, relevant and not excessive in relation to the purposes for which they are processed.[338] The data protection regulation also prohibits the automated decision-making by IT systems (Article 15 Data Protection Directive 95/46/EC) to help safeguard the values mentioned. Data protection is therefore, as De Hert and Gutwirth state, a transparency tool; it makes the powerful accountable for the decisions they and their IT systems make.

This is all reasonably well understood in the context of traditional data collection where the relation between data controller, data subject, purpose, relevant data, collection and use of personal data is fairly clear. The data protection legislation was introduced in an era when personal data processing mainly consisted in locally stored (large) databases under the control of an addressable entity, the company or government collecting and using data about their customers and citizens. The data protection legislation clearly shows its roots in the traditional files and folders concepts, despite Gutwirth and De Hert's claim that it captures the legislator's intuitive understanding of impeding changes. In my view, the legislator has not (sufficiently) anticipated the changes to come. The current practice, where data no longer typically reside within a single entity (enterprise, government) but where data instead are stored in distributed (networked) databases, data warehouses, clearing houses and so forth, does produce problems. Especially techniques such as data mining across databases and profiling, possibly undermine the assumptions of data protection legislation, as I will try to show in this contribution.

14.6.2   Personalised Profiling and Data Protection

Profiling complicates data protection. If the profiled data rightly represents the data subject, the situation is not too different from traditional databases containing customer data; this profile is just a complex record of a data subject. However, if the link between data subject and profile is more opaque, for instance because the profile is constructed by data mining techniques, or if rules about individuals or groups are inferred from data sets, then privacy is affected in a different way.

---

[338] Article 6 Data Protection Directive: Directive 95/46/EC of the European Parliament and of the Council of 24 October 1995 on the protection of individuals with regard to the processing of personal data on the free movement of such data, Official Journal of the European Communities, L 281, 23 November 1995: 31-50.

Rather, its constituent parts, such as autonomy and integrity are affected. Personalised profiles constructed by correlating multiple sources, including both identifiable data – which relate to the profiled individual and aggregated data (group level) that potentially does not relate to the subject at all – may well constitute incorrect representations of the profiled subject. If these (inaccurate) profiles are subsequently used to make decisions about these individuals and that seems to be their purpose, then there is a clear risk of unfair judgement. Especially in the case of automated decision-making, which, although limited by Article 15 of the Data Protection Directive, is common practice in industry and commerce.

De Hert and Gutwirth note this problem and point out that the set of principles in the European Data Protection Framework, which is primarily a transparency tool, is a good starting point to address the problems surrounding profiling. In their view, the use of profiles should be transparent and profiles should therefore be considered data for which the profiler has to be accountable. Data subjects should be entitled to similar rights as those for ordinary personal data: e.g., inspection, correction and deletion (Article 12 of the Data Protection Directive).

At the same time, they acknowledge that the EU Data Protection Directive does not always work well in practice. They point out that it is useful to consider the four modalities of regulation discussed by Lawrence Lessig (1999a): social norms, market, law and architecture ('code') – to construct the right mix to properly safeguard individuals against the potential harms of profiling. Although the authors are not explicit on this, I expect they primarily mean *code* as the modality to consider, because this is also Lessig's angle.

Although I subscribe to Gutwirth and De Hert's general conclusions, the application of these to a specific kind of profile, namely what they vaguely call "correlatable humans" and/or "traceable or detectable humans", raises two questions that I want to address in this contribution. First, what is the meaning of transparency tools in relation to these 'vague' profiles? Second, what can we expect of code in this respect?

14.6.3   Digital Persona

On the one hand, there are profiles that are linked to known or identified persons.[339] For instance, a supermarket chain may keep records of my purchasing behaviour on the basis of my customer loyalty card. On the basis of attributes, such as my purchasing history, new attributes may be inferred that could be added to my personalised profile. These new attributes could lead to predictions about my future needs and behaviour and be used by the supermarket to provide personalised services, discounts and so forth. The sudden addition of Pampers to my shopping list may signal that my family has acquired a new member. Apart from the obvious conclusion that

---

[339] Including user modelling and profiling of web users as described in chapters 2 and 9.

I most likely will also be in the market for baby food, a change in my behaviour may also be imminent. My wife and I may well develop a family life and become couch potatoes, instead of outgoing yuppies, which would lead to different purchasing habits. The supermarket has undoubtedly seen this behavioural transformation before and can use their knowledge to augment my profile. Transparency tools, as implemented in the Data Protection Framework, are useful and applicable here. The profile associated with a particular data subject can be identified and the data in the profile can easily be shown, corrected and so forth. It may even be possible to show why and how certain inferences were made, as required by Article 12 of the Data Protection Directive. I can see few problems here.

The profiles in this category represent attributes that constitute the individual or make them unique; you are what you read, eat, do, etc. The personalised profile to some extent is a *representation* of all of this and could therefore, be said to be a person's digital persona (Clarke, 1994).[340] Because the individual associated with the digital representation is known or identifiable, the profile is also related to this person's *idem identity*. More precisely, the digital representation has an identifier that allows it to be linked to one's idem identity. The supermarket can tell that it is me who pays at the counter and hence update my profile because I hand over the identifier included on my loyalty card, which allows this connection.[341]

14.6.4 Correlatable Humans

The other kind of profile, which includes most but maybe not all, kinds of group profiles, is more problematic in terms of transparency. Gutwirth and De Hert use the term "correlatable humans" to denote the kind of profiling and profile use that is not aimed at describing individuals in meaningful (stratified) terms. What they seem to mean is that individuals leave traces during their (on-line) activities and that these traces may be collected and correlated to devise new kinds of attributes that only derive their meaning through their use. They explain this idea by means of the metaphor of the bubble chamber. A bubble chamber, consisting of a saturated vapour, allows high-energy particles, which cannot be observed directly, to be visualised by the bubble traces they produce when hitting gas molecules, which consequently liquefy. Just like a thermometer is an indicator of temperature (which also

---

[340] Of course, most profiles are fairly limited in this sense because most likely Amazon has only a vague idea of my reading habits and does not know what I do (for a living). They have a very shallow and fragmented idea of who and what I am. In some cases, the profile is even rather contaminated, such as in the case of the supermarket, because this profile represents my family more than it represents me.

[341] Again, the supermarket is not the best example, as people at the supermarket where I buy my groceries, exchange loyalty cards, which results in incorrect identification and hence, contaminated profiles.

cannot be observed directly), the bubble chamber is an indicator for an unobservable phenomenon.

Similarly, our on-line behaviour produces data (traces) that can be observed and used to make sense of what we do. For instance, the fact that I was looking for a digital mirror reflex camera a year ago could be detected by following the traces that I left on-line; I visited news sites, browsed through reviews, compared prices, etc. I told no one that I was looking for a digital camera but this could easily be inferred from the traces I left. Someone who has only partial access to these traces would be unable to tell whether I was looking for a digital mirror reflex camera or for any other kind of digital camera, or that I was just interested in a particular report. The meaning of my browsing pattern holistically emerges when one sees the whole pattern. Profiling in this sense consists in trying to figure out what the data represent or signify; it is a process of making sense of the data. This can be performed on an individual basis, which requires being able to recognise the entity that produces the data but also on an unidentified or group level. For instance, Amazon produces book recommendations such as, "customers who bought the book: 'No place to hide' also bought a copy of, 'The Digital Person'", which could be based on this kind of unidentified profiling. These recommendations are not very intelligent: simply compare a couple of shopping baskets and the patterns emerge.[342] In a sense, this kind of profiling produces (very limited) prototypical digital personas – a set of attributes that represents the likely/possible preferences/needs of an actual or virtual individual – without being able to connect them to real individuals because there is no way of finding the 'real' person whose preferences it concerns. The profiles in question could potentially be very complex and relate both to known concepts, such as eating habits or 'crime novel reader preferences' but also to all kinds of novel and unlabelled statistical or correlated patterns. Because these patterns are not associated with particular individuals, they can only be used in the way group profiles are used: only after an individual is classified as being relevant to the pattern (triggering the pattern), can the pattern and the conclusions or inferences associated with the pattern be applied. The profiles discussed here resemble those discussed in chapter 2 of this volume and its reply but are not entirely the same. The profiles as discussed in this contribution can relate to anything, including but not limited to, groups of people that can meaningfully be labelled. Therefore, the relation between the profiles and known and meaningful concepts in this case can be very weak.[343]

This implies that one cannot use transparency tools at any particular moment in the process of construction, maintenance and use of a profile but only *after a particular profile is used* to make decisions about an individual. The classification

---

[342] In reality, the process may even work differently because one does not need real customer data to recognise that certain books are 'similar' in genre, author or topic. Furthermore, publishers probably even pay to be 'recommended' when a customer browses for particular books.

[343] This could particularly be the case in the example of Ami profiles, where the denotation 'data cloud' could be used to describe the set of sensor data that may be generated by an inhabitant of an intelligent house.

of an individual as matching a profile results in establishing the link between the profile and the individual. Hence, Amazon in presenting suggestions of the kind referred to above, may have made an implicit classification that I am a privacy aficionado on the basis of my browsing through their shop and the classification of the behaviour of many other Amazon shoppers (as well as information from the publishers, no doubt). Amazon may subsequently draw all sorts of conclusions on the basis of this classification. They may opt to show me only privacy related books and novels or offer different prices because privacy aficionados are wealthier than other customers.

Gaining access to one's profile to exercise data protection rights, as in the case of personalised profiles, is not possible because in essence, there are no identifiable profiles, only unidentifiable ones. The fact that I have a roadster may signify that I behave as a roadster owner but the behaviour of roadster owners is not a profile of me.

14.6.5 A Different Kind of Protection

In my view, this means that transparency tools probably need to function in a different way than currently provided for in the Data Protection Framework. The access to data and being able to correct the data in the profiles is not so important but rather, transparency with respect to the decision-making process. I concede with Koops (Chapter 15 of this volume), Johnson (1989) and others that an important value protected by privacy is fair treatment and judgement by others. The profiles discussed in this contribution are used to create heuristics and stereotypes. Stereotyping is a way of coping with complexity. People have to rely on them and use satisficing[344] as a way to overcome their cognitive limitations and cope with complexity. Heuristics and stereotypes are fallible by definition and so are the computerised variants in the form of the profiles. Therefore, in the case of automated decision making about individuals on the basis of profiles, transparency is required with respect to the relevant data and the rules (heuristics) used to draw the inferences. This allows the validity of the inferences to be checked by the individual concerned, in order to notice and possibly remedy unjust judgements.[345]

Accountability for profile use will probably not be welcomed by those using the profiles because it sheds light on the heuristics used in decision-making. However, doing so would be fair (or decent) to the individuals affected by the decisions.

---

[344] Satisficing can be defined as accepting a choice or judgment as one that is good enough, one that satisfies. The term was introduced by Herbert Simon (1982), who observed the tendency to satisfice in many cognitive tasks such as playing games, solving problems and making financial decisions, where people typically do not or cannot search for the optimal solutions.

[345] Compare this to the need for conscious reflection propagated in section 2.4 of this volume.

14.6.6   'Code' to the Rescue?

Let us briefly look at the second question I raised about Gutwirth and De Hert's contribution: the role of 'code' in the form of Privacy Enhancing Technologies (PETs) as a possible means to protect privacy (Lessig, 1999a:142-163).

By 'code', Lessig means "The software and hardware that make cyberspace what it is…". Together they "… constitute a set of constraints on how you can behave." (1999:89). He means that applications (and devices) can be programmed to facilitate or prohibit certain behaviour of both the application itself and the people using it. Digital Rights Management software embedded in applications such as Windows Media Player and Apple's iTunes, for instance, prohibit the unauthorised copying of copyrighted material. Legal norms, the traditional code, can be implemented in 'code' so that the software enforces the legal norms.[346]

The distinction in profiles made in this contribution also has consequences for the options to use 'code' as a means to prevent misuse. In the case of personalised profiles, PETs could be an option. Pseudonyms can seriously curb the construction of personalised profiles. Different types of pseudonyms can be used to prevent certain kinds of profiles from being constructed and maintained: session pseudonyms prevent linking individuals to different transactions or sessions with a particular service provider; relationship pseudonyms allow for profile construction and maintenance in a particular user service provider relationship and so forth.[347] 'Code' can be used to guarantee that the individual's privacy preferences are enforced.[348] 'Code' can act as an opacity tool. It can shield the individual's data from unauthorised use by others. It can even enforce the rules set by the individual, which makes it potentially powerful.

It is much more difficult though to envision a role for 'code' for the second type of profiles discussed. The data used to create the profiles do not relate to a particular user and in any case not necessarily to the individual to whom the profile applies. I fail to see how 'code' can prevent Amazon from labelling me as a privacy aficionado just because I searched for books by Franz Kafka and George Orwell and consequently triggered a privacy aficionado profile. The only way to be safe in this scenario is to not partake in the digital world at all.

14.6.7   Conclusion

Transparency and opacity tools are mechanisms in the traditional data protection context. Transparency requires the data controllers to justify their use of the data subject's personal data to protect the individual against unjust treatment. The basis

---

[346] As is the case in Digital Rights Management systems, albeit that these often go well beyond the provisions of copyright legislation and restrict the rights that consumers have on the basis of the same legislation. See, for example, Helberger (2006) on this topic.

[347] See Pfitzmann and Hansen (2006) for an overview of the terminological distinctions.

[348] This is what the PRIME project aims to accomplish. See http://www.prime-project.eu.

for transparency is that personal data can be used but this use needs to be justified. Opacity tools work the other way around; data may not be used, unless.... Opacity is particularly used to limit the powers of the state to monitor its citizens and invade their personal sphere.

Profiling complicates privacy protection because it moves away from the use of personal data as we know it. Instead of collecting personally identifiable data, such as name, address, telephone number, age and gender, profiling increasingly concerns data clouds consisting of data and attributes, which are not relatable to concrete individuals[349] but to creating digital persona instead. These profiles can subsequently be used in individualised decisions. Transparency in these cases can only be provided after application of such a profile to an individual, whereas traditional files allowed the data subjects to request inspection of the contents of their record even prior to application. Even after application of a profile, transparency may be an impotent tool because it presumes that the individual is aware that decisions are taken on the basis of these profiles. Unfortunately, this is often not the case. The application of profiles, even the simple ones used by Amazon.com, happens behind the screens. Users are unaware that decisions are constantly being made about their behaviour; opacity is the rule here. This opacity means that the use of profiles may relatively unnoticeably affect the individual's autonomy, individuality, integrity and in the end, dignity.

Could opacity rules be the answer? Given the freedom to process information, it would be hard to place a general or even relatively specific, ban on collecting data that by its nature is not personal data. This would also be undesirable in free societies. Opacity in the sense used by Gutwirth and De Hert therefore seems problematic. The possibilities for the legislator to use opacity as a regulatory instrument are consequently limited.

Individuals can also use opacity as an instrument. Privacy Enhancing Technologies allow its users to shield their data from peering eyes and unwarranted collection and use. This could indeed be the tool to prevent some kinds of profiling. However, as in the case of the transparency tools, it does not provide the solution for the kind of profiling addressed in this contribution. It is unlikely that 'code' can be of assistance for useful searches on sites such as Amazon, while at the same time preventing Amazon from invoking the profiles outlined.

In the end, the profiling problem discussed in this chapter may boil down to the question of how we can prevent the adverse effects of stereotyping. This has proved to be very difficult, if not impossible in the off-line world. I doubt whether we can do any better in the on-line world.

---

[349] This is even more the case for ambient intelligence, where ubiquitous devices collectively know a lot about users' preferences, moods etc. but can hardly be compared to a traditional filing cabinet, which has neatly organised records.

14.7   Bibliography

Ariès P. & Duby (eds.), *Histoire de la vie privée, Volume 4: De la Révolution à la Grande Guerre*, Perrot M. (dir.), Paris Seuil, 1987.

Broache, A., 'Judge: Google must give feds limited access', Special to ZDNet, March 20, 2006. Available at: http://www.zdnet.com.au/news/security/soa/Judge_Google_must_give_feds_limited_access/0,2000061744,39246948,00.htm

Bygrave, L.A., 'Minding the machine: art. 15 of the EC Data Protection Directive and Automated Profiling', *Computer Law & Security Report*, 2001, Vol. 17, pp. 17-24. Available at: http://folk.uio.no/lee/oldpage/articles/Minding_machine.pdf

Bygrave, L. A., *Data Protection Law: Approaching Its Rationale, Logic and Limits*, The Hague, London, New York: Kluwer Law International, 2002.

Clarke, R., 'The Digital Persona and its Application to Data Surveillance', *The Information Society*, Vol. 10, No. 2, Taylor and Francis, June 1994.

De Hert P. & Gutwirth, S., 'Interoperability of police databases within the EU: an accountable political choice?', *International Review of Law Computers & Technology*, Vol. 20, No. 1-2, March-July 2006a, pp. 21-35.

De Hert P. & Gutwirth S., 'Privacy, data protection and law enforcement. Opacity of the individual and transparency of power' in E. Claes, A. Duff & S. Gutwirth (eds.), *Privacy and the criminal law*, Antwerp/Oxford, Intersentia, 2006b, pp. 61-104.

De Hert P. & Gutwirth S., 'Making sense of privacy and data protection. A prospective overview in the light of the future of identity, location based services and the virtual residence' in Institute for Prospective Technological Studies - Joint Research Centre, *Security and Privacy for the Citizen in the Post-September 11 Digital Age. A prospective overview. Report to the European Parliament Committee on Citizens' Freedoms and Rights, Justice and Home Affairs* (LIBE), July 2003, IPTS-Technical Report Series, EUR 20823 EN, pp. 111-162. Available at: ftp://ftp.jrc.es/pub/EURdoc/eur20823en.pdf

De Hert P. & Gutwirth S., 'Grondrechten: vrijplaatsen voor het strafrecht? Dworkins Amerikaanse trumpmetafoor getoetst aan de hedendaagse Europese mensenrechten' in *Langs de randen van het strafrecht*, Haveman R.H. & Wiersinga H.C. (red.), E.G. Mijers Instituut-reeks 91, Nijmegen, Wolf Legal Publishers, 2005, pp. 141-175

De Hert, P., 'European Data Protection and E-Commerce: Trust Enhancing?' in J.E.J., Prins, P.M.A. Ribbers, H.C.A. Van Tilborg, A.F.L. Veth & J.G.L. Van Der Wees (eds), *Trust in Electronic Commerce*, The Hague, Kluwer Law International, 2002, pp. 171-230.

De Hert, P., Standard Briefing Note 'JHA & Data Protection', No. 1: 'What are the risks and what guarantees need to be put in place in view of interoperability of police databases?' (14 pages, written in January 2006 on behalf of the European Parliament). Available at: http://www.vub.ac.be/LSTS/pub/Dehert/006.pdf.

European Data Protection Supervisor (EDPS), *Annual Report 2005*, pp. 22-23. Available at: *http://www.edps.eu.int/publications/annual_report_en.htm.*

Etzioni A., 'Implications of Select New Technologies for Individual Rights and Public Safety', *Harvard Journal of Law & Technology*, Vol. 15, No. 2, 2002.

Foucault M., 'Deux essais sur le sujet et le pouvoir', in Dreyfus H. & Rabinow P., *Michel Foucault. Un parcours philosophique*, Paris, Gallimard, 1984.

Helberger, Natalie, Fence on Fence Can: Intellectual Property and Electronic Self-Regulation, in L.F. Asscher ed., *Coding Regulation: Essays on the Normative Role of Information Technology*, The Hague: T.M.C. Asser Press, 2006.

Hosein G., *Threatening the Open Society: Comparing Anti-Terror Policies in the US and Europe*, London: Privacy International 2005. Available at: http://www.privacyinternational.org/issues/terrorism/rpt/comparativeterrorreportdec2005.pdf.

Gandy O.H. & Lemi B., *'Racial profiling: they said it was against the law'*, University of Ottawa Law and Technology Journal, University of Ottawa, Vol. 3, No. 1, 2006, pp. 297-327. 14.10.2005. Available at: http://www.asc.upenn.edu/usr/ogandy/Gandy%20Baruh%20Racial%20Profiling%20Final.pdf.

Gutwirth S., *Privacy and the information age*, Lanham, Rowman & Littlefield Publ., 2002.

Johnson, J.L., 'Privacy and the judgment of others', *The Journal of Value Inquiry*, Vol. 23, No. 2, Springer Netherlands 1989, pp. 157-168.

Koops, B.-J., Leenes, R., 'Code' and the Slow Erosion of Privacy', *Mich. Telecomm. Tech. L. Rev*, Vol. 12; No. 1, 2005, pp. 115-188.

Lessig, L., *Code and Other Laws of Cyberspace*, Basic Books, New York, 1999a.

Lessig, L., 'The Law of the Horse: What Cyberlaw Might Teach', Harvard Law Review, Vol. 133, 1999b, pp. 519-521.

Pfitzmann, A. and Hansen, M. Anonymity, Unlinkability, Unobservability, Pseudonymity, and Identity Management - A Consolidated Proposal for Terminology v0.27, 20 Feb 2006.

Simon, H.A. 'Theories of Bounded Rationality', in Herbert Simon, *Models of Bounded Rationality. Behavioral Economics and Business Organization*, Vol. 2, Cambridge: MIT Press, 1982, pp. 408-423.

Tadros V., 'Power and the value of privacy' in Claes E., Duff A. & Gutwirth S. (Eds), *Privacy and the criminal law*, Antwerp/Oxford, Intersentia, 2006, p. 106-109.

Ward, M., 'Google data request fuels fears', 20 January 2006, *BBC News website*. Available at: http:/news.bbc.co.uk/go/pr/fr/-/2/hi/technology/4631924.stm.

Chapter 15
Profiling and the Identity of the European Citizen

Mireille Hildebrandt

Building on the fact that profiling technologies produce a new type of knowledge that will influence the lives of individual citizens in numerous ways, this chapter will elaborate the implications for the identity, subjectivity and agency presumed by constitutional democracy. After a brief excursion into the architecture of our European 'Rechtsstaat', the centrality of the human person of flesh and blood will be explored and its relationship with the *legal persona* and citizenship. The *legal persona* - a constitutive feature of this 'Rechtsstaat' - will be explained in terms of the negative freedom (freedom from) and the positive freedom (freedom to) that it creates for citizens to participate in public and social life and to retreat into their private and intimate relationships (with significant others and with themselves). The privacy that may be at stake with the advance of highly sophisticated profiling technologies concerns freedom to co-construct one's own identity in the face of feedback from the social and material environment. Apart from the outright abuse of profiles, e.g., discrimination, unauthorised use or violation of the presumption of innocence, one of the questions raised will be whether advanced, real time and ubiquitous customisation will be heaven or hell for a sustainable vital democracy.

15.1 A Changing Landscape for Democracy and the Rule of Law

Profiling technologies open up previously unknown opportunities to correlate data of individual persons and things. The resulting profiles can be used by government, commercial and other organisations to identify people, things or even situations. In addition, they may be used to assess possible opportunities and risks attached to these people, things or situations. As the chapters of part II of this volume demonstrate, the proliferation of automatically generated profiles could have a profound impact on a variety of decisions that influence the lives of European citizens. At the same time, it seems unclear whether and how a person could trace if and when decisions concerning her life are taken on the basis of such profiles.

As described in the second chapter, profiling is knowledge construction. It produces a new kind of knowledge about groups or individuals. Group profiles are

Vrije Universiteit Brussels and Erasmus Universiteit Rotterdam

M. Hildebrandt and S. Gutwirth (eds.), *Profiling the European Citizen:*
Cross-Disciplinary Perspectives.
© Springer Science + Business Media B.V. 2008

used to categorise persons - attribute to them a certain lifestyle, health risks, earning capacity or customer preferences. Even when a group profile does not necessarily apply to all the individual members of the group (non-distributive profile), it will often be used due to the probability that it does apply. Schauer's non-universal generalisations work for human profiling as well as machine profiling (chapter 2, section 2.4.1). As a result, service providers, insurance companies, forensic agencies, fraud detection agencies and even e-learning organisations use profiling technologies to identify and categorise their target populations. Personalised profiles contain knowledge about specific individuals, inferred from off and on-line behaviour, registration of birth and/or biometric data. The novelty or the invasiveness of this knowledge does not depend on the sensitive nature of the personal data that have been mined. Sets of correlated data that would be considered insignificant or even trivial, can provide intimate knowledge about, e.g., life style or health risks, if data mining is applied.

The vast expansion of databases and their content thus make possible new types of knowledge constructs that may develop into an infrastructure pervading most aspects of everyday life. If the visions of *Ambient Intelligence* (AmI) and *The Internet of Things* as propagated by e.g., the Information Society Technologies Advisory Group (ISTAG) and the International Telecommunication Union (ITU) materialise,[350] European citizens will live in networked environments, seamlessly connected with a variety of intelligent electronic devices that follow their movements and behaviour in real time, inferring wishes, desires and preferences. This networked environment will collect an enormous amount of data, which can be correlated via multiple data mining strategies, producing a continuous stream of profiles that can be tested and enhanced to better service those that 'use' them. This raises the question of who 'uses' these profiles: (1) the European citizen that is receiving personalised services and/or that can access personalised risk assessments or compare her own preferences with those of groups she is clustered with, or (2) the commercial service providers and government agencies that use profiles to obtain a better picture of the risks and opportunities concerning consumers, voters, potential criminals, terrorists or victims? Who is in control: (1) the European citizen (the subject, or end user) or (2) the organisations that invest in profiling technologies (the data user and the data controller, either commercial or governmental)?

In this chapter the changing landscape of our networked information society is assessed with regard to the identity of European citizens. The aim is not to provide a study in psychology but rather, to consider the impact of profiling on the subjectivity and agency of Europeans *as citizens of a constitutional democracy* from the perspective of legal philosophy and political theory. Does profiling change the mix of positive and negative freedom on which constitutional democracy depends? Are the machines taking over and if so, what are they taking over? In the second section some of the possible risks of profiling practices will be presented in terms of dataveillance, normalisation, customisation, privacy, equality, fairness and due process.

---

[350] Information Society Technology Advisory Group (ISTAG), 2001.

This means we will not focus on the famous twin set of privacy and security because we believe this may not provide much enlightenment. Privacy and security concerns are often framed in terms of fraud and abuse, while in this contribution we want to discover what the widespread use of profiling may do to the daily perception of our identity, with special regard to its potential impact on positive and negative freedom. In section 3 we will explore the centrality of the human and the legal person in constitutional democracy and indicate how the legal persona in fact creates both the freedom to act and the freedom from undesirable intrusion. In section 4 privacy will be discussed with reference to chapter 14, to clarify that privacy needs to be conceptualised as a public good that may need to be reinvented to function in a networked society where machines may take a host of decisions that impact our lives. In section 5 data protection will be discussed, claiming that it should aim to protect public goods such as privacy, equality, fairness and due process, taking into account the undesired processes of normalisation and customisation. The conclusion, in section 6, is that we need to reconceptualise data protection in terms of access to knowledge instead of data and that an effective protection against unfair use of such knowledge will demand a technologically embodied law.

15.2   Risks of Profiling Practices

15.2.1   Opportunities and Risks

In this section a set of relevant risks is presented, in order to assess the impact profiling practices may have on the identity of the European citizen. This does not mean that profiling is considered to be negative in itself. As indicated in the second and other chapters, profiling technologies may be the only set of tools to discriminate information from noise in a highly complex and dynamic environment and the only set of tools to make sense of the information in terms of knowledge. However, these technologies can be designed and used in different manners. We should not hesitate to anticipate the consequences of alternative ways of constructing and applying them in order to make informed choices in this respect – even if the actual consequences may turn out very different.

The majors risks discussed are those of ubiquitous dataveillance, normalisation and customisation: loss of privacy, equality, fairness and due process.

15.2.2   Dataveillance

On-line behaviour as well as parts of our off-line behaviour are under constant surveillance. This surveillance differs from 'old' types of surveillance because the data we 'leak' are collected, aggregated and stored in databases by a variety of data controllers, who can integrate them with other databases, mine them at any time and sell them to other interested parties. Human memory seems very limited compared to the seemingly endless possibilities for storage of ever more data. In this process of continuous *dataveillance* (data surveillance), a term coined by Clarke in 1994,[351] we seem to lose our 'right to oblivion'. One could argue that the limitations of human memory are a blessing, because they give us a chance to change without the prospect of a confrontation with what is inferred from the minute details of our past behaviour. Especially as all these trivial details can be mined to construct non-trivial knowledge that may deny the probability of such change, which could invite profilers to discard the change as not viable.

However, as Solove rightly argues, dataveillance should not be our greatest worry.[352] After all we are being watched by machines, not by people. The surveillance that targets us does not come from one central data controller, it rather consists in a distributed collection of private and public organisations that exchange and integrate data at the level of machines. The data controllers are not interested in ourselves or even in what we do, they simply want to assess their opportunities and risks regarding our future behaviour. *What they are interested in is knowledge, not our data.* Solove claims that the metaphor of Big Brother, often used to cast a spell on data surveillance, is inadequate to describe the risks of data mining. He suggests a reference to Kafka's process as a more relevant metaphor, describing in a more salient manner the indifference of the machines that collect and store our data, forming a multiplicity of 'dossiers' on our whereabouts, without accusing us – yet – of anything specific but capable of providing the evidence for a conviction at some point in time.

15.2.3   Normalisation and Customisation

Solove creates an atmosphere of technological doom around profiling, suggesting that anything we do is recorded, stored and processed and can be used against us in the future. It may be the case that in anticipation of such usage we will change our habits to fit the expectations of our profilers, hoping this will prevent them from bringing charges against us. This would mean that ubiquitous pervasive profiling has the effect of 'spontaneous' *normalisation*, an effect so well described by Foucault in his discussion of the panopticum. The point of being held in a panopticum is not whether we are actually being watched, rather it is that we may be watched any time without actually knowing it.

Lawrence Lessig also warns about normalisation as a result of profiling. His point is not, however, that we may fear accusations for which our present actions will provide the evidence. Lessig warns that the use of profiling for targeted servicing,

---

[351] Clarke, 1994: 2.

[352] Solove, 2004.

for instance in an AmI environment, implies that the continuous anticipation of consumer preferences engenders a process of normalisation:

> 'When the system seems to know what you want better and earlier than you do, how can you know where these desires really come from? (…) profiles will begin to normalize the population from which the norm is drawn. The observing will affect the observed. The system watches what you do; it fits you into a pattern; the pattern is then fed back to you in the form of options set by the pattern; the options reinforce the patterns; the cycle begins again'.[353]

Solove's normalisation is a matter of fitting oneself into inferred categories instead of developing unique characteristics. The other end of the spectrum is customisation, enabled by the construction and application of personalised profiles in order to adapt prices, goods and services to individuated consumers. Interestingly, customisation may lead to the same result as normalisation.[354] The reason for this is that consumer profiles contain preferences that are inferred on the basis of an extrapolation from past and present to future behaviour, based on a probabilistic calculation. Service providers will seek to profit by appealing to these extrapolations, thus invoking the probable behaviour they calculated. Hence, customisation that may seem the opposite of normalisation, in fact has a similar effect. The difference is that this time people will not attempt to fit the categories they believe to be safe (Solove's fear) but instead their probable preferences will be reinforced, thus normalising them without them even being aware.

A third effect of customised profiling is described by Sunstein.[355] In his Republic. com he warns us against the incompatibility of a customised life with the core tenets of democracy. He discusses profiling in terms of *filtering*: the process that enables us to filter incoming noise and information in order to receive only the information we appreciate.[356] After Solove's warning against spontaneous normalisation in fear of future use of our behavioural data against us and Lessig's warning against the normalising effects of customised consumer servicing, Sunstein detects two main problems with such personalised filtering (enabled by service providers but initiated by citizens to meet their self-perceived preferences):

> 'First, people should be exposed to materials that they would not have chosen in advance. *Unanticipated encounters*, involving topics and points of view that people have not sought out and perhaps find irritating, are central to democracy and even to freedom itself. Second, many or most citizens should have a range of *common experiences*. Without shared experiences, a heterogeneous society will have a more difficult time addressing social problems and understanding one another'.[357]

---

[353] Lessig, 1999: 154.

[354] In terms of the difference between personalisation and customisation, used in section 9.7.2 of Soenens, customisation is used here in the sense of automated personalisation, with little or no deliberate input from the person who's environment is being customised.

[355] Sunstein, 2001a.

[356] In terms of the difference between customisation and personalisation, as used by Soenens in 9.7.2 above, Sunstein refers to customisation in the sense of deliberate input from the user.

[357] Sunstein, 2001b.

Obviously, these three types of effects of profiling are deeply entangled, which may compensate negative effects or reinforce them, depending on the context.

15.2.4   Privacy, Equality, Fairness and Due Process

Negative effects of data collection, storage and processing are usually phrased in terms of privacy and security: the recording of personal data is thought to imply a loss of privacy and an increased risk of identity fraud. From the above it should be clear that the leaking of – mostly trivial – personal data is not equivalent to a loss of privacy. If I consent to provide such data, this should not be understood as giving up privacy because privacy concerns – amongst other things – the control I have over my data. Consent confirms this control and thus enhances my privacy. The problem is that we have very little access to which data are processed by which organisation, which knowledge is constructed with my data and how this may impact me. This is why the *principle of minimum information asymmetry* goes to the core of informational privacy: informational privacy is about mutual access to information, to counter the present state of affairs that provides information and knowledge to profilers without *adequate* feedback to those being profiled. Privacy is not the same as secrecy or isolation. It is both more and less: it refers to one's capacity to create and shift the borders with one's environments, allowing self-constitution in a dynamic environment.[358] To preserve or reinvent our privacy we will need to move our attention from the leaking of data to the construction and application of knowledge from these data.

However, the impact of profiling is not limited to privacy. It also concerns power relationships between, on the one hand, the organisations that can afford to profile citizens and consumers and, on the other hand, the citizens and consumers that are profiled but lack the feedback regarding what happens to their data and how the knowledge inferred from them may be put to use. Lessig has indicated how advancing profiling practices may impact these power relationships:

> All social hierarchies require information before they can make discriminations of rank. Having enough information about people required, historically, fairly stable social orders. Making fine class distinctions (…) required knowledge of local fashions, accents, customs, and manners. Only where there was relatively little mobility could these systems of hierarchy be imposed.
>
> As mobility increased, then, these hierarchical systems were challenged. Beyond the extremes of the very rich and very poor, the ability to make subtle distinctions of rank disappeared, as the mobility and fluidity of society made them too difficult to track.
>
> Profiling changes all this. An efficient and effective system for monitoring makes it possible once again to make these subtle distinctions of rank. Collecting data cheaply and efficiently will take us back to the past.[359]

---

[358] Self-constitution is the first and foremost characteristic of life in biological terms, in this sense privacy is constitutive of individual life forms. See Maturana and Varela, 1991. See section 2.4.5 in chapter 2.

[359] Lessig, 1999: 155.

The shift in power balance affects both equality and fairness. The *equality* of citizens in the face of government authority depends on countervailing powers that allow a dynamic balance, which is disrupted by the asymmetry of access to information and knowledge between profilers and profiled. One could of course claim that citizens – the ones being profiled – are equal in their submission to profiling practices but this is precisely the kind of equality we sought to overcome when we brought absolute monarchs under the rule of constitutional democracy. The *fairness* of practices that confront citizens with risks or opportunities is a matter of distributive justice: we want citizens to have an equal share of both, except if there is a justification to distribute them otherwise. This is the essence of the prohibition of unjustified discrimination, part of many constitutions and treaties that intend to establish the rule of law, human rights and constitutional democracy. On the other hand, one could claim that such a prohibition is only valid in dealings between a government and its citizens, not in dealings between a business enterprise and its consumers. Is not price-discrimination a central part of micro-economics?[360] The point that Lessig makes is that in a situation where the transaction costs to make consumers transparent for individuated price-discrimination are very high, the unfairness may not surface, while the age of personalised profiling could enable a type of price discrimination incompatible with the central values of constitutional democracy.

Equality is related to fairness and fairness is related to *due process*. In an interesting article Steinbock analyses the impact of profiling technologies on due process in a very broad sense (not limited to criminal law).[361] He starts by describing what he terms the 'age of decision by algorithm', referring to the host of trivial decisions taken by computers, such as a decision to refuse a request to lend books from a library without adequate explanation (thus making it difficult to solve the problem). As described in chapter 2, this concerns autonomic profiling: a process of decision making on the basis of data processing without human intervention.

15.3   The Human and the Legal Person: Positive and Negative Freedom

In this section we will seek to disclose the relevance of the concept of the legal persona for democracy and rule of law, highlighting the way the legal persona creates a mix of positive and negative freedom of citizens.

Democracy existed long before the modern state. The word itself is taken from the Greeks, who used it to refer to their aristocratic government (the Greek demos must not be equated with our conception of 'the people' because it concerned only a relatively small group of free men). Democracy basically means a kind of self-rule: those that govern and those that are governed are in principle the same, although those that are governed often participate only by means of representation.

---

[360] On (price) discrimination and data mining cp. Tal Z. Zarsky, 2002-2003: 22-35.

[361] Steinbock, 2005.

The free men of the Greek city-states enjoyed what Berlin has termed positive freedom[362]: the freedom to govern, or – even more generally – *freedom to* rather than *freedom from*. Historically, positive participatory freedom is probably older than what Berlin has termed negative freedom: freedom from interference by the state (or others). Negative freedom – or liberty - seems to be a modern invention, which celebrates the central position of the individual that arose in the renaissance and nourished on the French *Déclaration des droit de l'homme et du citoyen* and the American *Bill of Rights* at the end of the Enlightenment period.

To sustain democracy on a large scale, complex societies such as the European Information Society presume an effective rule of law. Democracy organises positive freedom for all its citizens, via a mix of representative, deliberative and participatory procedures. To be able to partake in the full range of democratic practices (voting, forming an opinion, defining a political common sense), a person must be able to retreat from the social pressures that impact and influence her in order to achieve some kind of autonomy, to come to her own conclusions, develop her own line of thought and her own lifestyle. This does not mean that people should or even can develop their opinions in sheer isolation. It is precisely in counterpoint to other practices, opinions and lifestyles that we build our own. However, to cope with the constant confrontation with others one needs space to reset; room for dissent and protection against asymmetric power relations. This is one of the things the rule of law provides for, by attributing to every citizen a set of human rights. Such rights give the individual citizen claim rights against the state, to be safeguarded by the judicial authority of that same state. This is often called the paradox of the 'Rechtsstaat': resisting the state by means of legal instruments that depend on the authority of that same state. The most evident legal instrument that makes this possible is the individual (subjective) right, a category invented in the civil law tradition in conjunction with the concept of objective law, being the positive law that attributes these individual rights.[363]

This brings us to a related central notion in modern law: the notion of the legal subject or persona. The legal subject has subjective rights that can be claimed in a court of law. The legal person is not congruent with the human person of flesh and blood, it is an artificial legal construction that aims to (1) provide the human person with access to certain individual rights whilst (2) enabling one person to hold another person liable (on the basis of tort or contract law) and (3) enabling the state to establish the guilt of a defendant (criminal law). However, the human person itself is fundamentally undefined and underdetermined. The legal person is the mould or mask (persona) that indicates the role one plays within the legal system, it basically shields the person of flesh and blood from undesirable definition from outside.[364] Besides

---

[362] Berlin, 1969/1958: 118-173.

[363] On the emergence of the category of individual rights: see Glenn, 2004: 140-143.

[364] The difference between the indeterminable, living person of flesh and blood and the artificial – objectified – construction of the legal person (which depends on objective law and the independent judge to function), has been explained in more detail in numerous publications of R. Foqué and A. 't Hart. It is part of a relational theory of law that describes both the human of flesh and blood and the legal person in relational terms, while explaining the importance of the distinction between both. See for instance (in Dutch) Foqué and 't Hart, 1990.

(1) providing access to the legal system, and (2, 3) making the subject accountable within it, the legal persona (4) thus also protects the indeterminacy of the human person by resisting the conflation of the artificial legal person and the human.

By providing individuals with the legal tools to participate - on an equal footing – in the public and private spheres, citizens are provided with positive freedom; by shielding the human person of flesh and blood from the inquisitive gaze of his fellow citizens and his government, citizens are provided with negative freedom. Thus, the legal architecture that institutes the European constitutional democracy protects the positive and negative freedom of the individual human person by attributing legal subjectivity to all its citizens.[365] This way one is at once protected against transparency (an aspect of negative freedom) and enabled to claim one's individual rights against other legal subjects in a court of law (an aspect of positive freedom).

15.4   Privacy: A Public Good

15.4.1   Legal Protection of Privacy

In this section we will explain the importance of conceptualising privacy as a public good. Legally speaking, privacy is not the same as private life, even though the protection of private life is one of the legal tools to protect privacy, e.g., art. 8 of the European Convention of Human Rights. To reduce privacy to private life would disregard the public nature of privacy and turn it into a commodity to be traded within the private sphere. For this reason it is important to acknowledge that besides the protection of private life, other human rights such as due process, prohibition of unlawful detention and inhuman or degrading treatment also relate to the protection of privacy, even if their first aim is to protect other public goods such as fair proceedings in criminal cases, legitimate use of state powers and the integrity of the person. Even the right to free speech has a dimension that protects one's privacy, in the sense that government should not consistently monitor the way I speak out in the public sphere, since the awareness of such monitoring may induce me to constrain myself in the expression of unconventional opinion. Therefore, privacy is protected by means of a set of human rights but it is also often protected by the criminalisation of unlawful entry, ill-treatment, assaults on bodily integrity and other actions that impact one's sense of privacy. Moreover, administrative law also often imposes obligations on natural and legal persons to safeguard the privacy of clients, consumers, voters or others, e.g., by prohibiting public exposure of what is

---

[365] Art. 17 Treaty of the European Community (TEC), art. I-10 of the EU Constitutional Treaty. Whether a human person that is not a citizen of the EU is protected as a legal subject is debatable, however the EU Constitutional Treaty speaks of 'everyone' and 'no one' in its Charter of fundamental rights.

nobody else's business, by prohibiting access to sensitive personal information or by regulating access to and processing of personal data in general.

If the entitlement to privacy can be facilitated by means of (1) a variety of human rights, (2) criminalisation and (3) administrative laws, privacy needs to be conceptualised in a way that invites contextual precision instead of reductive generalisation. In the next section we will provide a working definition for this purpose, taking into account the public nature of privacy. Obviously, public in this case does not refer to publicity but to the common interest, it indicates that privacy *should* be a matter of public concern.

15.4.2   Privacy and Identity: Idem and Ipse

Libraries are filled with books on the definition, scope and meaning of privacy.[366] Central features seem to be intimacy, anonymity, reserve, solitude and autonomy. This indicates concern with an individual's inner core. The more interesting definitions, however, focus on the relational core of privacy. In 1975, social psychologist Altman discussed privacy as a dynamic process of boundary control, taking place between a self and its environment.[367] Recently, Agre and Rotenberg build on such perspectives when they move beyond a 'static conception of privacy as a right to seclusion or secrecy', discussing privacy in terms of 'negotiated relationships'. They define the right to privacy as:

'the freedom from unreasonable constraints on the construction of one's own identity'.[368]

Besides providing a relational and dynamic picture, such a definition also links privacy to identity and identity construction, which is of great interest when discussing the impact of profiling technologies on the identity of European citizens.

The *term* identity refers to two different *concepts* of identity that are interrelated.[369] Firstly, identity derives from the Latin *idem*, meaning sameness in the sense of similarity or continuity. Two loaves of bread can be the same, or identical, in the sense of being similar (for example, both are ciabatta types of bread). One loaf of bread can be said to be the same, or identical with itself in the sense that this particular loaf of bread is the same loaf it was yesterday; this implies continuity and introduces the phenomenon of time. It should be obvious that sameness has to be asserted in opposition to *difference* or *otherness*: two ciabattas are the same because they differ from

---

[366] See for a discussion of the concept, the phenomenon and the right to privacy: Hildebrandt, 2006 and Solove, 2002: 1087-1156.

[367] Altman, 1975: 18 refers to another classic: Westin, 1970, who categorises four types of privacy: intimacy, anonymity, reserve and solitude.

[368] Agre and Rotenberg, 2001: 7.

[369] About identity, see Ricoeur, 1992; Rorty, 1976; Van Woudenberg, 2000; Glastra van Loon, 1987/1956: chapter VII; and Hildebrandt, M., 2006.

other types of bread; one individual loaf is the same loaf in the course of time because it differs from all other things. Group profiling technologies build on sameness in the sense of similarity (categorisation); personalised profiling builds on sameness in the sense of unique identification or continuity with oneself.

Secondly, the term identity refers to the concept of *ipse* or self. This concept overlaps with the *idem*-identity as it depends on a sense of the continuity of one's own existence: however much I may change in the course of time, I will still claim to be the same person. Apart from this, *ipse*-identity also concerns the *sense of self* that is constitutive of the human subject. This sense of self means that I view the world from a particular, situated, embodied perspective that I will never be able to discard completely. Interestingly, we experience ourselves simultaneously as *ipse* and *idem*: e.g., some philosophers speak of our body as *Leib* and *Körper*[370], as the experienced body that constitutes our sense of self (*Leib*) and as an object similar to other objects (*Körper*). The most interesting link between these two bodies – that are in fact one and the same - is that in order to perceive my body as an object similar to other objects (a *Körper*), I need a body to start from (a *Leib*). Objectification presumes a subject that objectifies. Profiling technologies cannot produce or detect a sense of self; they are built to detect sameness, even when they construct sophisticated personalised profiles that seem to define a person in many dimensions of her social, private and public life. They can, however, impact our sense of self. This is due to the fact that the construction of one's own identity depends on the confrontation with others, especially with the way other people seem to 'profile' us.[371] *I* learn about *me* because of the feedback I receive from my environment.[372] In the end this means that I have no privileged access to my own identity, as it is via others that I gain pictures or profiles of myself. This conception of identity presumes that most identity-building happens without conscious intention; it is not a voluntaristic project. Processing information about our self happens, as it were, under the skin.[373] This, however, does not mean that one has no control whatsoever; the ambiguity of our self as *Leib* and *Körper* already indicates that we have the capacity to become aware of our self as an object and become experienced in consciously accepting or rejecting particular influences on our identity.

Understood in this sense, *ipse*-identity is (1) inherently relational because it is constructed in confrontation with an environment[374], (2) fluid and dynamic, because this construction is an ongoing process as the environment changes and (3) while

---

[370] De Mul, 2003: 247-266.

[371] When put between inverted commas, I use the term profiling in the common sense of building stereotypes of friends, colleagues etc., called prototyping in cognitive psychology.

[372] About the difference between the I and the me, see Mead, 1959/1934. See also Nabeth, T., Hildebrandt, M. (Eds.), 2004, that refers to Mead's understanding of identity.

[373] About the emergence of consciousness and the identity of self in terms of neurosciences and phenomenology, see Cohen, Varela, A. E., 2002: 225-230.

[374] Idem identity is also relational, as the establishment of sameness builds on comparison.

mostly progressing at a pre-reflective level, identity-building can become part of conscious intention and reflection, indicating the particular capacity of human beings to be conscious of their own consciousness.[375]

As mentioned, when introducing the distinction between the concepts of *idem* and *ipse*-identity, the two are interrelated. On the one hand, *idem*-identity presumes the *ipse*-identity of the subject, which establishes *idem*-identity and on the other hand, our sense of self develops in counterpoint to and while accommodating the 'profiles' that others project onto us. This means that when Agre and Rotenberg define the right to privacy in terms of identity-construction they are talking about *ipse*-identity but we should remember that *ipse*-identity cannot emerge without the *idem*-identity we experience (our sense of continuity) and the *idem*-identity we are attributed by others (as this is how we establish our sense of self in contrast to others). It also means that while the human person of flesh and blood - in this context - refers to the *ipse*-identity of a person[376], the *idem*-identity that is provided by the legal person will impact this *ipse*-identity, for it creates and prohibits opportunities and risks that will shape our sense of self as we act on them. For instance, if the law considers me to be a father it will attach certain legal constraints to this status that enable me to exercise parental rights, obligate me to provide for my children and attribute liability for their actions if committed under a specified age. Apart from many other profiles that may impact me as a father (the expectations of my in-laws, those installed by education and other forms of enculturation, etc.), this will impact my sense of self. The difference between the role attributed to me as a father by law and the role of a father attributed by the common sense of those I live with, is that legal expectations are more explicit, while those internalised during my upbringing or education are mostly implicit. If profiles are generated by advanced profiling technologies, they may impact my sense of self without any awareness on my part, for instance by offering me targeted services otherwise not available. The point is not about whether those who profile us have good or bad intentions or whether they use profiles to manipulate our inferred desires but rather, the fact that knowledge is constructed that may impact our preferences while we are not aware of it.

15.4.3 Privacy and Identity: Freedom From and Freedom To

Following Agre's and Rotenberg's definition of the right to privacy, we shall now explore how privacy is related to freedom. Initially, we will explore the phenomenon and the concept of privacy in relation to identity-building. We take it that privacy is not a right but a *good* that can be protected by means of individual rights

---

[375] Plessner, 1975.

[376] In another context, a human of flesh and blood could be understood in a scientific, physicalist, objectified sense, exemplary for idem-identity.

and liberties[377]: in other words, privacy is the *object* of certain rights and obligations. In fact, we will claim that privacy as a *public* good does not precede such rights but depends on their effectiveness.

To argue this claim we have to briefly examine the history of the rule of law. Rule *by* law, the hall-mark of the modern state, was based on the positive freedom of the king to legislate and thus command his subjects. It demonstrates the freedom of the king to constrain the actions of his subjects. In a democracy, this positive freedom belongs to the citizens, who rule themselves by means of participation and/or representation.[378]

Complementary to democracy, the rule *of* law integrates the idea of positive freedom with that of negative freedom.[379] In a democracy, this means that citizens not only enjoy the freedom to rule themselves at the political level but can also claim freedom from governmental constraints on the way they wish to rule their own lives in private and social spheres. This is why rule *of* law – other than rule *by* law – implies that human rights are effectively guaranteed by an independent judiciary. Privacy is the combination of positive and negative freedom, which allows a person to negotiate boundaries in public, social and private life. In this sense, privacy is the result of individual legal rights that enable citizens to effectively ward off unwarranted intrusions.

However, if we acknowledge the fact that unwarranted intrusions upon our privacy may arise in both public, social and private life, it should be clear that the creation of negative liberty not only concerns non-interference by the state but also by other actors in the social and private sphere. From a social perspective for instance, life in a village can be more restrictive of one's privacy than life in a metropolitan city.[380] This is connected respectively with the transparency of the relationships in

---

[377] The discussion about the difference between privacy as a right and a liberty stems from the US jurisdiction that regards invasion of privacy as (1) a common law or statutory tort; (2) violation of the IVth Amendment of the Constitution that protects 'the right of the people to be secure in their persons, houses, papers and effects (…)' and (3) violation of the XIVth Amendment, in which the states are forbidden to 'deprive anyone of life, liberty, or property, without due process of law'. The first case does not relate to a human right but to an obligation under private law (to compensate damage caused by tort); the second reads a human right to privacy into the Constitution, even though it is not articulated as such; the third reads the human right to privacy into the prohibition to deprive anyone of his liberty.

[378] Articulating this as 'A people that rules itself' would perhaps presume that the collective decision-making process involves a consensus that is more than an aggregate of individual opinion (namely a kind of Rousseauean '*volonté générale*', or communitarian shared values). 'Citizens ruling themselves' can be understood in the same way but leaves room for an aggregative understanding of majority rule (a more liberal and/or pragmatic position).

[379] About the tensions between the pluralism made possible by the rule of law and the need for consensus inherent in democracy see Mouffe, 2000. This tension 'need not be visualised on the mode of a contradiction but as the locus of a paradox', Mouffe, 2000: 9; it must not be resolved but productively sustained.

[380] This obviously depends on the way village life is organised and not necessarily inherent in the concept of village life. See Altman, 1975: 15-16 on the difference between Javanese and Balinese societies.

a village community as far as it nourishes on gossip and social control and with relative anonymity in urbanised surroundings. In other words: in a village one may be 'profiled' continuously by one's fellow locals, while in a large city this is less probable.

There are, however, other ways in which social constraints can be imposed on those living in a metropolitan world, due to the development of the social public sphere created by the printing press and later on, the proliferation of mass media.[381] The advance of this type of social control has been one of the main worries of liberals and of the liberal strand of political philosophy, dating back to Constant and Mill in the 19th Century. They emphasise the intimidating effects of public opinion and plead a separation of public life (in which positive freedom is to bloom) and private life (where one can foster one's negative freedom).[382] Berlin articulated this in his influential *Two concepts of liberty* in the second half of the 20th century, warning against the totalitarian tendency of the positive freedom *of a government* on the social sphere if there is no space for negative freedom. More recently, Thomas Nagel built on this liberal defence of negative liberty by celebrating societal reticence in the face of political correctness and abrasive exposure of the private behaviour of public officials.[383] In law, the allergy against such exposure in the social public sphere has been articulated famously by two distinguished legal scholars, Warren and Brandeis, in their landmark article in the Harvard Law Review of 1890, where they pleaded a right of privacy against one's fellow citizens, articulated as the right to be left alone, based on tort (private law).[384] This privacy right must be distinguished from the US constitutional right or liberty that protects against government invasion; Warren and Brandeis were primarily concerned about the way private information of well-known public figures was disseminated into the public sphere by fellow citizens (notably the tabloid press).

The undesirable experience of living in a glass house may seem to be restricted to the rich and famous. Initially, the right of privacy was conceived as the right of those in power or fame to take action against the transparency of their behaviour (that is, when not intentionally put on stage for the public gaze). One can argue that the impact of public exposure on those living outside the realm of fame and power was rather marginal, since nobody was really interested in their private affairs and – more importantly – the means to observe their behaviour in any systematic way were absent. Continuous 'profiling' as occurs within small village communities, seems to have been out of the question. This is, however, not the whole story. From the 19th Century onwards, certain specific localities were artificially constructed to enhance the continuous visibility of their local 'inhabitants' and the recordability of their behaviours: schools, prisons, hospitals, offices and factories. The emergence of a particular type of detailed control of human beings inside such institutions has

---

[381] A classic on this topic: Habermas, 1962 / 1990.

[382] Constant, 1819 / 1980: 511-12, Mill, 1859 / 1974.

[383] Nagel, 1998: 3-30.

[384] Warren, and Brandeis: 1890. See also Alderman and Kennedy, 1997; Smith, 2004: 121-153.

been described by Foucault, who brilliantly related the advance of such loci of disciplinary control to the invention of modern social science (based on statistical inference).[385] Criminology has developed his notion of disciplinary institutions to what they term the 'society of control', in which the monitoring of individuals inside institutions has been replaced by a more pervasive tracking and tracing of individuals and their behaviour throughout society.[386] Big Brother is watching you. The present proliferation of profiling technologies could be described as a radicalisation of this control society but we may agree with Solove that the Big Brother metaphor is not adequate. It is not just state authorities that tend towards preventive monitoring of as many people as possible but also commercial business enterprises that like to know all about wishes and desires in order to provide us with customised services. Hence, quite apart from the 'traditional' loci of disciplinary control such as schools, prisons, hospitals, factories and offices, we now find many other social spaces that are embedded with intelligent electronic devices, which monitor our behaviour: airports, swimming pools,[387] hotel and catering services and, last but not least, the smart home.[388]

While liberals have traditionally been worried by the force of public exposure of what they consider their private lives and by the force of public opinion as it is transformed by the logic of mass media, others have worried about the interplay between monitoring infrastructures and the impact that the knowledge they produce can have on us. Could it be that consistent monitoring and processing of data will at some point in time destroy the negative freedom of citizens, because they nourish a process of normalisation (1) because we anticipate that whatever we do may be used against us, (2) because customisation leads to a situation whereas we are no longer sure which desires are our own and which have been produced by profiling technologies?

15.4.4 Identity, the Human Person and the Legal Persona

Identity building, as discussed above, depends on a mixture of positive and negative freedom: to reorientate our self-perception, to reassess our sense of self, we need both the active involvement with our social and other environments (exercising our positive freedom) and space to withdraw, to ignore the demands from outside, to rebuild the constraints or habits that enable us to deal with outside demands

---

[385] Building on earlier designs of disciplinary institutions such as the monastery: Foucault, 1975: 159-265.

[386] Cohen, 1985. For an analysis see Gutwirth, 2002: 71-78 with references to the work of Gilles Deleuze, Gary Marx and Stanley Cohen. See also Hudson, 2006.

[387] See http://www.poseidon-tech.com/us/system.html as an example of computer-aided drowning detection systems, promising constant and vigilant surveillance.

[388] See on Ambient Intelligence ISTAG, 2001 and Schreurs et al. (eds), 2005. Aarts and Marzano, 2003.

in our *own* way (exercising our negative freedom). Constant undesired intrusion could make us feel helpless and out of control, no longer able to decide who we are and/or want to be.

How does profiling affect this mix of positive and negative freedom? Firstly, profiling technologies may be particularly *un*obtrusive[389]: we may not be aware of the knowledge (profile) that is constructed on the basis of our data and we may not be aware of the impact it has on the risks and opportunities that are created for us by those that use the profile. The point is not just whether profiles are abused (e.g., unfair discrimination). The point is that (1) an abundance of correlatable data and (2) the availability of relatively cheap technologies to construct personalised knowledge out of the data, create new possibilities to manipulate people into behaviour without providing adequate feedback on how their data have been used. As indicated above in section 15.2.4, this may lead to major shifts in power relations between individual citizens on the one hand and commercial or governmental organisations on the other. The crucial issue is not abuse but rather the fact that we have no effective means of knowing whether and when profiles are used or abused. This seems to pose a greater threat to the mix of positive and negative freedom than outright, visible intrusion. As we do not know what opinions or preferences are inferred from our behaviour, both types of freedom may be impaired by constraints of which we are unaware.

It is not very difficult to see why this could create a type of human agency that is at odds with democracy and the rule of law as we conceive it today. This means that we may have to rethink human agency and find new ways to protect it. Privacy empowers a human person of flesh and blood to develop and reconstruct his identity, by protecting the indeterminacy of the human person; privacy rights, liberties and legal obligations provide the legal person with the legal tools to indeed seek such protection when it is violated. We shall now discuss one of these tools – data protection legislation – in more detail, because this is often presented as the panacea for informational privacy protection.

15.5 Data Protection

15.5.1 *Data Protection in Europe*

Directive 95/46/EC is entitled the *Directive on the protection of individuals with regard to the processing of personal data and on the free movement of such data.*

---

[389] Profiling techniques are unobtrusive because most of the data collection and data processing happens without the subjects cooperation or even awareness. We refer to Hildebrandt, M., Backhouse, J., (eds.) (2005) for an extensive description of the process of profile construction. See Lessig, 1999: 148 about three concepts of privacy: (1) preserving dignity, (2) protection against burdensome intrusions and (3) a way to constrain the power of the state to regulate. I would not limit this last concept to the power of the state but to anybody's power to regulate my life.

Data protection legislation thus entails at once (a) the constitution of an overall legal competence to collect, store and process personal data and (b) a set of restrictions upon which this general legal competence is conditional. This double instrumentality of data protection legislation is characteristic for the attribution of legal competence under the rule of law: whenever legal competence is created, it is at the same time restricted.

Data protection dates back to the 1970s when the first attempts were made to regulate the collection, storage, exchange and use of personal data.[390] Today's data protection legislation is generally based on a set of principles, first developed in the 1974 U.S. Privacy Act, later expressed in the (non-binding) guidelines of the OECD of 1980, CoE Convention 108 of 1981 and numerous national statutes on data protection (and also Directive 95/46/EC). Though several chapters in this volume have already referred to these principles, I will summarise them and indicate four pertinent issues related to European data protection legislation. The fair information principles comprise:

(1) the collection limitation principle, stating that collection of personal data should not be unlimited;
(2) the data quality principle, stating that personal data should be correct, complete and up-to-date;
(3) the purpose specification principle, stating that the purpose for which personal data are collected must be specified and that they may only be used for that purpose;
(4) the use limitation principles, stating that disclosure or use for other purposes is only allowed subject to the consent of the data subject or on the basis of the authority of the law;
(5) the transparency principle, stating that the data subject should be able to know about the collection and storage of personal data, its purpose and the identity of the data controller;
(6) the individual participation principle, stating that a data subject has the right to erase, rectify, complete or amend her data; and finally,
(7) the accountability principle, stating that the data controller should be accountable for complying with these principles.

First, for the European domain it is important to stress that D95/46/EC is only applicable in relation to community law. This means that the processing of data by the member states in the areas of criminal law or concerning public security *does not fall within the scope of the Directive* (as art. 3, paragraph 2 states explicitly), because these areas are not – yet – part of community law.[391] This raises many questions from

---

[390] Bennett, 2001: 99 -125.

[391] See, however, the draft Data Protection Framework Decision (DPFD) in police and judicial cooperation in criminal matters. When this chapter was finalised the DPFD was not yet decided upon, though it seems that the scope of its application will be limited to cross-border transmission of data. The DPFP has no equivalent of art. 15 and 12 of D 95/46/EC, implying that in the realm of justice and police, citizens have no right not to be subject to decisions based exclusively on automated data processing.

the perspective of the rule of law. Montesquieu frequently stressed that the way criminal procedure is organised determines to a large extent whether one lives in a free society. If the Directive is based on a default position of access conditioned by a coherent set of restrictions, the fact that data processing in the area of criminal law is excluded from application raises the question of which default position is applicable here and what restrictions apply.

Second, the Directive only concerns personal data, that is, data that can identify a person.[392] It should by now be obvious that in the case of profiling the limitation to personal data seriously hinders adequate protection of individuals with regard to the processing of data that are not yet, or no longer, considered to be personal data.[393] Individuals need protection regarding the *knowledge* that is constructed through profiling techniques on the basis of their and other data, whether personal or not. The transparency aimed at by data protection regimes is of the utmost importance in the case of this type of new knowledge.

Third, the consent of the data subject is taken quite seriously in the Directive. Art. 2(h) states: 'the data subject's consent' shall mean any freely given specific and informed indication of his wishes by which the data subject signifies his agreement to personal data relating to him being processed'. However, the reality of constant data exchange makes such consent utterly improbable, because (1) most of the time the data subject is not aware of data being recorded, stored and processed and (2) even if some awareness is present, the number of decisions to be taken would paralyse the data subject and only be feasible via an identity management device (IMD) or digital persona that serves as a proxy.[394]

Fourth, the Directive grants higher protection to a set of personal data that are usually referred to as sensitive personal data. Art. 8(1) states: 'Member States shall prohibit the processing of personal data revealing racial or ethnic origin, political opinions, religious or philosophical beliefs, trade-union membership and the processing of data concerning health or sex life'. The idea behind such special

---

[392] Art. 2 sub a: 'personal data' shall mean any information relating to an identified or identifiable natural person ('data subject'); an identifiable person is one who can be identified, directly or indirectly, in particular by reference to an identification number or to one or more factors specific to his physical, physiological, mental, economic, cultural or social identity'. After the text for this chapter was finalised, Opinion 7/2007 on the concept of personal data was published on 20th June 2007 by the Art. 29 Working Party (01248/07/EN, WP136). The interpretation proposed by the Working party is thus contextualised that legal certainty may be at stake. This reinforces the idea that the focus on personal data makes data protection an ineffective remedy for protection against unwarranted profiling.

[393] See Deadman, 2005: par. 4.1.2 on Identity and Identifiability, which propagates a wide scope for personal data, including for instance data about web users that can be correlated into a profile that makes them identifiable in the sense of the Directive. Custers, 2004: 28, 94, 124, 171-174 explains that it is not at all clear when data relate to identifiable persons, especially in the case of anonymity or pseudonymity. We should expect clarification on this point from the Art. 29 Working Party, which has placed the issue of what falls within the scope of identifiable person high on its 2006-2007 agenda (00744/06/EN, WP120).

[394] See Clarke, 1994.

protection is that in specific circumstances knowledge of such data can give rise to unjustified discrimination, obstructing both democracy and the rule of law. However, profiles can be constructed out of sets of insignificant data (not sensitive, maybe not even personal) and still contain a type of knowledge that can be used to discriminate between citizens, customers, clients, employees, patients, etc.[395] The problem of the Directive is that it builds on traditional ways of thinking about *data*, personal data and their possible abuse, without having a grasp on the new type of *knowledge* that is generated by data processing. The conclusion must be that even if data protection legislation were effective regarding personal data, it does not know how to deal with *patterns of correlated data*. This is the case because (1) group profiles are often inferred from anonymous personal data to which data protection regulations do not apply and (2) group profiles do not necessarily apply to identifiable persons but may, even so, affect the autonomy, privacy, security and equality of European citizens.

15.5.2 *Data Protection Against the Risks of Profiling*

Although data protection is not the only legal tool to protect citizens against the risks of profiling – and maybe not a very effective tool - it makes sense to assess to what extent it is an adequate tool to protect against risks detected in par. 15.2: dataveillance, normalisation and customisation, privacy, equality, fairness and due process. Other relevant legal tools are, e.g., attribution of liability or endorsing full-scale commodification of data and profiles. The problem is that these both presume the transparency of the actions taken by data controllers, which is precisely the main purpose of the Directive. For this reason we will focus on the Directive at this point in time, because this purpose has not been achieved regarding profiles.

In section 15.2 we discussed how government profiling may lead to spontaneous normalisation, based on the fear that anything we do can be tracked and used against us at some point in time (Solove). The Directive will not protect us against this risk because it does not apply to the area of criminal law or to public safety. In fact, a comparison of anti-terrorist policies and strategies in the US and the EU shows that Europe has developed far more invasive legal obligations for citizens to provide data, while allowing government authority to collect data without notifying citizens – it has been legalised to a much further extent in Europe then in the US.[396] US civil society's response and constitutional review turn out to be far more effective to counter invasive legislation, compared to the trust European courts and citizens seem to invest in the European way of protecting informational privacy. The second

---

[395] Custers, 2004: 19 and 57, discusses 'masking': avoiding applicability of data protection of sensitive data by the use of a piece of trivial information that correlates with sensitive information.

[396] Hosein, 2005.

way in which spontaneous normalisation may occur is by means of customisation of services, e.g., based on non-distributive profiles (Lessig). Again, the Directive provides little protection: the requirement of notification of consent in art. 7 has a set of exceptions that turn the requirement into a farce, e.g., art. 7 (f) and the exception of art. 6 section 1 (b) regarding statistical purposes can be read to legalise all types of profiling without consent. Actually, as we already mentioned above, the fact that the Directive only applies to personally identifiable information (PII) leaves all profiling on the basis of anonymised data outside the scope of the Directive, even if these profiles may be used to customise us. The essence of the customisation Lessig warns us about, is its implicit character: we have no idea how and what preferences are inferred and applied to us. As long as the Directive does not apply, we have no way of claiming access to these data (quite apart from the relevant question of whether the technological infrastructure allows the traceability of profiles by end users). The third risk of profiling discussed in 15.2 is filtering our access to information in order to receive only the kind of information that we judge to be interesting (Sunstein). On first sight this is not a risk to, e.g., our autonomy because it seems based on that. For this reason the Directive does not seem to offer anything here, because this is about filtering incoming information by data subjects from the rest of the world, not about disclosing data of the data subject. Of course, to allow such filtering service providers need personal data but there can be little doubt as to the consent of the subjects in this instance. Sunstein rightly argues that this is a risk to democracy, (1) as it allows us to avoid dissent by limiting our perspective on the world to what we agree to and (2) as it may cause fragmentation of the civil society on which democracy depends. On second thoughts, we should admit that since autonomy, like privacy and identity, does not develop in isolation, the absence of dissent and the fragmentation of civil society may weaken our personal autonomy in the end. Strong autonomy builds on serious confrontation with others, while it also needs a society that engenders trust and mutual understanding. Apart from this, the type of customisation by service providers discussed above will have the same effect that Sunstein describes: offering people a comfortable cage in which they can isolate themselves from undesired interaction with the environment.

These three types of risk – not seriously confronted by the Directive – all relate to the mix of positive and negative freedom that is crucial for a viable democracy. In a liberal perspective – traditionally inspired by some form of voluntarism – liberty is often defined as freedom from constraints in the exercise of choice; it concerns the question of whether we are in control. Thomas Nagel thus claims:

> 'The boundary between what we reveal and what we do not, and some control over that boundary, are among the most important attributes of our humanity.'[397]

In a less voluntaristic perspective one could claim that constraints are a necessary precondition for freedom.[398] This implies an important difference between liberty

---

[397] Nagel, 1998: 3-30.
[398] This is the position of Montesquieu. 1973 / 1748.

and freedom. Liberty has its focus on negative freedom, or absence of constraints. Freedom is more than that because it presumes the constraints that facilitate both negative and positive freedom and thus recognises that we cannot 'have' freedom without constraints. The pertinent question is always about which constraints enhance our freedom and which destroy it and this question cannot be answered out of context; it does not have one simple answer. Autonomy, which derives from auto (self) and nomos (law), means that I am capable of ruling my own life and participating in the life of others within the parameters that I have set for myself. Thus autonomy is related to the integrity and the identity of the person: am I acting as the kind of person I want to be?[399] This means that we must have some control over the constraints that regulate our interaction with others, especially if they concern boundary negotiations. In this case one may still agree with Nagel, to the extent that what becomes important is *which constraints establish our freedom and which destroy it.* Profiling is a risk in as far as it normalises and customises us without adequate feedback on what happens to our data and what types of profiles may be applied to us. This feedback – or rather the lack of it – is the central problem of the Directive's limited application and its mistaken focus on data instead of knowledge. As proposed in section 1.4 of chapter 1, autonomous human action presumes reflection and this reflection generates intentional action. Positive freedom, the freedom to interact with the environment – to make decisions and act on them – demonstrates autonomic behaviour. As long as the action is intentional it demonstrates autonomous human action. Without adequate feedback from our environment we cannot anticipate future interactions and may thus become a mere tool in the hands of those in the environment that manage to monitor, profile and manipulate our behaviour. We lose our autonomy and our positive freedom is restricted. This is true in biology but we cannot be arrogant about profiling machines: they may turn us into easy targets if we do not know what they are doing (if we do not know what they know). Our reflective capabilities are related to negative freedom, the liberty to ward off external interference in order to sit down and come to our own conclusions. If the profiles that interfere with us cannot be reflected upon because we are not aware of their application, we lose the chance to exercise this freedom – however comfortably we fit into our customised environment. It raises the question, what is being customised: the environment or the data subject?

If we look at privacy, equality, fairness and due process, the same problem surfaces. Above, privacy has been discussed in terms of positive and negative freedom. Equality is about the power (im)balances between profilers and their data subjects. According to Gutwirth and De Hert, data protection is mainly a tool of transparency. With transparency they mean the transparency of the profilers. However, since the default position of data protection legislation is access to information, its first aim is to regulate practices that in fact make the European citizen transparent. This transparency may seriously affect the balance of power between profilers and their subjects. If we were discussing the simple collection and aggregation of rather

---

[399] Taylor, 1976: 281-301.

insignificant personal data, this would not be a problem. *First*, the insignificance would prevent data users from storing such data on a large scale and, *second*, any massive storage of such data would soon render them inaccessible or unsearchable. However, this is not the case because profiling technologies are not interested in the data themselves but in the patterns and correlations that emerge between them, thus creating new knowledge and information. To a limited extent the Directive creates rights and obligations that allow some measure of transparency of the processing of data. For a number of reasons we should, however, not be too optimistic about the effectiveness of such obligations and rights in terms of the transparency they can provide. These reasons are both legal and technological. As shown by the legal analysis presented in chapter 13 above and in section 15.5.1 of the present chapter, the Directive has a rather limited scope and even if it were apt to deal with transparency of data, it offers hardly any transparency of profiles. Technological reasons concern the fact that, currently, data subjects do not have the technological means to track their personal data and trace what profiles are inferred from them, nor do they have the means to trace which profiles (based on their data and/or those of others) are used for or against them. Hence, even if the legal tools had a broader scope, we may still not have access to the information we want. Beyond that, if we had both the legal and the technological tools to access all the profiles that may impact our lives, we would be swamped by the sheer volume of it. This means we need to delegate the assessment of such profiles to an intelligent machine (personal digital assistant PDA), which could learn to function as a personalised filter. As long as these PDAs are not part of our daily life, fairness becomes difficult to achieve for the simple reason that in a world that fosters automated or even autonomic profiling, we have no way of knowing on what basis we are being offered opportunities, targeted as criminals or paying a different price. Due process suffers equally. First, whenever the Directive is not applicable and second because the technological infrastructure to access the information we need is lacking.

15.6   Concluding Remarks

Gutwirth and De Hert rightly conclude that data protection legislation was the lawyers reflex to cope with the increasing data explosion. It formed a first attempt to counter the powers that evolve from new technologies such as profiling. The question remains whether such an attempt can be effective. Data protection legislation is a form of administrative law, it imposes a set of obligations and prohibitions on data controllers and data processors and distributes rights to citizens. Many lawyers and policy makers suffer from a modernist reflex that calls for new legislation whenever a problem arises. The idea is that if we create new obligations and grant new rights, the world will organise itself accordingly. If not, even more rules are enacted to further the implementation of those that turned out to be ineffective. The problem with administrative law is that it exhibits the strengths but also the weaknesses of rule *by* law. The presumption that issues concerning the environment, biotechnology and profiling technologies can be solved by imposing rules on the stakeholders (enacting environmental law, prohibition of stem cell research or data protection legislation) is problematic, if the changing landscape in which such rules must apply is not seriously taken into account. If we turn back to the fair information principles, enumerated in section 15.4.1 and consider the unobtrusive and ubiquitous computing technologies that are already embedded in our environment, the principles seem written for another – less complex - age. If unlimited collection of data is technologically possible and profitable while effective control is an illusion and if the amount of data is such that no person would ever have the time to keep track of the collection and storage of her personal data, its purpose and the identity of the data controller, let alone to correct, complete and update her data and/or to erase, rectify, complete or amend it; if use of data collected for another purpose or disclosure of data for other purposes is technologically possible and profitable while effective control is an illusion; if consent is a burden for both the data subject and the data controller; and if, last but not least, the fact that data subjects are usually not aware of the data traces they leave behind makes it impossible to trace the data controller let alone hold her accountable for non-compliance with the fair information principles - then we may be fooling ourselves in thinking that such legislation will make much of a difference. Though chapter 13 concludes with moderate optimism, arguing for an extensive interpretation of the main tenets of the data protection Directive, this optimism must not lead us to believe that written administrative law will suffice.

What we need is an intelligent interplay between technological design and legal regulation, with a keen eye to market forces and business models as they will fit in with such design and regulation (legal regulation may invite predatory greed or responsible business enterprise; technological design may empower those that are already in charge or weaker parties). As Lawrence Lessig has argued extensively, the architecture of our world is not only a matter of enacted law but also a matter of the way we design our technologies. Similar to law, technologies regulate our world: constraining our actions while creating new options, enriching our world while also implementing certain choices. The challenge is to integrate these two aspects of our shared world: to construct common architectures, built of legal and technological constraints that intelligently interact. The central question should be how to construct infrastructures that enhance our freedom and reinvent democracy in a world that can no longer be ruled solely from the perspective of the national or supranational state. The point is not to weave a seamless web around us, integrating a legal network with advanced information and communication technologies in order to normalise us into a comfortable existence, where most choices are made for us by our intelligent agents.[400] Both law and technological design should be used to create an order that

---

[400] This may not be a problem if we can programme our own agents. However, in that case the problem is shifted to the design of the software and it presumes that we can anticipate the consequences of our predefined choices (issues of liability may arise here provoked by the complexity of the network of consequences that follow our agent's decisions). See M. Hildebrandt, 2008, forthcoming.

facilitates and empowers individuals to construct their identity in constant interaction with others, while participating in the construction of our common world.

Therefore, the disciplines of law and technological design need to create common ground and shared vocabularies that recognise both the similarities and the differences between the way law and technology regulate.[401] Lawyers will have to give up the attempt to rule the world as a voluntaristic project[402] and technologists will have to give up possible dreams of a technologically predefined world, however comfortable. It may be the case that the artificial construction of the legal persona as the mask that both protects the person of flesh and blood and enables her to take part in the life of the community as a legal person, is developing its counterpart in the digital persona, intelligent agent or identity management device that functions in a similar way: as a shield and a gateway, as protection and interface.

15.7   Reply: Some Reflections on Profiling, Power Shifts and Protection Paradigms

Bert – Jaap Koops*

This reply critically analyses the claims made by Hildebrandt, principally by distinguishing the various forms and stages of profiling and by analysing their impact on various constitutive features of the 'Rechtsstaat'. How serious is this potential impact in terms of legal protection, notably on privacy, data protection and *ipse* identity? Could the ability of weak parties to counter-profile the profilers restore the balance of power? If not, two other directions should be explored for containing serious profiling risks, both of which require paradigm shifts. First, protective norms should be built into technology, for instance through profile 'flags'. Second, legal protection should focus more on redressing wrongs than on preventing abuse, emphasising non-discrimination rather than privacy, for instance by stronger supervision mechanisms such as a Profiling Authority.

15.7.1   Introduction

In this chapter on profiling and identity, Mireille Hildebrandt sketches potential risks that profiling carries for European citizens and the rule of law. One should ask what exactly in modern profiling creates these risks, if we are to address them. Is it

---

* Tilburg Institute for Law, Technology, and Society (TILT)

---

[401] The challenge will be to overcome the voluntaristic presumptions prevalent in law and the deterministic assumptions prevalent in technology. Further elaboration of the work of Lessig, Reidenberg and others in this direction would be needed. See, Lessig 1999; Reidenberg, 1998: 553-585; and with contrary opinion Tien, 2005 and Brownsword, 2005: 1-22. A nuanced position is taken by Leenes and Koops, 2005: 329-340.

[402] Cp. Parker, C, et al., 2004.

the large-scale collection of personal – and non-personal – data in data warehouses, is it the data mining that seeks to uncover relations that are imperceptible to the human mind, is it the marketing of the resulting profiles, or is it the use of these profiles in various kinds of situations? Is it perhaps the impact of the use of profiles on the human person's sense of self, her *ipse*-identity?

In this essay, I provide some reflections on the impact of profiling on fundamental rights and the consequences this has on the protection of citizens. It is loosely conceived as a constructive critique of Hildebrandt's analysis on profiling and identity and, for the sake of argument, this essay tries to be succinct and provocative and, at times, exaggerating.

15.7.2   Distinctions in Profiling

We should make some distinctions, both conceptual and practical, before we begin to denounce profiling as a threat to the rule of law. We could start with three stages of profiling:

1. pre-profiling: the collection and storage of data;
2. profile-making: the analysis of data collections in order to make profiles;
3. profile use: the application of a profile in a concrete case.

However, to be able to assess the risk of profiling on the rule of law, we need more subtle distinctions. For instance:

1. pre-profiling: the collection and storage of
   a. non-personal data,
   b. personal data;

2. profile-making: the analysis of data collections in order to make:
   a. group profiles,
   b. individual profiles;

3. profile use: the application of a profile to:
   a. make a general rule:
      i. in science,
      ii. as a commercial and marketable asset,
      iii. which is used by the organisation to make general organisational decisions,
      iv. which is used by the organisation to make specific organisational decisions;
   b. apply in a concrete case:
      i. to decide to offer something to a group or not;
         1. which no-one is really remotely interested in,
         2. which most of the group members would actually like to have;
      ii. to decide to offer something to an individual:
         1. at all,
         2. with a discount,
         3. with a surcharge;

>   iii. to decide whether to grant a request by an individual:
>   1. which is not vital to the individual,
>   2. which is vital to the individual.

(Note the distinction in type 3 between a) a profile-based *rule* that is used for deci-sion-making and b) the *profile* itself that is used for decision-making. The use of rules is not evidently included in the term profiling, since the profile has done its work and is discarded but from the point of view of law or legal principles, it may be equally relevant).

This is just a sample taxonomy and a fairly simple one at that but it shows the importance of making distinctions in order to know what we are really talking about. I believe, for instance, that the distinction under 3bii is relevant because it specifies whether a profile is used to make an offer to someone or not (the profiled is not put in a position to choose), whether the offer is made with a discount (the profiled is rewarded for fitting the profile) or whether the offer is made with a sur-charge (the profiled is punished for fitting the profile). Making group profiles to generate general rules for scientific purposes is something quite different from applying an individual profile to deny someone a request. There is nothing wrong with many of the profiling actions in this taxonomy; only certain types of profiling are noteworthy because they may affect people's lives or fundamental legal princi-ples. Hence, the first step is to be precise in indicating what type of profiling we are concerned with.

The next step is to determine why a certain type indeed impacts on people's lives. Hildebrandt argues that profiling has serious consequences for human beings because it:

- creates stored histories 'capable of providing the evidence for a [Kafkaesque] conviction at some point in time' (dataveillance);
- surreptitiously changes their behaviour, both in anticipation 'to fit the expecta-tions of our profilers' (normalisation) and in being confirmed in their probable preferences through autosuggestion (customisation);
- negatively impacts privacy, equality, fairness and due process.[403]

Does profiling at large really have all these consequences? In my view, they largely occur only in profile *use* and *serious* consequences probably occur only in type 3biii2: applying a profile when deciding a request that is vital to someone and per-haps in type 3bii: applying a profile when deciding to offer something to an individ-ual. It is true that the threat of dataveillance relates to the first step (pre-profiling) but this is only a threat if the stored data are ever used in concrete decisions and thus, it is really profile use – or post-profiling – that is the serious issue. This is not to say that the other parts of profiling are irrelevant but the yardstick to judge profiling by lies in the use of profiles rather than in all the other steps. The risks of profiling lie in the misuse of profiles. Only if a serious risk of such misuse is demonstrated,

---

[403] See section 15.2.

should we do something about profiling, by containing the risk through actions that may target pre-profiling, profile making or profile use, depending on what is most suited to address the specific risk.

I shall not argue that profile misuse does not happen nor that ICT and the resultant correlatability of data has not greatly facilitated undesirable types of profile use. However, if it is to be shown that profiling poses significant threats, we need convincing qualitative examples and quantitative data of serious negative effects of profiling. In this chapter, Hildebrandt only posits the negative effects in the abstract. Therefore, there is a clear goal for further research: map the actual consequences of profiling on people's lives in reality.

15.7.3   The Effect of Profiling on Fundamental Legal Principles

For the time being, let us simply assume that there are cases in which profiling really has negative consequences for human beings. The core question is to what extent these negative consequences would impact the rule of law and fundamental rights of citizens. Hildebrandt discusses the core values of privacy, identity and data protection as being relevant in the field of profiling. These three could be called the fundamental legal principles that are tools for the high goals of democracy and the rule of law. They are interrelated but should be viewed separately because they each have somewhat different goals and characters. What is the impact of profiling-with-negative-consequences on these three principles?

15.7.3.1   Privacy is Dead (Requiescat in Pace)

How does profiling relate to *privacy*? Leaving aside data protection as a privacy instrument (because data protection should be viewed separately, as Gutwirth & De Hert rightly argue[404]), profiling as such does not – to me – seem a really significant privacy threat. That is, large-scale collection and storage of personal data can be seen as a privacy threat but privacy is not really affected if the data remain stored in computers and do not enter the heads of people who make decisions about other people. It is only when an individual profile is used in an individual case that privacy may be at stake because the profile user perhaps knows more about the profiled subject than she needs to know for the purpose of the particular transaction. However, does that really affect the profiled person in her private sphere? I appreciate the notion of privacy as a safeguard against – unjust – judgement from others (Johnson, 1989) because others should judge us only by relevant criteria and not by irrelevant criteria which, precisely because they are irrelevant in the particular context at issue, should remain private. However, why not call a spade a spade and say that in this respect,

---

[404] See Ch. 14.

it is not so much privacy that is at stake but fair judgement and equal treatment? Privacy may be a servant to many masters but here, I believe, it is largely the master of fair treatment, which privacy is serving. We risk blurring the discussion by bringing on board the multiple – and, to many people, confused – associations that surround the notion of privacy and hence, we had better turn to anti-discrimination law as the core issue in profiling and disregard privacy as being at stake.

Besides, privacy seems doomed anyway. Not because it is consciously being pushed aside in favour of other interests – although it often is nowadays – but because it is slowly but surely being eroded through ever-increasing advances in technology, which make people and society transparent and because somehow people do not notice or care that they end up with ever smaller opportunities to withdraw into a private sphere (Koops & Leenes, 2005). This, at least, is my vision for the next decade or so. Conceivably, a return-to-privacy wave may appear once the current era of technology push and security hype has passed. It may arrive too late, however, if privacy-destroying infrastructures have paved the world's ways by then.

15.7.3.2 Data Protection is Dead (Long Live Data Protection)

How does profiling relate to *data protection*? In many types of the profiling taxonomy given above, data are not traceable to unique persons and hence, not personal data subject to data protection law. Indeed, for many types of profiling, it is not necessary to process uniquely identifiable data; in many cases, data that correlate not at the individual level but at a more generic level or anonymised data will suffice. Data protection law typically plays a role in pre-profiling, when personal data are being collected and in profile use, when profiles are applied to unique individuals. What happens in-between may or may not legalistically fall under the scope of data-protection law but is insignificant as compared to the pre- and post-processing stages.

A more important issue is why we should really be concerned with data protection. The edifice of data protection principles and data protection laws that has been erected since the 1970s seems to be based on one major assumption: we need to prevent data processing as much as we can in order to prevent misuse of personal data. Only by allowing the minimum of data to be collected in the first place and by allowing the data to be processed only for the purpose for which they were collected, will we prevent data monsters from harming people by undue knowledge of them.

Admirable as this assumption may be, it is outdated and doomed to failure in the current information society. Data storage devices and data networks are here to stay. They create such huge opportunities for collecting and processing data and especially for interconnecting and correlating data that trying to prevent data collection and trying to restrict data processing is like banging one's head against a brick wall. The wall is not affected, as organisations happily continue large-scale data collection and correlation, with or without the blessing of data protection laws. However, the head is hurt over and over again as data protection laws and principles are infringed, without any material redress in practice.

Therefore, in my view, the focus of data protection should be radically shifted. Instead of focusing on the early, enabling stages of data processing, it should concentrate on the later usage stage of data processing. What data protection really is, or should be, about is decent treatment of people in society. The core value that I perceive is at issue in data protection is common decency. Decency that shows itself in using correct, up-to-date and relevant data, decency by adequately securing data against data snoopers, decency in using information in a correct manner. Only by stressing much more the use of data and adequately enforcing decency norms in that use, will data protection principles be able to survive the information age. If that is done, data protection may have a long and prosperous life as a core value in the information society. It may then become what it really fails to be now, a tool of transparency that enhances the rule of law.

Taking this view of data protection as input for an assessment of profiling, it is again the last stage of profiling – profile use – which we should be concerned with. The earlier stages of pre-profiling and profile making are either immaterial for data protection, because decency in human relationships is not at issue here, or they are elusive for data protection and uncontrollable in practice. Data protection might, on the other hand, help in the later stage of profiling to ensure anti-discrimination and fair treatment, which I indicated earlier to be the main concerns with profile *use*.

Hildebrandt seems to conclude that data protection legislation is ineffective to combat the negative aspects of profiling, stressing that most profiles are not personal data and the failure of the data protection principles in the face of unlimited collection, storage, and re-use of data.[405] In the case of profiling, however, I believe that data protection can still make a difference (at least to the extent that data protection is effective at all, which should not be overestimated). Regardless of how much data are collected and correlated and how many profiles are being made outside the scope of adequate data protection in the profile use stage, there are always personal data involved, which should be the target of protection. After all, when a profiler applies a profile to an individual, she must use one or more personal data as criteria that fit (or do not fit) the profile.

If someone applies for a bank loan and is granted or denied one on the basis of profiling, the bank must have used some of his personal data as input, for instance, his credit history, salary and whether or not he is wearing a tie. Data protection legislation applies to this use of personal data. The major issue here is that the bank should inform the data subject that the decision has been made by inputting his credit history, salary and 'tie-ness' into a profile. Ideally, if the loan was denied, the subject should be able to ask which of these three data were crucial so that he knows what he should do to alter the decision. If it turns out that not wearing a tie was the decisive factor, he should be able to appeal the decision, since it is unfair to judge people on ties. Of course, it is easier said than done that data protection should function in this way but I see some scope for effective protection against

---

[405] See sections 15.5 and 15.6.

unfair profiling by establishing mechanisms for enforcing data protection rules to
the serious types of profile use as applied to individuals.

15.7.3.3 Identity:Ipse and Idem

How does profiling relate to the sense of self, or *ipse*-identity? Hildebrandt makes the
crucial distinction between *idem* and *ipse* as two meanings of identity. I see a clear
connection between the human person and *ipse*-identity on the one hand and the legal
person and *idem*-identity on the other. In legal relationships (and I use this term
broadly: each relationship somehow has a legally relevant aspect), we act with legal
persons – the objectified construct that is the *external* part of a person that interacts
with and in society. Identification in this respect usually means *idem*-identity: we
want to know that we are dealing with the same – legal – person as last time, or with
a specific – legal – person with this name or attribute. It is immaterial in these transactions whether we are dealing with a – human – person whose *interior* entails a
well-developed or a crippled sense of self. Profiling, at least on the face of it, only
has to do with using profiles in legal relationships: you take a decision about someone by judging whether or not this person meets the profile or the profile-based rule.
This is *idem*-identity: are we talking about the right – legal – person? The profiler,
nor the profiled, is concerned with *ipse*-identity here: the question "are we talking
about a true human being?" simply does not arise.

    However, Hildebrandt argues that *ipse*-identity is related to *idem*-identity, since the
sense of self only develops in relationship to others, who interact with the person on
an *idem* basis, i.e., based on the knowledge or the perception that it is the same person
as before or as the one indicated by a name or attribute. As the *idem*-identity is used
by a profiler to interact with the person, the *ipse*-identity may be affected as a consequence: 'If profiles are generated by advanced profiling technologies they may impact
my sense of self without any awareness on my part, for instance by offering me targeted services otherwise not available'.[406] While I agree that this may be true, I do not
see this – as Hildebrandt implicitly seems to do – as necessarily consequential. The
sense of self is continually affected by a myriad of everyday experiences, albeit usually in minor and unnoticed ways. Is there a relevant difference between profiling and
'profiling'[407] here? We interact with people based on mutual perceptions and consequent reactions and the sense of self is just as much built on, for instance, being
offered a light by a stranger on the street or by getting a grumpy reaction from a bus
driver based on our appearance, as it is based on being offered a service after profiling. It seems to me that the sense of self is affected much more profoundly by, for
instance, witnessing a terrorist attack or an avalanche than it is by being offered any
kind of service. In other words: why should it matter that the use of a profile without

---

[406] Section 15.4.2.

[407] As Hildebrandt uses 'profiling': in the common sense of building stereotypes of friends, colleagues, etc.

the subject being aware of the profiling impacts his *ipse*-identity, given that many things happen, without our being aware of their rhyme or reason, which affect our sense of self just as much, if not more so?

According to Hildebrandt, this is largely because of the risk of people being 'manipulate[d] into behaviour without (...) adequate feedback on how their data have been used.' This may lead to 'major shifts in power relations between individual citizens on the one hand and commercial or governmental organisations on the other.'[408] For some types of profiling, this may be true and it is precisely these types of profiling that we must try to address if the risk of serious manipulation and a consequent power shift is high enough. Before we can do that, we must know which types of profiling in which situations actually carry such a risk. After all, manipulation of people's behaviour has a long-standing tradition in commerce, for instance, by placing candy bars near the cashier where people are queuing. When is manipulation serious enough to cause substantial shifts in people's sense of self? Moreover, when is such a substantial shift unwarranted, given that people's identity is shaped by numerous factors, which influence the ability to self-develop because they enhance or restrict opportunities and in that sense, 'manipulate' people's behaviour (genetics, nutrition, education, where you happen to be born, your mother's job, social surroundings, peer group, etc.). These questions merit further research before we can conclude that profiling is a serious threat to *ipse*-identity.

15.7.4 Counter-profiling by 'Weak' Parties

Concluding that some types of profile use impact privacy, data protection and – perhaps – *ipse*-identity is one thing but there may be another side to the story. We should have an eye for counter-developments. The rule of law is at stake, I would argue, if significant changes in balances of power occur without adequate reason - a changing conception of fairness, or a general acceptance of privacy as outdated, might be adequate reasons. It is probably true that profiling enables those in power – businesses, governments, employers – to enhance their power, by making ever more precise decisions that benefit themselves rather than the consumer, individual citizen, or employee. As yet I do not believe that this rise in power is very significant but it may be something to keep an eye on, so that we can intervene as soon as the current power balance threatens to tip too much in favour of those in power.

However, it should not be overlooked that, at the same time, consumers, citizens and employees also *gain* power through data storage and correlatability. This is particularly visible in the context of commerce: consumers are no longer dependent on the bookstore or camera shop on the village square but they can compare prices in an automated way and choose the cheapest offer or the best deal in as large a region as they care to explore from their desk chair. What is more, businesses are

---

[408] Section 15.4.4.

being profiled by ad-hoc collections of consumers who together build and maintain websites with assessments of their quality, service level and reliability. A hotel owner now must not only be friendly to Mr Michelin or Miss Lonely Planet when they visit once a year but to every customer with Internet access, lest he risks being allocated a bad profile.

In government-citizen and certainly in employer-employee relations, the empowerment of the traditionally weak party through technology is perhaps less clear. Nevertheless, the example of blogging is a case in point. Individual citizens can become famous bloggers, forcing local governments and government agencies to monitor how they are being talked about and 'profiled' on the web. Government decisions, much more than was the case before the wide adoption of the Internet, risk public denouncement by individuals, with a significant potential impact on their status and support. Increasingly, citizens also use mobile phones to photograph and film excessive actions by police on the street, thus providing a check on law enforcement that is stronger than traditional eyewitness statements have ever been. I am sure other examples avail of technology-facilitated empowerment that tugs at the power balance of governments and citizens by giving citizens an extra tool of transparency in practice.

Do not mistake me in arguing that profiling by the powerful is thus counterbalanced through 'profiling' by the power-poor, so that in the end, the balance of power remains the same. I doubt that this is the case but it is worth researching. My hypothesis is that technology causes shifts in existing balances of power in *both* directions but these shifts cannot exactly be measured against each other. The metaphor of a balance here falls short – it is not simply a matter of putting similar weights on both sides of a pair of scales. What the ultimate effect is on power relations remains to be studied.[409]

15.7.5   Two Paradigm Shifts in Protection

Not only should we look at counter-developments of new tools of transparency becoming available to citizens but more importantly, we should simultaneously take into account more of the societal context. It is conceivable that society is changing – not only through technology but also through internationalisation, commodification, anti-terrorismification and trivialisation and our notions of democracy, the rule of law, or fairness are shifting as well. They are not fixed notions and even within the continuing framework of a democratic constitutional state, the conception of what exactly constitutes democracy or fairness may vary.

Given the caveats of counter-developments and potential shifts in the social context, it is still possible that profiling poses a threat to citizens. This is not a general threat however: only some types of profiling might seriously impact one or

---

[409] See my project 'Law, Technology, and Shifting Balances of Power', described at http://rechten. uvt.nl/koops/files/page.asp?page_id=15.

more fundamental rights of citizens – privacy, data protection and perhaps the freedom to develop a sense of self (*ipse*-identity). In my view, it is only the *use* of profiles at issue here and particularly the use of profiles to offer or refuse vital services to groups or individuals and the use of profiles to grant or deny substantial requests by individuals. These types of profiling might undermine the legal protection that citizens enjoy and they could ultimately lead to a different kind of society in which citizen freedoms are crippled by judgements being constantly based on intransparent profiling embedded in an Ambient Intelligent world. The likelihood of such a scenario may not be great but the potential damage to society could be serious, resulting altogether in a non-negligible risk.[410]

Two lines of action can be considered to contain this risk. I agree with Hildebrandt that an integrated approach of technological and legal protection is called for: 'common architectures, built of legal and technological constraints that intelligently interact.'[411] The first challenge is to focus on building protection into the future technologies that will surround and profile us. 'Technology as law' is not an easy task, however, particularly not when it comes to 'building in' privacy norms into technology (Koops & Leenes, 2005). It requires a paradigm shift to convince technology developers and law-makers that norms can be – and are being – embedded in technology and that this should actually happen because increasingly, law fails to do the trick of regulating behaviour.

The second challenge is another paradigm shift. Legal protection must focus more on redressing wrongs than on preventing them. Traditionally, both privacy and data protection laws have a strong notion of preventing infringements, by general prohibitions of intrusion in the private sphere and by limiting data collection, storage and use of data processing that is 'necessary' and purpose-restricted. The legal norms fail to actually prevent privacy intrusions and data protection infringements, simply because technology and society have evolved to depend on large-scale and multi-purpose processing of personal data and profiles (this is why technology needs to take over, as far as possible, the preventative part of protection). The reactive part of legal protection – regulations to redress harm or award damages – is traditionally weak in privacy and data protection: privacy infringements can hardly be redressed and damages are rarely claimed and even more rarely awarded. Compensation for data protection infringements is unheard of.

Therefore, it seems to me that another paradigm shift is called for. Data protection is crucial in the information society but the legal edifice should shift from trying to prevent unreasonable data processing to trying to ensure that the knowledge arising from data is applied fairly. It is the *outcome* of data processing – the ultimate *use* of the data and the resulting knowledge – that should be the object of protection rather than the collection or processing itself. The key notion here is fair treatment rather than data control or informational self-determination. Data protection may be a sister of privacy but she is a twin of equal treatment.

---

[410] Risk equals likelihood multiplied by potential damage.

[411] See section 15.6.

15.7.6 Suggestions for Protection Measures in Profiling

To illustrate where these paradigm shifts might lead in the area of profiling, I will
conclude by giving a few tentative suggestions for enhancing protection with respect
to profiling, based on the hypothesis that some types of profiling pose a risk to citizens' rights and hence, to society at large. These are mere first thoughts to indicate
approaches we should explore, rather than ready-made policy recommendations.

A major task is to foster transparency. At the technological level, profile 'flags'
could be developed, which show up whenever a decision is based on a profile. In
on-line service delivery, for example, when someone is denied a request, the web
page could automatically show a 'profile icon', perhaps linking to information
about the profile used. In offers, a flag should show up indicating that the offer has
been made on the basis of a profile – comparable to on-line shops showing advertisements such as: 'People who bought The Da Vinci Code also bought The New
Testament'. Moreover, if profile use leads to *not* making an offer, this should likewise be mentioned somewhere by showing a profile icon. Ideally, a tool should be
available for people to click on a link showing the precise personal data that were
used as input in the profile, so that they know that the offer – or non-offer, or the
decision upon a request – was based on their clickstream, search words, IP-address-
inferred country of origin, credit history and/or use of a Microsoft browser, to name
a few possible criteria. Such 'profile flags' would never be developed by industry
without pressure from legislation or civil society but given that it is only serious
forms of profile use that we are concerned about, such pressure is not entirely
infeasible. Moreover, particularly the government itself could set an example by
embedding transparency tools in service-delivery procedures based on profiling.

Next, legal protection could be reinforced in several ways. First, there is a ger-
minal provision in the Data Protection Directive (Directive 95/46/EC) that merits
growing: art. 15 prohibits, in general, decision-making based solely on automated
data processing. This is a key issue in a ubiquitous profiling world, where decisions
are constantly being made by ambient surroundings based on profiles. Those decisions that have significant effects for the citizen should be subject to such a condition. However, this need not be done beforehand: in combination with a profiling
flag, the profiled person could, along with the decision made, be offered a mechanism to press a button to request 'human intervention'. Human intervention in
itself, however, is not sufficient if the human profiler, for example, simply acts as
an automaton on the basis of the profile and the few personal data used as input by
the system. Fair treatment can only be provided by someone who seriously takes
into account the context and the particulars of the case, including the relevant background of the individual. This can never be ensured, at least not completely, by
rules that regulate profiling as such.

Therefore, second and most importantly, effective control mechanisms should be
established. Legal norms on paper regulating the use of profiles will only work if
there is adequate enforcement. If sufficient transparency can be effected, enforcement
will be enhanced by appeal and complaint mechanisms with low thresholds for
profiled citizens. However, somewhat stronger supervision is called for, since

individual complaints have little power in a ubiquitous profiling world and transparency will never be completely achievable. Perhaps a Profiling Authority could be established with the official task of monitoring profiling in the public and private sectors, both by handling complaints and by active investigation into profiling practices in sectors or individual organisations. This might be placed within existing Equal Treatment Commissions, given the focus of supervising that profiles are being applied in a fair way. Several instruments could be borrowed from data protection regulation, such as stimulating the use of 'profiling statements' and requiring profilers to submit information about profiling practices to the Profiling Authority.

15.7.7 *Conclusion*

Profiling is multi-faceted and comes in many flavours. Some types of profiling can pose a threat to fundamental rights and freedoms, such as privacy, data protection and perhaps the freedom to develop a sense of self. Much should be researched before we can really answer the question of whether profiling seriously threatens citizens and could fundamentally alter the balance in power relationships that constitutes our current society and if so, which types of profiling. This research should include real-life examples and figures on profiling with negative consequences for citizens, an analysis of counter-developments that enable citizens to 'profile' the profilers and an analysis of changes in the social context in which all this is happening.

Let us suppose that such research would corroborate the hypothesis that profiling does carry a societal risk undermining citizens' protection, notably because profiles are used unfairly to take consequential decisions about individuals and groups. Rather, let us suppose that research would reject the hypothesis that there is no such risk. Then, measures should be developed to contain this risk, including a combination of technological and legal protection measures.

This is easier said than done, however. A paradigm shift is needed to effectively start building-in preventative protection measures in technology. Another paradigm shift is needed to turn legal protection away from stressing prevention and privacy-related data protection and to focus instead on effective legal supervision measures that target profile use and view data protection in the context of equal treatment.

15.8 Reply

Kevin Warwick*

Clearly the surrounding ethical issues are enormous. Although there are now some advisory European bodies, most practical ethical standpoints and approval mechanisms are still

---

* Reading University

organised on a national basis with considerable differences evident between them. These differences open up opportunities for some and appear as extra hurdles for others. The protective shield that ethical considerations can empower will therefore also be rather fragmented - most likely those wishing to benefit from the situation may seek ethical approval for data use and potential profile abuse from less discriminating countries. Moreover, the possibilities of the use of feedback in profiling are considerable - both in terms of individuals modifying their own identity in a direction of their choice in order to benefit themselves and also in terms of those wishing to modify and potentially control the identity of another individual or group. There is an interesting possibility of identity models being constructed as feedback mechanisms from which a detailed study of potential outcomes can be made.

15.8.1 *Classification*

One of the basic elements in the study of systems is the concept of a system type. Once classified a suitable method of controlling each particular type of system can be selected, dependant only on the choice of objective. For example, once classified as a second order dynamical system, if we want that system to optimally follow a changing required output value, then we can employ a controller with, possibly, proportional and derivative actions. However, this is merely one example of a trait that appears to be traceable back to the origins of humans and, judging by the antics of other creatures, further still. The important system to be considered here is humans themselves.

An overall inherent desire of many, and possibly all, species is to classify objects and other creatures into different groupings, the presumable aim being to simplify the thought processes involved in dealing with that entity. In terms of what can be witnessed, for many creatures visual evidence can provide an important first classifying measure. If it looks like a snake then run away. If she appears to be an attractive woman then persuade her to have sex with you. It is obvious from these examples that there are evolutionary pressures at work. A quick decision is important. If you are too slow then you may die or someone else will have all the fun. Those whose speed of classification and response are not adequate are unlikely to pass on their genes to the next generation.

Because of the historical importance of visual appearance, once it is roughly known what sort of response is likely to be invoked, so an appearance can be assumed, for the purposes of eliciting a desired output. We witness many creatures making use of evolved camouflage for safety or to capture prey – their lives depend on it. Humans have tales such as The Wooden Horse of Troy and the Wizard of Oz. All actors are pretending to be what they are not and as for politicians, well enough said. Essentially it is an everyday occurrence for someone or something to either attempt to appear to be what they are, or it is not and perhaps more so for an individual to highlight only certain aspects of their appearance and personality – I suspect humans have jewellery and make-up for this purpose.

In terms of Homo sapiens, the advent of the technological/computer era has completely changed the approach. As Hildebrandt pointed out in chapter 15 or was it Humphrey Bogart in the film Casablanca, the memory capability of the human brain does not amount to a hill of beans when compared to that of a stand alone computer. When the computer is networked, as the vast majority are, at least on a part-time basis, so the imbalance is even greater. As Marvin Minsky once said about a human: "It is ridiculous to live 100 years and only be able to remember 30 million bytes. You know less than a compact disc" (Hendricks, 2005: 81).

Now we are faced with a computer based profiling and classification system that has a direct impact on all humans who are part of the system and clearly this impact and influence is going to be more considerable and have a greater effect as the years pass.

15.8.2 Being Me

For humans, one distinct shift in the movement of a technological profiler is the ever increasing move away from the overriding importance of visual appearance. We can presently witness a rearguard action from fast food chains and action films in order to present a swift and effective visual cue, e.g., the colour red to sell food. Despite this, organisational databases for group classifications of 'individuals' are now the norm and are taking on increasingly more significance. This is partly due to commercial competitiveness and because the technology is there, so why not obtain the information anyway? For the individual the question, as always, is whether to make use of the system and profit by it or be abused by the system and lose out.

Peter Steiner once said "On the Internet, nobody knows you're a dog" (Hendricks, 2005: 114). If you become aware of what is on offer, then it is in your hands to change your (electronic/network) profile accordingly. This is not something new, it is only the method that is different because of the technology and the changing face of (apparent) identity.

Unfortunately, this land of future nirvana is not the bed of roses that I have pictured. Rather, it is filled with poisons the like of which we have never witnessed before.

It has, in the past, been the case that we cannot completely control the characterisation another individual holds of us, however in true Darcy fashion it has been possible to work on individuals to change their viewpoint of ourselves, which we believe them to hold. However, we are now faced with a global/networked structured definition of who we are.

We may not know what that definition is or even that it is being held by a specific group. When we do know of some characterisation we are perhaps the least powerful person to try to change that perception – anyone who has a "personal" Wikipedia entry will realise that anyone else in the world can input "data" on who you are but you cannot query this or modify it in anyway yourself, even if the "data" are more fictitious than anything written by Victor Hugo. The relative importance of pieces of information about yourself as an individual is also controlled by others, as indeed is your relative importance to and with others. Whilst those above 50 years of age are still operating on a basis of relative importance in which politics, film and sport perhaps plays an important role, those below 30 years of age focus more on a Google or Yahoo search – this will completely change the focus of power in the years ahead.

One enormous problem is that once we have built up sufficient confidence, as humans we completely believe the information given to us from a computer. Often this is without question and in many cases without regard for conflicting visual information. In other words, the characterised identity held by a computer will override any other potential information, including apparent visual ones. We are witnessing that our evolved dominant (visual) sense is being superseded by computer based profiling information. This is so evident that humans can behave in a completely sheepish way, believing any criticism reported about an individual, simply because they are told so on an obscure blog. This was aptly commented on by Pierre Gallois when he said: "If you put tomfoolery into a computer, nothing comes out but tomfoolery. But this tomfoolery, having passed through a machine, is somehow ennobled and no one dares criticise it" (Hendricks, 2005: 51).

15.8.3   Freedom

The evolutionary shift of human society towards a technological/networked world is incessant. For example, I predict that it will not be very long before we witness one global time for the entire planet, thereby discarding the time differences that are merely part of a world of individuality and individual freedom, which is now passing swiftly into history. This shift brings with it many differences compared to human lives of the past. These will appear as advantages and disadvantages to different people. What might be an advantage to one may well be a disadvantage to another. It should not therefore be our role to judge such goodness or badness but rather to study the changes and suggest ways to steer and control the system – as is the case with systems theory and design.

I believe that we have always been characterised by data rather than knowledge. What exists now is the means to rapidly spread conclusions drawn from data in a way that vast groups of society will believe the assessment to be an accurate one, a standpoint they may well continue to hold, even if they gather knowledge to the contrary.

Profiling is indeed a risk but I believe this is for reasons other than those given by Hildebrandt. As Clark discussed in his book *Natural Born Cyborgs* (Clark, 2003), the overall effect of such technological change is that our human brains are themselves evolving in order to adapt to the changes. By this argument, the overall effect of profiling is to actually change who we are. Those who do not adapt will lose out, those who rapidly adapt will benefit.

By far, the most important question in the argument on profiling and identity is who exactly is controlling the profile. If it is merely a supermarket with data on purchasing habits then it will effect your shopping and perhaps eating habits. If it is an on-line bookseller than it may well effect what books you purchase and read. Governmental profiling may determine what tax you pay or which countries you visit.

Like Hildebrandt, I believe that the most significant threat lies in the use of profiling machines, particularly when linked and networked with other profiling machines. Whilst retaining some humans in the loop one feels there is at least the possibility of bargaining or reasoning in order to modify a profile, albeit possibly futile in some cases. However, where a global profile is machine driven and controlled, then it would appear that we must become part of the machine ourselves. There would seem to be no alternative solution if we do not wish to be subservient to the machine.

15.9 Bibliography

Aarts, E. and Marzano, S., *The New Everyday. Views on Ambient Intelligence.* 010 Publishers, Rotterdam (Copyright Koninklijke Philips Electronics), 2003.

Agre, P.E. and Rotenberg, M., *Technology and Privacy: The New Landscape*, MIT Press, Cambridge, Massachusetts, 2001.

Alderman, E. and Kennedy, C., *The Right to Privacy*, Vintage Books, New York, 1997.

Altman, I., *The Environment and Social Behavior. Privacy Personal Space Territory Crowding*, Brooks/Cole, Montery, 1975.

Bennett, C.J., 'Convergence Revisited: Toward a Global Policy for the Protection of Personal Data?', in Agre, P.E. and Bramhall, G. (eds.), *Technology and Privacy: The New Landscape*: MIT Press, Cambridge, Massachusetts, 2001, pp. 99 – 125.

Berlin, I., 'Two concepts of liberty.' in Berlin I., Four essays on liberty, Oxford University Press, Oxford New York, 1969, pp. 118-173.

Brownsword, R., 'Code, control, and choice: why East is East and West is West', *Legal Studies*, Vol. 25, No. 1, SLS Publ. Southampton 2005, pp. 1-22.

Clark, A., *Natural Born Cyborgs*, Oxford University Press, 2003.

Clarke, R, 'The Digital Persona and its Application to Data Surveillance', *The Information Society*, Vol. 10, No. 2, Taylor and Francis Group, 1994, pp. 77-92.

Cohen Varela, A.E., 'Conclusion: 'Opening' ', *Phenomenology and Cognitive Sciences*, Vol. 1, No. 2, Springer, Netherlands, 2002, pp. 225-230.

Cohen, S., *Visions of Social Control*, Polity Press, Cambridge, 1985.

Constant, B., 'De la Liberté de Anciens Comparée a celle des Modernes.', in Marcel Gauchet (ed.), *De la liberté chez les modernes: Ecrits politiques*. Livres de Poche, Paris, 1819/1980.

Custers, B., *The Power of Knowledge. Ethical, Legal, and Technological Aspects of Data Mining and Group Profiling in Epidemiology*. Wolf Legal Publishers, Nijmegen, 2004.

Deadman, S., *Circles of Trust: The Implications of EU Data Protection and Privacy Law for Establishing a Legal Framework for Identity Federation*. Liberty Alliance Project, 2005.

De Mul, J., 'Digitally mediated (dis)embodiement. Plessner's concept of excentric positionality explained for cyborgs', *Information, Communication & Society*, Vol. 6, No. 2, Routledge, 2003, pp. 247-266.

Foucault, M., *Surveiller et punir. Naissance de la prison*, Gallimard, Paris, 1975.

Foqué, R. and 't Hart, A.C., *Instrumentaliteit en rechtsbescherming* (Instrumentality and Protection of Law, translation MH), Gouda Quint Kluwer Rechtswetenschappen, Arnhem, 1990.

Glastra van Loon, J.F., *Norm en Handeling. Bijdrage tot een kentheoretische fundering van de sociale wetenschappen*. Wolters-Noordhoff, Groningen, 1987/1956.

Glenn, H. P., *Legal Traditions of the World. Sustainable Diversity of Law* (second edition), Oxford, Oxford University Press, 2004.

Gutwirth, S., *Privacy and the information age*, Rowman & Littlefield Publishers, Inc., Lanham, 2002.

Habermas, J., *Strukturwandel der Offentlichkeit. Untersuchungen zu einer Kategorie der burgerlichen Gesellschaft*, Suhrkamp, Frankfurt am Main, 1962/1990.

Hendricks, V.F., *500CC Computer Citations*, King's College Publications, London, 2005.

Hildebrandt, M., 'Privacy and Identity'. in Claes, E., Duff, A., Gutwirth S. (eds.), *Privacy and the Criminal Law*, Intersentia, Leuven, 2006.

Hildebrandt, M., Backhouse, J., *Descriptive analysis of Profiling practices, FIDIS Deliverable 7.2*, European Union IST FIDIS Project, Brussels, 2005. Available at: www. Fidis.net.

Hildebrandt, M., 'Ambient Intelligence, Criminal Liability and Democracy', *Criminal Law and Philosophy* 2008, forthcoming.

Hosein, G., 'Threatening the Open Society: Comparing Anti-Terror Policies in the US and Europe', *Report Privacy International*, London, 2005. Available at: http://www.privacyinternational.org/issues/terrorism/rpt/comparativeterrorreportdec2005.pdf.

Hudson, B., 'Secrets of Self Punishment and the Right to Privacy', in Claes, E., Duff, A., Gutwirth, S. (eds.), *Privacy and the Criminal Law*, Intersentia, Leuven, 2006.

ISTAG (Information Society Technology Advisory Group), *Scenarios for Ambient Intelligence in 2010*, Brussels, 2001. Available at: http://www.cordis.lu/ist/istag-reports.htm.

ITU (International Telecommunications Union), *The Internet of Things*, Geneva, 2005. Available (for purchase) at: http://www.itu.int/osg/spu/publications/internetofthings/.

Johnson, J.L., 'Privacy and the judgment of others', *The Journal of Value Inquiry*, Vol. 23, No. 2, Springer Netherlands, 1989, pp. 157-168.

Koops, B.J., Leenes, R. ' "Code" and the Slow Erosion of Privacy', *Michigan Telecommunications & Technology Law Review*, Vol. 12, No. 1, 2005, pp. 115-188.

Leenes, R. and Koops B.J., ' 'Code': Privacy's Death or Saviour?', *International Review of Law Computers & Technology*, Vol. 19, No. 3, Taylor and Francis Group, 2005, pp. 329-340.

Lessig, L., *Code and other laws of cyberspace*. Basic Books, New York, 1999.

Mead, G.H., *Mind, Self & Society. From the standpoint of a social behaviorist*. The University of Chicago Press, Chicago – Illinois, 1959/1934.

Mill, J.S., *On Liberty*, Penguin, London, 1859/1974.

Montesquieu, *De l'Esprit des Lois*. Garnier Frères, Paris, 1973/1748.

Mouffe, C., *The democractic paradox*, Verso, London New York, 2000.

Nabeth, T., Hildebrandt, M., *Inventory of topics and clusters, FIDIS Deliverable 2.1*, European Union IST FIDIS Project, Brussels, 2004. Available at: www.fidis.net.

Nagel, T., 'Concealment and exposure', *Philosophy & Public Affairs*, Vol. 27, No. 1, 1998, pp. 3- 30.

Oksenberg Rorty, A., *The Identities of Persons*. University of California Press, Berkeley Los Angelos London, 1976.

Parker, C. et al. (eds.), *Regulating Law*, Oxford: Oxford University Press 2004.

Plessner, H., *Die Stufen des Organischen under der Mensch. Einleitung in die philosophische Anthropologie*, Frankfurt, Suhrkamp, 1975.

Ricoeur, P., *Oneself as Another*. Translated by K. Blamey, The University of Chicago Press, Chicago, 1992.

Reidenberg, J., 'Lex Informatica: The Formulation of Information Policy Rules Through Technology', *Texas Law Review*, Vol. 76, No. 3, Univesity of Texas School of Law, Texas, 1998, pp. 553-585.

Schauer F., *Profiles Probabilities and Stereotypes*, Belknap Press of Harvard University Press, Cambridge, Mass. London, England, 2003.

Schreurs,W., Hildebrandt, M., Gasson, M., Warwick, K. (eds.), *The Report on actual and possible profiling technologies in the field of Ambient Intelligence, FIDIS Deliverable 7.3*, European Union IST FIDIS Project, Brussels, 2005. Available at: www.fidis.net.

Smith, R.E., *Ben Franklin's Web Site. Privacy and Curiosity from Plymouth Rock to the Internet*. Sheridan Books, 2004.

Solove, D.J., 'Conceptualizing Privacy', *California Law Review*, Vol. 90, No. 4, 2002, pp. 1087-1156.

Solove, D.J., *The Digital Person. Technology And Privacy In The Information Age*, New York University Press, New York, 2004.

Steinbock, D.J., 'Data Matching, Data Mining, and Due Process', *Georgia Law Review*, Vol. 40, No. 1, University of Georgia School of Law, Athens, Fall 2005, pp 1 –84.

Sunstein, C., *Republic.com*, Princeton University Press, Princeton and Oxford, 2001a.

Sunstein, C., 'The Daily We. Is the Internet really a blessing for democracy?', *Boston Review*, Summer 2001b. Available at: www.bostonreview.net/BR26.3/sunstein.html.

Taylor, C., 'Responsibility for Self,' pp. 281-301 in Oksenberg Rorty, A. (ed.), *The Identities of Persons*, University of California Press, Berkeley, Los Angeles, London, 1976.

Tien, L., 'Architectural Regulation and the Evolution of Social Norms', *International Journal of Communications Law & Policy*, No. 9, Part 1, 2004. Available at: http://www.digital-law.net/IJCLP/index.html

van Woudenberg, R., *Het mysterie van identiteit. Een analytisch-wijsgerige studie*, SUN, Nijmegen, 2000.

Warren, S. and Brandeis, L.D., 'The Right to Privacy', *Harvard Law Review*, Vol. 4, No. 5, The Harvard Law Review Association, Cambridge, 1890, pp. 193 – 220.

Westin, A., *Privacy and Freedom*, Atheneum, New York, 1970.

Zarsky, T.Z., '"Mine Your Own Business": Making the Case for the Implications of the Data Mining of Personal Information in the Forum of Public Opinion', *Yale Journal of Law & Technology*, Vol. 5, 2002-2003.

Chapter 16
Knowing Me, Knowing You – Profiling, Privacy and the Public Interest

Roger Brownsword

16.1   Introduction

There is nothing like predicting the future and the future might turn out to be nothing like we predict. Even so, it is a fair assumption that, as the twenty-first century unfolds, we will know a great deal more about ourselves but, equally, others will know a great deal more about us. To put to a broader use the evocative terms of contrast employed by Serge Gutwirth and Paul De Hert, we might say that in the foreseeable future, there will be rather more transparency and rather less opacity.[412] When I say that there will be this shift from opacity to transparency, I mean not only that more raw data about ourselves and others will be available but that this data will translate into meaningful statements that impact our agency-based interests (particularly our interests in autonomy and privacy). Such is the prospect of profiling. A recurring theme of the essays in this book is that profiling promises benefits but, simultaneously, represents various threats.

For some, a future in which we might know more about ourselves will be a cause for concern; the transparency of a personal profile (for example, a profile of one's genetic make-up) will seem less than welcome. It is not simply that when one's profile is good it is good and when it is bad it is bad, some will see any such attempt at profiling as a violation of the dignity of human life. For others – which I believe to be a larger group - the principal cause for concern is not that we might know more about ourselves but that others, especially the State and powerful interests in the private sector, might come to know more about us. For this larger group, it is the loss of personal opacity and increased transparency relative to others that is the worrying prospect.

Prompted by the papers in this volume, my focus is the second rather than the first of these concerns. There are two general questions that I want to pose and pursue,

King's College London

[412] Above, chapter 14, 'Regulating Profiling in a Democratic Constitutional State', Gutwirth S. and de Hert P., 2006: 61.

M. Hildebrandt and S. Gutwirth (eds.), *Profiling the European Citizen: Cross-Disciplinary Perspectives.*
© Springer Science + Business Media B.V. 2008   345

both of which concern the identification of thresholds or limits. First, where precisely does an individual's interest in informational privacy engage? At what point does the right to control the outward flow of information about oneself begin? Is there anything that I can know about you without engaging your privacy interest? Second, where the State employs profiling techniques as part of its criminal justice strategy and assuming that such techniques enable the State to manage the risk of crime more effectively, is there a line beyond which the State should not go? Are there different lines to be drawn depending upon whether the State is using profiling ex ante to prevent the occurrence of crime, or to detect its commission, or ex post to correct offenders? I will deal with the first of these questions in Part II and the second in Part III of the paper.

In posing these questions, I will assume that the setting is a particular kind of moral community - a community of rights. By this, in brief, I mean a community, the developed members of which view themselves as agents (as capable of free and purposive action), where there is a general commitment to the principle that each agent should respect the generic rights of agency (essentially, the freedom and well-being) of fellow agents and that such rights are to be viewed under a will conception of rights.[413] This is not quite co-extensive with a community committed to human rights because the paradigmatic rights-holder is an agent (not necessarily of the human species) rather than a born human. For present purposes, though, the differences are not material, provided that the rights of a human rights community are also viewed under a will conception. So viewed, once (say) a right to privacy is engaged, a prima facie violation would be justified only where the right-holder has consented to the violating act (where the act is not against the will of the right-holder), where the act is necessary and proportionate in order to protect a more compelling right, or possibly where the State has special stewardship responsibilities.[414]

My conclusions are: firstly, insofar as the privacy interest is engaged where one "reasonably expects" the information in question to be no one's business other than one's own, it is important to distinguish between conceptions of privacy that are practice-led (where an expectation of privacy is reasonable provided that it is supported by practice) and those that are independent of practice (where the reasonableness of an expectation of privacy is not dependent upon support in custom, convention and practice); secondly, that a practice-led conception of privacy is unlikely to offer much (opacity) protection in a setting where profiling of one kind or another is the norm; and thirdly, that the deeper threat of the State employing a profiling strategy to manage crime is not that privacy interests will be routinely overridden by public interest considerations but rather that the State will jeopardise the possibility of the community functioning as an authentic moral community.

---

[413] For the development of these ideas spanning a couple of decades, see Beyleveld D. and Brownsword R., 1994, Beyleveld D. and Brownsword R., 2001, Beyleveld D. and Brownsword R., 2006: 141 and Beyleveld D. and Brownsword R., 2007.

[414] On this latter possibility, see Brownsword R., 2005: 435.

16.2 Privacy and Profiling

Privacy is a protean idea.[415] While spatial conceptions of privacy emphasise the right to be alone (the demand that others should keep their distance)[416], informational conceptions emphasise the right to control the outward (and perhaps inward) flow of information about oneself (the demand that others should mind their own business).[417] Insofar as profiling presupposes that data relating to an identifiable data subject has been collected before being processed for profiling in various ways,[418] then it is the individual data subject's interest in informational privacy that is primarily at issue. In this part of the paper, my intention is to try to identify the point at which this interest is engaged. Where precisely does the informational privacy interest begin?

16.2.1 Engaging the Right to Informational Privacy

If it takes just two agents to found a community of rights, then in its minimal form such a community comprises two individuated agents; there is a "me" and there is a "you" and that is all there is to our community. Ex hypothesi, we are committed to respecting one another's generic rights, including the right to informational privacy. Accordingly, I have a right against you that you do not, against my will, try to obtain information that is protected as personal to me and vice versa. In this particular setting, it is arguable that a privacy regime can function without the need for identifying names, numbers, marks or tags. Quite simply, if I have information about a person other than myself, it must be information about you and vice versa. If asked to whom the information relates or to identify the data subject, I can do so ostensively. In other words, in this minimal expression of a community of rights, there is little or no distinction or distance between the physically individuated agent and the agent's identifying metric (whether this is a whole, partial or non-biometric name or number, or the like).

However, as our community evolves into a modern complex society - the sort of society, in fact, where privacy claims are most forcibly articulated and pressed - each individuated right-holder will need his or her own identifying metric. In such a complex community of rights, it is still possible for information to be linked back to a data subject ostensively by a process of pointing out, or the like. Where this

---

[415] See, e.g., Laurie G., 2002, Ch. 1; Allen A.L., 1997: 31.

[416] Compare Warren S.D. and Brandeis L.D., 1890-91: 193.

[417] Compare Fried C., 1968: 475.

[418] For a working definition of profiling, see Hildebrandt M., this volume, Ch 2. Thus, profiling may be defined as "the process of 'discovering' correlations between data in data bases that can be used to identify and represent a data subject and/or the application of profiles (sets of correlated data) to individuate and represent a data subject or to identify a data subject as a member of a group or category".

happens, I know that the information in question is about "you" (qua the individuated physical agent pointed out to me), even if I do not know what your identifying name, number, mark or tag is. If a privacy regime can function by ostensive identification in a simple community of rights, it is arguable that it can also apply, to a more complex society. Even so, for present purposes, we can proceed on the basis that the typical case is not that of ostensive identification. Typically, an individuated agent (the data subject) is linked to the information non-ostensively, by reference to an identifying metric.

If the informational privacy interest typically presupposes that a wrong is done to an identifiable data subject, then the triad implied by the (engaged) privacy right is (i) a physically individuated right-holding agent, (ii) such agent being identified by an identifying metric and (iii) information of a protected class (private personal information) being obtained without the authorisation of the said agent - the wrong is done when the information so obtained can be linked back to the identifying metric and to the individuated agent. I am now going to assume that the informational privacy interest, as such, does *not* cover the individuated agent or the agent's identifying metric. Informational privacy demands respect for personal details concerning an individuated agent with that agent's identifying metric, not respect for the individuated agent or the metric as such. This should not be misunderstood. I do not mean that, in a community of rights, respect for the individuated agent does not matter, nor that there will not be concerns about the fragmentation and multiplication of identifying metrics. However, I do mean that such matters are not the concern of the right to informational privacy as such. Accordingly, if the informational privacy interest is not engaged by the agent's persona or identifying metric(s), this interest must begin at some point beyond the metric (where, of course, the protected information can be related back to the individuated agent via the metric(s)). The question, therefore, is this: what class of personal information, beyond the identifying metric(s) itself, is protected by the right to informational privacy?

Taking a broad view, David Archard[419] has suggested that personal information includes:

> One's age, address and phone number, income and purchasing habits, race or ethnic origin, medical history, blood type, DNA code, fingerprints, marital status, sexual orientation and history, religion, education, political allegiances, and membership of societies.[420]

If we follow this view, pretty much any of the details that we might include in our curriculum vitae constitute personal information. Some of the details might be judged to be more sensitive than others but, in principle, all such details are candidates for the protection of informational privacy. Archard, however, goes even further. In addition to the "relatively enduring features of an individual" of the kind listed, Archard includes as personal information those "occurrent properties that specify an individual's history, such as her location in some place at a particular time or her commission

---

[419] Archard D., 2006: 13.
[420] Archard D., 2006: 16.

of a particular act on a certain date".[421] Again, such details are candidates for the protection of informational privacy. If we exclude those details that serve as an identifying metric (for instance, the individuated agent's name or fingerprints) but only to the extent that such details function as a metric, then the question is: how much of this kind of personal information is protected by the privacy interest?

16.2.2 Two Approaches to a Reasonable Expectation of Informational Privacy

Following the strong lead given by the common law jurisprudence, let us suppose that the answer to this question is that personal information remains privacy-protected to the extent that this is in line with the claimant's reasonable expectations.[422] In a modern community of rights it might be argued that the range of personal information one can reasonably expect to be privacy-protected depends upon who the agent is (whether or not they are agents in the public eye, in public positions, or who court publicity and so on), where the agent is (whether or not one is in a zone that promises privacy), how the agent presents himself and so forth. Such an argument, though, may be grounded in two quite different ways. One argument is practice-led; the other is not and, in a community that is on a trajectory for ever more profiling, this difference might be extremely significant.

The practice-led approach treats an expectation of privacy protection as reasonable where it is supported by the practice of the community. Hence, if a particular community treats details of, say, one's age, address, blood type and religion as non-private personal information, then the default position is that such information (even when linked back to an identifiable agent) is not material to one's privacy interest. More pointedly, in such a community, I would do no wrong (or at any rate, no informational privacy wrong) if, without your consent or any other justifying reason, I sought to obtain details of your age, address, blood type or religion. In such a community, I could obtain such details from your curriculum vitae and, even without your consent, I would not violate your right to informational privacy. Of course, the practice of the community might be quite different, taking a more or less restrictive view than in the hypothetical case. The point, however, is that where the practice-led approach prevails, one's interest in informational privacy is engaged at whichever (contingent) threshold the community's custom, culture and practice designates.

If, by contrast, an expectation of privacy is judged to be reasonable or unreasonable by reference to some criterion that is not practice-led, what might this imply for the class of protected information? Clearly, in a community of rights, an

---

[421] Archard D., 2006.

[422] See, e.g., *Katz v United States* 389 US 347 (1967); *Campbell v MGN Ltd* [2004] UKHL 22; and, for a wide-ranging overview of the recent development of privacy protection in English law, see Phillipson G., 2003: 726.

approach of this kind requires the development of a theory that provides an account of how the protection of personal information (or specified items of personal information) contributes to the essential conditions of one's agency. Quite possibly, those attempts already made to theorise privacy by reference to autonomy, intimacy, dignity, or the like, will assist. However, this is too large an exercise to attempt in this paper. Nevertheless, it seems to me that in the absence of a better view, the default position must be that all items of personal information are prima facie privacy-protected. If so, this means that any personal information other than my individuated persona and identifying metric is exclusively my business and that you do me a wrong if, without my consent or other justifying reason, you seek to obtain any of this protected information. Once you have read my name at the head of my curriculum vitae, you should stop reading. Once you get beyond my name (or other identifying metric), my informational privacy interest is engaged.

Let us suppose, two communities operating with, in the first case, a practice-led conception of privacy and in the second case, an independent agency-based conception of privacy. In the latter, the privacy interest is engaged very quickly; in the former, let us assume, it is not. Even so, we might wonder whether there would be much practical difference because, in both communities, the benefit of the privacy protection would be waived where the right-holding agent so consented. However, how would this work? Consider, for example, Archard's example of information that locates an identifiable agent at a particular place at a particular time and let us suppose that in both communities, various kinds of technology are readily available to provide such locating information. In the former community, the fact that many agents acquiesce in the progressive embedding of such technology might be taken to signal a reduced expectation that locating information is a private matter; the culture changes to accept that there is no right to treat one's movements and whereabouts as a matter purely for oneself and those who expect otherwise are now judged to do so unreasonably. By contrast, in the latter community, such matters of acquiescence and acceptance are not relevant to the engagement of the informational privacy right; what matters is whether the collection of the details at issue touches and concerns the independently grounded interest in informational privacy. If obtaining locational details militates against the essential conditions for a flourishing agency, the privacy right is at least engaged and, in the absence of consent or overriding reasons, obtaining such details will not be justified.

16.2.3   Drift and Shift Arising from the Practice-Based Conception

In a very helpful paper, Bert-Jaap Koops and Ronald Leenes have anticipated the sting in this line of analysis.[423] According to Koops and Leenes:

---

[423] Koops B-J., and Leenes R., 2005: 115.

Technology affects the "reasonable expectation of privacy"....In the vast majority of technologies developed and used in real life, its influence is to the detriment of privacy. That is, technology often has the side-effect of making privacy violations easier....

....Examples in law enforcement and e-government show technology offers increasing opportunities for large-scale monitoring - from intercepting all telecommunications... to monitoring the movements of people. In the private sector, technology enables more control of people, from workplace and transaction monitoring to personalisation of consumer relationships, with new applications like facial recognition and RFID monitoring looming ahead.

....People gladly adopt the new possibilities. In fact, after a lapse of time, one gets so used to this new control mechanism that one may no longer perceive it as a side-effect but as an intrinsic - and perhaps intended - characteristic of the technology. This is when the "reasonableness" of a privacy expectation shifts: once the new technology is accepted as being inherently control-friendly, there no longer is a reasonable expectation that this control is not exerted....

The eroding effect of technology on privacy is thus a slow, hardly perceptible process. There is no precise stage at which one can stab a finger at technology to accuse it of unreasonably tilting the balance of privacy. Exactly because of the flexible, fluid nature of privacy, society gradually adapts to new technologies and the privacy expectations that go with them.[424]

With the benefit of these remarks, my point is an easy one to make. In a society that is not wholly technophobic and where the practice-based concept of privacy rules, then the technological developments that herald the emergence of a profiling community will modify practice and attitudes in a way that tends towards a reduction in the class of information that is judged to be privacy-protected. My point is not that prima facie infringements of the privacy right will more readily be taken to be authorised by consent (consent being implied or deemed on the basis of practice) or overridden by more compelling considerations (practice now downgrading the importance of privacy) - although all of this might well be the case. Rather, my point is the prior one - that the privacy right will be less quickly engaged. Quite simply, in a culture where agents have become de-sensitised to the routine obtaining and use of personal profiles, there will be little expectation of informational privacy and, when such an expectation is asserted, it will probably be rejected as unreasonable. Technology not only erodes privacy in practice, with the practice-based conception, it also erodes privacy in principle.

16.2.4   Marper and the Retention of DNA Profiles

These rather abstract reflections can be earthed by contrasting the approaches of the appeal courts in the recent English case of *R v Chief Constable of South Yorkshire, ex parte LS and Marper*.[425] This was a case in which there was a challenge to the

---

[424] Koops B-J., and Leenes R., 2005: 176-177.
[425] [2002] EWCA Civ 1275; [2004] UKHL 39. At the time of writing, Marper's challenge has been treated as admissible by the European Court of Human Rights and fast-tracked for hearing by the Grand Chamber.

legal framework that now permits the police to retain full DNA samples and identifying profiles even though the person from whom the sample has been lawfully
taken has not been convicted of any offence (indeed, not even brought to court). It
was agreed by the parties that the taking and use of such samples raises a privacy
question but it was moot whether *retention* of the profiles and underlying samples
raises such an issue. If the full sample were to be sequenced, this might yield a good
deal of sensitive medical information about the person but the profile itself does not
have such obvious privacy-engaging characteristics. Assuming that the profile
indicates only whether an identifiable individuated agent might or might not have
been at a particular crime scene, it is not so clear that privacy is engaged. Of course,
even if the right to informational privacy is engaged under Article 8(1) of the
European Convention on Human Rights, the State might justify the retention of a
profile either by relying on the consent of the right-holder or by reference to the
compelling public interest in the prevention and detection of serious crime. While
the courts in the *Marper* case are not quite at one in relation to the engagement of
Article 8(1), they have no difficulty in accepting a public interest justification for
the retention of the profiles.

In the Court of Appeal, it seems that a practice-based approach to privacy is
assumed. Lord Woolf CJ points the court in this direction by suggesting that,
whether or not retention is seen as engaging the privacy right, "depends very much
on the cultural traditions of a particular State."[426] If fingerprints are viewed as personal information, so too is DNA. This is not to deny that there might be a certain
shading of opinions. As Lord Woolf puts it:

> There is no doubt a rainbow of reactions that are possible to intrusions of this nature but at
> least for a substantial proportion of the public there is a strong objection to the State storing
> information relating to an individual unless there is some objective justification for this
> happening.[427]

Sedley LJ explicitly agrees, relying on the "strong cultural unease in the United
Kingdom about the official collection and retention of information about individuals".[428] Yet, is this correct? The DNA profiles held in the National DNA Database are
identifying metrics which can be employed to gather information about a particular
individuated agent. Where there is no match (between a profile and a crime scene
sample), we can say that the individuated agent was probably not at the scene of the
crime; where there is a positive match, we can say the opposite. Contrary to the views
of the Court of Appeal, I am not convinced that there is a cultural unease in the United
Kingdom about the State having the capacity to draw on such locating information
but, more importantly, I am not convinced that contingent cultural ease or unease is
the right way to distinguish between privacy engagement and non-engagement.

If we rely on a practice-based approach, it will often be a matter of impression to
determine at which precise point informational privacy is engaged. Thus, if, contrary

---

[426] [2002] EWCA Civ 1275, para 32.

[427] [2002] EWCA Civ 1275, at para 34.

[428] [2002] EWCA Civ 1275, at para 68.

to the Court of Appeal, privacy is not engaged where I am able to positively or negatively locate you, we might take a different view where there is either ongoing surveillance or an aggregation of locating particulars that disclose an agent's movement over an extended period of time. Furthermore, if the data collected are then used to develop a profile that discloses a latent pattern of conduct of which the agent is not aware, or which are used to place the agent in a category that carries with it certain disadvantages, then we might insist that, relative to our community's custom and practice, this has crossed the line. Somewhere between occasional location and deep profiling, there is an expectation (a reasonable expectation relative to practice) that privacy begins. Quite where and quite how securely privacy is engaged is moot, unless the community is rather conservative and homogeneous but even then, with the onslaught of technology, the balance shifts; there is less opacity.

When *Marper* was appealed, the House of Lords took a rather different approach to the engagement of privacy, distancing themselves from the culturally contingent view espoused by the Court of Appeal. Giving the leading speech, Lord Steyn said:

> While I would not wish to subscribe to all the generalisations in the Court of Appeal about cultural traditions in the United Kingdom, in comparison with other European states, I do accept that when one moves on to consider the question of objective justification under article 8(2) the cultural traditions in the United Kingdom are material. With great respect to Lord Woolf CJ, the same is not true under article 8(1)....The question whether the retention of fingerprints and samples engages article 8(1) should receive a uniform interpretation throughout member states, unaffected by different cultural traditions.[429]

Having rejected a custom-based approach and having reviewed the essentially identifying metric nature of a DNA profile (the profile as such, tells you nothing about the physical make-up, characteristics, health or life of the individuated agent), Lord Steyn concluded that retention either does not engage Article 8(1) at all or engages it only very modestly.[430]

Perhaps we should not read too much into Lord Steyn's judgment. Quite definitely, his Lordship is rejecting the idea that Article 8(1) is differentially engaged according to the particular custom and practice of each Contracting State. However, he might not be rejecting a practice-based approach as such, simply insisting that it should be applied only on a European-wide basis (Europe being the relevant area for a higher-level statement of shared practice). Equally, we cannot be confident that Lord Steyn has an independent non-practice based approach in mind. Even the idea that a profile, as a mere identifying metric, is not personal information *about* an agent is compatible with a practice-based approach.

The strongest support for the engagement of Article 8(1) is given by Lady Hale. For example, she states:

> It could be said that the samples are not 'information'....But the only reason that they are taken or kept is for the information which they contain. They are not kept for their intrinsic value as mouth swabs, hairs or whatever. They are kept because they contain the individual's

---

[429] [2004] UKHL 39, para 27.

[430] [2004] UKHL 39, at para 31.

unique genetic code within them. They are kept as information about that person and nothing else. Fingerprints and profiles are undoubtedly information. The same privacy principles should apply to all three.[431]

While the points made about the rich information-bearing potential of the DNA *samples* are extremely well-taken, it is not so clear that the same applies to the *profiles*. Arguably, the profiles are not so much "information about that person" but rather information that enables us to identify who "that person" is. Insofar as the profiles, in conjunction with crime-scene samples, yield information about an individuated agent's location, there is a question about whether the privacy right is engaged. However, that question needs to be squarely addressed rather than answered on the back of the privacy-engaging character of the full DNA sample.[432]

Finally, if the courts (as in *Marper*) are persuaded that the State has overwhelming reasons for maintaining profiles of its citizens, does it really matter where the privacy interest is engaged or whether we approach this by reference to practice or by reference to an independent account of agency? I believe that it does. For, when the technology of profiling is developing so rapidly, it is important that we are clear about where the privacy interest begins and why; if we lose sight of where privacy begins, we might find that it has ended sooner than we expected.[433]

16.3   Profiling and the Public Interest

Suppose that profiling of one kind or another is incorporated into the criminal justice system. The justification in the benign state is that such measures advance the public interest by strengthening the security of rights-holders. Consider the two

---

[431] [2004] UKHL 39, at para 70.

[432] It should be noted that there is also an interesting privacy issue arising from so-called familial DNA profiling. In some cases, although DNA samples taken from a crime scene might not fully match any profile held in the database, they might be a near-match to a particular profile. In such a case, there is a possibility that a close genetic relative of the person who has the near-match profile will be a full match. This was so, for example, in the "Shoe Rapist" case where the rapist was identified when a near-match showed up between crime-scene samples and the DNA profile of the rapist's sister (the sister's profile being taken in connection with a drink driving offence): see Norfolk A., 2006: 3. Quite apart from the investigative potency of familial DNA profiling, there is obviously the possibility that researching the DNA of family members might uncover embarrassing (and privacy-engaging) secrets about a person's genetic pedigree.

[433] Even if privacy (qua A's right to control whether A's personal information is accessed by B) is not engaged, confidentiality (qua A's right to control whether B, who legitimately holds personal information about A, may pass on that information to C) might still present some sort of barrier to the free circulation of personal information. For example, if the National DNA Database (B) legitimately holds information about A, it does not follow that such information may be legitimately passed on by B for retention by a third-party C (such as a commercial enterprise). For reports (by *The Observer* newspaper and Genewatch) of such possible breaches of privacy (in the broad sense) or confidentiality (in the more specific sense), see http://society.guardian.co.uk/crimeandpunishment/story/0,,1822354,00.html (last accessed July 31, 2006).

lead stories in a recent copy of *The Times*. The first story,[434] running over two pages, announces a proposed network of new generation synchronised speed cameras; if a car is driven through a restricted speed zone, the cameras will detect this, the car number plate will be identified, the information will be centrally processed and penalty notices will be issued within minutes of the offence. The second story[435] taking up a whole page, reports that a 58-year old architect, having been interviewed but not charged in connection with a complaint about theft and having had a DNA sample routinely taken, was found to have a DNA match with samples taken from crime scenes where young girls had been indecently assaulted many years earlier. In both cases these reports are implicit endorsements, indeed a celebration of the relevant technologies.[436] Even so, how far should we go with such a technological strategy in a community of rights?

In *Marper*, Lord Woolf CJ, appreciating the benefits of DNA sampling does not rule out the possibility of a national comprehensive collection. According to the Lord Chief Justice:

> So far as the prevention and detection of crime is concerned, it is obvious the larger the databank of fingerprints and DNA samples available to the police, the greater the value of the databank will be in preventing crime and detecting those responsible for crime. There can be no doubt that if every member of the public was required to provide fingerprints and a DNA sample this would make a dramatic contribution to the prevention and detection of crime. To take but one example, the great majority of rapists who are not already known to their victims would be able to be identified.[437]

Similarly, Lord Steyn is enthusiastic about the State making use of new forensic technologies. Thus:

> It is of paramount importance that law enforcement agencies should take full advantage of the available techniques of modern technology and forensic science. Such real evidence has the inestimable value of cogency and objectivity…It enables the guilty to be detected and the innocent to be rapidly eliminated from enquiries. Thus in the 1990s closed circuit television [was] extensively adopted in British cities and towns. The images recorded facilitate the detection of crime and prosecution of offenders….The benefits to the criminal justice system [of DNA profiling] are enormous. For example, recent…statistics show that while the annual detection rate of domestic burglary is only 14%, when DNA is successfully recovered from a crime scene this rises to 48%….[A]s a matter of policy it is a high priority that police forces should expand the use of such evidence where possible and practicable.[438]

With over 4 million profiles now held within the National DNA Database and with the average person being caught 300 times a day on CCTV, we might see the United Kingdom as a pilot for profiling-led criminal justice. My question is whether, in a community of rights, such a strategy can be assumed to be in the public interest.

---

[434] Webster B., 2006: 1-2.

[435] Bird S., 2006: 3.

[436] See also, the possibility of familial DNA profiling, note 421 (it should be noted that there is also an interesting privacy issue arising from so-called familial DNA profiling. In some cases…. etc.)

[437] [2002] EWCA Civ 1275, at para 17; similarly Sedley LJ at para 87.

[438] [2004] UKHL 39, paras 1-2.

16.3.1   The Chaplain's Concern

We start by reminding ourselves of a key moment in Anthony Burgess' remarkable novel, *A Clockwork Orange*.[439] Observing the successful results of young Alex's treatment at the State Institute for the Reclamation of Criminal Types, the chaplain laments:

> He [i.e., Alex] has no real choice, has he? Self-interest, fear of physical pain, drove him to that grotesque act of self-abasement. Its insincerity was clearly to be seen. He ceases to be a wrongdoer. He ceases also to be a creature capable of moral choice.[440]

To which Dr Brodsky, who pioneered the process of aversion therapy (the so-called Ludovico's Technique) to which Alex has been subjected, responds:

> These are subtleties…We are not concerned with motive, with the higher ethics. We are concerned only with cutting down crime….[441]

However, for the chaplain, the higher ethics really do matter. In his assessment, the principal objection to Ludovico's Technique is not that it might misfire but rather that it works and when it works, it succeeds in depriving the reclaimed person of the capacity for moral choice.

Of course, in *A Clockwork Orange* the technology is applied only ex post (Alex is a serial offender who has been convicted of his crimes). However, the chaplain's point can be generalised: too much technology, too much profiling, can be bad for moral choice. If we assume that some profiling *ex post* is acceptable in a community of rights (although this is certainly a matter for further consideration), we can concentrate on: (i) the development of panopticon profiling powers such that any criminal type is certain to be detected and (ii) the development of profiling technology that can be employed to ensure either that Alex-types simply are not born or that they are never released into the larger community.[442]

---

[439] Anthony Burgess, 1962. My page references are to the Penguin Classics edition, 2000.

[440] Burgess, A., 2000: 94.

[441] Burgess, A., 2000: 94.

[442] In principle, a profiling approach might be taken at one or more of the following three points in the criminal justice system:

> (a) Level One: *ex post* to those who have offended and who have been duly convicted of the relevant offence - possibly for the purposes of better-informed sentencing (the offending agent's records are mined so that the sentencing court has a better view of the person); or, possibly as part of the sentence (for example, by tagging and monitoring), or as a condition for early release, or possibly even after completion of sentence.
>
> (b) Level Two: for the purposes of investigation and detection and, by implication, deterrence (as with DNA profiles, CCTV, ambient environments and so on).
>
> (c) Level Three: *ex ante*, in order to prevent the commission of crime - for example, taking preventive action based on agent-specific DNA or brain-imaging profiles or the like.

In a community of rights, there is likely to be an ascending degree of resistance to the use of profiling as proposed for each of these levels. As explained in the text, in this paper, I am focusing on what are, in effect, Level Two and Level Three profiling strategies.

We know that the first of these developments re-introduces the privacy questions that we have already discussed but the particular concern raised by these profiling futures that I want to focus on is the one articulated by the chaplain. Once again, the point is that reliance on technology might have a corrosive effect not simply on a particular interest such as privacy but also on the underlying interest in the moral community itself.

16.3.2 Panopticon Profiling

Imagine that the State has access to a profiling technology, a technology of surveillance, locating and identifying that is so sophisticated and reliable that there is no chance that when a criminal offence is committed, the offending agent will not be detected. Even if such a community has a fairly limited criminal code, the fact that all crimes will be observed, all offenders detected, might be a cause for concern in a community of rights.[443] But why? If the code penalises the violation of those rights that are fundamental to a community of rights, what is the problem with such an effective detection strategy? For years we have bemoaned the fact that where crime and punishment is concerned nothing works, so why look for problems when we find a criminal justice strategy that actually works?

The problem, stated shortly, is that agents in a community of rights expect to make a choice between compliance and non-compliance with their legal-moral criminal code. To be sure, panopticon profiling presents agents with the paper option of non-compliance but the reality is that agents who do not obey most certainly will pay. Echoing the chaplain's concern, this real state of affairs might be thought to interfere with the development of agent virtue, particularly the virtue of choosing to do the right thing for the right reason. For, if agents comply only because they fear certain detection and punishment, there is little room for the promotion of the desired virtue.

Against this, it might be argued that such a view is "idealistic". Even without panopticon profiling, agents rarely do the right thing simply for the right reason. In practice, for many agents it is the background (albeit uncertain) threat of penal sanctions that deters the commission of crime. In this view, where agents rarely do the right thing for the right reason, panopticon profiling (by converting a low-risk threat of punishment into a high-risk threat of punishment) simply extends the logic of the existing arrangements - this is no real change in kind, simply a change in degree. Even in a morally disposed community, there has to be some sanction to compensate for the weakness of the will.

Against this injection of realism, those who hope for a morally progressive evolution in the community of rights will protest that panopticon profiling makes it much more difficult - in fact, nigh impossible - for that evolution to take place.

---

[443] Compare Tadros V., 2006: 105 (especially Tadros' discussion of what he calls Camerania).

For, when the threat of detection and punishment is relatively low, there is still space for moral reason to play a part in influencing the decision to comply or not. Indeed, in the Platonic fable of the Ring of Gyges[444] it was precisely where there was no risk of detection and punishment that moral reason came into its own. If, by extreme contrast, the threat of detection and punishment is overwhelming, this prudential consideration will dominate practical reason - inevitably, in most cases, the right thing will be done but not for the right reason.

The spirit of the chaplain's view that informs the idealist approach is that doing the right thing for the right reason speaks to what it is to be human. As Terry Eagleton explains:

> Being human is something you have to get good at, like playing snooker or avoiding the rent collector. The virtuous are those who are successful at being human, as a butcher or jazz pianist are successful at their jobs. Some human beings are even virtuosi of virtue. Virtue in this sense is a worldly affair; but it is unworldly in the sense that success is its own reward.[445]

However, if we argue against panopticon profiling on the grounds that it compromises what it is to be essentially human, or by asserting that the moral life is its own reward, this is liable to be rejected as mystical, metaphysical or just plain puzzling.[446] The danger with arguing that the virtue of doing the right thing has an expressive value is that we reduce what the community of rights prizes to little more than a modus vivendi, leaving the chaplain and advocates of this way of life simply to preach to the converted. Is it possible to put the case more convincingly?

Agents within a community of rights are committed to the ideal that their regulatory framework should present each developed agent with the option of doing the right thing for the right reason. In turn, agents should learn to act in other-regarding (fellow agent-respecting) ways because they understand that this is morally required. In a sense, agents who do the right thing for the right reason self-regulate.

To avoid any misunderstanding, it should be said that the community of rights is doubly different from a group bound together by the spirit of communitarian duty. Firstly, the ethic of the community of rights is rights-led, not duty-led and secondly, the ethic is foundationalist in the sense that its members hold that it is *irrational* for an agent to deny being bound by other-regarding principles. Specifically, it is held that an agent contradicts its own status as an agent if it denies a responsibility to respect the generic rights of fellow agents.[447] To be sure, such rationalist foundationalism is deeply unfashionable - and, indeed, has been so for

---

[444] Plato, 1974:105-106 (Book II).

[445] Eagleton T., 2003: 125.

[446] Not that this deters the (US) President's Council on Bioethics in its Report, *Beyond Therapy*, Dana Press, Washington, 2003, the leitmotiv of which is that reliance on biotechnology to go beyond therapy (towards "perfections" of one kind or another) may turn out to be at best an illusion but "at worst, a Faustian bargain that could cost us *our full and flourishing humanity*" (p. 338 emphasis supplied).

[447] Seminally, see Gewirth A., 1978, and Gewirth A, 1996.

some time.[448] However, if this view is correct, it follows that the commitment to doing the right thing is far more than a modus vivendi; doing the right thing is rationally required, other-regarding (and other-respecting) reason being a logical extension of self-regarding agency reason. What is more, although this argument develops the idea of an infrastructure for agency, its advocates may legitimately reject the claim that the reason for doing the right thing is merely instrumental. To the contrary, the reason for doing the right thing is not that this is in the longer-term interest of all agents (even though it might well be)[449] but that it is, so to speak, in the agent's own interests as a rational being - an agent who does the right thing for the right reason respects the logic of its own agency and maintains its own integrity as a rational being.

16.3.3   Exclusionary Profiling

Elsewhere,[450] I have used Lawrence Lessig's terminology to sketch two regulatory models. One, the so-called East coast model, is an approximation of the way in which regulators operate in modern societies; the other, the so-called West coast model, is a thought-experiment, purely ideal-typical. In the former, regulators rely on a mixture of regulatory strategies - traditional legal command and control techniques, informal social and peer pressure, market adjustment and so on[451]; in the latter, regulation is of an entirely technological kind - risk-management is handled exclusively by technological design of one kind or another. In the East coast community, Alex and his friends would not be out of place whereas in the West coast community, there would be no place for people like Alex. Not only would the West coast regulators either design-out people like Alex or design-in a control mechanism that eliminates the risk that Alex would otherwise present, they would also design-out the characteristic East coast choice between doing right and doing wrong. If we suppose that profiling is part of the West coast regulatory repertoire, we can capture the spirit of the West coast style by designating this as "exclusionary profiling". Even though the pattern and product of exclusionary profiling is a community that is regulated for compliance and agent security, the West coast model invites a range of objections.

First, as Lessig himself has perceptively pointed out, the perfect technology of safety has its price. Thus:

> Between [a] norm and the behaviour sought is a human being, mediating whether to conform or not. Lots of times, for lots of laws, the choice is not to conform. Regardless of what the law says, it is an individual who decides whether to conform.

---

[448] However, arguing against the tide, see the compelling commentary in Toddington S., 1993.

[449] Compare the strategy in Gauthier D., 1986.

[450] Brownsword R., 2005.

[451] Lessig L., 1999a : 53-54; and Lesig, L., 1999b: 533-534.

Regulation in cyberspace is, or can be, different. If the regulator wants to induce certain behaviour, she need not threaten or cajole, to inspire the change. She need only change the code - the software that defines the terms upon which the individual gains access to the system, or uses assets on the system. If she wants to limit trespass on a system, she need not rely simply on a law against trespass; she can implement a system of passwords....

Code is an efficient means of regulation. But its perfection makes it something different. One obeys these laws as code not because one should; one obeys these laws as code because one can do nothing else. There is no choice about whether to yield to the demand for a password; one complies if one wants to enter the system. In the well implemented system, there is no civil disobedience. Law as code is a start to the perfect technology of justice.[452]

Add to cybertechnology, biotechnology, nanotechnology, neurotechnology and a range of exclusionary profiling technologies and it becomes even more apparent that on the West coast, regulators simply manage their regulatees, by-passing practical reason to design-in a solution to a problem of which regulatees might not even be aware.[453]

The fact that exclusionary profiling operates in this way means that agents in such a community are not only excluded from the option of criminality, they are also excluded from the discourse and debate of regulatory standard-setting. Modern public law virtues, such as those of transparency, accountability and participation, are conspicuous by their absence.

Secondly, the objection to panopticon profiling that we have already analysed applies a fortiori to the model of exclusionary profiling. With panopticon profiling, there is no real chance of doing the right thing for the right reason; with exclusionary profiling, there is literally no chance of doing anything other than the right thing (as pre-coded by the regulators). It is true that exclusionary profiling might leave some space for minor moral decision-making and the possible significance of leaving such space merits further consideration. However, by excluding the most important moral matters, exclusionary profiling yields only an ersatz community of rights.

In this light, we might view some of the concerns about the administration of methylphenidate (Ritalin) and amphetamine (Adderall) to children whose conduct is outside the range of acceptability, as prefiguring concerns that we might have about exclusionary profiling. In its report, *Beyond Therapy*[454], the President's Council on Bioethics expresses just such a concern very clearly:

Behaviour-modifying agents circumvent that process [i.e., the process of self-control and progressive moral education] and act directly on the brain to affect the child's behaviour without the intervening learning process. If what matters is only the child's outward behaviour, then this is simply a more effective and efficient means of achieving the desired result. But because moral education is typically more about the shaping of the agent's character than about the outward act, the process of learning to behave appropriately matters most of all. If the development of character depends on effort to choose and act appropriately, often in the face of resisting desires and impulses, then the more direct pharmacological approach

---

[452] Lessig L., 1996: 1408 (emphasis added).

[453] A point made forcefully by Tien L., 2004.

[454] President's Council on Bioethics, 2003.

bypasses a crucial element....By treating the restlessness of youth as a medical, rather than a moral, challenge, those resorting to behaviour-modifying drugs might not only deprive [the] child of an essential part of this education. They might also encourage him to change his self-understanding as governed largely by chemical impulses and not by moral decisions grounded in some sense of what is right and appropriate.[455]

In other words, with the onset of exclusionary profiling, we observe a dramatic corrosion of moral community. As the President's Council graphically warns, once we take an interventionist biotechnological approach to respond to (or manage) our social problems, there is a danger that "we may weaken our sense of responsibility and agency".[456] Technological advances might be morally progressive but not necessarily so.[457]

Thirdly, when imagining a strategy of exclusionary profiling, I have assumed that regulators would be well-motivated. I have assumed that regulators would seek to design-in a pattern of conduct that would be, so to speak, community of rights compatible. We would find a rights-respecting practice even if agent regulatees have no real sense of what it is to respect a right - they simply act that way. Needless to say, this is a very generous assumption. Indeed, some might think it reckless. To put exclusionary profiling powers in the hands of regulators when there is no guarantee that such powers will be properly used (if proper use ever would be conceivable) is a hostage to fortune. Moreover, even if the precautionary principle has taken criticisim recently[458] there is good sense in being cautious about handing over irreversible powers of this kind to future generations of regulators.

Finally, I have also assumed that the technology would be perfectly effective and reliable. Again, this might seem like a rash assumption - *Minority Report* might move from the world of fiction into the world of fact.[459] As Michael Friedewald[460] has cautioned, in relation to ambient intelligence:

> The scale, complexity and ever-expanding scope of human activity within this new ecosystem present enormous technical challenges for privacy, identity and security - mainly because of the enormous amount of behavioural, personal and even biological data being recorded and disseminated....[Inter alia], there will be a constant struggle to defend this world of ambient intelligence against attacks from viruses, spam, fraud, masquerade, cyber terrorism and so forth.

Concerns of this kind are surely appropriate.[461] Perhaps, at this juncture, the prospect of workable exclusionary profiling is merely conjectural - and, in the light of the various concerns of a practical, principled and political nature that are associated with such a prospect, this is no bad thing.

---

[455] President's Council on Bioethics, 2003: 105-106.

[456] President's Council on Bioethics, 2003: 106.

[457] Compare Touraine A., 1995: 45.

[458] See, in particular, the powerful critique in Cass Sunstein, 2005.

[459] Compare Levi M. and Wall D.S., 2004: 194.

[460] Friedewald M., 2006: 10.

[461] Compare, e.g., Randerson J., 2006: 3.

16.4   Conclusion

The contributions to this volume highlight the potential benefits of profiling technology but also refer to the potential problems. As with all technologies, profiling is Janus-like: there is a face of opportunity but also a face of threat.

In this paper I have suggested that the threat is to both opacity and transparency. We lose opacity as technology erodes our privacy interest and we lose transparency as regulators rely on West coast style embedded strategies that threaten to undermine the dignity of moral choice. Moreover, the process is insidious; Big Brother does not announce itself with a big bang; it is simply a process of technological accumulation.

It follows that if we value privacy and dignity, we need to articulate these interests in terms that not only draw a clearer line in the sand but in terms that have stronger foundations than the shifting sands of local custom and practice. This might not arrest the development of profiling but knowing me and knowing you, it is probably the best we can do.

16.5   Bibliography

Allen, A. L., 'Genetic Privacy: Emerging Concepts and Values', in Rothstein, M.A., (ed), *Genetic Secrets: Protecting Privacy and Confidentiality in the Genetic Era*, New Haven, Yale University Press, 1997.

Archard, D., 'The Value of Privacy', in Claes, E., Duff, A, Gutwirth, S., (eds), *Privacy and the Criminal Law*, Antwerp and Oxford, Intersentia, 2006.

Beyleveld, D. and Brownsword, R. *Law as a Moral Judgment*, London, Sweet and Maxwell, 1986 (reprinted Sheffield: Sheffield Academic Press, 1994).

Beyleveld, D. and Brownsword, R., *Human Dignity in Bioethics and Biolaw*, Oxford, Oxford University Press, 2001.

Beyleveld, D. and Brownsword, R., 'Principle, Proceduralism and Precaution in a Community of Rights', *Ratio Juris*, Vol. 19, Blackwell Publ., 2006, pp. 141-168.

Beyleveld, D. and Brownsword, R., *Consent in the Law*, Oxford, Hart, 2007.

Bird, S., 'Architect who Dressed as Tramp to Attack Girls Trapped by DNA', *The Times*, June 15, 3, 2006.

Brownsword, R., 'Happy Families, Consenting Couples and Children with Dignity: Sex Selection and Saviour Siblings', *Child and Family Law Quarterly*, Vol. 17, No.4, Jordan & Sons Ltd., Bristol, 2005, pp. 435 – 473.

Brownsword, R., 'Code, Control and Choice: Why East is East and West is West', *Legal Studies*, Vol. 25, No. 1, 2005, pp. 1-21.

Burgess, A., *A Clockwork Orange*, London, William Heinemann Ltd, 1962/2000.

Eagleton, T., *After Theory*, London, Allen Lane, 2003.

Fried, C., 'Privacy', *Yale Law Journal*, Vol. 77, No. 1, The Yale Law Journal Company, 1968, pp. 475-93.

Friedewald, M., 'Introduction to the SWAMI Project', Friedewald and Wright (eds), *Report on the Final Conference, Brussels, 21-22 March 2006*, SWAMI Deliverable D5. A report of the SWAMI consortium to the European Commission under contract 006507, April 2006. Available at http://swami.jrc.es.

Gauthier, D., *Morals by Agreement*, Oxford, Oxford University Press, 1986.

Gewirth, A., *Reason and Morality*, Chicago, University of Chicago Press, 1978.

Gewirth, A., *The Community of Rights*, Chicago: University of Chicago Press, 1996.

Gutwirth, S. and De Hert, P., 'Privacy, Data Protection and Law Enforcement. Opacity of the Individual and Transparency of Power', in Claes, E., Duff, A. and Gutwirth, S. (eds), *Privacy and the Criminal Law*, Antwerp and Oxford, Intersentia, 2006.

Hildebrandt, M., 'Defining Profiling: A New Type of Knowledge?', in Hildebrandt, M., and Gutwirth, S., (eds), *Profiling the European Citizen* (Ch. 2), Springer Netherlands, 2008.

Koops, B.-J. and Leenes, R., ''Code' and the Slow Erosion of Privacy', *Michigan Telecommunications and Technology Law Review*, Vol. 12, No.1, 2005, pp. 115-188.

Laurie, G., *Genetic Privacy*, Cambridge, Cambridge University Press, 2002.

Lessig, L., 'The Zones of Cyberspace', *Stanford Law Review*, Vol. 48, No.5, 1996, pp. 1403- 1411.

Lessig, L., *Code and Other Laws of Cyberspace*, New York, Basic Books, 1999a.

Lessig, L., 'The Law of the Horse: What Cyberlaw Might Teach', *Harvard Law Review*, Vol. 113, 1999b, pp. 501 – 546.

Levi, M. and Wall, D. S., 'Technologies, Security, and Privacy in the Post-9/11 European Information Society', *Journal of Law and Society*, Vol. 31, No. 2, Blackwell Publishing Oxford, 2004, pp. 194 - 220.

Norfolk, A., 'Shoe Rapist is Trapped by Sister's DNA 20 Years After Serial Attacks', *The Times*, July 18, 3, 2006.

Phillipson, G., 'Transforming Breach of Confidence? Towards a Common Law Right of Privacy under the Human Rights Act', *Modern Law Review*, Vol. 66, No.5, 2003, pp. 726 – 758.

Plato, *The Republic*, Harmondsworth, Penguin, 1974.

President's Council on Bioethics, *Beyond Therapy*, Washington, Dana Press, 2003.

Randerson, J., 'Tighter Laws Needed on Sale of DNA Samples, Says Research Chief', *The Guardian*, June 15, 3, 2006.

Sunstein, C., *Laws of Fear*, Cambridge, Cambridge University Press, 2005.

Tadros, V., 'Power and the Value of Privacy', in Claes, E., Duff, A. and Gutwirth, S., (eds), *Privacy and the Criminal Law*, Antwerp and Oxford, Intersentia, 2006.

Tien, L., 'Architectural Regulation and the Evolution of Social Norms', *International Journal of Communications Law and Policy*, Vol. 7, 2004.

Toddington, S., *Rationality, Social Action and Moral Judgment*, Edinburgh, Edinburgh University Press, 1993.

Touraine, A., 'The Crisis of 'Progress', in Bauer, M., (ed.), *Resistance to New Technology*, Cambridge, Cambridge University Press, 1995.

Warren, S.D. and Brandeis, L.D., 'The Right to Privacy', *Harvard Law Review*, Vol. 4, No.5, 1890-1891, pp. 193-220. Available at: http://www-swiss.ai.mit.edu/6805/articles/privacy/ Privacy_brand_warr2.html.

Webster, B., 'Cameras Set to Catch Side-Street Speeders', *The Times*, June 15, 1-2, 2006.

Chapter 17
Concise Conclusions: Citizens out of Control

Mireille Hildebrandt and Serge Gutwirth

For a summary of the contributions we refer to the introductory chapter. In this chapter we undertake to draw some summary conclusions. It seems that profiling, especially in the context of smart applications and Ambient Intelligence, requires a focus shift from data to knowledge, while the type of knowledge that is at stake differs from more traditional knowledge production. We conclude that this shift has far-reaching implications for the relationship between citizens, commercial enterprise and governmental powers. This requires lawyers, policy makers, computer engineers and politicians to rethink the socio-technical infrastructure of constitutional democracy. Citizenship, participation in the creation of the common good and personal freedom cannot be taken for granted, they presume that citizens have some awareness of what is known about them and by whom.

Classification and Profiling

Profiling is a matter of pattern recognition, which is comparable to categorisation, generalisation and stereotyping. To understand what is new about profiling we must differentiate between classification (ex ante categorisation) and clustering (ex post categorisation). Classification is nothing very new, apart from the fact that databases allow more extensive queries; it does not deliver any new knowledge, it only permits a structuration of what was already known. Clustering and association rules, however, produce previously unknown patterns. This means that whoever controls the profiling machinery comes into possession of valuable knowledge and information. This knowledge is statistical and hence, not necessarily 'true' or adequating reality but it clearly has an added value.

Vrije Universiteit Brussels, Erasmus Universiteit Rotterdam

M. Hildebrandt and S. Gutwirth (eds.), *Profiling the European Citizen:*
Cross-Disciplinary Perspectives.
© Springer Science + Business Media B.V. 2008

Non-distributive Group Profiles and Non-universal Categorisation

Similar to non-universal categorisation, non-distributive group profiling reduces complexity without applying to all the elements of the category that is used. As we all know, categorisation allows segmentation and stratification: distribution of risks and opportunities on the basis of being an element in a category. Non-distributive group profiling causes problems whenever a person is categorised in a group while the relevant group profile does not apply. However, this does not mean that correct categorisation is without problems, as this may result in discrimination (if the categorisation is used for unfair distributions of risks or opportunities) or manipulation (if the categorisation is used to influence a person's behaviour without any awareness on the part of the person).

Data Processing: A Black Box?

The process of data mining is mostly invisible to the individual citizens to which profiles are applied. This is the case because the use of algorithms demands computing powers far beyond the limits of the human brain, requiring machines to do the work. As citizens whose data are being mined do not have the means to anticipate what the algorithms will come up with, they do not know how they will be categorised or the consequences. More complex types of profiling such as neural networks, process data without being able to predict the outcome; in this case the process is a black box even for the programmer and the data analyst. For individual citizens to regain some kind of control over the way they live their lives, access is needed to the profiles applied to them. This will require both legal (rights to transparency) and technological tools (the means to exercise such rights).

Risks and Opportunities

The risks and opportunities of profiling derive from the transparency of the personality, life-style, habits, desires and preferences of individual citizens. Such transparency allows: refined price-discrimination based on refined segmentation; refined criminal profiling, predicting criminal behaviour and/or recidivism; refined targeted servicing, aiming to reinforce or even initiate customers' behaviour that is profitable to the service provider; refined personalised support for e-learning in schools or workplaces. It should be obvious that these opportunities simultaneously entail risks. The most obvious risk is the inaccuracy of the data used to produce profiles, which may be caused by intentional actions, for instance data minimisation or identity fraud but also by unintentional actions such as human or technical error and the use of outdated data. The problem with such inaccuracy is not only that profiles will mismatch but also that the intelligence of an environment that depends on profiling technologies will diminish, causing irritating or even dangerous mistakes. Beside the obvious risk of inaccuracy the less obvious risk of accuracy relates to the finely-tuned segmentation that is made possible by profiling. The balance of knowledge (and power) between those that possess the profiles and those that are being profiled seems to shift in a substantive way. This may have far reaching consequences for basic notions such as identity, agency, liability, fair treatment and due process.

From Privacy Enhancing Technologies (PETs) to Transparency Enhancing Tools (TETs)

One way to deal with such risks could be the use of PETs, which anonymise personal data, provide contextual pseudonyms, create unlinkability and generate invisibility. PETs are tools of opacity because they tend to shield off the individual from scrutiny, focusing on minimising the exchange of personal data. However, even privacy preserving data mining (PPDM) does not provide transparency regarding the type of profiles that are constructed or applied. If we want to anticipate and/or change the way machines (and their masters) profile us, we will need transparency enhancing tools (TETs). Such technological tools would empower citizens to unfurl the profiling operations they are subject to. TETs, however, are still to be invented and their application may run counter to the intellectual property rights of the owners of databases, while the question remains of how humans could effectively communicate with the machines that provides transparency of the proliferation of profiles. This is a topic presently under investigation within the FIDIS research network.

Legal Framework

Informational privacy is not only protected by transparency tools that organise a conditional access to personal data but also by opacity tools, which as a rule prohibit access to sensitive personal data. As a default, however, the processing of personal data is not prohibited but made transparent, controllable and accountable by means of transparency tools, such as rights to access and correction of one's personal data, the establishment of special supervisory authorities and the obligation of data controllers to declare their processings. However, protection beyond one's individual personal data is not supplied. Moreover, anti-discrimination legislation also shows weaknesses when called upon in cases of profiling. Although data protection law theoretically applies to many facets of the profiling activity, in practice data mining techniques remain a technological black box for citizens and for this reason data protection is not effective. This situation demands the integration of legal transparency norms into technological devices that can translate what profiling machines are doing. In this way, citizens could be empowered to regain some control over the consequences of their interactions.

Main Conclusion: How to Empower European Citizens

Citizens are facing a new situation, in which they will mostly have no control, while most probably not one singly entity (governmental or private) will be in control. This is mainly due to the complex, fast and automatic nature of contemporary profiling techniques. Moreover, even if data protection legislation often applies, citizens are faced with profiling practices that make it possible to control and steer individuals without a need to identify them, thus escaping the data protection regime.

The time has come to explore the possibility of a new legal approach of profiling in which the approach based on the protection of personal data gives way to one focusing on the way profiles affect our behaviour and decisions. Such a shift would emphasise the issues of discrimination and manipulation of conduct through the use of profiles, as well as the transparency and controllability of profiles, rather than the more classical value of privacy and personal data protection. To empower European citizens, a paradigm shift is needed from data protection to knowledge transparency and from personal data to profiles. The legal status of profiles must be developed with respect to those to whom they may be applied, in order to counterbalance the legal status of profiles as trade secrets or intellectual property of profilers.

Summarising, further research is needed into the risks of the application of incorrect profiles in the case of data inaccuracy and/or non-distributive profiles; the risks of highly sophisticated accurate personalised profiles; the abuse of accurate and inaccurate profiles by private and governmental agents; the development of legal and technological transparency tools (proxies) and the way such tools can make accessible to humans the knowledge and information these TETs accumulate (by means of human machine interfaces).

Index